Politics and Religion in the United States

There is a complex relationship between religiosity and secularism in the American experience. America is notable both for its strict institutional separation of church and state, *and* for the strong role that religion has played in its major social movements and ongoing political life.

This book seeks to illuminate for readers the dynamics underlying this seeming paradox, and to examine how the various religious groups in America have approached and continue to approach the tensions between sacred and secular. This much-anticipated revision brings Corbett and Corbett's classic text fully up to date. The second edition continues with a thorough discussion of historical origins of religion in political life, constitutional matters, public opinion, and the most relevant groups, all while taking theology seriously. Revisions include fully updating all the public opinion data, fuller incorporation of voting behavior among different religious and demographic groups, enhanced discussion of minority religions such as Mormonism and Islam, and new examples throughout.

Michael Corbett was Professor of Political Science at Ball State University.

Julia Corbett-Hemeyer is Professor Emeritus of Religious Studies at Ball State University. She is a Community Minister with the Unitarian Universalist Church.

J. Matthew Wilson is an Associate Professor of Political Science at Southern Methodist University. He specializes in political behavior, religion and politics, and political psychology. Wilson is the editor of *From Pews to Polling Places: Faith and Politics in the American Religious Mosaic*.

Politics and Religion in the United States

Second edition

Michael Corbett,
Julia Corbett-Hemeyer,
and J. Matthew Wilson

Routledge
Taylor & Francis Group

NEW YORK AND LONDON

Second edition published 2014
by Routledge
711 Third Avenue, New York, NY 10017

and by Routledge
2 Park Square, Milton Park, Abingdon, Oxon OX14 4RN

Routledge is an imprint of the Taylor & Francis Group, an informa business

© 2014 Taylor & Francis

The right of Michael Corbett, Julia Corbett-Hemeyer, and
J. Matthew Wilson to be identified as authors of this work has been
asserted by them in accordance with sections 77 and 78 of the
Copyright, Designs and Patents Act 1988.

First edition published by Routledge 1998

Library of Congress Cataloging in Publication Data
Corbett, Michael, 1943–.
    Politics and religion in the United States/by Michael Corbett,
    Julia Corbett-Hemeyer, and J. Matthew Wilson.—2nd edition.
    pages cm
    Includes bibliographical references and index.
    1. Religion and politics—United States. I. Hemeyer, Julia Corbett,
    1945–. II. Title.
    BL2525.C68 2013
    322′.10973—dc23
    2013023824

ISBN: 978-0-415-64462-4 (hbk)
ISBN: 978-0-415-64463-1 (pbk)
ISBN: 978-0-203-07943-0 (ebk)

Typeset in Goudy
by Florence Production Ltd, Stoodleigh, Devon, UK

Printed and bound in the United States of America by Publishers Graphics,
LLC on sustainably sourced paper.

Contents

Figures

Tables

Preface

Politics and Religion in the United States seeks to provide a comprehensive view of the ways in which the sacred and civil spheres have interacted with one another in America from the early colonial period through the age of Barack Obama. In doing so, the book traces significant and recurring themes through a long span of time, illuminating for readers the roots and antecedents of today's controversies. As the volume makes clear, debates over America's national religious identity, over the influence of religion in public life, and over tolerance and accommodation for minority religious perspectives are not new; rather, they reflect the nation's ongoing struggle to harmonize a religious society with a secular government.

In dealing with these enduring questions, *Politics and Religion* takes a multifaceted approach. The interaction of faith and governance in America is amenable to, and indeed demands, a range of analytical perspectives. It is certainly a question of history, but also an issue of law; it touches on many dimensions of political philosophy, but also on modern empirical politics. Moreover, the relevant issues can be framed not simply in political terms, but in religious ones as well. The question of how people and institutions of faith ought to approach the state is just as interesting and important as how the state ought to approach people and institutions of faith. Religious communities are not just one more set of interest groups fighting for "goodies" in the political fray. They are, instead, bodies who speak to life's most fundamental questions, that have identities and purposes that transcend secular politics, and that make ultimate, supra-political claims on the loyalty of their members. As a result, it is critical that one take seriously their theologies, traditions, and doctrines if one is to understand what motivates their actions in the political sphere.

The authors' own diverse backgrounds and research interests facilitate this broad-based and interdisciplinary approach. Matthew Wilson and Michael Corbett, both political scientists, bring expertise in public opinion, elections, and statistical analysis of empirical data. Julia Corbett-Hemeyer, a religious studies scholar, brings an extensive background in American religious history and in comparative religion. All bring to the project an appreciation for the critical role that jurisprudence plays in adjudicating church–state questions in a constitutional democracy. This broad-based intellectual collaboration makes for a volume unique in the depth as well as the breadth of its coverage.

The book seeks to strike a balance between sophistication and accessibility. While we do not shy away from complex legal, theological, and political concepts, we seek to present them in a way that is jargon-free and intelligible to a broad audience. Our goal has been to produce a volume that will be simultaneously useful to scholars working in this area and engaging for students and interested general readers.

We advance a broad thesis in the book—namely, that American history and contemporary politics are generally characterized by a desire to separate church from state, but not religion from public life. Beyond that, however, the volume is not driven by any particular political or religious point of view. Many of the most critical questions surrounding the role of religion in public life are difficult issues on which reasonable people of good will can (and do) disagree. Our hope is that readers of various persuasions, from strong liberals to strong conservatives, from atheists and agnostics to evangelical Christians, will find the book's tone thoughtful and balanced, allowing them to draw their own conclusions from an even-handed presentation of the material.

The continually dynamic, contested, and evolving nature of the relationship between religion and politics in America is exemplified by the huge judicial issues looming as we completed work on this volume. The nation awaited word from the Supreme Court on the question of same-sex marriage, an issue in which many religious groups have been deeply invested. In addition, challenges to the "Obamacare" mandate that employers (including religious ones) provide insurance covering contraception, abortifacients, and sterilizations wend their way through the courts, as the administration and religious groups continue to seek an accommodation. These issues are discussed at length in the book, and provide but two examples of the continuing critical relevance of religious issues in American public life.

The first edition of this book, published in 1999, was a collaborative effort of Michael and Julia Corbett. Obviously, the passage of fourteen years and the intervening significant developments in American law, politics, and society have necessitated a very extensive updating and reworking of the manuscript. Matthew Wilson, who has come aboard as a co-author for this second edition, has both spearheaded this effort and added to the work elements of his own distinctive voice and perspective. Still, we hope that those familiar with the first edition will find that this new version remains consistent with the spirit and tone of the original—historically informed, interdisciplinary, grounded in contemporary data, and intellectually balanced.

This volume would not have been possible without the efforts (and patience) of the fine team at Routledge, most notably Michael Kerns and Darcy Bullock. Their efforts in bringing the book to fruition are much appreciated. In addition, Matthew Wilson would like to acknowledge the support and forbearance of his wife Carole and son Michael as he put in the sometimes long hours required to complete the necessary revisions.

Finally, we note with sadness the passing of Michael Corbett since the publication of the first edition. His contributions remain an integral part of the present volume. Our work in this new version is dedicated to his memory.

Abbreviations

ACLU	American Civil Liberties Union
AIPAC	American Israel Public Affairs Committee
CBN	Christian Broadcasting Network
CORE	Congress of Racial Equality
EEOC	Equal Employment Opportunity Commission
GOP	Grand Old Party
IRS	Internal Revenue Service
LDS	Latter-day Saints
NAACP	National Association for the Advancement of Colored People
NORC GSS	National Opinion Research Center General Social Survey
NRLC	National Right to Life Committee
PAC	political action committee
RFRA	Religious Freedom Restoration Act
SCLC	Southern Christian Leadership Conference
SNCC	Student Nonviolent Coordinating Committee
USCCB	United States Conference of Catholic Bishops
WISC	Washington Interreligious Staff Council

1 Politics and Religion
An Overview

> We know that part of living in a pluralistic society means that our personal religious beliefs alone can't dictate our response to every challenge we face. But ... we can't leave our values at the door. If we leave our values at the door, we abandon much of the moral glue that has held our nation together for centuries, and allowed us to become a somewhat more perfect union. Frederick Douglass, Abraham Lincoln, Jane Addams, Martin Luther King, Dorothy Day, Abraham Heschel—the majority of great reformers in American history did their work not just because it was sound policy ... but because their faith and their values dictated it, and called for bold action—sometimes in the face of indifference, sometimes in the face of resistance.
>
> (President Barack Obama, Speech at the
> National Prayer Breakfast, February 2, 2011)

As the above quote from President Obama suggests, religion is inextricably woven into the fabric of American political life. It has shaped the nation's self-conception, from the earliest colonies through the founding era to the present day. Communities of faith have been at the heart, both inspirationally and organizationally, of the most significant social and political movements in the nation's history. At the same time, however, America has always been religiously diverse and pluralistic; no single system of belief or way of worship has ever dominated the religious landscape, and people of faith have often been found on both sides of major national struggles. As a result, the relationship between religion and politics in America has always been complex, reflecting a delicate balance between respecting religious pluralism and acknowledging religion's significant role in public life. *Politics and Religion in the United States* provides a comprehensive view of this interaction, both historically and in America today. This ongoing story is told in several sections.

- This introduction lays the groundwork by *defining the terms of the relationship*, by providing working definitions of both religion and politics and demonstrating why they are necessarily related—especially in the United States. It also provides a brief typology of the logical forms that this relationship might take.

- Part I, *Religion and History*, examines *the nature of this relationship in the past*. Individual chapters deal with the colonial experience and intentions of the founders, the time period between 1800 and 1960, and the more contemporary era since 1960. The specific issues vary over time, but the deep interconnection of religion and politics is a continuing motif throughout our history.
- Part II, *Religion and the First Amendment*, traces the evolution of the *legal relationship* between politics and religion. The legal separation of governmental and religious institutions in the United States has meant that their relationship must continually be redefined as new situations arise. Separate chapters deal with the establishment clause and the free exercise clause, and the tension between the two clauses is examined.
- Part III, *Religion and Public Opinion*, uses information from leading public opinion surveys to explore *how the relationship between religion and politics is reflected in the social and political views of Americans today*. A chapter on religion and public opinion is followed by separate chapters that analyze religious–political links among white Americans and among racial and ethnic minorities, since these groups differ significantly in their understanding of how religion and politics are (and should be) linked.
- Part IV, *Effects of Religious Influences in Politics*, consists of two chapters that examine *how religion shapes public policy in America*, as religious groups try to affect the legislative process and as people reflect on what the relationship between faith and law should be.
- Two appendices profile major religious groups in the United States, with particular attention to features that influence their *participation in the relationship between politics and religion*, and also provide the wording of the survey questions used in our analyses.

Alongside the overarching theme of the contested and complex relationship between politics and religion, several groups of questions and issues recur throughout many of the above parts. Some of the key ones are enumerated below.

- Waging war and understanding or justifying it: From the American Revolution through the wars in Iraq and Afghanistan, religion has influenced peoples' views about warfare and has been used both to voice antiwar protest and to defend participation in military conflicts.
- The regulation of personal life: From Puritan restrictions on what one could and could not do on Sunday to contemporary restrictions on gambling, alcohol, and prostitution, people have sought to translate their vision of moral behavior into law.
- Relationships between groups of people: Religion was used to promote both slavery and abolition, as was cited in defense of both racial segregation and integration. It has, at different times and in different contexts, been the source of both ecumenical cooperation and sectarian strife.

- Attitudes toward government: In the United States, religious groups have most often been generally supportive of governmental authority. Throughout history, however, individuals and communities of faith have raised serious moral challenges to specific laws and decisions of political leaders and, less frequently, to the legitimacy of government itself on the basis of their religious views.
- Religion and the electoral process: Religion has long played an important role in American voting behavior. Catholics and Jews, for example, have tended to vote Democratic more frequently than white Protestants— though these patterns have evolved over time. It has also affected how candidates and elected officials present themselves and their proposals to the voting public.

Religion and Politics: Working Definitions

In order to describe relationships between politics and religion, we need first to be clear about the meaning of each of the two terms. The definitions we develop below are certainly not the only reasonable ones; they are, however, especially useful in the context of our particular discussions. They help us to understand how religion and politics are related and why this relationship is inevitable in the United States.

Description of Religion

For our purposes:

> [A] developed religion is an integrated system of beliefs, lifestyle, ritual activities, and social institutions by which individuals give meaning to (or find meaning in) their lives by orienting themselves to what they experience as holy, sacred, or of ultimate value.
>
> (Corbett-Hemeyer 2010: 13)

This definition is grounded in the social sciences in that it deals with human behavior in groups and with the beliefs and rituals that help to define those groups. It is also based in the humanities in its emphasis on the meaning that religion has for those who participate in it.

To say that a religion is an *integrated system* means that its various dimensions work together and reinforce each other. At least ideally, there are no "loose ends"; the multiple aspects of religious belief and practice fit together into a coherent worldview and way of life. This system can be thought of as being made up of four parts: *beliefs, lifestyle, ritual,* and *social institutions*.

The beliefs of a religion are found in its sacred writings and stories as well as in its doctrines, creeds, and hymns. Religious beliefs include beliefs about the sacred or holy, about the meaning of life in the world, about ethical and moral values, and about what happens after death, to name but a few common themes. These beliefs may or may not include explicit teachings about the proper relationship between religion and the political order.

Lifestyle and ritual are related in that they both have to do with activities. "Lifestyle" refers to how people live on a day-to-day basis. It is the ethical and moral dimension of religion. It includes activities that must be done and other behaviors that must be avoided (for example, the Ten Commandments of both Judaism and Christianity). Sometimes the lifestyle prescribed by a religion serves to set its members apart from the rest of their culture, to a greater or lesser extent. It may include directives about food and clothing (for example, the kosher dietary laws and distinctive dress of Hasidic Jews). It often prescribes participation in specific daily activities (for example, the expectation that Muslims will pray five times a day). Questions about the proper relationship between religion and the state inevitably arise when government interferes with these religious activities, or when members of one religious group seek to impose them on non-members.

Ritual, on the other hand, comprises those activities in which people focus explicitly on religion. In the United States, for example, attendance at corporate worship is a ritual in which people often participate. Rituals serve to make the sacred present and available to people. They also commemorate important historic events in the life of a community of faith, mark and celebrate the passages of the human life cycle, and celebrate and reinforce the connectedness of the community (to name but a few of their functions).

Social or institutional organization is an important aspect of any religion. Such organization is necessary to keep the life of the group going and to move it forward. The organizational structures of religious groups help express their self-understanding. It is often these institutional structures that interface with the political realm.

Religion is in some ways similar to other activities in which people find meaning, while being distinct in one critical respect. Like family, friends, work, leisure activities, and social organizations, religion is one of the things that make human life meaningful and rich for many people. The meaning that people gain from participation in religion is distinctive, however, in that it derives from contact and interaction with what they take to be holy, sacred, or of ultimate value—often transcending the physical, material world. It is this transcendent relationship with the sacred that sets religion apart from other human activities. While a person's membership in a religious community might in some respects be similar to membership in a professional organization or bowling league, it obviously has at least the potential to be much more significant and profound than that.

Definition of Politics

There are many different, though related, definitions of politics. Some political analysts have conceptualized politics primarily through the prism of government. For example, V. O. Key (1958) defines politics in terms of the workings of government, the impact of governments on people, the ways in which governments operate, and the processes by which governmental leaders attain and retain authority. While government is undoubtedly at the center of political activity, however, it does not encompass the entirety of what we might think of as political life. Direct citizen referenda, for example, can be very politically consequential, but take place largely outside the control of governmental elites.

A different approach focuses on the use of power. Dahl and Stinebrickner (2003: 3) define politics in terms of human relationships that "involve, to a significant extent, control, influence, power, or authority." Almost all political scientists would agree that politics involves the use of power. However, because there are different types of power in society (e.g., political power, economic power, and social power), some argue that the power approach is too broad. What is it about the use of authority and influence in political matters that distinguishes political power from other forms of power?

Another approach to understanding politics focuses on values. David Easton (1965) defines politics as the authoritative allocation of values for a society. This definition—or some variation of it—is perhaps the most widely accepted understanding of politics among political scientists. It is also the definition that we find most useful for the present work. It is important to note, however, that "values" in this context include not only intangible ideals, but also concrete, material resources that people value. In this sense, Harold Lasswell (1936) provided a useful framing of the political world in the title of his classic book *Politics: Who Gets What, When and How?* In our own book, we will use a combination of the Easton and Lasswell concepts as our working definition of politics.

Thus, politics concerns the allocation of values. Values are beliefs about what is good or bad, right or wrong, desirable or undesirable. People have many different values, such as wealth, power, health, religion, freedom, patriotism, justice, equality, love, friendship, tolerance, adventure, wisdom, beauty, security, peace, conquest, individualism, community, and so on. At times, these values conflict with one another; actions or policies that advance some may hinder others. Politics exists to resolve conflicts over these necessary tradeoffs. People might disagree on a value (as for example, the pro-life and pro-choice movements disagree about whether the value of human life is implicated in the abortion debate), and this disagreement may lead to political conflict. Conflict can also occur, however, even in situations where people have broad agreement about values. First, people might agree on a value but disagree on how that value should be achieved. For example, there is broad-based agreement that national economic prosperity is something to be valued. However, different people take different approaches to how it ought to be attained (e.g., increase government spending to directly stimulate the economy or decrease government spending to reduce debt and empower the private sector), and this leads to political conflict. Second, people might agree on a value but disagree on the priority of that value in relation to others. For example, although the great majority of Americans favor both clean air and economic growth, conflict arises when they must choose which is more important in a particular situation. Third, conflict can occur when people agree on a value but disagree on who should contribute toward its achievement. For example, people might agree that national security and a strong military are things to be valued, but try to shift as much of the cost for them as possible to others.

Since conflict concerning values is inevitable, not everyone can have everything that they want. Value conflicts must be adjudicated and resolved in the political process. In a particular situation, some people might win while others lose; alternatively, a compromise might result in everyone both winning and losing to some degree. In order for there to be any allocation of values, however, there must be at least some degree of cooperation among people. Further, the process by which these allocations are made has to be authoritative; in other words, people have to accept the decisions that emerge from the political process as legitimate and binding. People might not agree with the way that value conflicts have been resolved, but unless there is at least a minimal level of acceptance of the legitimacy of the resolution process, the political system will break down.

This, then, is our conception of politics. As we shall see, religious motivations have greatly affected the allocation of various values in American society. Religious faith powerfully shapes perceptions of what is valuable, and of how values ought to be ranked and prioritized. In addition, the social role of religion itself—the nation's identity as a religious or secular society—has been a source of significant political conflict, both historically and today.

Religion and Politics: Their Roles in Human Life

The Roles of Religion

Religion plays many roles, both in individual human lives and in the lives of societies and cultures. Its distinctive role for individuals is providing meaning that derives from human contact with what are believed to be sacred realities. Religion provides ways for people to live their lives in conscious relationship with what is to them the highest value. It helps them to connect with the transcendent in ways that illuminate mundane existence. Religion also plays many other roles, only a few of which can be discussed here.

One major function of religion, both for individuals and for entire societies, is the provision and sanctioning of moral guidelines. Religion provides both the "rules" for human behavior themselves and the rationale for those rules. It also frequently indicates punishments for disobedience and rewards for the obedient, thus encouraging compliance with moral norms. In addition, religion often defines appropriate roles for different members of a culture. Religion helps to mark the boundaries of acceptable individual and group behavior. These boundaries are defined and sanctioned with reference to perceived transcendent realities.

Religion contributes to the value system of societies and individuals in other ways as well. For example, Christianity and Judaism, the most prevalent religions in the United States, both emphasize the importance of helping other people, an emphasis that has led to a great deal of volunteer work in our society. Extensive research suggests that religiously observant Americans are significantly more likely to volunteer their time, contribute to charity, and be civically engaged than are others (Smidt et al. 2008; Putnam and Campbell 2010). More broadly, many have argued that Judeo-Christian religious values helped historically to shape the Western cultural emphasis on individual rights.

Religion also provides support for its adherents, both in their daily lives and at special times of crisis and celebration. Being a part of a like-minded group of people with similar values helps to provide the human context that all of us need. For many people, alongside family, their religious community is the primary face-to-face contact group with whom they celebrate births and marriages and mourn the deaths of loved ones. In addition, religious belief provides a cognitive framework that helps believers to find meaning both in their day-to-day activities and in the major events of human life.

The Roles of Politics

Politics can play different roles in different societies, and we focus our discussion here on the American political system. Sometimes politics is conceived as a means to achieve common goals for a society; this conception places the emphasis on cooperation in relatively non-controversial matters, and the overcoming of collective action problems to achieve widely acknowledged public goods. While this is certainly important, the most central role played by politics is one of conflict resolution. Disputes over public issues must ultimately achieve some sort of resolution that is widely regarded as legitimate and binding—though these decisions need not necessarily be regarded as "final." In America, resolutions based on notions of constitutionally circumscribed representative democracy carry inherent authority and legitimacy in the eyes of most citizens.

In a participatory democracy such as that of the United States, politics plays the important role of providing an avenue for people to express their views on public issues and to work for the advancement of their values in the public arena. Even if people do not actually attempt to advance their values by direct political action, the knowledge that they *could* try to do so might be intrinsically valuable to them and might serve as a constraint on the power of political elites. Even if people do make the effort and fail (as have, for example, advocates of strict gun control, an end to the death penalty, or a ban on abortion), the process itself might be satisfying to them; sometimes people derive satisfaction from expressing their values even if those values do not ultimately (or immediately) prevail in the political arena.

Another role that politics plays for some people is that it helps them to develop a sense of citizenship. Although most citizens do not participate in politics beyond the minimal level of voting (and some do not even consistently do that), politics can still make them more fully aware of their existence as part of a public whole. Political engagement can help people to realize that there is more to life than just their private goals. Aristotle and some other political philosophers have advocated that people take a very active role in public life in order to more fully develop themselves and to deepen their sense of connection to their community. In this sense, at least for those who actively participate, politics is similar to religion in that it can help to give meaning and purpose to mundane individual life.

Religion and Politics: Common Concerns

Although politics and religion are obviously not the same, their realms overlap. This is especially true with regard to the articulation and pursuit of values, and to the exercise of power over the lives of people. Reichley (2002: 10) argues that "the chief thing that religion and politics have in common is that both are concerned with the pursuit of values—personal, social, or transcendent." Chidester (1988: 1) begins his book on religion and politics by arguing that "religion and politics are dimensions of human experience engaged in the meaningful exercise of power."

Religions teach people certain values and, thus, have some degree of power over how people live their lives. Politics leads to the resolution of value conflicts in society; the decisions made in the political process are binding on people and exert some degree of control over what they can or cannot do. Chidester (1988) makes the further point that religion also provides an orientation for people to the powers that impinge upon their lives, and suggests that the way to distinguish between religion and politics is that religion concerns sacred power while politics concerns ordinary, mundane, or profane power.

Religion and politics inevitably become intertwined in a variety of situations. The values taught by a particular religion might become the authoritatively allocated values within a political system (if, for example, a nation bases its legal code on shariah law, as do many predominantly Muslim nations). Religious groups might attempt to use the power of the state to advance or enforce their religious values. Different religious groups with divergent values might engage in political conflict in order to have their own values prevail. The values generated or supported within the political system might permeate religious views—particularly if the state seeks to coerce religious communities into accepting values that it regards as desirable. Religious organizations might pursue their organizational interests (e.g., keeping church property exempt from taxes, or gaining support for parochial education) within the political system. Religion and politics each provide a point of reference by which the other can be judged, and the two may become intertwined as people engage in this evaluative behavior.

Politicians sometimes use religion to gain support for their own interests. Democrats eager for the support of African Americans have frequently sought the blessing of black churches, and the connection between the Republican Party and conservative religious groups is well known.

Both religion and politics are necessarily concerned with values and with power. Thus, they are almost inevitably intertwined to some degree in any society. Different people, however, have different views on what type of relationship should exist between these two realms. What kind of link should there be between religion and politics, between the sacred and the temporal spheres? The typology below surveys the different views on this subject.

A Typology of Views on the Relationship of Religion and Politics

> Believing with you that religion is a matter which lies solely between man and his God, that he owes account to none other for his faith or his worship ..., I contemplate with sovereign reverence that act of the whole American people which declared that their legislature should ... [build] a wall of separation between church and state.
>
> (President Thomas Jefferson, 1802)

> Somehow or another there's this ... steel wall, this iron curtain or whatever you want to call it between the church and people of faith, and this separation of church and state is just false on its face. We have a biblical responsibility to be involved in the public arena proclaiming God's truth.
>
> (Texas Governor and presidential candidate Rick Perry, 2012)

As these two quotations show, different perspectives on the proper relationship between religion and politics have been a feature of cultural life in the United States since the founding era, and the discussion continues to this day.

We present below a typology of the ways in which people through history and around the world have understood this relationship (see Figure 1.1). Some of the alternatives discussed have not been part of the American historical experience, and have few advocates in the United States. Others have existed here, or exist now, sometimes in a modified form. The typology should help to situate the debate about religion and politics in America in proper global and historical perspective. Every approach discussed here is in existence somewhere in the world today.

First, we present the opposing extremes of theocracy and government suppression of religion. We then consider the various types of religious establishments. Finally, we address views that typify the attempt to separate church and state.

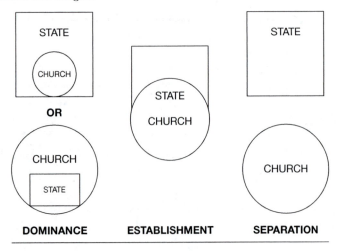

Figure 1.1 Typology of Church–State Relationships.

Complete Domination: Theocracy and Secular Suppression of Religion

As different as they are in substance, theocracy and the complete suppression of religion by government are formally very similar. In each instance, one of the two social systems completely overpowers the other, leaving it virtually no freedom or independent existence. Because they are extreme positions, they seldom appear in pure form. They are by no means absent, however, from the world stage; Afghanistan under the Taliban came quite close to a pure theocracy, while the communist government of North Korea represses religious institutions (and all other organs of non-governmental civil society) rather ruthlessly. While neither of these perspectives has many serious defenders in America, it is important to understand them, as they form the boundaries for the current discussion.

Theocracy

Theocracy is the government of a political unit by divine rule, usually thought of as operating through human rulers who receive immediate and direct guidance from God and/or sacred scripture. Theocracy assumes that religion and government are coterminous, and that every resident is subject both to the civil government and to religious authority. In one possible variation, the civil government and its officials may have some autonomy, but only as much as is granted by the religious hierarchy, which in turn may take it back at any moment. In a sense, the "state" as typically defined does not exist, since all political functions are performed by religious entities and all temporal power is ultimately held by religious authorities. While such an arrangement belongs in this typology, its embodiment in the modern world is rare. It presupposes a degree of religious strength and consensus that is unlikely in contemporary developed societies.

An example of a society with a theocratic system was the government of Moses among the early Israelites, as described in the Hebrew Bible and the Christian Old Testament. There was no distinction between the religious and the political in the life of the early Israelites. Both were subject to the all-powerful sovereign God who expressed his will for both the sacred and the secular life of the community in the law that he gave to Moses. A modern-day example of such thoroughly integrated political and religious authority is Vatican City, where the Pope is the temporal as well as the spiritual sovereign. A modified version of theocracy also exists in Iran, which styles itself an "Islamic Republic" where the elected civil authorities are ultimately subject to a Muslim cleric called the "Supreme Leader."

Governmental Suppression of Religion

In situations where there is governmental suppression of religion, the political state is typically a totalitarian entity, claiming jurisdiction over all dimensions of its subjects' lives and personhood. In such societies, the state seeks to permeate social life, taking over those functions that in other cultures are performed by religion and setting itself up as the highest value, the ultimate reality, in its subjects' lives. Usually such an arrangement leads to attempts to destroy institutional religion, since religion's claim on people's ultimate loyalties makes it an unwanted competitor for a totalitarian state.

Well-known examples of such totalitarian regimes litter recent history. Although Adolf Hitler's Nazi Party in Germany was not hostile to religion in theory, allowing the Christian churches to remain institutionally intact, in practice it subjected their leadership to constant coercion and attack. Religious people, including clergy, who resisted the Third Reich on grounds of conscience were often killed or imprisoned. Hitler's program also, of course, involved a direct attack on a particular religious group, the Jews, with the goal of total extermination.

The Soviet Union, especially under Josef Stalin, provides another dramatic example. For centuries an integral part of Russian life and culture, the Russian Orthodox Church was forced underground during the Stalinist regime. This example points up an important distinction: the suppression of religious institutions by a totalitarian government does not necessarily mean the extinction of religion, although it certainly lessens its public presence. Orthodoxy continued to exist underground in Stalinist Russia, as did a small evangelical Protestant movement.

Another twentieth-century example of a direct attack on religion by a totalitarian government was Maoist China. In the 1966 Cultural Revolution, there was a concerted effort to destroy all forms of religious practice: religious books were burned, temples destroyed, and religious leaders exiled or killed.

Death was the penalty for those who continued to openly practice their religion.

Establishments of Religion

A wide range of theories and actual practices comes under the heading of "establishments of religion." However, the basic principle is the same in all of them: The civil government supports religion, either directly or indirectly. Establishments of a stronger or weaker sort have existed at various times and places in the United States and in the colonies that preceded the revolution. Establishment also persists in many parts of the world today, and continues to have its advocates.

Protestant reformers Martin Luther in Germany and John Calvin in Switzerland advocated government support of religion, as did Henry VIII in England. The Catholic Church has often enjoyed favorable relationships with governments around the world. All were important predecessors of prominent religious groups in the United States today. Luther's teaching underlies the beliefs and practices of the Lutheran churches, and Calvinism gave rise to Presbyterianism, as well as influencing a number of other denominations. Catholics account for about a quarter of the population of the United States. None of these denominations today, however, advocate establishment in America. The most significant example of establishment in America was found in Puritan New England—to be discussed in Chapter 2.

Before discussing specific examples, it is important to consider the different forms that establishment might take. To begin with, government support for religion may be prescriptive or permissive. A prescriptive position holds that the residents of a given locale must support the religion favored by the government, by paying taxes to support its clergy, for example, or by attending its worship services. On the other hand, a permissive stance simply acknowledges the cultural predominance of a particular religion, by allowing its holy days and festivals to be celebrated in the public schools, for example.

Establishments may also exist with or without tolerance for other religions. An example of the former is the situation in which one religion receives support from tax monies while others are allowed to exist but receive no subsidy from public funds. In other circumstances, however, religions other than the official one are not even allowed to exist, or face varying degrees of discrimination.

Religious establishments may be exclusive, dual, or multiple. An exclusive establishment recognizes only one officially favored religion. At some points in the development of state constitutions in the United States, two different religions received the same treatment under a dual establishment (for example, Congregationalists and Unitarians in nineteenth-century New England). In other states during the very early statehood period, multiple establishments existed, in which taxes were paid to support whichever religious organization the taxpayer chose.

A final distinction can be made between general and specific establishments. General establishments are very broad. Full religious and political freedom might be granted to "all who believe in Jesus Christ," for example. On the other hand, specific establishments call for allegiance to a particular denomination.

Religious establishment has a long history in the Western world. The historic experience of Catholic establishment began with the dramatic conversion of the Roman Emperor Constantine in 312 and the subsequent establishment of Christianity as the official religion of the Roman Empire by 381. The Church thus began a long history of favorable relationships with civil government. In the late Roman Empire, for example, non-believers were barred from holding positions of authority, and Christian clergy received special privileges. The church also had the backing of the government in its quest to make converts. The Roman emperor was also declared the supreme authority in both civil and religious matters—a phenomenon called "caesaropapism."

The Catholic Church *was* the Christian church in the Western world until the Protestant reform movements beginning in the sixteenth century. Historically, Catholicism often took the position that the government must uphold the true religion, which, from the standpoint of the Catholicism of that time, was Catholicism. Thus, many European monarchs saw one of their roles as the safeguarding of Catholic orthodoxy within their domains.

The Catholic Church's Second Vatican Council in the early 1960s will be discussed in the section on disestablishment. Suffice it for now to say that it occasioned a rethinking of the desirability of religious establishment. While the pro-establishment Catholic view has been superseded in the teaching of the Church, it lingers as a source of uneasiness and sometimes prejudice in the minds of many non-Catholics in the United States who fear that Catholic loyalty to Rome undercuts Catholic loyalty to the United States.

We might think that, along with other sweeping religious reforms undertaken by Martin Luther (b. 1483) and John Calvin (b. 1509), they would have proposed doing away with the intimate connection between church and state that was so much a part of the Catholicism of their time. In fact, however, both Martin Luther and John Calvin supported some type of establishment for the churches that they helped found.

The pattern that finally prevailed in Luther's Germany and the Scandinavian countries was one of state churches, supported by the government. The prince of each state in the region had the right to select the religion that would be established in his kingdom, on the principle that the ruler's faith should prevail in his territory (*cuius regio, eius religio*—established with the Peace of Augsburg in 1555). What this meant in practice was that most of northern Germany and the Scandinavian countries became Protestant (Lutheran), while many of the southern German states remained Catholic.

John Calvin's view of the proper relationship between church and state was similar to Luther's. Calvin assigned a number of functions to civil government, some of which focused on the protection and advancement of religion. Civil government was to "cherish" and protect the outward worship of God, to defend sound doctrine (meaning Calvinist doctrine, of course), and to protect the position of the church (Calvin 1559: IV.xx.2). It was also responsible for preventing idolatry, sacrilege, and blasphemy, as well as "other public offenses against religion." "I now commit to civil government," Calvin wrote in his *Institutes of the Christian Religion*, "the duty of rightly establishing religion" (Calvin 1559: IV.xx.3). He also made civil officials responsible for enforcing the Ten Commandments as found in the Hebrew and Christian scriptures.

In Geneva, Calvin developed forms of both civil and church government based on what he believed was the pattern described in the Christian New Testament. The civil government was responsible in a very direct way for the affairs of the church. The line between the religious and the secular was blurred, but not erased. The same consistory that advised the city council on its actions also governed the church. The government of both the church and the city was in the hands of an elected group of officials rather than a single ruler. Calvin's belief in the sinfulness of human beings led him to believe that "men's fault or failing causes it to be safer and more bearable for a number to exercise government" (Calvin 1559: IV.xx.8). Luther, by contrast, favored a system in which princes ruled territories, but did not exercise authority over the church.

The English Reformation gave birth to the Church of England, which would become the Episcopal Church in the United States. The theological and liturgical religious reforms of the English or Tudor reformation were, at least in the beginning, slight. However, abrupt changes occurred in the relationship between church and state. Catholicism had been the established church in England, as in most of Europe. The Supremacy Act of 1534, however, created a fully separate national church in England. It declared that "the King's Majesty justly and rightly is ... the only Supreme Head in Earth of the Church of England"—thereby repudiating the ecclesiastical authority of the Pope. King Henry VIII had clearly become the head of a new national church. Under this arrangement, to dispute the legitimacy of the Church of England was to commit treason, punishable by penalties up to and including death. Thus, there was serious repression of Catholics, Lutherans, Calvinists, and Anabaptists.

Despite the power that the King or Queen exercised over the church in this system, however, there were limitations. The monarch was a layperson (not a member of the church hierarchy). He or she was in charge of appointing bishops and archbishops to their sees (area of church rule), but could not consecrate them, nor ordain men to the priesthood. The monarch was responsible for defending what the church taught was correct belief, but could not unilaterally determine what that correct belief was.

The Separation of Church and State

The separation of religious and political institutions, also known as *disestablishment*, has become a common feature of modern developed societies. While disestablishment can take various specific forms, it always involves two basic principles. First, religion is a matter of personal conscience and neither belief nor unbelief can be coerced by the government or by any religious group. Second, although peoples' religious beliefs may well influence their political behavior (as we will demonstrate throughout this book), there should be no formal connection between religious and political authorities. The state should neither directly support nor interfere with religious bodies, and political decisions should not be made according to the dictates of any specific religious leaders. In sum, disestablishment is legal separation between the institutions of religion and the institutions of government. A variety of religious and secular models have contributed to the understanding of disestablishment in the United States. Four influences in particular have been significant: the radical Protestant reformers, post-Vatican II Catholicism, Judaism, and humanism.

The Radical Protestant Reformers

Some of the Protestant reformers took a very different approach to issues of church and state than did either Luther or Calvin. These were the radical reformers (also called Anabaptists) in Germany, Switzerland, Holland, and Moravia. They opposed not only the Catholicism of their time, but also much of what Luther and Calvin taught. Their central belief was that Christians should seek to emulate the church at the time of the Christian New Testament, insofar as that was possible. The church, in their view, should be a voluntary association of believers with little hierarchy, and should shun any ties with the government (Dillenberger and Welch 1988). The ways in which Luther, Calvin, and Henry VIII had linked church and state were as unacceptable to them as were Catholic religious establishments.

Most radical reformation Christians did acknowledge the necessity of civil government and realized that they, too, benefited from it; few were out-and-out anarchists. They withdrew, however, from taking any active part in civil governance. They believed that a Christian could not be a magistrate and remain true to the faith. They generally refused to swear oaths and to participate in warfare. These positions set them against both the more mainstream churches and the civil governments of their day, and many died because of their beliefs.

Several small religious groups in America today (Quakers and Mennonites, for example) carry forward elements of Anabaptist belief. Among the larger religious denominations, Baptists are the most direct inheritors of the Anabaptist belief in the separation of church and state. As we will discuss more fully in Chapter 2, they were a significant part of a coalition that formed in support of religious liberty and disestablishment around the time of the American Revolution. Those (such as Baptists) who favored separation of church and state to protect religion from government interference joined with those (such as Thomas Paine) who sought to protect government from religious influences and with those (such as Thomas Jefferson) who simply favored individual autonomy in matters of conscience (Mead 1978).

Post-Vatican II Catholicism

Much later, in the 1960s, the Catholic Church emerged as a strong supporter of disestablishment. The Second Vatican Council, or "Vatican II" (1962–1965), was a meeting of Catholic bishops from around the world convened by Pope John XXIII to clarify and reform certain aspects of Catholic teaching and practice in order for the Church to more effectively engage the modern world. Of the many documents coming out of Vatican II, its "Declaration on Religious Freedom" is one of the most striking. It is addressed to the world at large, not just to the Catholic Church, and reflects on the relationship between individual conscience and state power.

The Declaration asserts that anything less than full freedom of religious belief violates the essential dignity of human nature. This right is derived both from human reason and from God's will for humanity made known in the Christian Bible. People should not be forced to act in ways that are contrary to their beliefs, nor should they be prevented from expressing and acting on those beliefs, within reasonable legal limits. Human nature is constituted such that people have both freedom and the responsibility that goes with it. Thus, we are all called to search for and to live by the truth. An authentic response to this inherent call, the Church argues, requires freedom from both external and psychological coercion in matters of faith.

Both the nature of religion and the social nature of human beings require that people be free to form and associate with religious groups. The same freedoms that apply to individuals apply to the groups of which they are a part, as long as these groups operate within just laws. The Declaration on Religious Freedom stipulates that, under certain circumstances, the government might choose to accord special preference to one particular religion. In that case, however, all other religious groups must have the benefits of full toleration. It also recognizes that "society has the right to defend itself against possible abuses committed on pretext of freedom of religion"—such as, for example, cynically labeling criminal practices "religious" in order to shield them from prosecution. Such protection must be carried out, however, with great care not to interfere more than is necessary with religious freedom (Second Vatican Council, 1966).

The Declaration also indicates that legal ties between religion and government can be bad for the church. It does not take the position that Christians must withdraw from worldly involvement (in fact, many documents of the Second Vatican Council argue just the opposite), but specifies that the church can fulfill its mission and calling only when it is free from undue government interference and coercion.

The Second Vatican Council's Declaration in many ways carries forward and systematizes Pope John XXIII's 1963 encyclical *Pacem in Terris*. That encyclical, in turn, built on some of Pope Pius XII's writing. During the course of the twentieth century, the Catholic Church made a remarkable journey from being the established religion in many nations, through acceptance of disestablishment in societies in which it had no choice, to a careful but powerful defense of the principle of religious freedom.

Judaism

Those of Jewish faith have often been a persecuted minority, without full civil rights, wherever they have lived since the Babylonian exile over 2,500 years ago. Owing in part to this history, many major Jewish thinkers have developed theories that advocate full separation of religion and government for the benefit of all persons.

The work of Jewish theologian Richard L. Rubenstein (1964) is an example. He notes that, ideologically, Judaism calls for a union between religion and government. That is certainly the pattern laid out in the Hebrew Bible, or what Christians would call the Old Testament. However, the realities of historical experience have led Jews—at least outside of Israel—to be nearly unanimous in their support for strong guarantees that the religious and political orders will remain separate. According to this view, political neutrality regarding religion is the only way that equality for all people can be guaranteed. Importantly, Judaism seeks more than simply the right of individuals to believe and practice their religion as they choose. It seeks their ability to participate fully in the civic communities of which they are a part, without any implication of "second-class" status because of their religious belief. This can come about only, many Jews believe, when governments maintain strict neutrality in matters of religion.

Rubenstein notes that absolute separation is not possible on an institutional level, and certainly not in the minds of most individuals. It is important, however, that the ideal be maintained as a goal and as a standard that actual practical arrangements seek to approximate. Anything less, he argues, threatens the civil rights of all.

Humanism

Although not a religion per se, humanism occupies a position in the lives of many humanists similar to that of religion in the lives of the more religiously oriented. Humanism endorses the complete separation of religion and government in the interest of both protecting the government and of guaranteeing individual rights in matters of conscience and religion. "A Secular Humanist Declaration," issued in 1980, is one of the most prominent documents that attempts to lay out the humanist viewpoint. Its authors advocate the complete separation of church and state, and make several specific points:

- Religious authorities ought not to be allowed to make their particular views into law for everyone.
- Tax money should not be used to support religious institutions.
- People should not be taxed to support religions in which they do not believe, and should be free to give financial support to organizations whose views they do share.
- Church properties should not receive special tax exemptions.
- Compulsory prayers and religious oaths in public educational or political settings violate the principle of separation.

(Kurtz 1981)

In recent years, a more aggressive humanist case for separation (and, indeed, for the complete marginalization of religion in social life) has been made by scholars often referred to as the "new atheists." This view, most prominently articulated by Sam Harris (2004), Richard Dawkins (2006), and Christopher Hitchens (2007), argues for disestablishment not only on the grounds of freedom, but because religion is socially pernicious. While there is certainly considerable overlap between self-proclaimed "humanists" and agnostics or atheists, they are not identical, and many humanists are careful to distance themselves from the sweeping claims and aggressive tenor of the "new atheist" arguments.

American Civil Religion

The discussion of the separation of church and state and its implications continues throughout this entire book. We will argue that a distinctive vision of the church–state relationship, which we term the *collaboration and cooperation* model, has grown out of the American experience of disestablishment. It sees church and state as parallel institutions, institutionally independent of one another, but working in tandem to accomplish shared goals. To be sure, Americans have disagreed historically and continue to disagree today about exactly how religion should manifest itself in our public life. Nonetheless, there has always been in America a broad-based, non-sectarian consciousness of and deference to The Divine in the life of the nation. It is embodied in what is often referred to as America's "civil religion."

The idea of a civil religion did not begin with sociologist Robert Bellah, but his work brought it to scholarly attention and ultimately to the American popular mind. In a 1967 essay, Bellah wrote that in the United States:

[T]here actually exists alongside of and rather clearly differentiated from the churches an elaborate and well-institutionalized civil religion in

America ... This public religious dimension is expressed in a set of
beliefs, symbols, and rituals that I am calling the American civil religion.
(Bellah 1967: 1, 4)

The American civil religion is a blend of the sacred and the secular that seeks
to imbue the elements of American nationhood with a reverential, universal,
and morally normative aura. The existence of a public religious dimension
in the United States begins with the founding documents of the nation,
and is carried forward through presidential addresses and similar utterances
that articulate the nation's "official" vision of itself. This religious (but
non-denominational) cast to American public life is reflected in George
Washington's declaration of November 26 as a national day of "public
thanksgiving and prayer," as well as in Congress's establishment in 1952 of
an annual National Day of Prayer, in which Americans are counseled to "turn
to God in prayer and meditation" (36 U.S.C. § 119). President Barack
Obama's speeches, like those of his predecessors, have repeatedly invoked
God's blessing on the United States.

The American civil religion has its own sacred texts (the Declaration of
Independence and the Constitution) and martyrs (Abraham Lincoln and
Martin Luther King). It has rituals such as the recitation of the Pledge of
Allegiance, as well as customs such as opening governmental sessions with
prayer. It is reflected in broad-based support for military and congressional
chaplains at public expense. It also appears in such songs (hymns?) as "The
Star-Spangled Banner," "America the Beautiful," and "God Bless America."
Most significantly, it gives rise to an American creed, which John Noonan
(1998: 245) describes as follows:

Its most salient features are these: it asks that America seek justice; it
recognizes that America is guided by divine providence; it acknowledges
that America stands under the judgment of God. In the Declaration of
Independence the founders appealed to "the Supreme Judge of the world."
The civil religion of America still makes this appeal.

Bellah's assertion of a common civil faith has been challenged and modified
by later scholars, but there remains little doubt that in the minds of most
citizens there is a religious dimension to the United States itself. It functions
as a genuine means of perceiving a sacred dimension to national life. The
inclusion of the phrases "In God we trust" on money and "One nation under
God" in the Pledge of Allegiance is criticized by some people as a violation
of the constitutional separation of church and state. The fact that these
phrases endure, however, indicates that civil religion does enjoy a type of
"permissive establishment" in the United States, despite the absence of formal
linkages between religious and governmental institutions. The collaboration
and cooperation model is based on a separation of church from state, but not
of religion from public life.

Summary and Conclusions

While this preliminary discussion necessarily paints with broad strokes, we can draw from it two key conclusions that will guide our examination of religion and politics throughout the book:

1. Politics and religion are, by their very natures, unavoidably intertwined. This connection can take many forms, as we have seen in the typology above, but there will always be a relationship.
2. Disestablishment—the legal separation of the institutions of government and those of religion—means that in the United States this relationship between government and religion can never be in a final sense "settled." It is always subject to negotiation and refinement.

The rest of this book can be seen as an exploration of the give and take, both over time and in contemporary American politics, between the deeply religious nature of American society and the nation's strong tradition of disestablishment.

In this introduction we have defined both politics and religion, discussed their common concern with power and with the provision of meaning in people's lives, and provided a typology of the relationships between them that might exist. We will now turn to the interaction of politics and religion throughout American history, beginning with the colonial experience and the intentions of the founders. We then trace this relationship during the periods from 1800 through 1960 and from 1960 through the present day. Throughout this historical section, we will demonstrate the relationship between politics and religion as it is reflected in a variety of movements and issues. These include questions of war and peace, the regulation of personal life, relationships between groups of people, and the electoral process.

Part I
Religion and History

2 The Colonial and Founding Eras

> If any man after legal conviction shall have or worship any other god but the Lord God, he shall be put to death . . . If any man shall blaspheme the name of God, the Father, Son, or Holy Ghost, with direct, presumptuous, or high handed blasphemy, or shall curse God in the like manner, he shall be put to death.
>
> (Selections from the *Colonial Laws of Massachusetts*, 1641)

> No man shall be compelled to frequent or support any religious worship, place, or ministry whatsoever, nor shall be enforced, restrained, molested, or burthened in his body or goods, or shall otherwise suffer, on account of his religious opinions or belief.
>
> (Thomas Jefferson, *Bill for Establishing Religious Freedom*, 1785)

The Puritans in the Massachusetts Bay Colony listed twelve crimes for which a person could be put to death, and the first three (blasphemy, witchcraft, and the persistent worship of "false gods") concerned religious matters. During its heyday in the seventeenth century, the Puritan system leaned toward the theocracy model discussed in Chapter 1. In this colony, the Puritan churches functionally controlled the civil government, and Puritans were very committed to using both religious and political institutions to create their vision of a "Holy Commonwealth." This Puritan idea of a community with a special, providential destiny and an over-riding obligation to do the will of God and model a rightly ordered society to the world has been very influential in American history, from the colonial era to the present day.

It is important to remember, however, that the Puritan worldview was not the only religious model in early America. Religious diversity increased and the Puritan influence waned markedly as one moved further south, with a significant Quaker presence in Pennsylvania, a strong Catholic element in Maryland, and a mixture of Anglican and Presbyterian believers in the southern colonies. Moreover, by the time of the revolutionary era in the late eighteenth century, Americans were quite diverse in their denominational affiliations, doctrinal beliefs, and levels of religious commitment, and states varied widely in their approach to the establishment question. The nation's early leaders, therefore, had to wrestle with how to accommodate this religious pluralism while at the same time maintaining a robust role for religion in American public life.

This chapter examines religion and politics in the colonies prior to the American Revolution, then explores religious–political linkages during the revolutionary era and the founding of the United States. To understand the relationship between politics and religion in the development of the United States—and especially how this relationship is dealt with in the Constitution—we must first examine some important colonial roots. Religious and political experiences in the early colonies had an important impact on the framing of the Declaration of Independence, the U.S. Constitution, and state constitutions. These arrangements in turn affected the course of political and religious history in the United States. As we have shown in Chapter 1, religion and politics can both be sources of meaning and power in people's lives; this was very much the case in the colonial and founding eras.

We will begin with the Puritans in the Massachusetts Bay Colony and describe their legacy for the nation's political development. Next we will examine important developments elsewhere in colonial America, such as the growth of religious tolerance in Rhode Island, the pluralism of the middle colonies, and the weakness of religious establishments in the southern colonies. Then we turn to two important eighteenth-century forces that helped shape the future of politics and religion in the United States: the Great Awakening (an evangelical religious revival) and rationalist religion (focused on the harmonizing of faith and reason). Here are some of the major questions to be approached in this chapter:

- How did Puritan views of covenant, congregation, and civil society influence the political development of the United States?
- What was the Puritan view of religious tolerance, and how did it differ from that expressed in other colonies (e.g., Rhode Island and Pennsylvania)?
- How did religious arrangements in the middle and southern colonies differ from those in New England?
- How did rationalist religion and the pietistic movement of the Great Awakening, though very different, join forces to support the American Revolution?
- What were the Founders' views on religion and on the proper relationship between religion and politics?
- How do America's great founding documents (the Declaration of Independence and the Constitution) treat religion?

The Puritans and the Massachusetts Bay Colony

Motives for the Colony's Founding

The Puritan colonists who founded the Massachusetts Bay Colony came to the New World for predominantly religious motives. They left England in order to live their lives and organize their communities more in accord with their own religious beliefs than had been possible in the mother country.

Prior to 1500, the Catholic Church was the only Christian religious body in western Europe. During the sixteenth century, however, religious leaders such as Martin Luther and John Calvin, who objected to various aspects of Catholic theology and worship, brought about the Protestant Reformation. Following the Reformation, some countries, such as Spain and Portugal, remained overwhelmingly Catholic, while others, such as Sweden and Norway, became predominantly Protestant. In England, for personal more than doctrinal reasons, King Henry VIII broke relations with the Catholic Church, established the Church of England (the Anglican Church), and made himself its head.

Because Henry VIII's quarrel with Rome was political rather than theological, the Church of England retained significant elements of Catholic doctrine and worship style. This displeased many in England who were sympathetic to the Protestant Reformation. The Puritans were among these, and their name derives from the fact that they sought to "purify" the Church of England of its remaining Catholic influences. While some Puritans (like the Pilgrims) wanted to separate from the Church of England completely, the Puritans who settled the Massachusetts Bay Colony were content to maintain a formal affiliation with the Church of England as long as they could shape the Church in accordance with their own Protestant beliefs. During the reigns of James I and Charles I, who had more Anglo-Catholic sympathies, many Puritans decided that their vision of the Church could only be realized outside England. Thus, Puritans established the Massachusetts Bay Colony in 1630; over the next decade, more than 20,000 Puritans migrated there.

The Puritans in the Massachusetts Bay Colony were *Congregationalists*. Various settlements in the colony had their own churches, each of which was based around its congregation. Each congregation selected its own minister and made its own decisions, within broad limits. While all congregations were tied together by an overall structure and a generally similar set of beliefs and practices, congregational autonomy did result in some significant variations. In Salem, for example, women were permitted to speak publicly in church meetings, while this was not allowed in Boston (Schneider 1958). This sort of congregational self-governance, without significant oversight from bishops or other high clergy, was a key part of the Puritan conception of the properly ordered Church.

The Puritan Conception of Covenant

The Puritans saw themselves in a very special light. In the biblical exodus, the Children of Israel fled bondage in Egypt to travel to a new land promised to them by God. The Puritans saw themselves as the new chosen people and America as the new Israel. They made a covenant with the Lord: if God brought them safely to the New World and helped them to prosper there, they would build a society—a Holy Commonwealth—governed by divine laws. John Winthrop, the first governor of the Massachusetts Bay Colony, likened the colony to a "City set upon a Hill," a model of Christian community with the eyes of the world upon it. The Puritans would set an example for the world. This kind of thinking has persisted in the United States, if in a more secular form; Americans often view themselves as having a special mission to serve as an example for the rest of the world.

Given the conspicuous position of the Puritan experiment in the eyes of the world, God would punish the colony severely if it strayed too far from divine law. The covenant was an agreement of the colonists with each other and with God; thus, the contract obligated the whole community. This covenant was to be reflected in both religious and political organizations. While separate institutions, the church and the state were each to support and protect the other. Church attendance was required of everyone, and everyone contributed to the financial support of the church.

This concept of a covenant among people became very important in the later political history of the country. When the Founders wrote the Declaration of Independence, the concept of a social contract was crucial: individuals entered into a contract with government in which they submitted to the law in return for protection of their inalienable, God-given rights. This social contract was certainly different from the Puritan covenant, and was based on the writings of John Locke rather than the ideas of the Puritans. However, two points are in order. First, covenant theology preceded the work of John Locke and probably influenced his thinking about the social contract between citizens and the government. Second, the covenant theology of the Puritans had prepared ordinary Americans to think in terms of a social contract. To a people accustomed to thinking of making commitments to God and each other in return for certain benefits for all within the community, the idea of a covenant or contract between the people and the government was not such a great leap.

Indeed, the democratic element in Puritan covenant theology is clear. Cowing (1971) has noted that there are three classic forms of church organization: episcopal (government by bishops), presbyterian (government by elders), and congregational (government by the whole church membership). Many scholars have associated these three with (respectively) monarchy, republicanism, and democracy in terms of secular governance. The idea that the congregation itself is the basic source of authority in the church certainly had implications for later notions of democracy in the civil sphere.

One should not, however, push the notion of a democratic Puritan society too far. Only full-covenant church members could participate in church and civil governance. Such members constituted no more than 20 percent of the colony's population (Miller and Johnson 1938), and perhaps even less than 10 percent (Reichley 2002; Fowler et al. 2010). In order to be a full-covenant church member, one had to demonstrate evidence of spiritual regeneration, or a dramatic personal conversion experience. This involved elaborate testimonials, before both the church elders and the entire congregation, that those seeking membership knew and understood the substance of Christian faith and that they had been "wounded in their hearts for their originall sinne" (Schneider 1958: 20). Only by virtue of such an ordeal could it be established that a person was truly one of "the elect," those predestined by God to receive spiritual regeneration and to become a community of living saints.

While everyone in the community was a member of a congregation and was expected to attend services and support the church, only those who went through the arduous process of demonstrating their spiritual regeneration could become full-covenant members, thus gaining a say in both ecclesiastical and secular government. The civil government had authority over everyone in the community, but was controlled by the minority of the population that had achieved full church membership.

Puritan Intolerance

The Puritans believed that they had a mission, and they were very concerned about the spiritual health of their "New Jerusalem"; thus, they enforced strict conformity with their beliefs and practices. Efforts to maintain this religious conformity resulted in intolerance, persecution, and exile for those who strayed (Gaustad and Schmidt 2002). In addition to conformity with orthodox religious views, Chidester (1988) points out that everyone was expected to attend church, to live in a family setting rather than singly, to read the Bible, to be modest in behavior and dress, and to monitor each other's moral behavior. Any departure from the established pattern was regarded as a danger to the entire social fabric, placing the whole community in peril of God's judgment.

The Puritans did not believe in tolerance for differing religious views; to them, the very idea of religious pluralism was absurd (Miller and Johnson 1938; Miller 1989; Reichley 2002). They believed that only the truth should be heard, and that it was dangerous and immoral to allow false religious ideas to be expressed. They were, it is only fair to note, hardly alone in this idea. At that time, support for the idea that a society should tolerate diverse religious views was rare in the world, except perhaps in the Netherlands. The Puritans' intolerance of religious diversity cannot simply be dismissed as ignorance; on the contrary, the Puritans placed great emphasis on learning, as their founding of universities such as Harvard and Yale indicates. Such learning, however, needed to be rightly directed toward what they saw as the proper worship of God.

The Puritans did not come to the New World to celebrate religious diversity; if anything, they came to escape it, to find virgin territory in which a like-minded community of believers could build a Holy Commonwealth. Religious liberty in the eyes of the Puritans was the freedom of other believers to keep away, as indicated by the following declaration from Puritan clergyman Nathaniel Ward (1647: 97):

> I dare take it upon me, to be the Herauld of New-England so farre, as to proclaime to the world, in the name of our Colony, that all Familists, Antinomians, Anabaptists, and other Enthusiasts, shall have free Liberty to keep away from us, and such as will come to be gone as fast as they can, the sooner the better.

Believing that their own religious views represented God's will, the Puritans took pride in punishing transgressors. Miller and Johnson (1938: 185) describe the puzzlement of Puritans at the end of the seventeenth century when the idea of religious toleration was becoming more acceptable in the world:

> They could hardly understand what was happening in the world, and they could not for a long time be persuaded that they had any reason to be ashamed of their record of so many Quakers whipped, blasphemers punished by the amputation of ears, Antinomians exiled, Anabaptists fined, or witches executed.

There was little tolerance in Massachusetts Bay Colony for visions of Christianity that differed from Puritan orthodoxy. The banishment of heretics such as Roger Williams and Anne Hutchinson, as well as the anti-witchcraft hysteria of Salem, are well known. The practice of Roman Catholicism was strictly forbidden, and in 1647 Jesuit priests were barred from the colony on penalty of death (O'Connor 1998). At first, Quaker missionaries who came to Massachusetts to spread their views were simply banished. However, as Quakers kept coming, harsher punishments were introduced for them, such as cutting off their ears or boring a hole in their tongues with a hot iron— and then banishing them. When even this didn't stop Quaker missionary activity, the death penalty was added. Between 1659 and 1661, four Quakers were put to death by the Puritans (Miller 1976). It appeared that the persecution would become even more deadly; however, in 1661, King Charles II intervened and prohibited any corporal punishment of Quakers.

To understand this behavior, it is important to keep in mind the worldview of the Puritans. They were the new chosen people in the new Israel. They had a covenant with God to establish religious and political institutions in accord with divine law. This covenant community of saints had to be kept as pure as possible given the realities of human depravity. The Puritans worked hard and led ascetic, self-disciplined lives to produce their City upon a Hill. It could not be corrupted by false doctrines or religious indifference. The religious intolerance they demonstrated was not new in the world; on the contrary, until the eighteenth century, it was more the rule than the exception.

The Erosion of Puritanism

By the eighteenth century, "pure" Puritanism had faded, and was giving way even in New England to religious rationalism and evangelism as the dominant forces in colonial religious life. As the first generations of Puritans passed on, Puritanism was unable to retain its original form and ardor. In 1684, the British government took away the charter of the Massachusetts Bay Colony and brought it under more direct control by the government in London; this lessened the power and independence of the Puritans. Further, the idea of religious toleration was becoming more acceptable in the world, and the British Act of Toleration of 1689 extended religious tolerance to all Protestants. Finally, church membership ceased to be a prerequisite for voting for civil government, and as religious zeal decreased, church membership began to dwindle.

Miller and Johnson (1938) argue that a very serious problem developed with regard to the covenant idea as time passed. As religious ardor cooled, it became more and more difficult to distinguish between citizens (in the original Puritan sense of full-covenant church membership) and inhabitants. As this happened, many people began to view the covenant in a different way—as a compact among people rather than as a compact of people with God. This shift moved the covenant concept closer to the idea of a secular social contract, and lessened the importance of Puritanism in both religious and civil matters.

As Puritanism in its original form declined, some church leaders took a pragmatic approach to try to preserve as much of it as they could (Cowing 1971). Given less interest among people in achieving the rather daunting full church membership, the "Half Way Covenant" was introduced. This plan reduced the requirements for a kind of partial membership in the church. Baptized Christians received this type of membership until they could demonstrate their spiritual regeneration. For many, this was the final plateau of membership; they never attempted the more difficult task of publicly demonstrating their spiritual rebirth. Allowing people to become partial church members in this way did increase membership in the Puritan congregations. Ultimately, however, the predominance of Puritan thought and practice in the colonies—even where it had once held sway—could not be maintained. According to one estimate, on the eve of the American Revolution, only 22 percent of the population of Massachusetts were formal members of church congregations, and in all the colonies combined only about one fifth of churches were congregational (Finke and Stark 1992).

Puritanism's Legacy

Most Americans today reject significant aspects of the Puritan worldview—most notably its rigid religious intolerance. Some Puritan beliefs, however, have had a tremendous impact on American political and religious culture. We will briefly review several of these influential ideas.

Covenant Theology and the Social Contract

As indicated before, the covenant concept—that the Puritans had formed a compact with God and with each other to establish a society in accord with divine law—preceded and perhaps influenced John Locke's social contract views, which were so important in the Declaration of Independence. The social contract described in the Declaration of Independence differed significantly from the Puritan conception, but the Puritans had laid the groundwork for thinking of a covenant among and between people and the government as the basis for society. This idea has persisted in American political thought and rhetoric, as reflected by Bill Clinton's call at the 1992 Democratic National Convention for "a New Covenant—a solemn agreement between the people and their government."

The "City upon a Hill" and American Destiny

The Puritans came to the New World thinking of themselves as a chosen people with a mission. America was the new Israel, and the Puritans had formed a covenant with God and each other to build a society based on divine law. They were to stand in sharp contrast to the corruption, decadence, and depravity of the world they had left behind, to be a morally shining "City set upon a Hill" and an example to all of what a godly commonwealth could be. Today, many Americans continue to think of their country as having a special mission and providing an example to the world, if not necessarily in explicitly religious terms. This view has been echoed by presidents throughout American history, from President Lincoln's characterization of the American ideals of freedom as the "last, best hope of earth," to President Reagan's frequent references to the United States as a beacon for oppressed nations. It is reflected in the desire of American leaders as disparate as Woodrow Wilson and George W. Bush to model and promote American ideals of the good society globally.

Congregationalism and Democracy

Within limits, the individual congregations in the Massachusetts Bay Colony had autonomy in religious matters; decisions were made democratically and openly by all full members of the church. In addition, church members also elected the colony's civil government. Individuals in Puritan communities were under an obligation to learn; literacy, for example, was required of everyone so that they could study the Bible. These practices contributed significantly to the development of a democratic political culture in America. To be sure, full participation in civil government was limited to the small minority who were full church members, and Puritan leaders stopped well short of a full embrace of popular sovereignty. The Puritans remained at least outwardly loyal to the King, and Chidester (1988: 34) reports that Governor John Winthrop regarded democracy as one of the "meanest and worst forms of government." Even so, it is no coincidence that ideals such as popular empowerment and local autonomy, so critical to the American founding, flourished in a place where religious congregationalism had held such sway.

Original Sin and Limited Government

The Puritans believed strongly in original sin and in the pervasiveness of human depravity. This skeptical view of human nature significantly influenced the development of American political culture. While the Declaration of Independence did not emphasize this negative view, the writers of the Constitution—notably James Madison—were powerfully shaped by it. In recent times, there has been criticism of gridlock in American government; it appears very difficult to get all branches of the government to agree enough in order to solve the problems of the country. The preconditions for this gridlock, however, were deliberately built into the constitutional framework by the Founders. Given a negative view of human nature, they formulated a limited government with restrictions, checks and balances, and separation of powers. There is more than a whiff of the Puritan legacy in Madison's discussion, throughout the *Federalist Papers*, of the pervasiveness of greed, ambition, and the will to dominate others, and of the unreliability of good intentions. The Founders did not have faith in full-fledged, unlimited democracy; they intentionally sought to check and counterbalance all powers, including that of the people. According to Madison in *Federalist* 51, it is "a reflection on human nature that such devices should be necessary to control the abuses of government."

The Other British Colonies

While Puritanism was the predominant religious influence in colonial Massachusetts (and, to a lesser extent, in New Hampshire and Connecticut as well), markedly different religious arrangements prevailed in the other British colonies of North America. These served to temper and mediate the Puritan influence on American political culture, and also contributed much to the American understanding of church–state relations.

Roger Williams, Rhode Island, and Religious Liberty

Roger Williams was a Puritan minister who came to the Massachusetts Bay colony from England in 1631. Soon after his arrival, he began to run afoul of local leaders because of his outspoken condemnation of many aspects of religious and political practice in the colony. While his points of contention with the religious and political establishment were many, Gaustad and Schmidt (2002) identify three principal ones. First, Williams advocated separation of church and state in order to purify the church even further; he greatly feared that true religion would be (and, to some extent, had already been) corrupted by intertwining with the civil power. Second, Williams wanted the Massachusetts Puritans to break completely with the Church of England; even the loosest association with its hierarchical governance and liturgical conventions brought with it, in his view, the taint of "popery." Third, Williams was concerned that the Puritans had simply taken land from the Native Americans without any agreement with them or any compensation for the land; he further argued that King Charles I had no right to give the land to the Puritans because it did not belong to him in the first place.

Because Williams was quite vocal about these and other criticisms, he was officially banished from the Massachusetts Bay Colony in 1635. In January 1636, Williams was to be arrested and returned to England; however, he fled the colony. Later that year, he and a small group of followers bought some land from Native Americans in what is now Rhode Island and founded Providence.

Roger Williams and the Rhode Island experiment are today generally associated with religious tolerance. This is rather ironic, however, given Williams's own religious views; his eventual grudging embrace of toleration evolved out of a quest for an even purer, more exclusivist form of Puritanism than existed in the Massachusetts Bay Colony. He despised both Quakers and Catholics, castigated the religious practices of both the Church of England and the Massachusetts Puritans as insufficiently "reformed," and was convinced that the Native Americans were in the thrall of demons and in need of immediate conversion. In the end, however, Williams essentially threw up his hands and consented to religious toleration in Rhode Island, even doing away with the Puritans' notorious persecution of witches, because those who he regarded as free from significant doctrinal error were so few. As Wills (1990: 347) explains:

> If he started hanging witches, he would be forced to proceed thence to Quakers and afterward, by degrees, through almost the whole population. Once he had resigned himself to the prospect that Rhode Island would fill up with consorts of the Whore of Babylon, wearing almost every guise imaginable, there was not much he could do but get along with them, day by day, as he had with the devil-worshiping Indians.

In Rhode Island, Roger Williams put into practice his evolving political and religious views. First, he bought the land from the Native Americans rather than simply getting title for it from the British government. Second, he helped to found a church that was not tied to the Church of England. This church, however, was not formally established; the colony's government had a role to play in providing for the social order, but it was not to control religious life. It was Roger Williams—not Thomas Jefferson—who first used the metaphor of a "wall of separation" between church and state, but his purpose was to protect the church from being corrupted by the world (Barry 2013).

Paradoxically, despite his own strong and intolerant religious convictions, Roger Williams became a champion of religious liberty and the separation of church and state. As we noted in Chapter 1, one of the arguments for separating civil and religious authority is that it will protect religion from governmental interference. This was certainly Williams's view. He believed that efforts by the state to compel people to accept specific religious beliefs would only lead to hypocrisy; he also felt that it was morally wrong to persecute people for their religious beliefs, no matter how deeply erroneous he believed them to be. The state, governed by democratic means, provided for the public order; within that state, people were free to hold their own religious beliefs, and to work out their own paths to Heaven (or Hell).

As a result of this freedom of conscience in Rhode Island, the colony became diverse in religious beliefs. Roger Williams helped to found a Baptist church, and was a Baptist himself for a while. In addition to Baptists, there were Quakers and, later, Anglicans and Congregationalists. A variety of Protestant viewpoints were represented, and eventually there were also Jews and Catholics in Rhode Island. This example of religious pluralism provided a sharp counterpoint to Massachusetts in colonial New England.

Religious Pluralism in the Middle Colonies

As one moved south of New England in colonial America, the Puritan influence declined considerably. The middle colonies of New York, New Jersey, Pennsylvania, Delaware, and Maryland exhibited a great deal of religious diversity, and this pluralism no doubt had a great impact on the development of religious tolerance in America during the eighteenth century.

Pennsylvania was founded by William Penn, a Quaker, as a "Holy Experiment." Penn believed that people should receive spiritual salvation independently rather than through an established church. He believed strongly in religious toleration, and he deliberately incorporated religious diversity into the development of Pennsylvania. Penn did not establish a colony for Quakers alone; on the contrary, he welcomed (and, indeed, actively recruited) a diversity of religious groups to Pennsylvania—although he did enforce the Quakers' views of moral standards on all residents. In addition to Quakers, the Pennsylvania colony contained significant settlements of Mennonites, Amish, German Lutherans, German Reformed, Scotch–Irish Presbyterians, Welsh Baptists, free African Methodists, Irish Catholics, deists, and Anglicans, among others (Miller 1976; Gaustad and Schmidt 2002). This diversity helped to protect religious freedom, as no single group was predominant. Further, to the surprise of some, the colony thrived.

In New York and New Jersey, religious diversity developed despite some official efforts to discourage it. New York (originally New Netherland), for example, was originally settled by the Dutch West India Company, and Dutch Reformed Calvinism became the established faith. The Dutch, however, were fairly tolerant and loose in their religious establishment. At any rate, the area was quickly filled by people of diverse religious views. When the director general, Peter Stuyvesant, later tried to reduce the diversity (e.g., by keeping Jews out and by punishing Quakers), he was rebuked by the West India Company and by his own people. In 1664, the British captured New Netherland and, under the control of the Duke of York, it became New York. For a while, there was even greater religious tolerance in the colony because of the Duke's Catholic sympathies. While the Church of England was eventually established in New York following the Protestant triumph in England's "Glorious Revolution" of 1688, the colony's governors were never able to bring about religious uniformity through this establishment. The religious diversity that had frustrated Peter Stuyvesant continued to thwart efforts to create a unified church in the colony (Gaustad and Schmidt 2002).

A bit further south, Maryland was originally founded as a haven for Catholics, but it did not remain so for long. Cecil Calvert (Lord Baltimore), a Catholic, founded Maryland in 1634. He wanted to attract both Catholics and Protestants to Maryland, but to protect Catholics from the discrimination that they faced in England. Protestants soon outnumbered the Catholics in the colony, and in 1649, Calvert persuaded the Maryland Assembly to pass the Toleration Act, providing religious liberty for all persons who professed to believe in Jesus Christ. Eventually, however, Protestants took control in Maryland and excluded Catholics from holding public office. Further, after the Glorious Revolution of 1688, Maryland became a royal province, and the Church of England was established as its official church.

The Southern Colonies: A Weak Anglican Establishment

The first permanent British colony in what is now the United States was established at Jamestown, Virginia, in 1607. Unlike the New England settlers and some of those in the middle colonies, those who came to Jamestown (and, indeed, to most of the South) did so for primarily economic rather than religious reasons. The Jamestown colony was founded in order to seek profit (and thus to strengthen the British empire). The Anglican Church was formally established; people were usually required to attend its services and to help pay for its support. For at least the first half of the century, however, the Anglican Church in Virginia was very weak. The church's resources were not great, and the great expanses of territory meant that the ecclesiastical presence was spread very thin. Adding to this was the fact that there were few Anglican clergy in early Virginia, and these were, for the most part, neither industrious nor particularly good role models. Generally, the only clergy who could be persuaded to leave England and come to Virginia were those who wished to escape from problems (e.g., debts) in the old country (Gaustad and Schmidt 2002). The situation improved in the second half of the century as the colony took root, and the Anglican organization became stronger. However, after the British Act of Toleration of 1689, Protestant religious diversity increased in Virginia. During the eighteenth century, Baptists, Presbyterians, and Methodists flowed into the colony. Because of the tensions that resulted between Anglican establishment and religious pluralism, Virginia gave rise to men such as Jefferson and Madison who were firmly committed to religious liberty.

In 1663, King Charles II gave to some of his supporters the land that was to be called Carolina, which was later divided into North Carolina and South Carolina. Settlement in this area, however, was very slow. Gaustad and Schmidt (2002) report that by the end of the seventeenth century the population in Carolina was only about 8,000, and half of these people were black slaves. The owners of Carolina were concerned with profit rather than religion, and they granted religious freedom to anyone who would come to settle in the area. In the "wild, sparsely settled and ill-governed expanses of early Carolina," churches had a very weak hold (Ahlstrom 1972: 196). The Anglican Church was the primary church in the Carolinas, but attempts to establish it were unsuccessful. There was simply too much (Protestant) religious diversity and too little institutionalization of any sort for a relatively weak church to impose uniformity.

Georgia, the last of the British colonies to be established in what is now the United States, was not founded until 1733. While the Anglican Church was the official religion, it was weak. At the time of the American Revolution, the population of Georgia was small, diverse, and relatively scattered, and tended to be under-served by the clergy and institutions of the established church.

Eighteenth-Century Religious Movements

By the end of the seventeenth century, the British empire had taken direct control of all the colonies. While this strengthened the official position of the Anglican Church in some areas, the British Act of Toleration of 1689 helped to preserve a significant degree of religious pluralism. During the eighteenth century, two important religious forces emerged with strong implications for the American Revolution and for religious liberty: the Great Awakening and religious rationalism.

The Great Awakening

The Great Awakening was an evangelical Protestant religious revival that saw its greatest flowering in America in the 1730s and 1740s. The movement was an expansive, broad-based religious movement in that it attempted to bring into the church many who would not have qualified under older Puritan standards. In this, it was largely successful—church membership increased substantially during this period. The Great Awakening was also marked by highly emotional and dramatic preaching; the movement emphasized religious fervor and personal conversion more than theological study or religious reasoning. Conversion was seen as a sudden, dramatic event that instantaneously and profoundly changed a person through religious rebirth.

Leaders of the Great Awakening

While the Great Awakening is generally seen as a movement of the mid-eighteenth century, many of its roots were planted by the earlier work of Solomon Stoddard (1643–1729), a Congregational minister in Northampton, Connecticut (Cowing 1971). In essence, Stoddard brought people into the congregation by not discriminating between those who had made a public testimony of their spiritual regeneration and those who had not. The congregation included both those who had been saved and those who wanted to be saved, and Stoddard did not make distinctions between the two groups in worship and communion. His goal was to bring virtually everyone into the church and then to help lead them to the fullness of Christian faith and life.

Stoddard's approach to bringing people to the faith was unusual for its time. The substance of his preaching was not much different from traditional Puritan ideas, but his style was emotive and evangelical. Stoddard's view is reflected in his often-quoted statement: "The Word is as a hammer and we should use it to break the Rocky Hearts of Men" (Cowing 1971: 43). In order to convert souls, Stoddard skillfully and dramatically invoked fear of damnation on one hand and the possibility of salvation on the other. Stoddard first terrorized people (this is what God will do to those who reject His grace), then gave them the good news (here is how you can be saved).

Stoddard's work was carried on in part by his famous grandson, Jonathan Edwards (1703–1758), who is well known for his sermon "Sinners in the Hands of an Angry God." After Stoddard died, Edwards took over his pulpit in Northampton. While Edwards's manner was less dramatic than Stoddard's, he developed a very effective style of expressing complex and profound theological ideas in a plain manner so that they were easily understood. Edwards has been classified by some (e.g., Noll et al. 1989) as the most important theologian of the Great Awakening.

Reichley (2002) argues that Edwards's chief influence on politics was his part in relating the millennial expectations aroused by the Great Awakening to the American nationalism that was developing in the eighteenth century. While he clearly believed in the pervasiveness of sin and corruption, Edwards also held that civil society could be used to build—very gradually—God's kingdom on earth. He believed that as time passed, progress toward this goal would be achieved. This belief in gradual progress toward a better society was very important in the beliefs of American evangelical Christians in the eighteenth century, and it clearly had an impact on their willingness to support social and political change. As we will see in Chapter 4, this belief in the power of people of faith to change society for the better continues to have significant resonance today.

An even more central figure in the Great Awakening than Jonathan Edwards was George Whitefield (1714–1770). He was the movement's greatest preacher, and was probably the most widely known person in all of the colonies by the time of his death. Whitefield traveled around the colonies preaching between 1738 and 1770, and was instrumental in driving the evangelical religious revival of those times.

Whitefield was by all accounts a spellbinding orator, and had great power over those who heard him. His powerful voice could reach crowds of thousands who gathered to hear him; Benjamin Franklin calculated that Whitefield's voice could reach 30,000 people at one time. Whitefield's presentation of Christianity, while clearly rooted in Calvinism, was a bit gentler than that of his Puritan forbears, focusing more on inspiration and religious enthusiasm than on human depravity. While Whitefield was not the theologian that Jonathan Edwards was, he provided an enduring model for revivalist preachers and carried the revival message to the people more effectively than anyone in America had done before.

Effects of the Great Awakening

Whitefield's revivals represented the peak of the Great Awakening, and there is no doubt that the movement had a significant effect on religious, social, and even political life in the colonies. Noll et al. (1989) argue that the Great Awakening had three major effects: it converted many new Christians; it energized many churches and made them more active; and it shaped colonial culture (e.g., by spurring a greater interest in education for both religious and secular purposes). Chidester (1988) argues that the Protestant pietism (the personalized, inner emotional experience of religious power) of the Great Awakening supported a more democratic distribution of political power.

This pietism of the eighteenth century was used to undergird the efforts of the American Revolution. Kidd (2010) concludes that the large evangelical element in the American population was crucial in spurring both revolutionary fervor and a desire for religious freedom. Kidd (2010), Chidester (1988), Cowing (1971), and others argue that the Great Awakening contributed directly to the American Revolution is several key ways:

- The pietism of the movement gave people a sense of personal religious power; this feeling of religious empowerment led to a desire for empowerment in other areas of life as well, and specifically to support for more democratic political practices.
- In clashing with more traditional religious establishments, evangelicals strove to achieve religious freedom. This, in turn, led to support for

political freedom and ultimately for independence of the colonies from Great Britain and the Anglican Church.

• Those who accepted the millennialism of the movement—the belief that progress would be made, through human effort, toward achieving God's kingdom on earth—were eager to help bring this about by establishing a better social order.

There is no doubt that the pietism and religious fervor of the Great Awakening supplied much of the energy and impetus for the American Revolution. The intellectual rationale and underpinnings, however, were largely supplied by a different movement: religious rationalism.

Religious Rationalism and the Enlightenment

The European Enlightenment, an intellectual movement of the seventeenth and eighteenth centuries, revolved around the use of human reason to discover and understand the laws that governed nature and society. This movement encompassed a range of thinkers, from those whose primary accomplishments were in the physical sciences (e.g., Isaac Newton) to those whose major contributions were in the philosophical realm (e.g., John Locke). Their approach to understanding all aspects of the universe—whether the laws of motion or the laws of God—was to use the human intellect to discern rational answers based on observable reality. Rationalists expected that their approach would lead to progress in improving the human condition.

Obviously, European rationalism would not be adopted by the average farmer or tradesman in the colonies. While the Puritan heritage valued learning and required people to be able to read, common people in America would not know about or care about European intellectual currents. However, people in relatively well-to-do families did have the resources and the time to read broadly, and thus to be influenced by the European Enlightenment. Men such as Thomas Jefferson and Benjamin Franklin are prominent examples of the application of rationalism to both the physical world (in terms of their inventions) and to the social world (in terms of their political theories). Many of the elite who adopted Enlightenment viewpoints developed a very non-traditional view of religion; religion itself was to be analyzed through the prism of human rationality. This led to the development of religious approaches that have been termed "rational religion" or "religious rationalism."

Enlightenment Religion

Some clergy in the colonies were educated at colleges in which they were exposed to Enlightenment philosophy. Their liberal, rationalist religion rejected the traditional Calvinist outlook with its emphasis on the depravity of human nature, predestination, and the necessity of conversion. Instead, they took a more benign view of human nature and human prospects; the emphasis was not on the next life, but on what people could do in the here and now. There was more emphasis on questions of ethics (how should people act towards one another?) than of theology (what is the nature of God?). Ahlstrom (1972) notes that there was no uniformity in the ideas of Enlightenment theology, but certain ideas were widely shared, and he describes seven chief characteristics of "enlightened Christianity." In brief, they are as follows:

1. It emphasized the role of humans in their own redemption and it rejected predestination.
2. It stressed simplicity in Christian doctrine.
3. It emphasized the importance of leading an ethical life.
4. It saw little value in sacraments and clerical ministry outside of moral instruction.
5. It placed great emphasis on reason, rather than revelation, as a source of knowledge.
6. It stressed the idea of human progress, and downplayed the limitations imposed by circumstance.
7. It viewed God as an impersonal power that ruled the universe through natural laws, rather than as a personal God who related to humans.

Political Implications of Religious Rationalism

This rationalist religion, of course, was naturally suited for a political system that expanded power beyond the few. Rational religion and Enlightenment philosophy were very much in tune with the establishment of new ways of doing things in the governance of human beings. A rejection of traditional authority in religion led very easily to questioning the legitimacy of existing political arrangements, especially monarchy and hereditary aristocracy. Of course, it is important to stress, religious rationalism remained much more an elite-level than a mass phenomenon. It did not by itself have sufficient adherents or influence to spur a revolution. In tandem with the currents stirred up by the Great Awakening, however, it could become quite powerful. Despite their obvious differences, rational religion and pietistic evangelicalism shared some key features—most notably a belief in human agency in producing some ideal state of affairs on earth—and they joined forces temporarily in support of the revolutionary cause (Mead 1978).

Religion and the Revolution

During the 1760s and 1770s, a variety of political and economic tensions contributed to an increasing estrangement between the American colonies and the British government. These strains were due in large part to an increasing sense among the colonies that they could rule themselves and that they needed neither the benefits nor the restraints of a distant government in which they had little say. Considerable resentment was also engendered by the British government's attempts to shift the costs of colonial administration and imperial defense to the colonists themselves. The debt of the British government was staggering, and much of it stemmed from military expenses incurred during the French and Indian War, which ended in 1763. As a result, the British government enacted the Sugar Act in 1764, the Stamp Act in 1765, and the Tea Act in 1773—all of which imposed significant new taxes on the American colonies. For both political and economic reasons, many colonists strongly opposed these measures, giving rise to the "No Taxation Without Representation" slogan and, ultimately, to armed rebellion.

In addition to these well-known political and economic issues, some important religious concerns also drove a wedge between the colonies and the Mother Country. First, some colonists feared that Britain would appoint an Anglican bishop in America. Recall that the Anglican Church was the official, established church in England. Many Anglicans in America wanted Britain to appoint a bishop for the colonies; however, many people of other faiths (and some Anglicans) feared such external control of religious institutions and the accompanying strengthening of religious establishment. Second, the Quebec Act of 1774 caused an uproar among many colonists. Having acquired Quebec from the French as a result of victory in the French and Indian War, the British came to an agreement with the French Catholic population of Quebec. This agreement gave the Catholics some degree of autonomy (e.g., the ability to raise tax money for religious schools) and the kind of protected status that Catholics had in Catholic countries in Europe. Many American colonists saw this arrangement as the establishment of a "hostile" religion in North America, and reacted angrily. There was strong anti-Catholic sentiment in this period among American Protestants of virtually all stripes, and many balked at any official recognition of Catholicism. Thus, ironically, one of the motivations for the American Revolution was colonial objection to the excessive religious tolerance shown by the British government in a neighboring province.

As a result of these political, economic, and religious grievances, a period of colonial resistance against the British government began. This resistance initially took the form of defiance of British tax laws and harassment of tax collectors. In response, the British government escalated its use of force in order to bring the defiant colonists to heel. This escalation led, in turn, to greater resistance from the Americans and to a growing desire for complete separation from the British empire.

The process of declaring political independence from Britain changed church–state relations in America. In the first place, the emphasis in political and religious rhetoric on personal and local autonomy carried over into debates about the proper relationships among the individual, religious bodies, and political institutions. Further, as the colonies declared their independence from Britain, they transformed themselves into independent states, and this process opened certain questions for debate. As each of these newly created states drafted its own constitution, questions of church–state relations inevitably arose. On the eve of the American Revolution, most colonies had some provision for an establishment of religion, and often these provisions were simply carried over into the new state constitutions. However, the spirit of religious freedom engendered by these discussions would be very influential in the framing of the national Constitution, and most of these state-level religious establishments were eliminated by the end of the century.

After declaring independence, the states formed a loose association under the Articles of Confederation; after the war was over, this government continued functioning for a time. However, many leaders in the states wanted a stronger national government for various reasons (e.g., to aid economic development, to present a stronger front in international relations, and to provide more effectively for national defense). With great political skill, these leaders brought about a new Constitution. As we will see, the development of the Constitution and the Bill of Rights had enormous implications for church–state relationships then and later. Further, relationships between individuals, churches, and governments were necessarily affected by the creation of a larger political entity with much greater overall religious diversity than existed within any individual state.

Religious Elements of the Revolutionary Coalition

The American Revolution did not arise out of any single political or religious viewpoint. The motives and worldviews of those who carried out the revolution were diverse and at times conflicting. Further, within almost every American religious grouping, some supported the Revolution and others did not. However, an informal religious coalition did come together that generally agreed on independence from Britain and on a substantial degree of autonomy for the individual. Two major components of this coalition were discussed previously: pietistic evangelical Christians and religious rationalists. We will reiterate here some basic points about these two groups and expand the discussion to include a third key element of the revolutionary coalition: the deists.

Pietists

The evangelical pietists who emerged out of the Great Awakening emphasized the role of the individual in achieving salvation. This emphasis gave people a feeling of personal power in religious matters that could be transferred to their roles in government and society. In their clashes with traditional religious establishments, the pietists worked to achieve religious freedom. This desire for religious autonomy for themselves led them to support a broader conception of religious freedom generally, and it led to support for independence from Britain. Further, many pietists held a millennial view of American society: breaking with Britain was a step toward creating a better social order in which gradual progress could be made toward achieving God's kingdom on earth.

Religious Rationalists

Religious rationalism, growing out of the European Enlightenment, emphasized the use of God-given human reason to determine the optimal forms of government, society, and human behavior. While it did not—at least in what Miller (1976) terms its "liberal" variant—explicitly reject orthodox Christianity, it tended to downplay doctrinal sophistication, personal piety, and the emotional experience of religion in favor of simple Christian ethics and an emphasis on social progress. Religious rationalists, such as John Locke, saw God as the source of human rights, but emphasized the need for human beings to build rational political orders to secure those rights. This naturally gave rise to a desire to replace tradition-bound monarchies and aristocracies with simpler, more egalitarian political and social arrangements, an attitude that helped fuel the American revolution.

Deists

Some people, inspired by the spirit of religious rationalism, carried its ideas and tendencies further. While liberal religious rationalists sought to reconcile Christian faith and the ideas of the Enlightenment, deists were much less interested in retaining anything from traditional Christianity. They tended to deny, explicitly or implicitly, the divinity of Jesus, and to embrace a very abstract, impersonal notion of God. While deism never became a widespread popular movement in America, it did attract some of the most significant founders (notably Thomas Jefferson and Benjamin Franklin). As a result, deistic perspectives represent one important element of the revolutionary coalition. They can be generally summarized as follows:

- Deists believe in a deity who created the universe.
- The deity was sometimes called simply "God," but more often was referred to as "The God of Nature," "The Governor of the Universe," "The Great Architect," "The Great Legislator," or some other such grand, impersonal formulation.
- The nature and attributes of the deity were largely beyond the ability of human beings to comprehend.
- The deity governed through the orderly regulation of nature rather than through direct intervention in human affairs. As Albanese (1976: 118) puts it, "The Creator God had wound the springs of a great natural machine which worked according to prescribed and predictable laws."
- These laws of nature that ordered the universe could be discovered through reason, and people had a duty to use their talents and intellect to discern these laws and thereby to improve the human condition.

The deistic religious worldview obviously departs significantly from that found in Christianity, Judaism, or indeed any of the world's great traditional religions. It places little, if any, emphasis on acts of worship or on prayer. It also looks skeptically at communal moral norms derived from sacred texts or teachings, leaving individuals to discern ethical principles as best they can through the use of their own reason. As a result, those founders who were deists generally did not publicize their views, in order to avoid conflicts with more orthodox believers. In the public mind, it was not a long step from deism to atheism, and deist founders such as Franklin and Jefferson were often attacked as atheists by their political adversaries.

The Basis for the Coalition

Clearly, significant differences in religious worldview separated the pietists, religious rationalists, and deists who formed the revolutionary coalition. However, all of them shared two key characteristics that made an alliance possible, at least for a time: an emphasis on individual autonomy in both civil and religious matters, and a tendency to reject both hereditary monarchy and religious establishment. Miller (1976: 57) argues that Americans of various religious stripes around the time of the Revolution were beginning to think of themselves as free beings who chafed at institutional control, whether political, economic, or religious: "Would not things be better, they reasoned, if men could be trusted to attain their own goals, find their own religion, manage their own economy, and even govern themselves?"

The coalition between pietism, rationalism, and deism lasted long enough to see the Revolution through and to bring about a substantial degree of religious freedom and church–state separation in the new republic. It was only afterwards that the theological strains and contradictions within the coalition became too much to bear, leading pietism (the largest element in the coalition) to "discover its latent incompatibility with rationalism, divorce itself, and remarry traditional orthodoxy" (Mead 1978: 162).

Wrapping the Revolution in Religion

Patriot leaders frequently used religious appeals to inspire and justify the movement for American independence (Chidester 1988; Novak 2000; Reichley 2002). The rationale and motivation for the war were often presented using religious imagery. Drawing, as the Puritans had, on the biblical account of Jews escaping from Egypt to seek the new land promised to them by God, the American colonies became the new Israel and Britain became the new Egypt. While the pietist side of the revolutionary coalition provided more of the ardor and the rationalist side provided more of the intellectual rationale, both groups wrapped the revolutionary effort in religious language.

These efforts to identify the American revolutionary effort with religion stemmed not only from the founders' sense that the cause was indeed morally just, but also from political necessity. Very few of the Americans who would be asked to fight, to die, and otherwise to sacrifice for the revolution had read John Locke; virtually all, however, had read the Bible. Thus, if people were to be inspired to take up arms against the Mother Country, and then sustained during the trying times that would inevitably follow, the revolutionary movement would need the support of religion and the churches. This, in large measure, it got; American preachers of various denominational stripes got behind the revolution and contributed their religious endorsement to the cause of liberty. "Pulpit oratory ran like a shock of electricity through the whole colony" wrote Thomas Jefferson in praising the churches' contribution to the revolution (Novak 2000: 164). Whereas later revolutions in Europe were often directed at least in part against religion, the American revolution never took on that sort of anti-clerical cast, in large part because so many American churchmen were ardent promoters of the patriot cause.

Of course, the religious diversity of the revolutionary coalition required the obscuring and papering over of some differences. The cultural environment of that time was infused with both the pietism of the Great Awakening and the rationalism of the Enlightenment. The pietists tended to speak of what Albanese (1976) terms the God of History or Jehovah, while the rationalists spoke of the God of Nature. The common goals of the revolutionary coalition, the infusion of the environment with both pietism and rationalism, and the emotionally charged situation gave rise to an interesting blurring of both theology and religious language, at least publicly. Albanese (1976: 139) argues that during the revolutionary era, "both leaders and followers acknowledged the God of Nature, while many of the leaders and most of the followers cheerfully venerated Jehovah as well." The people of the time often moved comfortably between the God of History framework characteristic of traditional Christians and pietists and the God of Nature framework favored by rationalists and deists, and sometimes did not perceive any difference. The identities of the two became fused in much of the thinking and rhetoric of the time. This is an important point to keep in mind when trying to interpret the religious motives and beliefs of leaders during the revolutionary and founding eras. Sometimes a deist such as Jefferson or Franklin might use the language of traditional Christianity, while a more orthodox Christian such as Washington or Hamilton might use the general "God of Nature" formulation.

The Declaration of Independence

The fundamental philosophical statement of the American revolutionary movement is the Declaration of Independence. Like much of the rest of revolutionary rhetoric, the Declaration is replete with references to God. But to which God, exactly—the Christian God of History or the deistic God of Nature? The document mentions the Divine in four different places, using four different phrases: "Nature's God," "Creator," "Supreme Judge of the

World," and "Divine Providence." Overall, these terms sound more like the God of Nature than the God of History. Further, the document was written primarily by Thomas Jefferson, who was in the deistic/rationalist camp. On the other hand, there were plenty of the more traditional Christians in the Continental Congress that revised and approved the document, and they raised no objection to these phrases. Ultimately, while the Declaration of Independence allows for a specifically Christian interpretation, it does not require one; in that sense, it was ideally suited to the revolutionary coalition. The deistic phrasings serve as a useful "least common denominator" between those who regard God as only the Creator and Architect and those who see him as that, but also much more.

What is in the Declaration of Independence? One way to view it is in terms of five sections:

- The first paragraph says that the representatives of the United States of America are declaring independence from Britain and this document will give the reasons for the separation.
- The second paragraph presents the political theory justifying the right of the colonies to declare their independence.
- The next twenty or so paragraphs list specific grievances against the government of Great Britain.
- The next two paragraphs say that the colonies have repeatedly asked for a redress of grievances and received only further injury in return.
- The last paragraph declares the independence of the colonies from Britain and declares that each of the colonies is now an independent state with all the rights and powers that that implies.

The political theory in the second paragraph is extremely important because, although it was not explicitly included in the Constitution later, it has become a semi-official rationale for the United States government; many people refer to the ideas in the Declaration of Independence as if they were legally binding or perhaps even sacred. These ideas have come to form the justification for liberal government—one in which individuals are given a great deal of freedom and responsibility. In writing this concise summary of his political theory, Thomas Jefferson clearly borrowed heavily from English Enlightenment philosopher John Locke. At the same time, however, we can also see the distinctly American legacy of Puritan covenant theology transposed into the social contract basis of government. These come together in the Declaration of Independence to produce the following basic philosophical argument:

- All men are created equal.
- Humans are endowed by their Creator with certain fundamental (natural) rights, among which are life, liberty, and the pursuit of happiness.

- Governments are created for the purpose of securing these rights, deriving their powers from the consent of the governed.
- If a government doesn't secure these rights, it is the right (and duty) of people to alter or abolish it and to institute a new government.

This philosophy, it is important to note, represented a dramatically different conception of the relationship between God, people, and government than that which had traditionally prevailed in Europe. Under the theory of divine right monarchy, widely embraced by European sovereigns, God gave to kings and queens the right to rule, and those monarchs might in turn choose to grant certain rights and liberties to their subjects. The Lockean/Jeffersonian formulation, however, turns this view on its head. Instead of giving monarchs the right to rule, God gives people the rights to life, liberty, and property (or the "pursuit of happiness"); the people in turn may choose to grant governing authority to magistrates. This view of God as the source of the people's rights and liberties, rather than of the government's mandate, is perhaps the Declaration's most profound philosophical statement.

Of course, there are tensions, contradictions, and ambiguities underlying this noble philosophy and grand rhetoric. At the same time that he was writing that all men were created equal and endowed by God with an unalienable right to liberty, Jefferson owned hundreds of his fellow human beings as chattel slaves (an irony of which Jefferson himself was acutely aware, and with which he struggled all of his life). In addition, the equal rights envisioned in the Declaration did not for some time extend to women or to those without land. Finally, the document leaves ambiguous the relationship between these philosophical ideals and the specifically Christian religious faith held by the great majority of Americans in the founding period. Despite these issues, however, the Declaration is unquestionably the best-known and most inspiring document of the American revolutionary era, and is an important complement to the later, more prosaic text of the Constitution.

Religious Views of the Founders

In order to understand the views of individual, church, and state that underlie the Constitution and the Declaration of Independence, it is useful to examine the specific views of some of the most prominent leaders of the era. In doing so, however, one must keep in mind some very important qualifications. First, the Founders, while they shared certain core convictions about individual liberty and republican government, differed significantly among themselves on matters both political and religious. It is very clear from the historical record that some important Founders were orthodox, traditional Christians, while others were not. Thus, blanket statements such as "the Founders were Christians" or "the Founders were deists" or "the Founders were secular" are all over-simplifications more suited to a modern cultural argument than to a nuanced appreciation of the religious and political climate of the late eighteenth century. Second, it is important to remember that the Founders were engaged in the difficult political enterprise of building a new nation, and politics often involves compromise. While the Founders were generally principled people, they were also very goal-oriented and pragmatic. In order to achieve the over-riding goal of making the new nation work, they sometimes bent their principles, obscured their true views on controversial matters, or compromised one ideal completely in order to further another that they regarded as more critical. Thus, one should not take every public act or utterance of the Founders at face value as an indication of their most deeply held beliefs. A deistic founder might at times find it expedient to use the language of traditional Christianity to rally political support or to insulate himself from religious criticism, while a Christian founder might at times use the broad, abstract language of deism in order to minimize sectarian tension.

Thomas Jefferson (1743–1826)

As the son of a wealthy Virginia planter, Jefferson had the time and resources to develop his education broadly and deeply. He was very familiar with—and affected by—the currents of the European Enlightenment. Jefferson was very much a "renaissance man," with interests in history, philosophy, science, architecture, literature, and music. Aside from his other pursuits, Jefferson was deeply involved in state and national politics, and in the question of the proper relationship between church and state. The epitaph inscribed on Jefferson's tombstone reads: AUTHOR OF THE DECLARATION OF INDEPENDENCE, OF THE STATUTE OF VIRGINIA FOR RELIGIOUS FREEDOM, AND FATHER OF THE UNIVERSITY OF VIRGINIA. All three of these accomplishments involve religion and politics in one way or another.

Jefferson's own religious views can best be classified as deist—although at various times he also referred to himself as a "theist," a "unitarian," or a "rational Christian" (Reichley 2002: 92), and his political enemies labeled him an atheist. As a deist and as a creature of the Enlightenment, he placed great emphasis on the use of reason to discern truths that would improve the lot of humanity.

Jefferson also considered himself a Christian, but not in any orthodox sense. In an 1803 letter to Benjamin Rush, he wrote that "I am a Christian, in the only sense in which he wished; sincerely attached to his doctrines, in preference to all others; ascribing to himself every human excellence; and believing he never claimed any other" (Wills 1990: 357). Jefferson rejected the divinity of Jesus, seeing him as a moral teacher rather than as Savior or Redeemer. He believed that there was great insight in the philosophy of Jesus, but that this simple wisdom had been perverted and complicated by others (e.g., the clergy and organized religious institutions), often for selfish reasons. He argued that people should read the Bible in the same way that they read any other book; they should take the gems of wisdom from it and discard the "wrong" parts. Thus, Jefferson culled from regular Bibles his own slim

"Jefferson Bible," entitled *The Life and Morals of Jesus*. In it, he eliminates all references to miracles, the supernatural, and the resurrection, leaving only a simple book of ethical precepts.

Given his distrust of the clergy and religious establishments, Jefferson believed strongly in freedom of conscience and in the separation of church and state. The phrase "wall of separation between church and state," while originating with Roger Williams, was made famous by a Jefferson letter of 1802; he used the term in response to a question from the Baptist Association in Danbury, Connecticut, asking about the interpretation of the First Amendment. In this letter, Jefferson affirmed his views on religious liberty for the individual and gave his interpretation that the religious clauses of the First Amendment (to which we will return later) created a strong barrier between the political and religious spheres.

While Jefferson distrusted the clergy and opposed the establishment of any church, he nevertheless advocated religion as a useful support for achieving civic virtue. This view, as we will see, was shared by most political and religious leaders of the time of whatever persuasion. In order that liberty not degenerate into license, Jefferson felt that it was necessary that people view their rights and freedoms as divine gifts. While Jefferson was committed to individual liberty, he also strongly believed that people—for the good of society and for their own good—needed to act in a moral and responsible fashion. Religion, in his view, helped them to achieve this. Despite his own unorthodox views, Jefferson regularly attended Christian religious services while president, in part to set what he viewed as a good example for the people. Ultimately, Jefferson's view of religion was quite utilitarian; it was useful and to be encouraged insofar as it helped to build a virtuous republican citizenry. He was much more interested in how people behaved than in what they believed.

James Madison (1751–1836)

James Madison, the Father of the Constitution and the fourth president of the United States, was very quiet about his personal religious views. As a result, it is difficult to place him with precision on the spectrum between deism and orthodox Christianity. On one hand, he studied theology for several years at Princeton, and regularly attended Episcopal religious services. On the other hand, some scholars have discerned a deistic bent in some of his later writings (Murrin 1990), though the evidence is limited because of Madison's reticence to speak publicly about personal faith. In any event, as Wills (1990: 373) writes, "His own religious views were either more conventional or less disclosed than Jefferson's. He was not widely accused of atheism by his enemies. He has not regularly been called a 'deist' by those who equate that adjective with 'irreligious.'" What *is* clear about Madison is that he believed strongly in individual political and religious freedom, and he was eager to see them protected in the new nation.

As the chief architect of the Constitution, Madison helped to construct a government structure with countervailing forces to prevent it from becoming too powerful and to prevent it from oppressing individual freedom. In the Tenth and Fifty-first Federalist Papers, he laid out a skeptical view of human nature which some argue is rooted in the concept of original sin. Without restraints, the selfishness of human nature would lead to government policies in which factions would trample upon the rights of other people. The masses might, for example, use the power of the government to stifle unpopular opinions or to undermine the property rights of the wealthy. On the one hand, protection from such abuses was to be promoted by the sheer size and diversity of the new nation; given the number of different factions in America, it would be difficult for any one of them to gain enough power to become oppressive. Thus, political pluralism—the existence of a great number of competing factions—would help to prevent tyranny. In addition, however, there were structural safeguards built into the Constitution: the separation of powers in the three branches of government and the system of checks and balances so that each branch could counterbalance the power of the others. Further, within the legislative branch, the method of dividing power between the two houses—the Senate favoring the small states and the House favoring the large states—would also provide countervailing forces.

Reimer (1989) argues that Madison's earlier experience with the religious liberty issue provided him with the political pluralism ideas for the national government. In his 1785 fight in the Virginia legislature against religious establishment and for religious liberty (which we will discuss later), Madison had come to the conclusion that religious pluralism—based on the variety of different religious sects—would protect the religious freedom of individuals provided that there was no oppressive coalition among these sects. Thus, in both religion and politics, pluralism—the existence of a variety of different competing groups—was to help safeguard the freedom of the individual.

Madison strongly opposed any form of religious establishment, even of the Anglican or Episcopal Church (of which he himself was a member). In Virginia, Madison and Jefferson together succeeded after the Revolution in preventing the reestablishment of any church and in giving official sanction to a broad concept of religious liberty. While he was an equally ardent church–state separationist, however, Madison's view of religion was not nearly so utilitarian as Jefferson's. Madison's writings on the subject reflect a genuine concern for the well-being of the churches, not merely as supports for republican virtue, but as important institutions in and of themselves.

George Washington (1723–1799)

George Washington's religious views are open to various and contradictory interpretations; his speeches and religious observances contain enough ambiguity that some have claimed that he was an orthodox Christian (Lillback 2006; Novak and Novak 2006), while others maintain that he was basically a deist (Boller 1963; Schwartz 1987). On one hand, he attended church, favored the reestablishment of religion in Virginia, made frequent religious references in his public speeches, and as president issued proclamations of national thanksgiving to God. He also required his soldiers to attend religious services on Sunday unless they were on active duty, and expressed his hope that "every officer and man will endeavor so to live and act as becomes a Christian soldier" (Meacham 2006: 77). On this basis, one might certainly conclude that Washington was a fairly orthodox Christian. On the other hand, his church attendance was irregular, his religious references were "ecumenical rather than specifically Protestant or even Christian" (Reichley 2002: 102), he seldom cited the Bible, and he often spoke of God in terms (e.g., Providence, the Grand Architect, the Great Ruler of Events, the Governor of the Universe) that resembled the language of deism more than that of traditional Christianity. Washington was even labeled an atheist by some during his presidency. In short, Washington, like Madison, defies definitive religious classification.

There is also some degree of ambiguity about Washington's views on church–state relationships. Washington supported Patrick Henry's failed attempt to restore a religious establishment in Virginia, he asked Congress to institute chaplains in the military, and as president he proclaimed national religious holidays. On the other hand, he apparently supported a religious establishment in Virginia only because it would be a very broad one encompassing Christian churches in general; as military commander during the Revolution, he was very careful to avoid any partiality or offense with regard to the various religious views of the soldiers; and as the first president of the United States, he set the tone for religious freedom in the future by making it quite clear that the government would not support religious bigotry or persecution. While it is clear that Washington did not share Jefferson and Madison's ardor for church–state separation, he was also obviously no sectarian zealot.

After Washington became president, various religious groups (e.g., Catholics, Jews, Baptists) that had been the targets of persecution in the colonies wrote to him to determine what his view would be on religious discrimination. One by one, he responded to their queries by writing that the government would not support religious bigotry. His August 17, 1790 response to a Jewish group summarizes his position well:

> For happily the Government of the United States, which gives bigotry no sanction, to persecution no assistance, requires only that they who live under its protection should demean [behave] themselves as good citizens, in giving it on all occasions their effectual support.

Benjamin Franklin (1706–1790)

Benjamin Franklin—politician, writer, inventor—can probably best be described within our present examination as a tolerant Christian deist who felt that religion—all religions in general, but especially Christianity—served a good purpose in society. His own basic beliefs are indicated in his autobiography and in a March 9, 1790 letter—written shortly before his death—to Ezra Stiles, president of Yale University. In that letter, Franklin expressed what he considered to be the fundamental principles of all sound religion:

> I believe in one God, Creator of the Universe. That he governs it by his Providence. That he ought to be worshiped. That the most acceptable service we render to him is doing good to his other children. That the soul of man is immortal, and will be treated with justice in another life respecting its conduct in this.

Franklin continued in this letter that he believed (like Jefferson) that the system of morals and religion left by Jesus were the best in the world, but that they had been corrupted by others. Further, Franklin doubted the divinity of Jesus but had not really given much attention to the issue; he also indicated that he would not busy himself with the question now since he would soon know the truth with less trouble. In line with his view that religion helped support a moral society, Franklin indicated that he saw no harm in people believing that Jesus was divine. He added that he didn't believe "the Supreme" punished the unbelievers of the world. Franklin also added that he had experienced the goodness of that Being in this life and had no doubt that it would continue in the next.

As indicated before, many deists conformed to a greater or lesser degree to the religious customs around them. It was not generally their goal to convert people to religious rationalism. They were very concerned about the protection of religious liberty; they did not want the religious views of others imposed on them and they did not attempt to impose their views on others. At various times, many of the Founders, including Jefferson, Franklin, and even Washington, were labeled atheists by their political adversaries. In order to avoid fights over such matters, they usually kept their views to themselves. This is very evident in the postscript to the letter to Stiles, in which Franklin requests: "I hope you will not expose me to criticism and censure by publishing any part of this communication to you." Franklin asserted that he himself had always let others hold their own religious sentiments without criticism even when he strongly disagreed with them. He had contributed money to many religious groups in his area to help build their places of worship, and since he had never opposed any of their doctrines, he hoped to go out of the world at peace with all of them.

Like Jefferson, Franklin felt that religious views should be judged on the basis of their effectiveness in making people good citizens (Chidester 1988). Along with some other deists, he held the admittedly elitist view that many ordinary people were weak and required traditional religion to restrain vices and support virtue. Any religious doctrine that contributed to this goal was a good one, in his view.

John Adams (1735–1826)

Like Franklin, John Adams, the second president of the United States, could also be described as a Christian deist, one who believed in the moral teachings—but not divinity—of Jesus. In Massachusetts, Adams was one of the religious liberals who split off from the orthodox Congregationalists to become a Unitarian. He believed that the Christian religion was the best, but he viewed this in terms of its promotion of moral behavior; in his July 26, 1796 diary entry, he referred to Christianity as the religion of wisdom, virtue, equity, and humanity. These qualities concern human characteristics rather than dealing with divinity or salvation. In a diary entry on August 14, 1796, Adams wrote that one great advantage of the Christian religion was that it was able to spread to everyone the great principle of the law of nature and nations: Love your neighbor as yourself, and do to others as you would that others should do to you. Like Jefferson and Franklin, Adams emphasized the behavior of people rather than their religious beliefs. Adams believed that all good men (whatever their religious beliefs) were Christians; this is different from saying that a man had to be a Christian in order to be good.

Like many deists, Adams was suspicious of institutional religion, believing that it often got mired in unproductive theological disputes. Adams believed in—and worked for—religious freedom. He did not believe that any group had a right to impose its religious doctrines on others. The human mind was to be left free from dogmatism. In a May 22, 1821 letter to David Sewall, Adams expressed the view that progress had been made in various areas during his lifetime; the list of such areas included the abatement of superstition, persecution, and bigotry.

Despite his wariness of religious institutions, however, Adams did believe that people should go to church, and that widespread religious devotion was a very good thing for the nation. In his August 28, 1811 letter to Benjamin Rush, Adams expressed an idea that he had long held: religion and virtue are the foundations of all free governments and the basis for social happiness under all governments. Adams believed very strongly in the use of religion to support both individual morality and civic virtue; religion tended to make people more responsible and moral in their behavior as individuals and in terms of their duties as citizens. In this view, Adams went farther than Jefferson or Franklin; without religion as a support, he believed, a republican government simply could not exist.

Brief Comments on Other Founders

By this point, certain patterns have become clear with regard to the Founders discussed so far. They tended to be religious rationalists—and sometimes deists—who believed strongly in religious freedom but also saw religion, especially Christianity, as an essential source of moral and ethical guidance for a decent society and an enduring republican government. While the

Founders supported religious liberty, they overwhelmingly believed that religion was a necessary support for a free society, and thus should be encouraged among the people in a non-dogmatic, non-sectarian way.

It should also be noted that this tendency toward deism and religious rationalism, while very influential with some of the most important founders, was hardly universal in the founding generation—even among the elites. Alexander Hamilton, for example, the brilliant author of many Federalist Papers and the first Secretary of the Treasury, was a relatively orthodox Christian. John Jay, who penned some of the Federalist Papers and served as the first Chief Justice of the Supreme Court, was quite conservative in matters both political and religious (though he was a strong supporter of religious liberty). Finally, prominent and enthusiastic patriots such as Patrick Henry in Virginia and Samuel Adams in Massachusetts aggressively championed an explicitly Christian vision of the new nation (Noll et al. 1989).

At the other end of the spectrum, a few in the founding cohort dissented from the general view of religion as a benign and useful social force. Most prominent among these was Thomas Paine, whose deism was much more pronounced and aggressively proclaimed than the religious rationalism of any of the other Founders. In *The Age of Reason*, written in 1794, Paine trumpeted his deistic views, criticized church institutions, and ridiculed the Bible and all revealed religion. To him, all religious institutions of whatever kind were tools by which some humans terrified, enslaved, and exploited others. Most deists among the Founders did not attempt to convert others to their way of thinking about religious matters; they had other political goals, and in the religious realm they simply tried to bring about broad-based religious liberty. However, by the time he wrote *The Age of Reason*, Paine was different in this respect; he did want people to turn away from traditional religion and become deists. Instead of turning away from traditional religion, however, most people simply turned away from Paine.

Overall, it could be argued that the most effective Founders combined elements of Christianity and the Enlightenment and did not use confrontational tactics in reaction to either side of the religious spectrum. Those who took a strongly sectarian viewpoint (e.g., Samuel Adams) and those who pushed the deistic view aggressively (e.g., Thomas Paine) were more limited in the impact that they could have in the new national environment.

The Founders and Religious Establishment in the States

Despite the widespread preference among the founders for religious liberty, almost all colonies on the eve of the Revolution had some provision for an establishment of religion. In New England, the Congregational Church was established in Massachusetts, Connecticut, and New Hampshire. The Anglican Church was established in New York, New Jersey, Maryland, Virginia, North Carolina, South Carolina, and Georgia. Only Rhode Island, Pennsylvania, and Delaware had no single established religion. Furthermore, in almost all of the colonies there was discrimination against Catholics and Jews, who were generally banned from voting and holding office. Many also imposed religious tests for office, such that to hold an elected position one had to belong to a particular religious group or profess belief in certain religious doctrines (Curry 1986).

As the states drew up new constitutions after independence was declared, many of these establishments were weakened or eliminated, and many of the religious restrictions were relaxed. Disestablishment was not universal and immediate, and the pace of change was not uniform; some state support for particular denominations, and some explicitly anti-Catholic and anti-Semitic provisions, lingered into the nineteenth century. Nonetheless, the general trend set in motion by the Revolution was clearly one of increasing religious liberty and toleration, and of decreasing sectarianism on the part of the states.

Most notable in this regard is the case of Virginia, which many scholars argue provided a model for other states to follow later. The Virginia case is also of particular interest because some of the key players in its battle over establishment were nationally prominent Founders: Thomas Jefferson and James Madison on one side, Patrick Henry and George Washington on the other. In the process of fighting religious establishment in Virginia, Jefferson and Madison developed important arguments for religious freedom that would later influence the U.S. Constitution. Indeed, Mead (1978) argues that the two most fundamental documents of American religious liberty were produced during this debate: Madison's *Memorial and Remonstrance* and Jefferson's *Bill for Establishing Religious Freedom*.

The Reestablishment Effort in Virginia

Prior to the Revolution, the Anglican Church had been established in Virginia, and was supported by taxes and tracts of land (glebes) given to it by the government. Other Protestant churches were allowed to exist, however, and this relative tolerance had attracted a number of Baptists and Presbyterians. With the coming of the Revolution, the Anglican Church (rooted in the Church of England) came to be called the Protestant Episcopal Church. By this time, Episcopalians constituted only 35 percent of all church members in Virginia, according to the first U.S. Census taken in 1790. There were almost as many Baptists (30 percent), and there was a substantial group of Presbyterians (22 percent). Further, there was a non-trivial presence of smaller religious groups, including Quakers (7 percent) and Methodists (2 percent).

When the state constitutional convention met in 1776, George Mason proposed that the Virginia Declaration of Rights include a phrase providing for "the fullest Toleration in the Exercise of Religion." James Madison, however, wanted the language to go beyond mere toleration. To him, the concept of toleration implied that those with greater power would put up with and indulge those with less; Madison wanted a fuller expression of true equality for the range of groups comprising Virginia's religious pluralism. Thus, he succeeded in replacing Mason's formulation with the following phrase in the Virginia Declaration of Rights: "All men are equally entitled to the free exercise of religion according to the dictates of conscience." This put the emphasis on individual rights rather than on governmental toleration of diverse religious views.

This statement did not totally and unequivocally settle the question of state support for the church. However, the legislature soon suspended the Act for the Support of the Clergy, and made this suspension permanent in 1779 (Miller 1976). At that point, the Anglican Church had been effectively disestablished for all practical purposes. However, when Jefferson first proposed his Bill for Establishing Religious Freedom in 1779, which would have explicitly prohibited the state from ever having an established church, it was defeated by being tabled. The failure of the bill to pass left the question of possible religious establishment in limbo.

In 1784, after the Revolution, Patrick Henry (with the support of George Washington) introduced an assessment bill that would create a broad establishment of the Christian religion and provide for its tax support. The proposed arrangement was similar to the plural establishments of Christian churches in several other states at the time. People would be taxed to support Christian churches generally, and they could then specify which particular church was to receive their support.

This bill was popular, and Henry apparently had enough votes to get it passed. Madison, however, led the opposition and was successful in getting a vote on the bill postponed until it could be submitted for public comment. By the time the bill finally did come up for a vote, Madison had successfully marshaled opposition to it. He mustered a coalition of religious rationalists and two Christian groups—pietists (mostly Baptists) and Presbyterians—who had borne the brunt of discrimination under the Anglican establishment, and he provided an extensive rationale for religious freedom in his famous *Memorial and Remonstrance*.

Madison's Memorial and Remonstrance

In his *Memorial and Remonstrance*, Madison presented fifteen arguments against the bill to make Christianity the established religion in Virginia and to provide tax support for it. In its basic outline, his argument is as follows:

- Religion should be directed by reason and conviction, not by government coercion, and the free exercise of reason and conscience is the unalienable right of every person.
- We should be careful about any infringement of our civil liberties; minor transgressions now might grow into much larger usurpations in the future.
- Giving favored status to the religious views of some people violates the principle of equality of all citizens.

- When a church is guaranteed the support of the state, its clergy become corrupt and complacent.
- The Christian religion does not need state support; it existed and flourished for centuries without the support of laws, and indeed even in the face of persecution by the state.
- Establishment would actually hurt the spread of Christianity by making unconverted people defensive toward it; further, it would hurt the faith by increasing disharmony and resentment among the different Christian denominations.
- Creating a less hospitable environment for religious diversity would discourage immigration to Virginia and might even cause some non-Anglicans to leave the state.
- The enforcement of a law considered obnoxious and invalid by so many people would undermine respect for the laws in general and weaken the legitimate powers of government.
- If the legislature can infringe on freedom of religion, then it can infringe on other individual rights as well.

Some of Madison's arguments were not specific to the question of religious freedom per se. He argued, for example, that if a state can infringe on any freedom a little now, it might completely usurp all freedoms later. Some arguments concerned practical consequences (e.g., possible economic development problems resulting from decreased immigration and increased emigration). At the core, however, Madison argued that religious establishments were not good for the individual, the state, or even the established churches themselves. Individuals have an unalienable right to freedom of conscience, and their religious beliefs should be developed from their own reasoning, faith, and voluntary commitment rather than being imposed on them by law. State establishments violate the rights of those who don't share the established religion, and this violates the principle of equality of all citizens. When the government involves itself in religion, the resulting intermingling of sacred and secular can corrupt both state and church. Finally, when the state enforces laws in favor of one religion, it alienates some people and reduces its own legitimacy in their eyes; this makes it more difficult to obtain citizen compliance with laws in general. Further, the established churches and their clergy are harmed by establishment because of the complacency and even corruption that a privileged position can engender.

Madison's arguments helped to win the fight against Patrick Henry's religious assessments bill. Further, this victory paved the way for a reintroduction of Jefferson's Bill for Establishing Religious Freedom.

Jefferson's Bill for Establishing Religious Freedom

Soon after Patrick Henry's assessment bill was defeated, Jefferson's Bill for Establishing Religious Freedom was called up again, and the state legislature enacted it—in slightly modified form—into law in 1785 by an overwhelming majority. Jefferson's statute had three sections.

The first section provided a rationale for the law. Jefferson argued that God had created the human mind free and wanted to keep it that way. Attempts to force people to conform outwardly to certain beliefs and practices only result in hypocrisy and meanness, and such attempts are not in accord with the plan of the deity, who sought to have people accept religion through their own reason. It is an "impious presumption" of civil and religious leaders —who are themselves fallible—to impose their views on others. Compelling people to help pay for the propagation of religious views with which they disagree is sinful and tyrannical. It is even wrong, Jefferson argued, to force people to contribute to their own religious institutions; such contributions should be freely given. It is wrong to deprive people of civil rights, or to prevent them from holding public office, simply because of their religious views. By making rights and privileges dependent upon believing particular doctrines or belonging to a particular church, one corrupts religion itself by creating incentives for insincerity and mere outward conformity. Ultimately, the divine truth is great and will prevail unless free argument and debate have been stifled.

The second section constitutes the actual policy. It provides a very extensive statement of religious liberty. It first expresses a negative, a restriction on what government can do to the individual:

> [N]o man shall be compelled to frequent or support any religious worship, place, or ministry whatsoever, nor shall be enforced, restrained, molested, or burthened in his body or goods, or shall otherwise suffer, on account of his religious opinions or belief;

The Bill then provides an affirmative statement of religious freedom:

> but that all men shall be free to profess, and by argument to maintain, their opinions in matters of religion, and that the same shall in no wise diminish, enlarge, or affect their civil capacities.

The third section begins by acknowledging that it would be futile for the present legislature to try to keep future legislatures from revoking this statute. However, it does declare that these religious freedoms are natural rights; if any future legislature repeals the statute or narrows it, such action would be an infringement of the innate, God-given rights of conscience.

Thus, Virginia went from a colony with an established Anglican Church prior to the Revolution to the forefront of religious liberty on the eve of the development of the United States Constitution. Three of the men involved in the fights in Virginia—Madison, Jefferson, and Washington—went on to have a substantial voice in individual–state–church relations in the national arena. They brought from this debate over religious establishment in Virginia critical perspectives that would shape the national Constitution and Bill of Rights.

Religion in the United States Constitution

In its original version drafted by delegates to the Philadelphia convention in 1787, the United States Constitution makes almost no mention of religion. With the exception of the document's date ("the Seventeenth Day of September in the Year of our Lord one thousand seven hundred and Eighty seven"), the Constitution makes no mention of the deity whatsoever—neither the orthodox God of History nor the deistic God of Nature.

Religion is referenced only once in the main body of the Constitution. Article 6 stipulates that "no religious Test shall ever be required as a Qualification to any Office or public Trust under the United States." At the time the Constitution was drafted, many states still had religious tests of various sorts for public office, generally intended to bar "Papists" (Catholics), Jews, "Mahometans" (Muslims), and atheists. While the Constitution did not prohibit the continued use of such tests for state offices, it did mandate that no such requirements be imposed for national office-holding. The people were free, if they wished, to take such religious considerations into account when choosing their leaders, but a national Protestant hegemony would not be required by law.

Why a Secular Document?

Given the extensive use of religious language and images by both religious rationalists and pietists during the Revolution, in the Declaration of Independence, and in their later public statements, it might seem odd that many of those same people put together a Constitution with such minimal reference to religion. Of course, the Constitution is in many ways a "nuts-and-bolts" document laying out a detailed plan of government, as opposed to a philosophical treatise; in that sense, it is inherently less amenable to religious language than, for example, the Declaration of Independence. Beyond this, however, there are other reasons why the Founders largely avoided religious questions in the drafting of the Constitution.

First, the Founders were well aware of the great religious pluralism that existed in the new nation. Perhaps in no country in the world at that time was there as much religious diversity as there was in the combined population of the different American states. Any attempt by the delegates at the Constitutional Convention to establish a national church or to require religious tests for public office would have led to intense opposition, both within the convention itself and in later efforts to obtain ratification.

Second, the Founders were well aware of the various religious persecutions that had taken place historically in the colonies and in the world generally; they had seen how established churches had often treated dissenters. Thus, they did not want to provide any basis for such sectarian persecutions by the American national government.

Third, the Founders were primarily interested in achieving their over-riding goal—the creation of a stronger central government—and they did not want to raise issues that might derail this effort. The Constitutional convention was already beset with major battles over representation and slavery, and few were eager to add religious disputes to the mix. As Wilson (1990: 84) argues, "The Founding Fathers' overriding concern was to neutralize religion as a factor that might jeopardize the achievement of a federal government." Thus, the Founders' avoidance of religious concerns in the Constitution signaled neither support for nor opposition to any particular religious values; it was simply a pragmatic strategy to avoid stirring up another hornets' nest. This is demonstrated somewhat oddly in the reaction to Benjamin Franklin's request that each day's session of the Constitutional Convention be opened with a prayer; the unsuccessful request was opposed by Alexander Hamilton. Recall that Franklin was a deist and Hamilton a more orthodox Christian, yet Franklin had called for prayer and Hamilton had opposed him. Despite his deism, Franklin felt that this common religious observance might help lift the convention out of the deadlock it was in at that particular time. Hamilton, conversely, opposed the measure on pragmatic grounds: a resort to prayer, he feared, might signal to the rest of the country that the convention was having problems (Murrin 1990).

Fourth, the Founders generally shared the belief that religious liberty was good for religion itself (Castelli 1988; Reichley 2002). Therefore, any promotion of a particular set of beliefs within the Constitution itself would ultimately prove unhelpful to the chosen creed. Most of the founders, regardless of their own religious views, believed that widespread religious observance among the people provided an essential support for republican virtue and good government. This flourishing of religion in civil society, they believed, would be best assured if government refrained from supporting any particular religious institutions.

Finally, given the concern of many at the convention with the economic development of the country and given the need to deal effectively with other nations, it was very pragmatic for the delegates to avoid the matter of religion in the Constitution. The establishment of any religion might have discouraged immigration to this country by those not of the favored faith, hampered foreign investment, and made it more difficult to enter into agreements and treaties with some foreign powers. Noll et al. (1989: 131) emphasize the importance of this non-sectarianism to the 1797 treaty with the Islamic state of Tripoli. This treaty—which was negotiated under President Washington, ratified later by the Senate, and signed by President John Adams—states that the harmony between the two countries would not be interrupted on the basis of religious difference because the United States "is not in any sense founded on the Christian Religion."

Adding the Bill of Rights

In order to go into effect, the proposed Constitution required ratification by nine of the thirteen states. As soon as the delegates signed the document and left the Philadelphia convention, ratification battles began in earnest all over the country. Supporters and opponents of the proposed stronger central government marshaled their arguments to persuade the undecided. In these debates, one argument frequently raised by those skeptical of the Constitution was that it lacked a bill of rights.

Most of the Founders at the Constitutional Convention apparently felt that a bill of rights was unnecessary, because the Constitution was not empowering the government to violate individual liberties, because governmental power was to be hemmed in by checks and balances, because many of the state constitutions already had some sort of bill of rights, and because the enumeration of some rights in the Constitution might imply that those were the only rights individuals possessed. Nevertheless, the absence of a bill of rights became one of the most widespread and persuasive arguments raised by the Constitution's opponents. Some who raised this objection (e.g., Patrick Henry) apparently did so simply to prevent ratification of the Constitution; others (e.g., Thomas Jefferson) did not necessarily oppose the document on the whole, but were genuinely concerned about the absence of a bill of rights (Curry 1986). In discussions of the need for a bill of rights, one recurrent theme was the imperative that religious freedom be explicitly guaranteed.

While he did not originally think a bill of rights was necessary, Madison ultimately changed his mind and promised that drafting one would be one of the first actions of the new government. This helped smooth the way for ratification. After the Constitution was ratified, the new United States government began in 1789, and Madison was elected to the first House of Representatives. In June, he submitted a series of rights-oriented amendments to the House; after debate and modification of the amendments in the House and Senate, a final set of ten amendments was passed on September 25. These first ten constitutional amendments, the Bill of Rights, were ratified by the states and took effect on December 15, 1791.

The first Congress had many pressing issues with which to deal, and many of its members did not want to spend a great deal of time in abstract discussions of individual liberties. As a result, the amendments were modified, compromised, and passed without a great deal of debate. The language of the amendments was often very general, leaving them open to interpretation by future generations. However, there was some discussion of the proposals in Congress, and Madison kept notes on this debate. These notes reveal broad-based agreement on the desirability of both religion and religious freedom, but some differences of opinion on exactly how this should be enshrined in the Constitution.

The "first freedom" of the First Amendment prohibits Congress from making any laws concerning an establishment of religion or from interfering with its practice: "Congress shall make no law respecting an establishment of religion, or prohibiting the free exercise thereof." Thus, at the national level, there was to be no religious establishment, and individuals were to have religious freedom.

It is important to note that this amendment, like all of those in the Bill of Rights, applied only to the national government; it did not apply to the states and, as discussed earlier, there were still states at that time that had Protestant religious establishments and that discriminated against Catholics, Jews, and others in various ways. Not until the adoption of the Fourteenth Amendment in 1868 were the guarantees in the Bill of Rights applied to the states. At least at the national level, however, adoption of the First Amendment represented a broad-based commitment to religious freedom.

The final wording of the religion clauses in the First Amendment came about after a series of changes and compromises. Madison's original proposals concerning religion in the Bill of Rights were broader. He originally envisioned two amendments concerning religious freedom. The first would prohibit any violation of individual rights on the basis of religious beliefs or practices, prohibit any national religious establishment, and guarantee full and equal rights of conscience:

> The civil rights of none shall be abridged on account of religious belief or worship, nor shall any national religion be established, nor shall the full and equal rights of conscience be in any manner, or on any pretext, infringed.

These ideas were modified and compressed into what became the religion clauses of the First Amendment.

Madison's second amendment relating to freedom of religion extended conscience protections, along with other important rights, to the states: "No state shall violate the equal rights of conscience, or the freedom of the press, or the trial by jury in criminal cases." Madison himself considered this to be the most important of all his proposed amendments (Curry 1986). While this proposal passed in the House of Representatives, it was rejected in the Senate. Thus, the Bill of Rights, at least until the adoption of the Fourteenth Amendment, applied only to the national government.

The debates concerning the religious clauses of the First Amendment indicate that there was no single dominant viewpoint on church–state relations during the founding era. Further, given the religious pluralism and the variety of church–state relationships in the individual states, Congress tried to avoid much controversy in the proposed amendments (after all, three fourths of the states had to agree in order for them to be ratified). Perhaps the clearest agreement among members of Congress during the debates about the religion clauses was the idea that the national government ought not to legislate in religious matters. Beyond this, they largely agreed to disagree, and state-level variations in the relationship between political and religious institutions continued into the nineteenth century.

Summary and Conclusions

Religion clearly played a central role in the foundation and early development of what would become the United States, and the legacy of this role continues to affect political–religious linkages in America today. Religious motives combined, at times inextricably, with economic and political ones in the settlement of many of the original colonies. Puritanism dominated religious life in early New England, and certain aspects of Puritan thought (e.g., the concept of covenant and a skeptical view of human nature) have permeated American political culture ever since. As the dominance of the relatively pure strain of Puritanism faded, two other religious movements (the Great Awakening and religious rationalism) emerged, temporarily joining forces to support the American Revolution. These two movements subsequently influenced American political development in different (and sometimes conflicting) ways.

Political leaders in the founding generation were clearly shaped, to differing degrees, by both of these religious movements. As a result, there are tensions, conflicts, and ambiguities in their approach to religious questions. Part of the difficulty that we have today in interpreting the intentions of the Founders with regard to individual–church–state relationships is that they did not speak with a single voice. They held a variety of viewpoints, not only on theological questions, but also on the proper mix of religion and politics. This situation was further complicated by the fact that, during the process of making a revolution and building a nation, leaders had to form coalitions among groups that held conflicting views on religion and on church–state relations, often papering over differences on these issues with vague language and inconsistent policies.

Thus, Thomas Jefferson wrote the Declaration of Independence in such a way that it could garner support from both religious rationalists like himself and from those who held pietistic or orthodox religious views; the God in the Declaration of Independence was general enough to be interpreted as either the God of History or the God of Nature. The coalition that created the Constitution, on the other hand, was held together partly as a result of taking a neutral stance toward religion; it largely avoided any mention of the deity at all. In formulating the religion clauses in the First Amendment, Congress simply affirmed that the Constitution did not give the national government any power to legislate in matters of conscience.

Despite the problems in attributing a single set of intentions to the Founders, we can say that the major figures among them shared a certain set of beliefs about relationships between the individual, the church, and the state. These are, briefly, as follows:

• Individuals have an inherent, unalienable right to form their own religious views without external compulsion.

- There should not be an established church arrangement—neither a single established church, nor even a multiple establishment. Support for churches should be completely voluntary.
- There should be no religious test for public office, and individuals should not be deprived of any of their rights on account of their religious beliefs or practices.
- Any religion that helped to bring about moral behavior in people was good, and the Christian religion is the best one in this respect.
- A republican government required a fairly high level of morality and ethical conduct from citizens.
- Religion was needed to lay the moral foundations for good government—especially a republican government in which a comparatively large proportion of the population would have a say in public policy.

Overall, the Founders simultaneously emphasized the desirability of flourishing religious life in the new nation, and the imperative that individuals have freedom in matters both spiritual and political.

In this chapter we have examined the development of religion and politics in America during the colonial and founding eras, from the narrow sectarianism of the Puritans to the strong endorsement of religious liberty in the First Amendment. In the next chapter, we will see how this framework played out in the historical period from 1800 through 1960, as the nation engaged such issues as slavery, prohibition, war and peace, and religious inclusion.

3 Religion and Politics in American History 1800–1960

> By human law, under the Christian Dispensation, in the nineteenth century, we are commanded to do what God more than three thousand years ago, under the Mosaic Dispensation, positively commanded the Jews not to do ... How long the North will thus shake hands with the South in sin, I know not ... but one thing I do know, the guilt of the North is increasing in a tremendous ratio as light is pouring in upon her on the subject and the sin of slavery. As the sun of righteousness climbs higher and higher in the moral heavens, she will stand still more and more abashed as the query is thundered down into her ear, "Who hath required this at thy hand?"
>
> (Angelina Emile Grimké, *Appeal to the Christian Women of the South*, 1836)

The previous chapter examined the cultural, institutional, and ideological framework, established during the colonial and founding eras, that has shaped the interactions between religion and politics in America. This chapter briefly reviews the evolving nature of those interactions as the United States grew from a small, odd experiment in democracy at the margins of the global power structure to the most economically, militarily, and culturally powerful nation in the world.

A general overview like this one cannot possibly discuss all of the ways that religion shaped politics (and vice versa) in more than a century and a half of national life. Instead, it will focus on a few key issues central to the story of religion and politics in America during this period: the role of religion in the debates over slavery and Prohibition, religiously inspired movements for broad-based social reform, religious approaches to questions of war and peace, and the struggle to accommodate America's growing religious pluralism. In doing so, it will address a range of questions:

- In what specific ways did religion and religious groups shape the American political process?
- What particular social movements involved linkages between religion and politics, and what kinds of social reforms did religious groups seek?

- What religious divisions resulted from the slavery issue, and what were the long-term effects of these divisions?
- What role did religious groups play in the temperance movement and the push for prohibition of alcohol?
- What were the religious–political ramifications of the New Deal during the 1930s?
- What different views of war and peace have been advanced by American religious groups, and how did religious groups react to specific wars in which the nation was involved?
- How did American society treat religious groups outside the Protestant mainstream during this period, and what were the political implications?

Religion and American Political Development: An Overview

During the course of American history, religious institutions and beliefs have shaped politics in a whole host of ways. Among these, religious historian Robert Swieringa (1990) identifies three particular channels of religious influence that have been especially important:

1. Religious groups' identities provided important reference points that people used to help make sense of the social and political world.
2. Religious organizations worked to advance their values, extend their influence in society, and protect their interests from attack by using the political process.
3. Religious beliefs often shaped the way that citizens evaluated political issues, parties, and candidates.

One important vehicle in which all of these forms of religious influence came together was the development of social reform movements, or extended, organized campaigns that attempt to bring about change in social institutions, law, and human behavior through deliberate action. While such movements did not really arise in America until the late eighteenth century, over the next 200 years they became a powerful and recurrent feature of the nation's political life. Indeed, Noonan (1998) sees the frequency and prominence of such movements, along with their invariably strong religious overtones, as a key distinguishing feature of American political culture. America was uniquely well suited for the development of a social movement culture, as the nation combined the political efficacy and individual responsibility that come from democracy with strong institutions of civil society (clubs, associations, churches, etc.) and relatively widespread religious piety. Thus, Americans tended to believe that: (1) People could bring about effective social change, rather than having to passively await government action; (2) True religion necessarily involved both personal piety *and* social action, rather than simply the former; and (3) Maintaining the social order and making needed changes was everyone's obligation, not just the responsibility of political and religious elites. These sentiments continually fueled a broad-based reformist impulse in America during the nineteenth and twentieth centuries.

The Benevolent Empire

The term "Benevolent Empire" is sometimes used to refer to the reforming organizations and movements that harnessed the religious energies loosed by the Second Great Awakening (a religious revival of the 1790s through the 1830s) to bring about significant social reforms. The Society of Friends—more commonly known as the Quakers—was one of the first religious groups to explicitly link personal piety with responsibility for improving the social order. Quakers were active from the earliest days of the American republic in their distinctive advocacy for pacifism and in movements for poor relief, prison reform, temperance, and the abolition of slavery (Goldman 2012).

In a similar vein, a number of general movements to better society through improved education and strengthened morals began in New England in the early 1800s, sponsored primarily by Congregationalists and Presbyterians. Most focused on the distribution of Bibles and religious tracts, along with teaching literacy so that people could read them. In addition, the Unitarians—whom the Congregationalists and Presbyterians regarded as heretics—sponsored humanitarian reform efforts of their own, believing that such work was the most (and perhaps only) genuine piety. Unitarians were active in the establishment of public education and in working for more humane care for the mentally ill, the deaf, and the blind (Cayton 1988).

Revival and Perfectionism

A second religious movement played into the growing reform wave as the Benevolent Empire peaked in the 1830s. Revivalists such as Charles Grandison Finney, a New York Presbyterian, preached perfectionism and holiness. These new doctrines held that people could actually avoid sinning in this life, and that moral perfection and true holiness were indeed possible for human beings. Further, Finney emphasized that true religious conversion and genuine spiritual rebirth would be accompanied by a zeal to reform society. Like the Benevolent Empire reformers, the perfectionists primarily advocated pacifism, temperance or prohibition, and abolition (Cayton 1988). Their program, however, was even more comprehensive. Finney's list of political issues that the churches must address included "Abolition of Slavery, Temperance, Moral Reform, Politics, Business Principles, [and] Physiological and Dietetic Reform" (Sweet 1988: 893).

Despite his insistence that the churches must address a number of pressing social issues, Finney avoided direct political involvement. Government reforms, he believed, were useless without the regeneration of people's souls. He thought it best to rely primarily on preaching, conversion, and sanctification of each individual to gradually eliminate social evils. William Lloyd Garrison, on the other hand, who followed Finney into the abolition movement, thought preaching and conversion important, but believed that churches should engage in direct political action as well, lobbying government to get abolitionist views enacted in law (Mayer 1998).

The Social Gospel Movement

The period between 1865 and 1930 saw a continuation and expansion of the religiously motivated social reform efforts of the antebellum era. Religious organizations of various denominational stripes became increasingly involved with advocating social change and developed active programs to better conditions for the poor and marginalized. Perhaps the best known of these efforts is the Social Gospel movement. Especially with the presidency of Theodore Roosevelt, whose progressive social views were well known, "new progressive suggestions from Christians for more comprehensively reforming the social and economic order" arose (Marsden 1991: 29). What was distinctive about the Social Gospel movement was that it understood the Christian Gospel as essentially social in its message, rather than seeing social reform as a by-product of individual conversion. For many in the Social Gospel movement, action on behalf of the disadvantaged occupied center stage, with personal piety, theology, and individual conversion pushed to the margins. This is where theological conservatives, many of whom were in evangelical or "fundamentalist" churches, parted company with theological liberals. As Wilson (2009: 195) argues, "many evangelicals grew concerned that the economic agenda of their mainline counterparts had become detached from its Christian moorings, abandoning a theology of personal responsibility for one of collectivism." These concerns signaled the "beginning of the end" for social reform movements that could span the theological gamut of American Protestantism.

This break between liberal and conservative Christians over social justice efforts was part of a broader split within American Protestantism developing at that time. The dramatic "revolution in morals" in the 1920s engendered a "climate of crisis" that led to deep theological divisions within many churches (Marsden 2006)—divisions that continue to be felt almost a hundred years later. In the 1920s, the divide took the form of a schism between "fundamentalism" and "modernism." While many issues divided liberal and conservative Protestants, one focus of the debate was increasingly paramount: differences over the Darwinian theory of biological evolution.

The "Climate of Crisis" and Its Results

The campaign against Darwinism was largely a political one, since it focused on attempts to prohibit the teaching of evolution in public schools. In that sense, it anticipated battles later in the twentieth century to require the teaching of "creation science" alongside evolutionary theory. There was no clear "winner" in the 1920s battle over evolution, symbolized by the famous Scopes trial in Tennessee. The state's prohibition on teaching evolution was not overturned, and such bans in Tennessee and many other states lingered into the 1960s (when the Supreme Court found them unconstitutional in *Epperson* v. *Arkansas*). On the other hand, the media's treatment of fundamentalism and their portrayal of evangelicals seriously discredited conservative Christians in the minds of many people, widening the divide between mainline and evangelical Protestants.

The 1920s looked in some ways like the end of fundamentalism as a major cultural force in America, but this was not to be the case, as subsequent chapters will show. Fundamentalists, by and large, returned to what had always been their strength—evangelization and building local congregations—to re-emerge as important political players in the closing decades of the century.

One important result of the religious and cultural turmoil of the 1920s was that American Protestantism was divided into a politically and theologically conservative branch and a politically and theologically liberal one. While the divisions between evangelical and mainline Protestantism had previously been loose and predominantly stylistic, the differences over the course of the twentieth century became increasingly stark, in both theological and political terms.

Another change occurred during this period that would be highly significant for the role of religion in social reform movements in succeeding decades. Up through the early twentieth century, the language of social reform in America was predominantly religious, if not explicitly theological; it assumed a common set of generally held beliefs. By the end of this era, however, the language used to address social issues had become much more secular. The growth of pluralism played a role in this shift; there was increasing religious diversity in America, and if political coalitions were to be formed, language had to appeal widely and avoid potentially divisive theological implications. The shift was also aided by a retreat from social activism on the part of evangelical and fundamentalist Protestants; increasingly, progressive Christian social reformers were making common cause not with their theologically conservative fellow believers, but with secular liberals who preferred the language of social science to that of the Bible.

Between the Great Depression and 1960, mainline Protestantism in the United States was closely bound up with the prevailing culture, producing a high level of complacency. In addition, the economic crisis of the Depression forced religious congregations to concentrate on their own economic survival while doing what they could to assist their own members during hard times. Following that, World War II and the Korean War tended to put a damper on domestic social reform activism. As a result, the period between 1930 and 1960 represented a relative hiatus for religiously motivated political action in America. Not until the civil rights movement, the anti-war movement, and the other social upheavals of the 1960s did religion again become intimately involved in the process of political and social reform (Bucher and Tait 1988).

With this general overview of the evolving relationship between religion and politics in mind, we turn now to a specific examination of some notable areas in which the two interacted during this time period.

Religion and the Slavery Question

Slaveholding had been a part of life in most of the colonies, both North and South, before the American Revolution. The little organized opposition that existed had come mainly from the Friends (Quakers) and Mennonites, both small and often marginalized groups. The first known written public protest against slavery in North America was that published by the Monthly Meeting of Friends in Germantown, Pennsylvania in 1688 (Edel 1987). As the abolition movement grew stronger, it would see increasing participation by Quakers, whose belief in the inviolability of each individual's conscience made slaveholding anathema. The Friends banned slaveholding among their own members and worked actively to help slaves escape, even in explicit defiance of federal law (Goldman 2012). Widespread opposition to slaveholding, however, did not begin to appear until the 1770s, when the spirit of liberty manifested in the Revolution and articulated in the Declaration of Independence began to seem incongruous with the denial of freedom to the slaves. As John Jay, President of the Continental Congress and later Chief Justice of the United States, put it, "That men should pray and fight for their own freedom and yet keep others in slavery is certainly acting a very inconsistent as well as unjust and perhaps impious part" (Johnston 1891: 168).

Slavery, the Bible, and the Churches

Both pro-slavery forces and abolition advocates cited the Christian Bible and the teachings of their churches in support of their views. The slavery issue proved quite disruptive for the churches, in large part because stridently vocal pro-slavery and anti-slavery movements existed side by side in denominations and sometimes in local congregations. In addition, pro-slavery sentiments were not confined to the South, nor was opposition to slavery an exclusively Northern phenomenon. Although many southern churches defended slavery as a necessary and even beneficial institution (especially as a part of the cotton economy), and most of the northern churches decried it, there were exceptions. Typical of the apologists for slavery was Richard Furman (1755–1825), President of the South Carolina Baptist Convention. Furman declared that "the right of holding slaves is clearly established in the Holy Scriptures, both by precept and example" (Young 2006: 230). On the other side of the debate, the Presbyterian General Assembly of 1818 stated that slavery was "utterly inconsistent with the law of God" and "totally irreconcilable with the spirit and principles of the Gospel of Christ" (Murray

1957: 259). Finally, the South Carolina Lutherans refused to stake out either a pro-slavery or anti-slavery position, believing that churches should not interfere in economic issues. They cited the "impropriety and injustice of the interference or intermeddling of any religious or deliberative body with the subject of slavery or slaveholding, emancipation or abolition" (Gaustad and Schmidt 2002: 191).

Clearly, American Christianity was divided over the slavery question, and this division was eventually reflected in religious institutions. The Methodist Church was the first to split over slavery. While the immediate cause of the break was a debate over whether a slaveholding minister could be appointed a bishop, tensions within the denomination had been building for some time. Although the founder of Methodism, John Wesley, had spoken out against slavery and the founding conference of the church had provided for the expulsion of slaveholders who refused to free their slaves, Methodism had gradually backed away from this view as it extended its membership in the American South. The General Conference of 1836 named slavery as an evil, but also condemned abolitionism. Two conferences later, in 1844, the church adopted a strong anti-slavery position. Given the charged climate of the time, this made division inevitable, and the Methodist Episcopal Church, South, formally separated and staked out a pro-slavery platform.

The Presbyterian Church did not actually divide until somewhat later, officially separating in 1857, but slavery was one of the issues underlying the Old School versus New School controversy in the late 1830s. The Old School was solidly centered in the South, while the New School drew its strength from the North. In 1849, the official statement produced by the General Assembly was that slavery was a matter for the civil government to deal with, and the church should stay out of it. This attempt at compromise was ultimately unsatisfactory, and the church divided into the Presbyterian Church, United States, and the United Presbyterian Church in the United States of America, a regional split that would not be reconciled until 1983.

The Baptists, the third major denomination with strength in both North and South, were in a somewhat different position. While both the Methodists and the Presbyterians had national judicatories that made decisions and set policies for the entire church, Baptist church polity was altogether congregational. By the mid-1800s, however, churches in the North and the South had become more polarized in their views of slavery. In 1845, the southern churches seized the opportunity to break away and form their own, more connectional association, with a pro-slavery stance, becoming what would eventually be known as the Southern Baptist Convention. Meanwhile, the northern churches had also consolidated into a closer union, although still without the connectionalism of their southern counterparts, eventually becoming the American Baptist Churches and excluding pro-slavery members.

The Disciples of Christ were so thoroughly local in their organization that there was literally nothing on the national level to divide. This meant that the Disciples escaped any serious institutional division over slavery. Another group of churches was not particularly disrupted because they did not have meaningful membership in both regions. The Congregationalists, Unitarians, and Universalists were largely confined to the North, and thus moved easily into the abolitionist camp. Most Quakers were without question abolitionists, though a few did own slaves and the Quaker John Woolman's *Considerations on the Keeping of Negroes* (1754) dealt with how to keep slaves humanely without considering the moral acceptability of slave-owning itself. The Lutheran and Episcopal churches remained undivided until the country itself split in 1861, despite their having membership in both regions and devoted proponents of both points of view. The Catholic Church, despite consistent doctrinal objections to slavery stretching back to the middle ages (at least from Rome, if not always from local clergy), was generally reluctant to provoke conflicts with civil authorities over the issue—and in any case had too small a presence to do so meaningfully in any antebellum southern state other than Louisiana. As a result, the Catholic Church did not "confront government head-on over the issue and attempt to force an end to slavery . . . in practice, the Church settled for attempting to ameliorate the conditions of slaves as much as possible" (Stark 2003).

The perfectionist theological tendencies described earlier in this chapter were especially prominent among the major denominations that divided over the slavery issue, as well as among the Lutherans, whose territorial organization kept them together by preventing a clash of opinions in any national meeting. Increasingly, perfectionists of whatever denomination came to identify slaveholding as the sin of sins, utterly incompatible with religious conversion. By the early 1800s, however, many of the perfectionists had adopted the attitude that the churches should deal with spiritual matters and leave civil matters in the hands of civil governments. They thus focused more of their efforts on the spiritual care of slaves and provision for their physical welfare than on political efforts at emancipation.

The obvious exception to this generally apolitical approach to the slavery question was the abolition movement, a largely religious effort spearheaded by northern Protestants such as William Lloyd Garrison, Henry Ward Beecher, and John Brown, along with the aforementioned Quakers. In addition, it should be noted that Christian women played a very prominent role in the abolition movement. Harriet Beecher Stowe, daughter of a minister and a skilled lay theologian in her own right, awakened the conscience of many people with her impassioned *Uncle Tom's Cabin* (1852). After the Civil War began, Julia Ward Howe wrote "The Battle Hymn of the Republic," couching the conflict in apocalyptic religious imagery. Howe's work became as much the anthem of the northern cause as "Dixie" was for the South. Other, lesser-known women contributed greatly to the anti-slavery cause with their time, money, and organizing ability, often taking on roles and responsibilities that reached beyond what was common for women at the time.

Long-Term Effects of the Slavery Battle

The anti-slavery movement was the site of the first open conflict between cautious religious reformers and the more radical perfectionists, as outright abolitionism emerged from the humanitarian movement that intended simply to improve the lot of slaves, not necessarily to end the institution of slavery. It was a split that would be echoed by divisions between advocates of temperance and supporters of complete prohibition, between moderate and radical factions within the peace movement, and between more and less aggressive elements of the anti-abortion movement.

More broadly, there were enduring effects of the profound religious engagement with politics represented by abolitionism. Charles Dunn (1984) lists a variety of such legacies, of which five seem especially important. (1) The abolition movement could scarcely have existed without the active, religiously motivated involvement of believers; thus, a template was established for religious leadership of major American social movements. (2) The battle against slavery left the churches with a legacy of direct political action as a tool for achieving their vision of the good society, a legacy that continues to have an impact right up through the present. Religious groups emerged as political interest groups, a position they would continue to occupy. (3) The different views of theological liberals (direct action) and conservatives (indirect action) of what was appropriate laid the groundwork for a difference in approach that continued into the 1970s. As a result, until that time, the main religious lobbies in Washington were liberal. (4) The concepts of equality and its corollary, social reform, raised during this era laid the groundwork for a continuing political emphasis on these issues, and the formation of political party platforms that emphasized them. (5) Emancipation brought with it identification of African Americans with Lincoln's Republican Party, but the accompanying social reform emphasis set the stage for most blacks to become Democrats in the New Deal era when Roosevelt took on the mantle of egalitarianism and the economic cause of the "little guy."

Religion, Temperance, and Prohibition

The crusade for regulation of liquor or for total prohibition was part of a much larger middle-class support for "social Christianity" that had begun to emerge after the Civil War and that, by the early twentieth century, had aligned itself with Theodore Roosevelt's progressive, "Bull Moose" Party. The 1912 Progressive Party convention, which nominated the former President for a third-party bid for another term in office, used "Onward, Christian Soldiers" as its theme song. The party advocated reforms including:

> [D]irect primaries, women's suffrage, the initiative, referendum, recall, regulation of interstate commerce, revision of banking and currency laws, effective antitrust legislation, municipal ownership of public utilities, the

income tax, the eight-hour day, prohibition of child labor, safeguards against industrial accidents and occupational diseases, and either strict regulation of the liquor traffic or its outright prohibition.

(Hudson and Corrigan 1992: 303)

This was a representative laundry list of turn-of-the-century progressive priorities, and highlights the increasing convergence of mainline Protestant causes with secular progressive ones. Prohibition, however, was one item on the agenda that tended to unite liberal and conservative Protestants of the time. Strong drink had come to be regarded in much the same way that northern evangelicals had viewed slaveholding in the previous century—as clear evidence of an unconverted life, and as a ripe object for social and legal reform.

Two strands of religious thought came together in the campaign against "Demon Rum." Progressive social Christianity was motivated primarily by the harms that stemmed from overuse of alcohol, by the strains on families and on society that resulted from the unregulated sale and consumption of liquor. This often gave rise to working for temperance and regulation, without total prohibition. Temperance advocates often distinguished between wine and beer, on one hand, and distilled spirits on the other, and encouraged moderation in the use of the former with total avoidance of the latter. Perfectionist evangelicalism, conversely, was motivated more by its view that any use of alcohol was clear evidence of an unredeemed life, and anything short of prohibition was evidence of an unredeemed society. For most in this movement, temperance was not enough; abstinence (for individuals) and prohibition (for society) were the only satisfactory approaches.

A Protestant Crusade

The push for prohibition was largely a Protestant initiative, though it ran the theological gamut of American Protestantism. One author has dubbed the Anti-Saloon League, founded in 1895, as "virtually a branch of the Methodist and Baptist churches" (Dabney 1949: 35). While neither Episcopalians nor German Lutherans officially supported the prohibition cause, both did advocate temperance. Some individual Episcopal parishes and leaders did support prohibition, as did Scandinavian Lutherans of a more pietistic inclination (Ahlstrom 1972). Congregationalists and Quakers had been strong supporters of prohibition for decades, and remained so in the early twentieth century. Even as evangelical Protestantism was beginning to back away from much of its previous zeal for social reform, its determination to see a prohibition amendment enacted remained intact (Sweet 1988).

Catholic responses to the push for prohibition ranged from ambivalent to hostile. Tensions between Irish and German Catholics had festered in the United States at least since the Civil War, and the prohibition battle highlighted this conflict. German Catholics, like their Lutheran counterparts, felt that prohibition amounted to fanaticism. Irish Catholic leaders in general—and those who advocated rapid assimilation into American culture in particular—were more open to the idea. They regarded the drinking habits of Irish Catholic laity as a serious obstacle to progress and integration into American culture, and saw prohibition as a potential aid to their cause. Divisions over prohibition within Catholicism continued until Protestant domination of the movement and the 1919 passage of a constitutional amendment—widely regarded as a failure and repealed in 1932—brought about nearly unanimous Catholic opposition (Ahlstrom 1972).

Jews were usually in the forefront of reform movements well into the 1900s, and the fight for temperance was no exception. Jewish participation in such efforts was usually disproportionate to the size of the Jewish population, for a number of reasons. The prophetic tradition of the Hebrew scriptures emphasizes social justice and providing for the needs of the entire community. As one Jewish author put it, "The Jewish outlook . . . prods Jews constantly to strive for a better world, to be in the thick and at the front of movements for social reform" (Bernstein 1950: 419). Secular and Reform Jews, especially, for whom the essence of Judaism lay in its ethical directives, supported temperance on the grounds that it would benefit the entire community. On the other hand, many were not wholly favorable toward prohibition, because it advocated a level of puritanical asceticism that was and is foreign to Judaism.

Women, Religion, and Prohibition

As discussed previously, American women were actively and extensively involved in the crusade against slavery. Women were also central figures in the temperance movement, again in ways that reached beyond the social and political norms of the day. In addition to the reasons for opposing alcohol common to all temperance advocates, women's groups that rallied to the cause also emphasized the connection between drunkenness and domestic violence. The Women's Christian Temperance Union, founded in 1874, was the "first nondenominational mass women's organization." Led by founder Frances Willard, whose concerns reached far beyond prohibition, the organization provided women with a "base for their participation in reformist causes, [and served] as a sophisticated avenue for political action, as a support for demanding the ballot, and as a vehicle for supporting a wide range of charitable activities." There was a conscious attempt to "integrate women's moral outlook into the public policy arena" (Mayer 1988: 1447). Women who had begun to gain a sense of their own power and effectiveness in the fight against liquor were also involved in working more directly for women's rights, including suffrage. Involvement in the successful abolition and temperance crusades made women more aware than ever before of their political power and its potential.

The Churches and Broad Programs for Social Reform

Religious organizations and people have been heavily involved in single-issue efforts, such as the crusades for abolition and prohibition, throughout the course of American history. At times, however, they have also formulated multifaceted, far-reaching programs for social reform. It is precisely these sorts of programs that motivated the efforts of the Benevolent Empire and the Social Gospel movement. Two specific articulations of such wide-ranging policy agendas are found in the 1919 U.S. Catholic "Bishops' Program of Social Reconstruction" and the statement "The Social Ideals of the Churches," adopted by the Federal Council of Churches (predecessor of the National Council of Churches of Christ in the U.S.A., and, like it, closely identified with liberal Protestantism) in 1932.

The Bishops' Program of Social Reconstruction

Beginning in earnest with Pope Leo XIII's encyclical letter *Rerum Novarum* in 1891, the global Catholic Church sought to address the moral and social challenges posed by industrial capitalism. In keeping with this growing emphasis on social conditions, the American bishops were increasingly motivated to speak, in a wide-ranging way, to the moral implications of America's changing economic order. Catholicism has always advanced an organic view of society, in which all people and institutions are intimately interconnected, as opposed to the more characteristically Protestant emphasis on individualism. This theological position has often been the foundation for Catholic support of social programs.

The 1919 Bishops' Program of Social Reconstruction touches on a wide range of social concerns. In the face of proposals for a general wage reduction, the bishops supported labor's efforts to resist such reductions on grounds of both justice and economics. While acknowledging that there were limits to the government's ability to construct public housing, they did assert a governmental obligation to provide decent housing for all, especially in the burgeoning cities. While eschewing government price controls, they championed continued reduction of the cost of living, primarily by the prevention of monopolies. They promoted the concept of a legal minimum wage and of government-provided insurance against "illness, invalidity, unemployment, and old age."

The bishops also supported labor's right to organize and to deal with management through representatives chosen by the workers, as well as labor's right to have a say about workplace policies, practices, and conditions. Specifically, they advocated extension of workplace safety and sanitation regulations, and of vocational training, along with the elimination of child labor.

Like the Vatican, the American bishops did not seek to undermine the basic architecture of the capitalist economic order (indeed, they echoed *Rerum Novarum*'s explicit rejection of socialism). They did, however, cite three major moral defects of the existing system: it was inefficient and wasteful in both production and distribution, it provided inadequate financial security for many workers, and it afforded "unnecessarily large" incomes to the privileged few. This wide-ranging critique of existing economic arrangements in America represented the most significant social statement that the U.S. bishops had ever made, and in that sense represented a watershed moment for America's growing Catholic population (Byrnes 1993).

The Social Ideals of the Churches

Around this same time, support was coalescing in the mainline Protestant churches for a similarly wide-ranging program of social reform. Indeed, the Federal Council of Churches list in 1932, which in many ways echoed a social statement approved by the Methodist Church in 1908, was even more comprehensive. It called for the "practical application of the Christian principle of social well-being" to various aspects of the economic system: credit, monetary policy, capital acquisition, distribution of wealth, and the minimum wage, among others. Worker safety in both industry and agriculture, as well as unemployment insurance, were also listed. The Council called for a reduction in the number of hours worked daily, and encouraged all employers to limit their employees' work week to six days, "with a shorter working week in prospect." The legitimacy of labor organizations and the right of collective bargaining were upheld. Economic justice for farmers and the extension of the cultural opportunities available in cities to those in rural areas were also listed as priorities.

The statement also advocated special provisions to safeguard working women, as well as the complete abolition of child labor, the "protection of the family by a single standard of purity," and "educational preparation for marriage, homemaking, and parenthood." The Council sought to protect society from the effects of "any traffic" in alcohol or illegal drugs, and encouraged reform of the criminal court and prison systems.

Finally, the Council sought to promote a "cooperative world order" by the renunciation of war and dramatic armament reductions, as well as the establishment of international agencies for settling disputes. More generally, they embraced toleration and goodwill toward all, along with the safeguarding of the rights and responsibilities of free speech, free assembly, and a free press, holding the "free communication of mind with mind as essential to the discovery of truth."

Two things stand out in an examination of both the Bishops' Program and the Federal Council of Churches list. First, though they were written almost a century ago, many of the problems that they address still exist in one form or another. Second, the solutions suggested then are often very similar to those being suggested now; for example, a call for government-funded health insurance appears in both documents, and was the legislative centerpiece of President Obama's first term in office. Likewise, battles over the minimum wage and over the distribution of wealth in America are recurrent features of our political landscape.

Religion and the New Deal

The political opportunity to implement many aspects of the churches' social reform agenda was presented by the Great Depression of the 1930s. During his presidency, Franklin Roosevelt changed the role of government to one of much greater direct responsibility for the economic welfare of individuals and society. His "New Deal" included programs to assist people in terms of jobs, disabilities, pensions (Social Security), and other matters—very much in line with what both the Catholic bishops and the Federal Council of Churches had called for. While religious people and institutions were divided over the wisdom and scope of these programs, they ultimately passed with widespread support from people of faith, especially from clergy in the more liberal Christian denominations.

Religious involvement in the politics of Roosevelt's New Deal had ramifications that would linger into the twenty-first century. First, religious liberals had carried the day, largely because their more conservative counterparts did not make common cause with political conservatives, believing that "religion's business is religion." This general aversion toward political activism on the part of religious conservatives would endure into the 1970s, when the pattern would change dramatically.

Second, Catholics, Jews, and African American Protestants became important elements of the New Deal coalition, and would continue to be so for decades. These previously marginalized religious groups came to occupy a more central place in American political life, and to play a more prominent role in shaping the interaction between religion and politics in America.

Third, this particular time period drew battle lines between religious liberals and conservatives on what type of government each favored—lines that still exist. While liberals sought to use the power of government to reform society and promote economic equality, conservatives advocated a much more limited role for government and worried about the morally corrosive effects of collectivism. This difference, too, is still relevant in the twenty-first century, as exemplified by current debates over the proper size and scope of the welfare state.

Fourth, the ascendance of religious liberalism contributed to the rise of internationalism, as isolationist sentiment was more characteristic of the conservative Protestant churches. This would fuel the post-World War II push for the United Nations, as well as for a variety of international organizations and governance structures.

Finally, prohibition's repeal just as the New Deal was beginning signaled a reduction—at least temporarily—in the American churches' emphasis on personal morality in their political engagement. This shift in emphasis would persist until the last quarter of the twentieth century, when political activism around morality issues would be reignited by debates over abortion, homo-sexuality, drugs, and gender roles.

Religion, War, and Peace

The religious roots of American attitudes toward peace and war are found in the scriptures and teachings of Judaism and, especially, Christianity. These religious traditions have given rise to three basic perspectives on warfare: the "holy war" approach, just war theory, and pacifism. Until the reign of the Roman Emperor Constantine in the fourth century, pacifism, or the complete rejection of military conflict, was the dominant Christian position. As Christianity made the transition from a persecuted minority sect to a religion of empire, however, many Christians began to believe that an absolutist pacifism was overly simplistic and unsuited to the realities of civil governance. Led by Augustine of Hippo, they developed a doctrine of "just war," which argues that Christians may take part in military conflicts if the war is declared by proper authority and meets a set of strict ethical criteria in its rationale and conduct. Finally, the idea of the crusade or holy war—a conflict against evil in which Christian participation is not only morally permissible, but a positive good—first arose during the Middle Ages, but never became the predominant Christian approach to warfare.

Holy War

The crusade, or "holy war," approach has been a significant aspect of attitudes toward some conflicts in American history. In this conceptualization, a holy war is one waged by the righteous on behalf of God and his justice against unbelievers, heretics, or evildoers. When it came to interpreting and making sense out of the carnage and destruction of the Civil War, the crusade model apparently worked for both sides, although understandably somewhat better for the North. It was easy enough for the victors to regard their triumph as God's vindication of the anti-slavery position, and the South's defeat as a manifestation of divine wrath (Faust 2008). For the vanquished, however, it was harder to see God's hand at work in what appeared to be the destruction of their entire way of life. Many Americans saw World War II as a righteous moral struggle against the evils of fascism; indeed, General Eisenhower characterized the D-Day landings as part of a "crusade" against the Nazis. Finally, President George W. Bush famously characterized America's struggle against terrorism, including the war in Afghanistan, as a "crusade"—a remark that generated some controversy, given the sensitivity of that term in the Arab world (Ford 2001).

Just War: The Predominant Model

While bellicose "holy war" rhetoric has appeared at times in American history, the more common prism through which communities of faith have viewed military conflicts has been one or another version of just war theory. In this approach, war is regrettable, but if it is declared by the proper authorities, and carried out justly, people may in good conscience participate; in fact, they may be obligated to do so. Protestant reformers Martin Luther and John Calvin each supported a version of the traditional Catholic just war doctrine elaborated by Augustine, Aquinas, and others. According to Luther, the sword is a legitimate weapon of the state to be used in safeguarding its citizens and preserving order. Calvin was somewhat more militant: in his view, the state is responsible for supporting the church, and he comes close to describing warfare to this end as a holy war. However, in the long run, his emphasis is on the right to take up arms in a just cause, including the defense of "true religion."

While different Christian thinkers and denominations have offered somewhat varying articulations of just war theory, a few general criteria governing *jus ad bellum* (right entry into war) and *jus in bello* (right conduct in war) are common to the approach (Corey and Charles 2012):

1. A just war must be declared by duly constituted governmental authority.
2. The cause must be just, such as resisting aggression or combating significant human rights abuses.
3. The intention in going to war must be rightly ordered (e.g., righting a wrong or alleviating suffering, not pursuing material gain).
4. There must be a realistic prospect of success in achieving the war's objectives.
5. War must be entered into only as a last resort, after all other reasonable avenues of conflict resolution have been exhausted.
6. The use of force must be no greater than necessary, and must be proportional to the expected gain.
7. Every reasonable care must be taken to minimize civilian casualties resulting from military actions.
8. Enemy combatants who no longer pose a threat (e.g. prisoners of war) must be treated humanely.

Of course, it can in practice be difficult to determine whether these criteria are being met in the conduct of an actual war; none except the first is easily decided, and even that is subject to some ambiguity. Thus, a small but significant minority within the Christian tradition has always rejected the very idea of "just war."

Pacifism

In the United States, the primary locus of pacifism, the third viewpoint, has been the "historic peace churches," though they have at times received support from elements within other denominations. Certain strictly pacifist religious groups have been present in the United States from early in its history, most notably the Society of Friends, the Mennonites, and the Brethren. One of the Friends' "Queries" serves as an example of this perspective: "Are you faithful in maintaining our testimony against all war as inconsistent with the spirit and teaching of Christ? Do you live in the life and power that takes away the occasion of all wars?" The Seventh-day Adventists and the Jehovah's Witnesses are later pacifist denominations (although the Witnesses say they will fight in "God's war," so their pacifism is, at least in theory, not absolute).

The Fellowship of Reconciliation, founded in 1914, is the primary interdenominational Christian pacifist organization. It was founded on five basic principles:

1. Love, as shown in the life and death of Jesus Christ, is the only power strong enough to overcome evil with good, and the only sufficient basis for human society.
2. In order to establish a world order based on this love, people must accept the principle fully, even though this means taking risks, since most of the world does not accept the law of love.
3. Christians cannot participate in war, and must instead live a life based on love in all respects, as an embodiment of their national loyalty and their loyalty to Jesus Christ.
4. The power, wisdom, and love of God are far greater than human beings can know, and are always seeking to be embodied in human life in more decisive ways.
5. God works in the world through people; therefore, Christians must offer themselves to Him for whatever peaceful use He will make of them.

Attitudes Toward Particular Wars

Given the three very different approaches to war outlined above, it is inevitable that the responses of specific American religious groups to specific national conflicts have varied considerably. Chapter 2 has already reviewed the strong role that religion played in supporting the American Revolution (despite the objection of some groups, such as Quakers, to the idea of armed conflict). The general religious enthusiasm for that conflict, combined with the pervasive patriotic spirit of the time, gave rise to the beginnings of what would be called "American civil religion," that union of religion and nationalism that would color—but not completely dominate—religious Americans' response to the nation's later wars.

The Civil War

Both North and South, supporters of the Union and of the Confederacy, slaveholders and abolitionists, used religious rationales in support of their positions in the Civil War. Religious historian Sydney Ahlstrom has described the Civil War as an uniquely "moral war," not necessarily because one side was clearly in the right and the other clearly in the wrong, but because "it sprang from a moral impasse on issues which Americans in the mid-nineteenth century could no longer avoid or escape" (Ahlstrom 1972: 649). Chaplains supported soldiers and consoled those at home on both sides. The war became a central topic of sermons and pastoral prayers. Revivals were a frequent feature of military camp life.

We have already noted that "holy war" ideology and the rhetoric of judgment and punishment helped many to make sense of the war and its carnage. This was certainly the tone of Julia Ward Howe's "Battle Hymn of the Republic," the unofficial anthem of the Union war effort. There were also, however, more theologically nuanced views. Connecticut Congregationalist minister Horace Bushnell saw a war in which the nation's divisions were purged and its oneness strengthened. He compared it with Jesus' atoning sacrifice, in which suffering and death brought salvation. Historian Philip Schaff interpreted it as divine judgment on the entire nation's participation in the institution of slavery and as an event that readied America to play a decisive role in the extension of human freedom. Abraham Lincoln, whose second inaugural address reflects elements of Schaff's view, also believed the war to have been an ordeal to test the nation's moral purpose, leading to a new birth of freedom in the land (Ahlstrom 1972).

World War I

When England and France, with their allies, declared war on Germany and its allies, religious leaders and laity were divided in their opinions of the war effort. Divisions were not along denominational lines so much as over the morality and likely long-term consequences of the war. President Wilson's decision to enter World War I in 1917 received nearly the full support of the nation's religious groups, even of those usually committed to pacifism. His depiction of U.S. involvement as completely disinterested, an engagement solely on behalf of human rights, made it easier to accept. Even many of those who had been pro-German earlier in the European conflict changed their minds. It was generally seen as a situation in which war was a necessary evil, the only way to ensure long-term peace. Religious organizations and their leaders very shortly were caught up in feverish support of the war effort. To a large extent, the war became a crusade: God had called the nation into the battle, to promote the final triumph of "Christian civilization," and the allied combatants were glorified as champions of right against the devil's minions (Endy 1988).

Protestant, Catholic, and Jewish religious organizations and chaplains served the needs of both military personnel and their families. World War I was the first time that significant non-Christian services had been made available by the military. Concerned not only with spiritual issues, religious organizations worked alongside secular ones to help provide for the various needs that the wartime situation engendered. The American Friends Service

Committee was formed in 1917 both to counsel and assist Quakers and others in remaining strong in their peace witness and to support humanitarian activity for the benefit of all engaged in the war. It has endured to the present day as a significant peace and humanitarian service organization.

The Selective Service Act of 1917 (the "draft") did provide exemptions from combatant service for clergy and seminary students. Members of the historic peace churches were exempt as well. Interestingly, although many thousands were granted certificates of exemption, only a fraction used them. The majority of those drafted went to war. Two factors together were probably responsible: the churches' hold on their members had weakened somewhat, and there was fervent public condemnation of those who did refuse to fight, even on religious grounds.

Religious support for the peace movement increased in the interval between World War I and World War II, among both Protestants and Catholics outside the historic peace churches. The Fellowship of Reconciliation grew to 12,000 members by the 1930s, and the Catholic Association for International Peace was formed in 1927. As peace activism in America expanded beyond its traditional base into larger religious groups, churches worked on new ways to counsel and provide assistance and support to conscientious objectors.

World War II

Prior to the Japanese bombing of Pearl Harbor in 1941, almost all religious groups opposed the United States becoming involved in yet another European conflict. However, the attack on the U.S. base led to widespread religious support for intervention in World War II. Just war ideology carried the day, generally focusing on the necessity of opposing the fascist regimes more than making the war into a crusade against demonic evil. Religious organizations responded in two wide-ranging ways (Gaustad and Schmidt 2002). Protestant, Catholic, and Jewish chaplains (over 8,000 of them) led worship, encouraged the living, comforted the dying, and provided spiritual services to all. Their assistance went beyond what is usually defined as "spiritual," however, as they also helped provide for the physical and emotional needs of soldiers and their families, focusing on humanitarian efforts intended to soften the war's effects. Clothing, food, housing, and medicine were all provided to those in need. Religious organizations also helped deal with the tremendous refugee problem occasioned by the global conflict.

Mennonites, Brethren, and Friends helped run Civilian Public Service work camps where those who claimed conscientious objector status could do alternative service. The Selective Training and Service Act of 1940 extended the right of conscientious objection to members of any religious organization who "by religious training and belief" objected to all warfare. This meant, for example, that Seventh-day Adventists could opt out of combat; they made up between one fourth and one half of conscientious objectors. The Jehovah's Witnesses were more difficult for the draft boards to deal with, since they did not oppose all wars, but only those of human origin. When God's final battle of Armageddon came, they anticipated being on the front lines. Many were imprisoned for their beliefs, even after the 1942 Selective Service Act provided for them to be granted ministerial standing if religious duties occupied them for at least eighty hours a month. Beyond these groups, conscientious objection became an option for members of mainline religious organizations. Methodists and Baptists accounted for the majority of mainstream Protestants claiming such standing. Some Catholics and a few Jews also joined in this form of peace activism. Since the Nazi persecutions had turned World War II into a virtual holy war for Jews, however, conscientious objectors were often regarded as traitors by fellow members of the Jewish community.

World War II had an immensely unifying effect on the American Jewish community, as it did on Jews throughout the world. As the atrocities of the Nazi death camps came to light, Jews, who before had been divided in their support for a Jewish state of Israel, came to favor it overwhelmingly. One of Theodor Herzl's key points in *Der Judenstadt* ("The Jewish State"), the book that gave the first voice to the Zionist movement in the late nineteenth century, was that Judaism would not be safe in the world until a permanent Jewish homeland was established. The Holocaust brought this point home in a tragic and dramatic way. Jews in the United States, as elsewhere, laid aside differences in order to focus on supporting this crucial goal.

When the United States dropped atomic bombs on Hiroshima and Nagasaki in 1945, it not only brought a rapid end to World War II, but also posed significant challenges for just war theory. The widespread killing of innocents and the unimaginable horror of near-total destruction seemed to make many traditional just war criteria obsolete. Could a nuclear war be "winnable" in any meaningful sense? Could civilians ever be sufficiently protected in the event of a nuclear exchange? Where even the remote possibility of nuclear escalation existed, could conventional wars be justified as easily as they had been in the past? Increasingly, these questions became a prominent part of American religious thinking about war and peace.

In the mid 1950s, the United States and Soviet Union's testing of nuclear weapons, fear of nuclear fallout, and the very real prospect of worldwide destruction led to a resurgence of peace activism. Liberal religious leaders, especially, joined scientists in SANE, a prominent anti-nuclear advocacy group. This laid the groundwork for increasing skepticism by religious groups about American involvement in military conflicts in the nuclear age.

The Challenges of Religious Pluralism

As American religious groups grappled during this period with weighty social issues such as slavery, temperance, economic justice, and war and peace, the nation also struggled to come to grips with a growing diversification of the religious landscape. From its inception, as discussed in Chapter 2, the United

States had been more religiously pluralistic than most nations of the world, and by the nineteenth century there was broad toleration for all of the sects within mainstream Protestantism. As fresh waves of immigrants arrived, however, and as new religious movements arose, the boundaries of this toleration were tested. Groups outside the Protestant mainstream increasingly sought an equal place at the national table, and were often greeted with considerable resistance. Moreover, these battles over inclusion frequently took on an explicitly political, as opposed to simply social and religious, dimension, because dominant religious groups often used the law to coerce, marginalize, and disenfranchise members of minority faith traditions.

The experience of three American religious groups—Catholics, Mormons, and Jehovah's Witnesses—is particularly illustrative of this struggle for acceptance and inclusion. This is not by any means to suggest that these were the only religious groups facing hostility and discrimination in nineteenth- and early twentieth-century America. Instances of anti-Semitism abound, for example, as do localized cases of some Protestant denominations marginalizing others. The experiences of these three groups, however, are especially revealing of the political and legal issues involved in the nation's struggle to accommodate increasing religious pluralism, and thus merit brief consideration here.

American Anti-Catholicism

As noted in Chapter 2, anti-Catholic sentiment in America dates back to the earliest colonial experience. The largely English Protestant settlers of the colonies brought with them, to varying degrees, an antipathy toward Catholicism born out of the Reformation, the English religious unrest of the sixteenth century, and geopolitical struggles with Catholic Spain and France. These sentiments were reflected, in the extreme, by the death sentences for Catholic priests in Puritan Massachusetts, and in milder form by the widespread disenfranchisement of Catholics in other colonies. A strong anti-Catholic bent is evident even in the writings of generally tolerant founders such as Jefferson, who argued that Catholic priests were "hostile to liberty," and John Adams, who believed that Catholicism damaged people by "reducing their minds to a state of sordid ignorance and staring timidity" (Winters 2010). This anti-Catholic animus was largely abstract in eighteenth-century America, since the nation's Catholic population was so small. This changed significantly, however, during the course of the nineteenth century, as waves of immigration, first from Ireland and Germany in the antebellum era, then from Italy, Poland, and elsewhere in southern and eastern Europe between the Civil War and World War I, swelled the ranks of American Catholics. While Catholics were less than 2 percent of the U.S. population in the founding era (Middleton 2002), they were the nation's largest single denomination by the time of the Civil War, and by the early twentieth century had come to comprise the roughly one quarter of Americans that they do today (Paulson 2008).

Native Protestant reaction to this influx of Catholics took many forms. The Catholic immigrants were variously accused of being drunken, violent, and undemocratic, and salacious tales proliferated in the popular press accusing priests and nuns of multiple offenses, including sexual depravity, kidnapping, and even cannibalism (Lockwood 2000). Whole political and social movements were spawned by fear of the Catholic "menace," including the Know-Nothing Party of the 1850s (which included a former president, Millard Fillmore) and the second incarnation of the Ku Klux Klan in the 1920s. Periodic local anti-Catholic uprisings, often including violence against the Catholic population and the destruction of Church property, were a feature of nineteenth-century American life (Massa 2003). The anti-Catholic impulse in American culture found its most tangible legislative manifestation in opposition to Catholic schools, as efforts to prevent them from receiving any government assistance began in earnest with the proposed Blaine Amendment of the 1870s and culminated with Oregon's attempt to ban Catholic education outright in the 1920s (Tyack and Hansot 1986). While this initiative was ultimately struck down by the U.S. Supreme Court, it is revealing of the depth of anti-Catholic sentiment lingering in America well into the twentieth century.

Despite strong and persistent resistance from the religious majority, the American Catholic community continued to grow and thrive, and eventually began to flex its political muscle. It did so first at the local level, becoming a major force in the urban politics of immigrant centers such as New York, Boston, and Chicago, followed by the election of Catholic Governors and Members of Congress. Finally, in 1928, a major party for the first time nominated a Catholic candidate for president, as the Democrats chose New York Governor Al Smith to run against Republican Herbert Hoover (who was himself a Quaker). Smith's nomination provoked an avalanche of anti-Catholic invective. Conservative Protestants and liberal secularists alike decried Smith as a representative of an "alien culture" hostile to American liberties and beholden to a "foreign despot"; some went so far as to suggest that the Pope planned to move to Washington if Smith should be elected (Slayton 2001). Hoover won the election easily, even carrying several Southern states that had not voted Republican since Reconstruction.

The next opportunity for a Catholic to win the presidency would not come until 1960, when the Democrats nominated Massachusetts Senator John F. Kennedy to oppose Vice President Richard Nixon (by coincidence, a Quaker like Hoover). The election would provide a test of how far America had come in accepting its largest religious minority. Kennedy faced many of the same objections that Smith had decades earlier, and felt compelled to reaffirm repeatedly his commitment to separation of church and state and to downplay the role of religion in his worldview (to the point that some in the Catholic hierarchy regarded him as "spiritually rootless and almost disturbingly secular"—Hennesey 1981: 308). Nonetheless, Kennedy's eventual victory in a very close election (aided by the overwhelming support of his co-religionists, which helped him to overcome strong opposition from conservative Protestants—see Wilson 2007) was a watershed moment in American Catholicism. The election of one of their own to the presidency signaled to American Catholics that anti-Catholicism, if by no means dead in America, had at least lost its stranglehold over national politics.

Mormonism and Polygamy

Another group that faced significant resistance from the American religious mainstream during this period was the Church of Jesus Christ of Latter-day Saints (LDS), or the Mormons. Mormonism is a home-grown American religion, originating with Joseph Smith in upstate New York in the 1820s. Smith claimed to have received a special revelation from God, which he published as The Book of Mormon, and he began to attract followers to his new religion. Smith's unorthodox beliefs, however, including his promotion of extra-biblical scripture, assertion of links between Native Americans and ancient Israelites, and claims to have received religious visions, brought him and his followers into conflict with conventional Protestants, ultimately causing them to leave New York in search of a more hospitable environment in Ohio, Missouri, and then Illinois.

The Mormons encountered strong opposition at each of these stops, often facing violence over their unorthodox beliefs and perceived insularity. This included a "Mormon Extermination Order" issued by Missouri Governor Lilburn Boggs in 1838 (DeVoto 2000), and the murder of Joseph Smith by an Illinois mob in 1844 (Bushman 2008). Smith's murder had been motivated in part by a new practice that he had introduced at the Mormon settlement in Nauvoo, Illinois—polygamy, or having one man take multiple wives. The general outrage of non-Mormons over polygamy convinced the LDS community that they would have to go far from established settlements to practice their religion freely. This prompted a great migration by the bulk of the Mormon community to the Utah Territory, led by Joseph Smith's successor, Brigham Young.

As the Utah Territory was still under the jurisdiction of the United States, however, battles over polygamy continued. In 1862, Congress passed, and President Lincoln signed, a law criminalizing polygamy and prohibiting any church in the territories from acquiring more than $50,000 worth of property. The target of the statute could not have been more obvious. In subsequent decades, federal and territorial laws were passed to prohibit polygamists from voting and from serving on juries; virtually all of those affected were Mormons (Noonan 1998). Mainstream Christian opposition to Mormon beliefs and practices, especially polygamy, was so strong that it delayed Utah's admission to the Union for decades.

When Mormons challenged the statutes targeting them in court on religious freedom grounds, they were uniformly unsuccessful. In *The Late Corporation of the Church of Jesus Christ of Latter Day Saints v. United States* (136 U.S. 1,

1890), a unanimous Court rejected the Mormon challenge to anti-polygamy laws on explicitly religious grounds. Justice Bradley, writing for the Court, argued that polygamy was "contrary to the spirit of Christianity, and of the civilization which Christianity has produced in the Western world" (Noonan 1998: 254). Shortly thereafter, the LDS Church changed its teaching on polygamy, formally disavowing the practice (and provoking some "fundamentalist" sects to splinter from mainstream Mormonism). This shift paved the way for a gradual diminution of the most intense anti-Mormon sentiment, and for Utah's admission as a state in 1896.

The combination of the Church's disavowal of polygamy and the post-1850 concentration of Mormons in the relatively isolated Mountain West meant that violent expressions of anti-Mormonism were largely confined to the nineteenth century. A general suspicion of and ignorance about the Mormon faith, however, persisted for much longer—so much so that it became a hindrance to Mitt Romney's presidential aspirations. As recently as 2007, about one in four Americans said they could not support a Mormon for president, many more than said the same about a woman, an African American, a Jew, or a Catholic (Jones 2007). Moreover, the nineteenth-century battle over polygamy remains relevant today, as the right of a majority to codify its understanding of marriage in law has taken on renewed importance in light of contemporary debates over recognizing same-sex relationships.

Jehovah's Witnesses and American Civil Religion

A final example of clash between a religious minority and the mainstream Protestant majority is provided by the Jehovah's Witnesses, another American home-grown religion. Founded in the 1870s in Pennsylvania by Charles Taze Russell, the Witnesses (originally known as the Watchtower Bible and Tract Society) held a variety of beliefs that would be deemed unorthodox by mainstream Christians—rejecting the Trinity, questioning the immortality of the soul, refusing to celebrate Christmas and Easter, and holding blood transfusions to be immoral (Holden 2002). What really aroused the ire of their fellow Americans (and citizens of other countries to which the Witnesses spread), however, was their refusal to participate in any rituals of patriotism. Not only did they, like members of the historic peace churches, refuse to serve in the military, but they also declined to say the pledge of allegiance, sing the national anthem, or salute the flag, viewing all such acts as idolatrous. This refusal to participate in America's civil religion of nationalism earned the Witnesses considerable enmity. As international tensions escalated in the 1930s, Americans became less and less tolerant of those in their midst who would not publicly profess their loyalty to the nation. Over 200 Witnesses children were expelled from public schools in the 1930s because they refused to say the pledge—a practice that the Supreme Court affirmed in 1940. While the Court would later reverse this decision (as Chapter 6 will discuss), it served at the time to validate the general national prejudice against the Witnesses. This prejudice was no mere intellectual phenomenon, but took very tangible, violent form. As Noonan (1998: 242) writes:

> Before the decision came down on June 3, 1940, they had been victims of several incidents of mob violence in Texas. After the decision, individual Witnesses were attacked in Maine (beatings, burning of the Kingdom Hall in Kennebunk), West Virginia (forced drinking of castor oil), Wyoming (tarring and feathering), Nebraska (castration), Arkansas (shooting), Illinois, Indiana, Maryland, Mississippi, and Oregon (mob attacks).

After World War II ended, the anti-Jehovah's Witness hysteria receded, and violent persecution of the sect became rare. Still, their ordeal at the hands of both their fellow citizens and of the government serves as a cautionary tale from the not-too-distant past about the perils of defying American civic rituals on religious grounds.

Summary and Conclusions

As this chapter has made clear, religion played an important role in many major political movements between 1800 and 1960. Religion figured prominently in:

- the abolition movement;
- temperance and prohibition efforts;
- the push for broad, progressive social reform; and
- attitudes toward war and peace.

It is very clear that events during this period laid the foundations for relationships between religion and politics that persist in the twenty-first century. Perhaps the most important of these was the churches' discovery of the political process as a way of enacting social reforms that they sought. Fundamental differences in how conservative and liberal religious groups relate to politics also developed during this time. Of crucial significance was the firm establishment of the principle that religion would interact with the political order in an effort to advance its vision of the good society. There were then and there are now religious groups that try to limit their contact with politics, but they do not represent the main thrust of religion in the United States, on either the left or the right.

Beyond these broad principles, however, more specific echoes of this historical period appear in religious–political interactions since 1960. The wide-ranging social programs espoused by many religious liberals as well as by the evangelical progressives (e.g., Sojourners) are quite similar to those of the Bishops' Program of Social Reconstruction and the Social Ideals of the

Churches. On the other hand, the concern with personal morality and virtue that marked the advocacy of temperance and prohibition echoes today in conservatives' support for traditional values in the area of family and sexuality. The fundamentalist–modernist controversy reappears, with modifications, in the "culture wars" of the late twentieth and early twenty-first centuries, as well.

Events that took place during this period continue to affect the relationship between politics and religion in the new millennium. The experience of slavery and emancipation, for example, helps to explain differences in how religion and political views are related among white and black Americans, to be discussed in Chapters 8 and 9. Moreover, the experience of religious discrimination against Catholics, Mormons, Jehovah's Witnesses, and others continues to resonate, both for these groups themselves (albeit in milder form) and for other minority religious communities—most notably Muslims.

A final important conclusion to be drawn from this discussion of the relationship between religion and politics from 1800 through 1960 is that their interaction is seldom simple and straightforward. Those who differ on religious matters may be drawn together in a common social or political cause—a phenomenon that continues today. Similarly, as Chapter 9 will show, those who concur on religious questions do not always agree on political ones.

4 Religion and Politics in America Since 1960

> As a pastor and as a parent I am calling my fellow American citizens to unite in a moral crusade for righteousness in our generation . . . It is time to call America back to God . . . I am convinced that God is calling millions of Americans in the so-often silent majority to join in the moral-majority crusade to turn America around in our lifetime . . . Let us unite our hearts and lives together for the cause of a new America, a moral America in which righteousness will exalt this nation.
>
> (Jerry Falwell, *Listen America!*, 1980)

> Society as a whole, acting through public and private institutions, has the moral responsibility to enhance human dignity and protect human rights. In addition to the clear responsibility of private institutions, government has an essential responsibility in this area . . . In a democracy, government is a means by which we can act together to protect what is important to us and to promote our common values.
>
> (USCCB, *Economic Justice for All*, 1986)

This chapter examines relationships between religion and politics in America as they have developed over the last fifty years. Some of the most significant issues raised in recent decades echo themes from the previous chapter:

- The struggle over civil rights for African Americans demonstrates that the abolition movement left an incomplete legacy of racial equality.
- The Vietnam War (and, to a lesser extent, the Iraq War) again raised questions about just wars and the legitimate use of military force.
- The resurgence of political involvement by Christian conservatives and their emphasis on personal morality echoed in some ways the temperance and prohibition crusades.
- At the same time, the re-emergence of a social justice agenda among Christians across the theological spectrum hearkens back to the broad-based reform impulse of an earlier time.

As in earlier periods, religion and politics in modern America interact in complex ways; religion helps to shape both the political questions asked and the answers given, while political controversies can both divide religious traditions and bring them together. The modern era, bringing with it significant technological and cultural change, has presented both new opportunities and new challenges for people of faith seeking to influence American politics, law, and society.

The decade of the 1960s serves as the starting point for this examination, as those pivotal years changed forever the ways that people in the United States looked at their society and their government, and drew moral and cultural battle lines that in many ways survive today. We proceed from there to an examination of the major religious groups in America today, and what their policy priorities have been over the last several decades. Having laid this foundation, we turn to consideration of specific issues, such as the role of religion in the civil rights movement, the development of the New Christian Right and responses to it, and America's continuing struggle to accommodate religious diversity. Some of the major questions guiding this examination are:

- What dramatic events and trends that occurred during the 1960s affected the relationship between religion and politics—and the American culture in general?
- During the time period from 1960 to the present, how have America's major religious groups sought to have their values reflected in public policy?
- How did religion and politics interact in the context of the civil rights movement?
- Why did the New Christian Right emerge, and how has it evolved over time? What has been the cultural and political response to a resurgent Christian conservatism?
- How has the experience of American Muslims, especially in the last decade, compared with those of other minority religious traditions?

The Decade of the Sixties

Following a relatively calm period after the end of World War II, the 1960s saw dramatic change and upheaval in America on a variety of fronts. The implications of the social, cultural, and moral changes sparked in that decade are still being worked out in the twenty-first century.

The Civil Rights Movement

Although various analysts of the 1960s give different lists of the social changes that are most significant from the period, there are several on which nearly all agree. Certainly first among these is the civil rights movement, the concerted effort by African Americans and their allies to claim fully for black people the freedom and equality to which all Americans are entitled under the Constitution. The civil rights movement shook the nation out of its complacency and brought about political and religious changes whose legacy is still evident today. We will discuss in detail later in the chapter the profound interconnection of religion and politics in this epic movement. For now, however, the key point is that the civil rights movement ushered in an era of broad social transformation in America, and became the first in a series of efforts by women, Hispanics, Asians, migrant farm workers, and homosexuals, among others, to expand legal protections for their rights. The decades since the 1960s have seen political battles over charges that efforts at social change have gone either too far or not far enough, along with political attempts by religious groups and individuals to either increase the pace of change or to rein it in.

The War in Southeast Asia and Questioning of the "Establishment"

After 1965, the war in Vietnam became an increasingly divisive issue in America. Religious groups through their Washington offices weighed in on both sides of the argument. Both supporters and opponents of the war cited religious rationales for their views, and many believed that they were truly "on God's side." Although war had never been declared officially by the Congress, the conflict escalated by executive order, especially after the alleged attack on U.S. warships in the Gulf of Tonkin in 1964. Some people opposed the war on the grounds that they believed it to be illegitimate because undeclared. Others questioned the underlying "domino theory" that held that if South Vietnam fell to the Communists, the rest of southeast Asia would not be far behind. Still others saw it as a "white man's war" against Asians, fought disproportionately by black soldiers. Some people questioned motives of defense contractors, who had an economic incentive to keep the nation on a war footing. Finally, and most significantly, a growing number of Americans began to balk at the escalating body count, questioning whether whatever might be achieved in southeast Asia was worth tens of thousands of American lives (not to mention Vietnamese casualties). Although protest against the war was outspoken, at times violent, and increasingly widespread, it was by no means universal; a large number of Americans supported the war as necessary to stop the advance of atheistic communism and "make the world safe for democracy."

   Along with increasingly sharp questioning of the war, the military, and the government, the 1960s saw a more generalized rebelliousness on the part of some young people against what they saw as a racist, militarist, materialistic, elitist, and essentially meaningless culture. "The establishment" became a catch-all term of contempt for the existing order in virtually every sphere of

American cultural life. Increasing disillusionment with what seemed to be enormous gaps between what was said and what was done, between the ideal and the actual, joined with serious doubt that the existing social, religious, educational, and political institutions were capable of doing anything to close the distance. These attitudes paved the way for a growing cynicism about virtually all of our national institutions (government, churches, universities, businesses, unions, the media, etc.) that persists today.

Murders and Moral Mayhem

The 1960s also witnessed a shocking series of assassinations, including three well-known and widely beloved leaders—President John F. Kennedy in 1963, and both Robert Kennedy and Martin Luther King, Jr. in 1968. Many, if not most, of those who were older than young children at the time can still recall exactly where they were and what they were doing when they heard that President Kennedy had been shot. The connection of television made people's individual grief over Kennedy's death into a truly national mourning in a way that had not happened before in America. These assassinations, in tandem with the general cultural ferment of the time, collectively fed a national sense of grief, anger, and fear, and a general perception that something of America's innocence had been lost (Lytle 2006).

Adding to this general sense of social and cultural insecurity was the rise among many Americans of a "new morality," or a different paradigm for understanding right and wrong. The new approach of "situation ethics" (Fletcher 1966) shifted the groundwork of moral decision making for many people, and helped to lay the foundation for some of the religious and political conflicts that persist today. Traditional teaching in most religions holds that there are clear and constant moral laws that should govern human behavior in all situations. Some things are absolutely right and others are absolutely wrong, regardless of circumstance. This view is sometimes described as an "ethic of the right," because of its emphasis on bedrock moral truths. Situation ethics, by contrast, emphasizes circumstantial and contingent determinations of morality. It can be characterized as an "ethic of the good," because it prioritizes the best outcome to a given situation over adherence to fixed principle. Flexible and alterable moral guidelines are only one element of moral decision making; the other is the situation itself. Situation ethics not only allows for variations according to context, but requires that these circumstances be given prominent consideration if moral reasoning is to be legitimate. While some people welcomed this loosening of moral strictures as evidence of a "humanity come of age," others feared that it would bring moral chaos, anarchy, and the rationalization of evil. Perhaps both have proven true. At any rate, this controversial revolution in moral thinking helped set the stage for the emergence of the religious right in the last decades of the twentieth century.

Technology Outstripping Ethics

Finally, major technological advances that emerged in the sixties and spilled over into the following decades profoundly changed the way that people interacted with their world. While technological advance is a constant feature of human existence, its pace began to increase dramatically in the 1960s, and both political and religious institutions struggled to keep up with the new legal and moral questions raised. Humans went into outer space at the same time that advocates of psychedelic drugs claimed to have discovered "inner space." The development and increasing use of computers and the beginnings of satellite transmission technology made communication much more rapid and far-reaching. The "industrial age" began to be superseded by the "age of communications." Medical advances greatly increased the capacity to sustain physical life, and soon outdistanced our capacity and willingness to think ethically about their meaning. While some technological developments cast doubt on traditional ways of thinking about the end of life, others, in the areas of conception and fertility control, required a re-examination of the moral issues surrounding its beginning.

America became aware of at least the beginnings of the "energy crisis," and of the ways in which the surge of technology and prosperity threatened the environment. Nuclear weapons, known since the United States bombed Hiroshima and Nagasaki in 1945, proliferated, and fears of their use proliferated with them. Machines began to displace people in the labor force, and increasingly dictated how people did their work. The pace of technological advance, in these and other areas, has only increased since the 1960s, and has continued to raise ethical questions that must be addressed by both politics and religion.

In sum, the years between 1960 and 1970 witnessed more social change more quickly than America had ever seen before, transformations that added up to a dramatic metamorphosis in the world in which people lived and worked, voted and prayed. These changes required a rethinking of social and cultural arrangements, of the nature and purpose of human life itself, and thus necessarily engaged both religion and politics. The process of negotiating and responding to these changes, of sorting out the genuine advances from the missteps, and of developing coherent moral and political responses to a dramatically new set of issues continues today.

Contemporary Religious Groups and Their Political Priorities

Chapter 3 argued that perhaps the most important discovery that religious groups made in the nineteenth and early twentieth centuries was that they could effectively use the political process to advance their social and moral agendas. This realization continues to shape the behavior of American religious groups in the twenty-first century. American religion has come increasingly to be characterized by the proliferation of organized interest groups and by concerted efforts to shape law and policy, a development that sociologist Robert Wuthnow calls "a significant form of social restructuring in American religion" (Wuthnow 1988: 101). This trend has led to both a more explicitly political consciousness on the part of many religious believers, as well as an expanded presence for religious organizations among the ranks of Washington lobbyists. To be sure, these religious lobbies are not, for the most part, fighting for their own tangible, material benefit. Instead, they are seeking to advance through public policy their visions of the good and just society, pursuing what E. E. Schattschneider (1960) would call "public interests" and often focusing on what Ronald Inglehart (2008) terms "postmaterial" questions of rights and values.

Here, we seek to provide a brief overview of the political priorities of America's largest faith traditions as they have evolved in the late twentieth and early twenty-first centuries. Chapters 7, 8, and 9 will explore in much more detail the opinions of religious Americans on specific policy questions, and Chapter 10 examines the political dynamics of religious interest group activity. In order to understand the interactions of religion and politics in America over the last several decades, however, it is important to have at least a general sense of what policy objectives the nation's major religious groups have pursued in recent years. This brief examination focuses on the recent political priorities of five major religious traditions with distinctive social and political outlooks: mainline/liberal Protestants, evangelical/funda-mentalist Protestants, Catholics, Jews, and African American Protestants. Each of these groups "reflects a characteristic way of interpreting and responding to the world that is evident among people who are affiliated with religious bodies that are interrelated in some historical and organizational fashion" (Smidt 2007: 30); moreover, they clearly reflect the major players in the interaction of politics and religion as it has developed since the 1960s. None of these traditions, it should be noted, is monolithic; all are composed of elites and rank-and-file constituencies with a variety of views on both religious and political matters, as well as on the proper relationship between the two. However, they clearly exhibit sufficient commonality in their approach to these questions to examine them as discrete clusters.

Mainline/Liberal Protestants

Of all the religious traditions discussed here, the mainline Protestant group is the most heterogeneous. As Chapter 8 will show, the largest mainline groups—Methodists, Presbyterians, Lutherans, Episcopalians—contain signifi-cant numbers of people at both the liberal and the conservative end of the political and theological spectrums. Over time, however, the unmistakable trend within this group has been leftward—especially among the clergy (Guth et al. 1997)—as many more conservative members have left for evangelical or Catholic churches. Thus, mainline Protestantism today, particularly at the elite level, can generally be described as theologically, socially, and economically liberal, very ecumenical and willing to form partnerships across denominational lines, frequently critical of American foreign policy, and generally opposed to the regulation of personal morality. In addition to the major denominational groups mentioned above, it includes also those smaller sects that have traditionally focused on issues of peace and social justice, such as the Mennonites, Friends, and Brethren. Institutionally, the National Council of Churches is representative of the mainline/liberal Protestant group. Working for socially and economically liberal causes within the mainline Protestant tradition goes back at least to the Social Gospel movement (discussed in the preceding chapter). This emphasis was supported and increased by the tide of liberal theology that swept seminaries in the 1920s, and was renewed in the 1960s as "radical theology" focused on the social dimension of Christianity, sometimes to the exclusion of nearly everything else. Liberal theology, with its emphasis on life in this world, its optimism about human nature, its eagerness to accommodate religious thought to prevailing cultural and scientific trends, and its willingness to cooperate with other like-minded groups, was well suited to engage with social issues on a continuing basis.

The civil rights and anti-war movements of the 1960s dramatically increased the involvement of liberal Protestants in lobbying and other activities to promote social justice. As Hertzke (1988: 31) argues, the political emphasis of liberal Protestants can be summarized as support for "peace and justice." This includes working on behalf of the poor at home and abroad, seeking to expand the scope of the American welfare state, and increasing funding for international development. Working for peace "translates into frequent criticism of American military and foreign policies, nuclear arms strategies, and military spending generally," on the grounds that money spent on defense is diverted from better uses in humanitarian development programs.

Liberal and mainline Protestants have generally been strong supporters of racial and gender equality, and other characteristically liberal social positions such as legal abortion and civil rights for homosexuals—including, increasingly, support for a right to same-sex marriage.

Mainline Protestantism's leadership still provides a consistent religious locus of support for liberal social and economic positions, as it has for decades now. However, the potential power of their political advocacy has been sapped in recent years by several significant issues:

- In the larger mainline denominations, there are often significant differences between clergy and laity on social and economic questions. Ministers in these churches are much more uniformly liberal on political issues than the people in the pews (Smidt 2004). While the disparity is not as acute as it was twenty years ago, the political divide between clergy and congregations remains significant enough to hamper mainline Protestant political activism (Wilson 2009).

- More than members of any other Christian group in America, liberal Protestants tend to be separationists when it comes to questions of religion and politics. They have become generally suspicious of organized efforts by churches and clergy to influence the political process, a reality that often undercuts the effectiveness of their denominational lobbying efforts (Olson 2002).

- While there are many nuances, variations, and exceptions to the story, mainline and liberal Protestant denominations have generally been declining in America for decades, as many of their members have moved in one of two opposite directions: either away from organized religion altogether and towards secularism, or into more conservative churches (Wuthnow and Evans 2002). Liberal Protestants are significantly more likely to report that their congregations are declining in size than are fundamentalists and evangelicals (Olson 2007). These trends have translated into a significant decline in financial support for national denominational offices and especially for the National Council of Churches, all of which have had to curtail their staffs and initiatives sharply in the face of these cutbacks.

- To some extent, liberal Protestant political activism has been a victim of its own political success. With battles won against segregation and the Vietnam War, and with a generally liberalizing climate on women's rights, gay rights, etc., the "religious left" during the 1980s and beyond lost much of its impetus for political action. Self-identified liberal Protestants are now much more likely to report general contentment with the status quo in America than are religious conservatives (Olson 2007). This lack of "fire in the belly" for social change is a significant inhibitor of religion-based political activism.

Evangelical/Fundamentalist Protestants

Since the 1970s, evangelical Protestants—found principally in the Southern Baptist Convention, the Missouri and Wisconsin Synods of the Lutheran Church, the various Pentecostal denominations, and a growing number of non-denominational "Bible churches"—have both significantly increased their share of the American religious market and found their political voice. Many, but by no means all, of these Christians would call themselves "fundamentalists," highlighting their attachment to the basics of the Christian faith such as scriptural authority (though many have begun to shy away from this label as it has become a pejorative term in the usage of cultural elites—see Bolce and De Maio 1999, 2007). The primary political emphasis of these conservative Protestants has been "traditional values." Concerned with what they see as an increasingly acute moral crisis in America, they defend the traditional family, orthodox religion, and strong patriotism, and emphasize the importance of personal moral virtue. Their support for traditional values has tended to pit them against such things as the changes in the family brought about by the liberalization of divorce laws and the movement of women into the work force, the increased availability of pornography, increased cultural and legal acceptance of homosexuality, and the legalization of abortion. Many evangelicals are especially concerned with what they see as a culturally destructive secularization of the public schools, and thus support a return of prayer to the schools, voucher programs that allow parents more choice in their children's education, and freedom for Christian schools (and, increasingly, home-schoolers) to operate with minimal government interference. Believing that America is and should be a Christian nation in some meaningful sense, they typically seek to have the basic precepts of Christian morality enshrined in the civil law. Major political advocacy groups representative of this perspective include the Moral Majority and Christian Coalition (both now defunct), Focus on the Family, the Family Research Council, and Concerned Women for America.

The problem as many evangelicals see it is not so much secularization in general as "elite secularization." America's social elites—the media, government, the educational establishment, and other gatekeepers and agenda-setters—are more secular than is the mass public. This means that the elites that determine policy and make laws are out of touch with the values of the majority, and are inclined, in the view of many evangelicals, to make relentless assaults on traditional moral norms. These secular elites have set standards and made policy for too long, according to this view; it is time to restore the values of the still-extant (if admittedly diminished) "moral majority."

In addition to this strong and pervasive emphasis on the social and moral issues of the "culture wars," however, a growing number of evangelicals in recent years have also begun to give more attention to questions of social justice. Many evangelicals believe that there is a genuine biblical imperative for action on behalf of the poor and oppressed, both in America and abroad. This cause has been most prominently championed by Jim Wallis (2005), an evangelical leader and founder of the Sojourners movement. This charitable imperative is complicated, however, by the general evangelical ethic of individualism and suspicion of "big-government" programs. While evangelicals are very generous toward charities that seek to help the poor (Brooks 2006; Smidt et al. 2008), they are often reluctant to support expansions of the welfare state, preferring programs such as President George W. Bush's faith-based charitable initiatives. This creates, as Wilson (1999: 434) notes, something of a paradox: "evangelicals seem simultaneously more anxious to help disadvantaged people and more hostile toward government programs that seek to do exactly that." Nevertheless, an openness to social-justice liberalism, while still not the dominant position in the movement, has been increasing in contemporary evangelicalism. This trend is reflected currently in increasing evangelical advocacy on behalf of immigrants, both legal and illegal, and in growing evangelical openness to comprehensive immigration reform (Huey-Burns and Cannon 2013).

To be clear, this growing concern with social justice has not displaced the long-standing conservatism of American evangelicals. As Chapter 8 will show, they remain strongly committed to traditional positions on abortion, homosexuality, pornography, etc., and they disproportionately supported the Iraq War and the "Bush Doctrine" of pre-emptive military strikes (Guth 2009). As Wallis (2008) has described it, the ethos of social-justice evangelicalism is "traditional or conservative on issues of family values, sexual integrity, and personal responsibility, while being progressive, populist, or even radical on issues like poverty and racial justice." This combination of conservatism and progressivism, traditionally a hallmark of Catholic thought (as discussed below), bears watching as an emerging trend in the political orientation of American evangelicalism.

Catholics

Traditionally, the official teaching of the Catholic Church has been a politically and ideologically mixed bag. As discussed in Chapter 3, the Bishops' Program of Social Reconstruction laid the foundations for what has been an enduring concern for the rights of workers and the poor. At the same time, however, some important voices in the American Church were closely associated with the political right. One of the most prominent among these was Francis Cardinal Spellman (Archbishop of New York from 1939 to 1967), whose views largely mirrored those of mid-century secular conservatives: anti-Communist, suspicious of leftist elements in organized labor and the civil rights movement, and strongly pro-military (Cooney 1984). Similarly, the anti-Communist crusade of Joseph McCarthy (himself a Catholic) drew some support from Catholic conservatives, as did the John Birch Society, a secular right-wing organization (Lipset 1964). Catholic intellectuals, most prominently William F. Buckley, were also instrumental in developing the intellectual foundations of a more mainstream modern American conservative movement (Allitt 1993, 2009). Clearly, American Catholicism and American conservatism developed a profound interconnection in the second half of the twentieth century, especially at the elite level.

There were, however, more left-leaning currents in the American Catholic Church as well. Robert F. Wagner, a Catholic senator from New York, contributed significantly to establishing the welfare system in the United States (O'Brien 1968). During the same time period that Cardinal Spellman was providing a strongly conservative Catholic political voice, Dorothy Day—whose cause of sainthood has been endorsed by the U.S. Conference of Catholic Bishops—co-founded the Catholic Worker movement, which identified the church with increasingly progressive economic views, especially on issues affecting labor (Piehl 1982). From the founding of that movement during the Depression until her death in 1980, Day and her colleagues worked tirelessly on behalf of the poor and oppressed. *The Catholic Worker,* a publication that she founded in 1933, remains a prominent voice for very liberal Catholic social and economic thought.

It is difficult to overestimate the role that the Second Vatican Council played in encouraging liberal elements among American Catholic leaders and laity. The Council, convened by Pope John XXIII between 1962 and 1965, did two things that directly stimulated the growth of liberal Catholic social involvement. The first was to encourage laity and leadership alike to apply their religious values to life in the world, especially on behalf of the poor and disadvantaged. The second was to reorganize the Catholic Church in the United States, empowering the American bishops to establish the United States Conference of Catholic Bishops (USCCB). This helped to give the American church a unified voice on social issues, along with a degree of autonomy for the American bishops. This organization gave the bishops a platform from which to speak much more boldly and directly about important social and political questions than had been their wont in the past (Byrnes 1993).

The American Catholic bishops have used that platform to take positions that have encouraged and enraged people on both ends of the political spectrum. Two of the most famous statements from the Conference were their pastoral letters *The Challenge of Peace* (USCCB 1983a) and *Economic Justice for All* (USCCB 1986), which staked out positions sharply critical of American nuclear deterrence strategy and of the insufficiency of the American economic safety net. More recently, in *Strangers No Longer* (USCCB 2003), the bishops called for a significant liberalization of American immigration law, and also spoke out against the Iraq War, arguing that it did not meet the traditional "just war" criteria discussed in Chapter 3. All of these positions aligned the bishops, to one degree or another, with the American political left.

At the same time, however, the bishops have also maintained a strong and consistent advocacy on behalf of the right to life (manifested principally in their opposition to abortion, but also to euthanasia and the death penalty). Their unequivocal public stance against legalized abortion dates back at least to *Human Life in Our Day* (USCCB 1968), a decade before the evangelical Protestant churches would coalesce around a pro-life position. In addition, American bishops have taken an increasingly visible role in the fight against same-sex marriage, and have typically supported educational voucher and school-choice bills in states around the country. Finally, despite their support in principle for the idea of universal health insurance, the bishops ended up opposing President Obama's health care reform proposals, on the grounds that they contained insufficient guarantees against publicly funded abortions. After "Obamacare" eventually passed despite their objections, the bishops ended up in a very public, bitter legal battle with the Obama administration over the requirement that religious employers provide their employees with insurance policies that cover contraception, sterilization, and abortifacients. On all of these issues, the bishops' stances are consistent with those of the American political right. Thus, today's USCCB is a multidimensional lobby that shares concerns with a number of other very diverse political and religious groups. Its focus can be described as "peace, justice, and traditional values." It makes common cause with liberal Protestants and the secular left on issues of war and peace and international development, but its social issue stands—on abortion and homosexuality, for example—align it with conservative Protestants, Orthodox Jews, and Mormons. This diversity of interests and of coalition partners represents what is sometimes referred to as a "seamless garment" of Catholic social teaching that transcends the categories of secular politics.

One important social factor increasingly shaping the political face of American Catholicism is the growing Latino presence in the Church. Because the Catholic Church in the United States is historically a church of immigrants, it has always paid special attention to the marginalization of immigrants and immigrant rights. About half of American Catholics are now of Hispanic descent, and many are not native English speakers (Corbett-Hemeyer 2010). As a result, contemporary Catholic political involvement has often revolved around issues affecting the Latino community. Cesar Chavez, who organized Mexican American migrant farm workers in California in the 1960s and 1970s, was a Catholic layperson. His work led to the founding of the National Farm Workers Union to protect the rights of these workers wherever they worked. In a 1983 pastoral letter entitled *The Hispanic Presence*, the U.S. Catholic bishops sought to draw attention to "those social concerns which most directly affect the Hispanic community, among them voting rights, discrimination, immigration rights, the status of farm workers, bilingualism, and pluralism" (USCCB 1983b). These issues, of course, do not affect only Hispanics; most of them apply as well, for example, to Asian immigrants, whose numbers are also increasing in the United States (and some of whom, particularly Vietnamese and Filipinos, are Catholic).

While the teaching of American Catholic leaders is clearly rich and wide-ranging, it has not had as much policy impact as one might imagine given the Church's strong organization, skilled representation in Washington, willingness to engage in coalition building, and large grassroots numbers. There are several potential explanations for this limited influence. First, despite the increasing boldness of their social policy statements beginning in the 1980s, American Catholic leaders are still more reticent about direct and explicit political engagement than clergy in white evangelical and African American churches (Byrnes 1993). In addition, since 2000, the bishops' moral authority has been undermined to some degree (among both their own faithful and the society at large) by revelations about their often inadequate responses to sexual abuse allegations against priests in their dioceses. Finally, public opinion data suggest that a large segment of the American Catholic population—particularly those who attend Mass infrequently—ignore their leaders' guidance on many questions. American Catholic laity are neither as uniformly liberal on social justice issues nor as uniformly conservative on life and family questions as are the bishops (Mockabee 2007). It appears instead that many American Catholics take their cues more from the surrounding culture than from their ecclesiastical leadership (Corbett-Hemeyer 2010). This may suggest a widening gap between Catholic laity and clergy on issues that involve both politics and religion, a divide that parallels the experience of mainline Protestants.

Jews

Jewish Americans' religious values and their historical experience have combined to involve Jews in politics in numbers far higher than their proportion of the population. The "Jewish view" on political and social matters is more complex than it may seem at first, and, like Jewish religiousness itself, is not monolithic. Secular Jewish intellectual and cultural leaders also have a far greater influence in formulating the Jewish viewpoint than is the case with either Protestant or Catholic Americans. The "Jewish civil religion" (Woocher 1986) that largely unifies America's religiously diverse Jewish population does not require that one be religiously observant in order to be Jewish. This view, nevertheless, deserves inclusion here because it represents Jewish religio-cultural interests and is rooted in the traditional religious orientations of the faith.

Jewish groups usually side with liberal Protestants on church–state questions and many social/moral issues, and with both liberal Protestants and Catholics on military policy, national economic issues, civil rights, and immigration. Where many Jews—especially the more religious—part company with these groups is on questions pertaining to Israel (Greenberg and Wald 2001). Many Catholics and liberal Protestants believe that any lasting Middle East peace will include far-reaching Israeli concessions to the Palestinians. These attitudes place them profoundly at odds with many Jews who believe that such a compromise would inevitably mean injustice and insecurity for Israel. In this view, they find support among American evangelical Protestants, whose endorsement of Zionism is at least as strong as that of Jews themselves (Spector 2008).

Characteristically, Jews have had and continue to have a very positive attitude toward social change and toward the use of government as a primary means to bring about that change (Djupe 2007). For the most part, their views have been considerably to the left of the American center on most sociopolitical issues. For at least some Jews, this view comes close to being a religious as well as a political outlook (Fuchs 1956; Sklare and Greenblum 1967). This is one reason that the Democratic Party has held the allegiance of most Jews in America since at least the middle of the twentieth century.

Whether social and political liberalism is an inherent aspect of Jewish religious thought has become a topic of debate among scholars. The relationship advanced by Fuchs (1956) and Sklare and Greenblum (1967) has been questioned by scholars who have found that the most religiously observant Jews are also the most politically conservative (Lazerwitz et al. 1988; Cohen and Liebman 1997; Greenberg and Wald 2001). There remain, however, good grounds for including social justice liberalism within the compass of the Jewish theological tradition. Theologically, such liberalism arises from the tradition of the Hebrew prophets. Time and again, they enjoined their people to care for the unfortunate, the oppressed, the widow, and the orphan as an integral aspect of their devotion to a God who is concerned for the welfare of all people. That those Jews who are more religiously observant are the least politically liberal is not surprising: traditional Judaism focuses heavily on Judaism's ritual and legal component, which the Orthodox hold to be at least as important as the ethical precepts. The emphasis here is on the "vertical" dimension of the faith, or the relationship between the people and God. Religiously liberal Judaism, by contrast, epitomized in the Reform and Reconstructionist variants, places predominant emphasis on the faith's ethical commandments. Religion here becomes virtually identical with social ethics, and the emphasis falls almost entirely on the "horizontal," or human-to-human, aspect of religion. Despite being one of the more affluent populations in the United States, Jews have tended less than other prosperous groups to vote for their own economic self-interest; in the colorful formulation of Milton Himmelfarb (1985: 40), American Jews "earn like Episcopalians and vote like Puerto Ricans."

The history of persecution endured by those of Jewish faith, and their continuing minority status, has led them to be ardent supporters of individual civil liberties and of the separation of church and state. Their concern for civil rights led them to be early allies of African Americans in the struggle against racial discrimination. Tensions arose between the Jewish and black communities, however, with the establishment of affirmative action programs, which gave advantages in college admissions and hiring to African Americans. To Jews, historically the victims of exclusivist "quota systems," affirmative action seemed to give unjust advantage to one group over others. When Jews allied themselves with those who opposed affirmative action programs as a means of racial advancement, some blacks leveled charges of racism, in response to which some Jews accused African Americans of anti-Semitism.

Tensions also arose over relations with Israel, as indicated above. In 1975, the United Nations declared that Zionism—Jewish support for the creation and maintenance of a Jewish homeland in Palestine—was a form of racism, and compared the actions of Israeli Jews against the Palestinians to those of white South Africans against blacks. This declaration, coupled with African American sympathy for the Palestinian cause, further eroded relations between Jews and blacks in the United States.

These issues, and others less important, caused a small group of Jewish intellectuals to rethink traditional Jewish attachments to political liberalism and the Democratic Party. High-profile Jewish conservative commentators such as William Kristol, Norman Podhoretz, and Michael Medved are a visible manifestation of this development. While Jews remain generally to the left of the American population as a whole, they are less uniformly so on economic questions than they once were, and conservative self-identification in the group has been increasing since the late 1980s (Djupe 2007). In addition, while a strong majority of American Jews supported Barack Obama in both of his presidential bids, their enthusiasm for his presidency has been tempered by concerns about his insufficient support for Israel (Wisse 2012). However, as Chapters 7 and 8 will show, on questions of church–state separation and personal morality, American Jews remain overwhelmingly liberal. These preferences have, at least thus far, kept most of them in the Democratic camp.

African American Protestants

The black church (a term generally used to refer to predominantly African American congregations across many denominations of Protestantism—see Lincoln and Mamiya 1990) occupies a unique position in the American religio-political landscape. While generally similar to white evangelicals in terms of theology and worship style, black churches look much more like liberal Protestant and Jewish congregations in terms of their issue emphases and partisan leanings. The historically black churches (e.g., the African Methodist Episcopal, African Methodist Episcopal Zion, Christian Methodist Episcopal, and several black Baptist churches) maintain their own Washington offices, which focus primarily on lobbying for civil rights for African Americans and other minorities, as well as for programs designed to assist the poor. This political focus on civil rights and economic liberalism has clearly been the predominant one for the black church in recent decades, and was most evident during the civil rights movement of the 1950s and 1960s (discussed below).

At the same time, however, many African Americans (as Chapter 9 will show) hold quite conservative positions on issues such as abortion, homosexuality, and drug legalization. When it comes to presidential voting and party affiliation, racial and economic liberalism clearly wins out over these attitudes for the vast majority of African American Protestants—both clergy and laity—who have been overwhelmingly Democratic for over fifty years. When given an opportunity to take positions on individual issue referenda, however, black church leaders and their faithful will often stake out morally traditionalist positions. Efforts by African American religious leaders were widely credited with helping to defeat same-sex marriage efforts in California in 2008 (Vick and Surdin 2008) and in North Carolina in 2012 (Kaufman 2012). In addition, George W. Bush in 2004 was able to increase his vote share among African Americans (albeit only to about 12 percent) by working directly with some black clergy and emphasizing traditional values themes. At the same time, however, the vast majority of black voters and religious leaders supported the presidential bids of Barack Obama, who himself endorsed gay marriage during the 2012 campaign. Thus, while the social conservatism of the black church can sometimes be a factor in state-level issue politics, the big-picture story of contemporary African American religious activism remains dominated by the quest for racial and economic equality—a quest that, in its modern incarnation, has its roots in the civil rights movement.

Politics, Religion, and the Civil Rights Movement

The civil rights movement has been called "the most important recent example of a political movement where religious forces played a tremendous role" (Fowler 1985: 154). While not all churches and religious people were in favor of ending segregation and expanding rights for African Americans—and some were vocally opposed—African American religious leaders and their white allies in Jewish, Catholic, and liberal Protestant congregations were at the forefront of the movement for civil rights from its inception.

The civil rights movement as a major national phenomenon is generally held to have begun in the 1950s with two major events. First, in 1954, the United States Supreme Court held in *Brown* v. *Board of Education of Topeka* that racially segregated schools were inherently unequal, and were thus a violation of the U.S. Constitution. The Court ordered that school desegregation proceed as rapidly as possible—an order that would meet with considerable resistance in many states. The following year, in an atmosphere already tension-charged, Rosa Parks, a Montgomery, Alabama, domestic worker, boarded a city bus to return home after a tiring day. Finding no seats available at the rear of the bus, where black people were required to sit, she took a seat nearer the front. She refused the driver's order to move to the rear, where she would have had to stand, and was arrested. Dr. Martin Luther King, Jr., pastor of Montgomery's Dexter Avenue Baptist Church, was soon thrust into the leadership of what would become known as the Montgomery bus boycott, an ultimately successful year-long protest of segregated bus seating that was largely organized and orchestrated by the city's African American churches.

King's Approach to the Civil Rights Struggle

King's tireless and inspirational leadership of the civil rights movement continued into the following decade, until his assassination in 1968. King's religious outlook combined warm Baptist piety and enthusiasm with a personalist theology acquired during his graduate school days. While King combined religious and secular arguments in favor of civil rights, he always saw the movement first and foremost as a Christian moral crusade for racial justice in America (Lischer 1997). His approach was guided by his commitment to positive change at as rapid a pace as possible, on the one hand, and his equally strong commitment to non-violent methods. In studying the lives and teachings of Jesus of Nazareth and Mohandas Gandhi, the Indian reformer, King had concluded that the way to lasting results was through cooperation and non-violent confrontation, coupled with a readiness to accept the consequences of one's actions.

King and his followers made use of the non-violent technique of "civil disobedience." There are, he argued in his famous 1963 "Letter from Birmingham Jail," four necessary steps in such an effort:

- careful collection of the facts to verify that injustice does exist;
- negotiation—always to be attempted before more confrontational methods are used;
- self-purification—a necessary prelude to civil disobedience so that participants are clear about their own motives and strong enough within themselves not to return violence for violence; and
- direct action—marches, sit-ins, boycotts, and protests.

The purpose of direct action is to force a community or group to confront an issue that they have refused to confront, about which they have refused to negotiate. Such an approach had worked for Gandhi in freeing India from British colonial rule. Privileged groups seldom relinquish their privilege voluntarily; freedom is seldom given by the oppressor without something to force the issue. Thus, King argued, non-violent protest as a form of political action must often be part of efforts for positive moral change.

As a general matter, King said, people should obey just laws. At the same time, however, he argued that God calls people to resist and to disobey unjust laws. Citing Saint Thomas Aquinas, King explained in his "Letter from Birmingham Jail" that "a just law is a man-made code that squares with the moral law or the law of God," and that "any law that degrades human personality is unjust." Resistance to such laws was, in King's view, not only permissible, but obligatory. This approach came to inform the social activism of the black church in the civil rights movement and beyond.

The Black Church and Civil Rights

The roots of King's political action were sunk deeply into his religious convictions and experience. A key result of the civil rights activism of the 1950s and 1960s was the passage of the Civil Rights Act in 1964 and of the Voting Rights Act of 1965. In addition to King's influence in bringing these about, the vast majority of white religious leaders in Washington also worked for the passage of these bills, as they had stood arm-in-arm with King and other black religious leaders in Selma and Montgomery. It is notable that a white Catholic priest, Theodore Hesburgh of The University of Notre Dame, came to serve as chair of the federal Civil Rights Commission in 1969.

Despite all of this support from sympathetic whites, however, the black church remained at the heart of the civil rights movement. Not only Martin Luther King, Jr., but Ralph Abernathy, Andrew Young, Jesse Jackson, and other charismatic leaders were drawn from the ranks of the black clergy. Before abolition, black religion had helped the slaves retain a sense of being "somebody" in God's eyes, a powerful antidote to being "nobody" in the eyes of the slaveholding world. After emancipation, it had provided necessary services to assist freed slaves, and continued to strengthen the sense of peoplehood and worth in the African American community. With its emphasis on the biblical story of the Exodus and on the sufferings and eventual triumph of Jesus, the black church provided a forum in which the yearning for freedom could find expression and organization, with little outside support from the white culture.

In practical terms, black churches became the "command centers" of the civil rights movement. They organized transportation for people who were not riding buses, or who wanted to travel to protest rallies. They had dedicated people who were ready to volunteer for all sorts of difficult and potentially dangerous tasks in support of the movement. They became information centers, emergency housing coordinators, food providers, and places of encouragement. Finally, they provided constant reminders that the civil rights struggle was not just a political one, but a transcendent moral one—a critical reinforcement to the spirit of people facing imprisonment, beatings, economic hardship, and occasionally even death because of their participation in the movement.

A Diversity of Views

While the black church was indisputably central to African American political life in the civil rights movement and beyond, it should not be viewed as monolithic. There was and is a range of views within the black churches, from those who believe that the "business of religion is religion" to those whose members and leaders believe that they should be at the forefront of social justice activism. Studies done during the 1960s found that there were at least three types of attitudes among black clergy, reflected among black laity as well. Traditionalists held to a view that churches should be concerned with spiritual matters and the salvation of souls, and steer clear of political involvement altogether. Moderates, while believing that religion must be deeply concerned with worldly as well as spiritual affairs, preferred to work for change gradually, without causing significant social turmoil. Militants believed that God called them to direct political action, including disruption and disturbance, if it was required to bring about a more just and moral society. A minority even condoned violence (Johnstone 1969; Marx 1969). On this spectrum, King and his followers fell somewhere between the moderate and militant camps.

This diversity of views notwithstanding, some black church scholars understand political action as an inherent aspect of black religion, as an embodiment of its prophetic mandate to criticize society in the name of God (Paris 1985). Other scholars point to the transformation of the "Negro" church by its participation in the civil rights movement. In answering the call to full personhood posed by the movement, they argue, the traditional, somewhat passive black church had to give way to a more assertive, race-conscious vehicle of black empowerment (Frazier and Lincoln 1974).

These sentiments gave rise to the development of Black Liberation Theology, a religious movement within African American Christianity that emphasized the struggle for black social advancement as the core of the Christian mission. This view, initially advanced shortly after the classic "civil rights era" (Cleage 1968; Cone 1969; Roberts 1974) offered a version of Christianity that was highly racialized and inherently activist, focusing almost exclusively on social reform over personal morality and spirituality. In more recent years, a prime example of this sort of thinking would be the Reverend Jeremiah Wright, whose incendiary and controversial preaching caused political problems for Barack Obama during his 2008 campaign.

The Black Liberation Theology approach, it is important to note, is by no means universal in African American Christianity; in fact, it has been much more influential at the elite level and in seminaries than among the masses of black churchgoers. In recent years, a countervailing "prosperity gospel" has emerged in many black churches, emphasizing personal moral betterment as a source of health and wealth and downplaying the group-struggle worldview of the civil rights era (Harris-Lacewell 2007). Prosperity gospel theology offers a much less politicized version of African American religious experience, suggesting that the divisions between traditionalists, moderates, and militants of the civil rights era remain relevant today.

The politics of the civil rights movement created divisions not only within the black church, but within white American religion as well. While there was widespread support for the movement's aims from leaders of white churches and synagogues, it was far from universal. Their disagreements were not so much over whether an integrated society should eventually become a reality—a point on which most agreed—but over how best to go about it, and what roles were appropriate for clergy to play. As a general rule, the more theologically conservative groups, and laypeople more than clergy, favored very gradual change brought about by the passage of resolutions and proclamations, without direct action and certainly without the involvement of clergy in practical politics.

In its effect on mainline religion, the civil rights movement precipitated an increase in direct political action on the part of the elites, which then led to dissent by many laypeople. It also heightened conflict between more conservative and more liberal religious groups. The more conservative sought to mold individual values and thus to influence society indirectly, while the more liberal took the more direct route of political activism (Wuthnow 1988). This divide, which echoes the tension within the prohibition movement described in the previous chapter, is still a source of some conflict between religious groups, but to a lesser extent, as conservative religious groups have increasingly come to espouse direct political action as well. This shift was seen most dramatically in the late twentieth century with the rise of the New Christian Right.

The New Christian Right

The civil rights movement of the 1950s and 1960s was followed by another extremely significant, organized effort to bring religious values to bear in the political sphere—the emergence of the New Christian Right. In the 1970s, evangelical Protestant congregations began to grow significantly, fueled in part by former mainline Protestants disturbed by the leftward drift (both politically and theologically) of their previous churches. At the same time, there was a growing sense among religious conservatives that America had lost its moral bearings, and that direct political action (often viewed with suspicion by religious traditionalists in the past) was necessary to combat the cultural forces of relativism, immorality, and godlessness. Thus, the New Christian Right movement developed from the confluence of a "swing toward conservatism" in American religion in the 1970s and of conservative religion asserting its political voice. In many ways, the emergence of this movement —and of responses to it—structures the relationship between religion and politics in America today more than any other single factor.

The Emergence of the New Christian Right

Why did the New Christian Right emerge when it did? There are any number of explanations, some theological and some sociopolitical. It is not possible here to survey all of them, nor to trace their historical development in detail. We can, however, suggest the broad outlines. A thorough analysis of these developments can be found in sociologist Robert Wuthnow's *The Restructuring of American Religion* (1988), an account that informs the discussion that follows.

The rise of the New Christian Right and the widening chasm between conservative and liberal religion in the 1970s and 1980s is in some ways the legacy of the fundamentalist–modernist controversy discussed in the previous chapter. However, the relationship is not direct. The earlier controversy provides only a beginning point, a legacy that has been dramatically modified over time. Yet the legacy is important.

By the 1950s, religion in the United States was marked by divisions between Christians and Jews, between Catholic and Protestant Christians, and between various Protestant denominations. Conservative religion was consciously moving away from doctrinaire fundamentalism, while liberals were moving away from modernism; both were approaching a more centrist position. Further, most were agreed that the "business of religion is religion," and that their focus should be on nurturing the faithful and gaining new converts. Largely gone from both camps was the social crusading impulse that had animated the push for prohibition, workers' rights, and other early-century moral causes.

The Decade of the 1960s

The social turmoil of the 1960s dramatically altered this picture. The civil rights movement and American involvement in the Vietnam War helped bring about a sharp division in the approach to religious activism: liberals came to embrace direct action—sit-ins and other sorts of demonstrations—while conservatives believed that religion's role was to form individual consciences, not to push directly for policy change. This division cut across denominational lines, laying the groundwork for the increasing intradenominational divides that characterized subsequent decades.

Events in the 1960s also shook the foundations of the (at least apparent) moral and cultural consensus that had prevailed in America in previous decades. Growth in higher education, coupled with the increasing secularization of the American university, gave rise to perceptions on the right of an America divided between "ordinary people" and an "intellectual elite" that was viewed as morally permissive, unpatriotic, and largely godless. This perception of a profound values divide (and, in the view of religious conservatives, a values crisis) was fueled by a remarkable series of dramatic cultural changes over a short period of time. The decade from 1963 to 1973 saw the end of public school prayer (as discussed in Chapter 5), the birth of the gay rights movement in the Stonewall riots, the increasing assertiveness of the feminist movement, the national legalization of abortion in *Roe* v. *Wade*, and the rise of a counter-culture that glorified "free love," drug use, and the rejection of authority. The divides created by these developments laid the groundwork for a "politics of cultural differences" (Leege et al. 2002), as attitudes toward the changes split along lines of age, education, class, and region, but tended to cut across denominational boundaries.

Into the 1970s and the 1980s

The 1970s and 1980s were a time for the consolidation of these cultural cleavages, which made the time ripe for the development of the New Christian Right. Conservative evangelical Protestants, who had retreated into relative political quiescence (at least at the national level) following the fundamentalist–modernist split in the 1920s and the repeal of prohibition, felt like they could not sit idly by in the face of what they regarded as existential threats to American civilization and a recognizably Christian moral order.

These developments, again, were a result of both religious and social forces at work. Religious conservatism had gained a national identity with the founding of a number of "parachurch" organizations such as the Campus Crusade for Christ and the founding in 1942 of the National Association of Evangelicals as an umbrella organization for those denominations that were dissatisfied with the theological liberalism of the National Council of Churches. The national prominence of Billy Graham's "crusades"—a huge cultural phenomenon that drew millions to revivals all over the country—added to this identity.

Interestingly, the growth of mass media and the use of polling techniques also contributed to this sense of national identity. Polls made it possible to measure conservative religious sentiment and commitment with new precision. National surveys revealed that up to a third of the population regarded themselves as conservative Protestants (depending upon the criteria for inclusion). These figures easily gained the attention of the media elites, who had previously been inclined to regard evangelicalism as something of a fringe cultural phenomenon. They also helped to reinforce among Christian conservatives a sense of their own potential political and cultural power. Finally, evangelical Christian television blossomed in the 1970s and 1980s, driven first by the development of UHF stations, then by cable and satellite broadcasting. Programs such as Jerry Falwell's *Old Time Gospel Hour*, Pat Robertson's *700 Club*, and the broadcasts of Jimmy Swaggart, Oral Roberts, and others had by the 1980s become a prominent feature of the American television landscape (Peck 1993). These programs helped to cultivate a national, as opposed to merely congregational, evangelical identity, and often blended implicit or explicit political messages with their religious content.

The presidential candidacy of Jimmy Carter, a Southern Baptist who spoke openly of his "born-again" experience, and his subsequent victory in 1976 also helped to raise the public profile of evangelical Christianity. *Time* and *Newsweek* declared 1976 the "year of the evangelical." This was underscored further by the fact that Carter's opponent in 1976 (Gerald Ford) and both opponents in 1980 (Ronald Reagan and John Anderson) also openly professed their born-again status. Clearly, a religious and cultural movement had arrived.

The New Christian Right and the Republican Party

By the 1970s, it was increasingly clear that evangelical Protestants (and, to a lesser extent, their conservative allies in the mainline, Catholic, and even Jewish traditions) had both a definite sociopolitical agenda and significant potential political power. It was not immediately apparent, however, what if any partisan form the incipient religious conservative activism would take. As late as the 1970s, there were no significant, consistent relationships between party identification and religious commitment in America; more devout citizens were just as likely to be Democratic (or Republican) as more secular ones. This began to change, at least at the elite level, in 1972, when the Democratic Party decisively embraced the cultural left with the candidacy of George McGovern. More than a third of the white delegates at the 1972 Democratic National Convention were self-identified atheists, agnostics, or people who seldom or never attended religious services (Layman 2001), a figure much higher than that in the national population at the time. McGovern was widely identified as the candidate of "acid, amnesty, and abortion" (Noah 2012), and was decisively rejected by conservative Christians (along with most of the rest of the nation—he carried only one state). Jimmy Carter's candidacy in 1976, however, temporarily checked the evangelical migration toward the Republican Party, as Carter was himself an evangelical and it was by no means clear that he stood to the left of his Republican opponent, Gerald Ford, on moral issues such as abortion (Byrnes 1993). A decisive and definitive embrace of the Republican Party by conservative Christians would await the arrival of Ronald Reagan's 1980 presidential campaign. It was the Reagan era that saw a deep and enduring bond forged between the GOP and the religious right.

The association between Republicans and evangelical elites did not arise out of nothing with Ronald Reagan; the relationship between Billy Graham and Dwight Eisenhower is well known, for example, as are the White House "prayer breakfasts" of the Nixon years. However, Reagan both broadened and deepened these ties and, more critically, expanded them beyond the religious elites to enlist rank-and-file evangelicals as foot soldiers in the "Reagan Revolution." The following is an illustrative, though not exhaustive, list of Reagan's concrete steps to woo the religious right:

- Almost immediately after the 1980 nominating convention, Reagan endorsed the work of Christian conservatives in a speech to a ministerial meeting in Texas.
- Reagan forged a close partnership with the Revered Jerry Falwell and his Moral Majority organization, a relationship that generated considerable media attention during the campaign.
- Several New Christian Right favorites were appointed to prominent (including cabinet-level) positions by Reagan.
- In a 1983 speech to the National Association of Religious Broadcasters, Reagan supported tax credits for parents whose children attended religious schools and the return of prayer to the public schools, and condemned *Roe* v. *Wade*, all items close to the heart of the New Christian Right.
- Also in 1983, a new political action group, the American Coalition for Traditional Values, was founded to get out the conservative vote for the Reagan–Bush ticket in 1984. Its focus was the registration of religiously conservative voters, and it received direct support from the Reagan White House in the form of a million-dollar grant through Leadership '84 (Jorstad 1993).

The political linkages that Ronald Reagan developed between the Republican Party and religious conservatives have only deepened over time. Bill Clinton, despite being at least a nominal evangelical himself, seemed to embody all of what the religious right saw as the cultural missteps of the 1960s, with his serial infidelity, admitted drug use, avoidance of military service, support for abortion, and endorsement of expanded gay rights. As a result, religious traditionalists gravitated even more in the direction of the GOP, fueling a Republican takeover of Congress in 1994 for the first time in forty years (and becoming a critical foundation of the coalition that sustains a Republican House majority even today). Evangelicals found a champion for the new millennium in George W. Bush, whose personal conversion story and embrace of conservative positions on social issues resonated strongly with them. As a result, the association between religious conservatism and Republican vote choice (and, conversely, between secularism and Democratic allegiance) continues strong in the era of Obama (as Chapter 8 will show).

In practical terms, the New Christian Right's partnership with the Republican Party has yielded mixed results for both sides. From the Christian conservative standpoint, their association with the GOP has given them unprecedented access to the corridors of power, including having some of their own appointed to high governmental office (the most notable recent example being John Ashcroft, Attorney General under President Bush from 2001 to 2005). They have also seen Republican presidents use executive orders to restrict funding for international family planning efforts that include abortion and for embryonic stem cell research (though these restrictions have been reversed during Democratic administrations). They also won a victory with President Bush's establishment of the Office of Faith-Based and Community Initiatives, which facilitated governmental partnering with churches to address community problems and help the poor (an initiative that President Obama has continued). Finally, and in some ways most significantly, religious conservatives have worked with Republicans in many state and local government contexts throughout the country to advance their agenda, including restrictions on abortion, support for school choice and home schooling, and various sorts of public religious expression.

At the same time, however, the religious right's partnership with the Republican Party has failed to achieve their principal national policy objectives. Despite three Republican presidencies and years of Republican control of Congress, abortion remains legal in the United States, legal recognition of homosexuality is expanding rapidly, prayer has not been returned to the schools, and the general secularization of American public life seems to be proceeding apace. This has led many Christian conservative leaders to question what exactly they have gotten for their years of staunch support for the GOP, at least at the national level. Moreover, there are real costs to the very visible public association with Republican politics; to take just one example, it makes coalition-building with blacks and Latinos, many of whom share white evangelicals' core values on a variety of issues, much more difficult.

The Republican Party is likewise somewhat ambivalent about its decades-long relationship with the Christian right. On one hand, religious conservatives have provided critical grassroots support for GOP candidates, giving the party a "boots on the ground" activist presence in many congressional districts that they would not otherwise have. In addition, evangelical Christians were critical in the realignment of the South from solidly Democratic to solidly Republican, a political phenomenon that fueled the party's rise from clear minority status in the 1960s to a national majority in the 2000s. At the same time, however, a strong, public link with religious conservatives has hurt the GOP in the Northeast and on the West Coast, and makes it difficult for the party to reach out to suburban swing voters, who are generally sympathetic to Republican positions on economic issues but are often wary of the religious right. Thus, each side of the Republican Party–religious right partnership has gained undeniable benefits from its association with the other, but both are now beginning to question the ongoing utility of such a close linkage.

The Evolution of the New Christian Right

Like any sociopolitical movement that endures over decades, the Christian Right has passed through several distinct phases in its growth and development. Matthew Moen (1996) describes four key stages in the movement's rise to national prominence and political influence. His core thesis is that, even as the New Christian Right has shaped politics, the demands of political life have shaped the New Christian Right. The 1970s through 1984 were the expansionist period, highlighted by Jerry Falwell's "Moral Majority," and were marked by steady growth in the number of people identifying with the movement, the building of organizational infrastructure, and reliance on direct-mail fundraising. A brief transition phase ran from 1985 through 1986, and was a time distinguished by retrenchment. Although the New Christian Right's effectiveness seemed to wane during this time, its leaders were working toward the next major stage.

Moen names this stage the institutionalization phase, dating it from 1987 through 1994. This stage was notable for the maturation of stable organizations that were well positioned to accomplish their political goals. Their financial situation was more secure, with less reliance on direct-mail fundraising. Several Christian Right groups (e.g., Concerned Women for America and Focus on the Family) matured into genuine membership organizations having regular membership lists, meetings, dues, and benefits for members, as opposed to merely vehicles for political advocacy. Theological orientations within the New Christian Right diversified, as the movement began to seek allies beyond the evangelical base, reaching out to sympathetic mainline Protestants and Catholics (Finucane 1995). Further, the New Christian Right gained political savvy, learning to frame issues in a way that would resonate beyond its core supporters. Last, it gathered strength at the grassroots level, fueled by aggressive efforts by the Christian Coalition (in many ways a spiritual successor organization to the Moral Majority) to distribute voter guides, register religious conservatives, and elect sympathetic (largely Republican) candidates—an effort that bore considerable fruit in 1994, with the GOP takeover of both houses of Congress for the first time in a generation.

The mid- and late 1990s saw a transition to a devolutionary phase, driven both by choice and by necessity. In most ways it was similar to the preceding phase, except that the locus of action shifted from the national scene to the states and the de facto partnership with the Republican Party became more wide-ranging and entrenched. The Christian Coalition, which had become the primary vehicle for religious right activism, was dealt a significant setback in 1999, when the Internal Revenue Service (IRS) denied it tax-exempt status (on the grounds that it was a political, rather than a religious, organization). This forced a legal reorganization into a series of state-level affiliates, and spelled the beginning of the end for the group as a national-level political player. In addition, the Christian Right movement was coming to realize that policy victories would come more easily in sympathetic state legislatures than in the U.S. Congress (no matter which party was in charge). Increasingly, the political priorities of the religious right became intertwined with those of secular conservatives, and the GOP became the vehicle for this union. The Republican emphasis on curbing the power of the federal government in favor of state and local government power accords well with the New Christian Right's own beliefs that "big government" harms families, while more limited, local government helps them (Moen 1994, 1995). The Republican and New Christian Right emphases thus dovetail nicely on this point.

By the beginning of the twenty-first century, the political agenda of the Christian Right had become both wide-ranging (adding less obviously religious GOP priorities to their previous core of moral issues) and well-defined. It includes:

- Family issues: strong support for traditional family structures and sexual norms, including opposition to abortion, pornography, and any redefinition of marriage, as well as resistance to governmental interference with how parents raise their children.
- Education issues: support for prayer and devotional exercises in the public schools, the teaching of creation science alongside evolution, elimination of teaching about unconventional lifestyles, the establishment of a network of Christian schools free from government regulation, and increasing support for the rights and autonomy of home-schoolers.
- Foreign and military issues: support for the United States as the primary world military power, and for the notion that the U.S. has a special and unique role to play in the world; also strong support for Israel in its conflicts with the Muslim world.
- Economic issues: strong support for the free enterprise system, preference for private-sector over governmental efforts to alleviate poverty, and opposition to government control over the health care system.
- Crime issues: support for a tough "law-and-order" position, and for the notion that individuals are responsible for their misdeeds; opposition to drug legalization.
- Directly political goals: lobbying, voter registration, funding candidates with whose priorities they agree, and making certain that information is

available to conservative Christians about politicians' voting records (Corbett-Hemeyer 2010).

Thus far in the twenty-first century, the New Christian Right has seen mixed results in terms of its policy priorities. The passage of the Partial-Birth Abortion Ban Act of 2003 (upheld as constitutional by the Supreme Court in 2007) was a significant victory, as have been the proliferation of state and local-level school voucher programs. In addition, U.S. support for Israel continues strong, and even the Obama administration has endorsed the idea, strongly favored by evangelicals, of church–government partnerships to combat poverty and other social ills. At the same time, however, religious conservatives have been frustrated in some of their other key priorities. Their efforts to secure constitutional amendments permitting school prayer and banning same-sex marriage have been unsuccessful, and the legislative trend seems to be against them on homosexuality and drug issues, at both the state and national levels (2012 saw the first successful state-level referenda legalizing gay marriage and recreational marijuana use). Moreover, while they have chipped away at the edges of abortion through a series of national and state-level regulations, abortion in general remains legal in America despite forty years of religious conservative efforts. Finally, the passage of "Obamacare" in 2009 was widely seen as a defeat by religious conservatives (and by those on the right generally).

Entering its fifth decade as a movement, the New Christian Right faces some significant challenges to its role in American politics and society. There is a widespread perception that, while religious conservatives remain a significant portion of the electorate (there are more than twice as many evangelical Christian voters as Latino voters, for example), they are no longer the rising, dynamic political force that they were fifteen or twenty years ago. This is true for a variety of reasons. First, the movement's leadership is aging; Jerry Falwell, the one who in many ways started it all, died in 2007, and Billy Graham, Pat Robertson, and James Dobson are all over 75 years old. No figures of similar national prominence and stature have risen to take their place, resulting in a religious conservative movement that is more devolved and localized. Second, demographic changes in American religion pose significant challenges; religious non-identification is growing, particularly among the young (perhaps as high as a third in this demographic), and many of these secular voters define themselves politically specifically in terms of opposition to the Christian Right and its agenda (Bolce and De Maio 2007). Moreover, many Americans who do share religiously conservative values are black or Latino, and the Christian Right movement has a hard time drawing them in on a sustained basis because of its close association with the Republican Party and its embrace of conservative economic policies. Finally, some important voices within the movement have begun to question whether the whole project of trying to reshape America through the political arena is worth it in the first place (Thomas and Dobson 2000). According to this view, the inevitable sordidness and compromises of politics have sullied the movement and damaged the credibility of evangelical churches, who would do better to focus on changing hearts and minds than on winning elections. All of these issues are very significant considerations for a movement that has been and remains politically important, but is beginning to feel its age.

American Muslims and the Struggle for Inclusion

As discussed in Chapter 3, a recurrent feature of American cultural and political life has been the challenge of dealing with increasing religious diversity. At various times and in various ways, Catholics, Quakers, Mormons, Jews, Jehovah's Witnesses, and others have all struggled against laws, policies, and prejudices that marginalized them and questioned whether they were authentically American. For these particular groups, the prejudices have abated (though certainly not vanished entirely). For one contemporary religious group, however, the battle for acceptance is very much ongoing: American Muslims.

While Islam is the world's second-largest religion and dates back to the seventh century, it has historically had very little presence in the United States. This has begun to change, however, in the last fifty years, as immigration from Muslim countries and conversion efforts (especially among African Americans) have increased the U.S. Muslim population to about three million, or 1 percent of the national total (Neal 2012). While this may not seem significant, it means that there are as many Muslims in America as Episcopalians. Moreover, Muslims are one of the nation's fastest-growing religious groups, and are expected to top six million by 2030 (Grossman 2011).

The distinctive dress of religiously observant Muslims (especially women), as well as their predominantly immigrant origins, serve to set them apart from other Americans and to engender a certain level of nativist suspicion and mistrust. Moreover, hostilities between the United States and various Muslim nations (dating at least back to the Iran hostage crisis of 1979) fed the sense that there was an inevitable tension between America and Islam. What really stoked the fires of Islamophobia in the United States, however, were the September 11, 2001 terrorist attacks against the Pentagon and the World Trade Center. In the wake of those strikes by radical Islamists (some of whom had lived for extended periods in the United States), many Americans reacted with anger toward the Muslim community, and toward Islam as a whole. In a 2002 speech to the Southern Baptists' annual convention, the Reverend Jerry Vines (a past president of the group) said that Allah was the kind of god who would "turn you into a terrorist that will try to bomb people and take the lives of thousands and thousands of people," and referred to Muhammad, the great prophet of Islam, as a "demon-possessed pedophile" (Sachs 2002).

Reverend Vines was not alone in these sorts of remarks or sentiments. The last few months of 2001 saw a surge in anti-Muslim violence in America (Kaplan 2006), with attacks on mosques, businesses, and individuals. While the most violent expressions of Islamophobia abated thereafter, significant hostility and suspicion toward the group remained. Only 30 percent of Americans reported a favorable view of Islam in a Pew Research Center survey (Esposito and Lalwani 2010), while 43 percent admitted to Gallup that they felt at least "a little" prejudiced against Muslims (Gallup Center for Muslim Studies 2010). In a 2004 survey, 44 percent of American Muslims reported that they had experienced verbal abuse on the basis of their religion (Djupe and Green 2007). Finally, this climate was reflected quite clearly in the widespread outrage over plans to build in lower Manhattan a "Ground Zero mosque"—an incendiary misnomer (the proposed project was neither at Ground Zero nor principally a mosque) that is in itself revealing.

These anti-Islamic sentiments have political implications as well. In a Gallup survey, 40 percent of Americans reported that they would not support a Muslim presidential candidate under any circumstances, far more than said the same about a Mormon, Jew, Catholic, or homosexual (Jones 2012). In addition, attempts to paint President Obama as a "secret Muslim" (which continued well into his presidency—see Pipes 2012) testify to the powerful negative connotations that his opponents believed any association with Islam would have. Clearly, Islam has become the latest in a series of faiths whose adherents have had to struggle to show that fidelity to their religion can be compatible with genuine "Americanness." This demonstrates that the challenge of responding to religious pluralism is not merely an historical reality in America, but a contemporary one as well.

Summary and Conclusions

The decade of the 1960s represented a major turning point in the relationship between politics and religion in the United States. In some ways, the social, cultural, and moral conflicts of that decade continue to resonate in the twenty-first century. Some of the major groups and approaches that developed in the 1960s continue, while others have arisen in response to them, or as modifications of them. Religion—among both blacks and whites—was instrumental in the civil rights movement, and was in turn deeply influenced by it. Cultural shifts resulted in the rise of the New Christian Right, which in turn spawned a variety of religious and (especially) secular forces arrayed in opposition. The conflicts discussed in this chapter can safely be predicted to remain relevant into the foreseeable future.

What lessons can we draw from this survey of the relationship between politics and religion over the last fifty years? This chapter provides strong support for three major conclusions:

- This time period has witnessed an ever-greater diversity of voices clamoring to be heard and to get their agenda on the table of national discussion. On one hand, this has led to what may appear to be a "confusion of tongues." On the other, however, it has led to increased coalition-building among religious groups and between political parties and faith-based organizations. We can reasonably expect that this pattern will continue.

- A second inescapable conclusion is the resilience and adaptability of the religious conservative perspective in the United States. It has been a part of the American religious scene since the colonial period, and while it waxes and wanes, it seems continually to re-emerge as a force during periods of social upheaval. While the religious right now faces serious challenges after its heyday in the 1990s, it is unlikely to disappear as a force in American political life.

- A third conclusion seems to follow from the second. While religious conservatives remain a political force, so too do religious liberals, represented by Jews, Catholics (in some contexts) and, increasingly, mainline Protestants. Their championing of liberal social justice causes, especially in the economic sphere, has increasingly won support even from some otherwise conservative evangelicals.

The religious climate in the United States, always relatively diverse, has become even more so over the last fifty years. The mainline Protestant hegemony of previous eras has collapsed in the face of increasing pluralism, with groups as disparate as evangelical Christians, Mormons, Muslims, and atheists all seeing increases both in numbers and in cultural assertiveness. In addition, both African American Protestants and American Catholics, long present in significant numbers but previously rather quiescent, found their political voice in recent decades. This pluralism has inevitably given rise to sharply differing visions of the proper role for religion in American public life. While these differences are sometimes resolved in the political arena, they also often find their way into the courts, which are called upon to resolve contests over applications of the First Amendment's religion clauses. It is to these sorts of issues that we turn in the next two chapters.

Part II

Religion and the First Amendment

5 The Establishment Clause

> The First Amendment has erected a wall between church and state. That wall must be kept high and impregnable. We could not approve the slightest breach.
>
> (Justice Hugo Black, *Everson* v. *Board of Education*, 1947)

> The First Amendment forbade the establishment of a particular religion or a particular church. It also precluded the federal government from favoring one church, or one church group, over another. That's what the First Amendment did, but it did not go further. It did not, for example, preclude federal aid to religious groups so long as that assistance furthered a public purpose and did not discriminate in favor of one religious group over another.
>
> (Attorney General Edwin Meese, Address to the
> Christian Legal Society, September 29, 1985)

As discussed in Chapter 2, the framers of the Constitution (and of the First Amendment) held differing views on the proper relationship between religion and government in the new republic. While there was virtually unanimous consensus that there should be no official national church, the founders diverged on just how far separation of church and state should go beyond that. Religious liberty was written into the United States Constitution from the beginning, with Article Six, which prohibits requiring religious qualifications for holding public office. It was substantially augmented with the adoption of the Bill of Rights in 1791. The First Amendment limits the national government's power to intervene in religious affairs, requiring that "Congress shall make no law respecting an establishment of religion, or prohibiting the free exercise thereof." The freedoms of speech, of the press, and of peaceful assembly guaranteed in the First Amendment also contribute to religious freedom.

Throughout American history, but especially in the twentieth and twenty-first centuries, courts have struggled to define exactly what "establishment" means, and to balance the competing claims of non-establishment and free exercise. This chapter will examine the application and interpretation of the

First Amendment establishment clause in various types of cases involving connections between religion and government (the next chapter will consider the free exercise clause). The major questions guiding this examination of the establishment clause are:

- What was the constitutional background of the religious liberty clauses in the First Amendment?
- What major developments since the adoption of the Bill of Rights have affected the way in which those religion clauses are applied and interpreted?
- What are the major Supreme Court cases concerning establishment issues, and what criteria and standards did the rulings in these cases articulate?
- What principles guide government aid to religiously sponsored schools?
- What religious activities are permitted in public schools, and what religious activities are forbidden?
- How have taxation issues for religious organizations been decided? For example, are a religious organization's buildings exempt from taxes?
- How have religious holiday display issues been decided? For example, is it legal to have a nativity scene in a city hall?

Background and Context

Because the founders were not of one mind concerning the role of religion in public life, the language of the Constitution on religion (as on some other matters) was left somewhat vague in order to gain support from a range of people who might not have agreed on more precise statements. However, it is safe to say that, because of the nation's considerable religious diversity, the founders were in general agreement that the national government should minimize its involvement in religious matters. The matter of whether and how state and local governments ought to involve themselves with religion, however, was left completely ambiguous, and was not addressed until religious liberties began to be "incorporated" by the courts in the twentieth century (discussed below).

The First Amendment and Religious Liberty

The First Amendment itself was drafted largely by three Virginians: James Madison, Thomas Jefferson, and George Mason. While their personal religious convictions differed, none was hostile to religion; all, however, tended to regard it as a private matter, outside the realm of government. Although they believed that a religious culture provided critical support for republican government (Novak 2000), they also believed that religion stood to gain little and lose much if it were officially linked with government. Likewise, government could only suffer from a formal tie with religion.

Thomas Jefferson's statement (echoing Roger Williams) that there should be a "wall of separation between church and state" has become well known and is often cited as the guiding principle behind the First Amendment. However, as Mead (1977: 40) points out, James Madison wrote thirty years later that there should be a "line of separation between the rights of religion and the Civil authority." Madison's more judicious articulation is more accurate, Mead argues, since in the United States there is no single church (but a variety of sects and religious interest groups) and no single state (but rather the dispersal of civil authority throughout a wide range of agencies at multiple levels of government). The image of a moving point drawing a constantly shifting line also reflects more accurately than does the wall metaphor the reality of changing interpretations, and the inevitable permeability of any boundary between the sacred and the secular.

By including freedom of religion in the Constitution, the Founders effectively removed religion (at least at the national level) from the realm of majority rule, and made it subject instead to the courts. Writing for the majority of the Supreme Court in *West Virginia State Board of Education* v. *Barnette* (319 U.S. 624, 1943), Justice Robert H. Jackson made this point succinctly:

> The very purpose of a Bill of Rights was to withdraw certain subjects from the vicissitudes of political controversy, to place them beyond the reach of majorities and officials and to establish them as legal principles to be applied by the courts. One's right to . . . freedom of worship . . . and other fundamental rights may not be submitted to vote; they depend on the outcome of no elections.

The authors of the Bill of Rights, while conscious of religious pluralism, could never have imagined the profusion of religious groups and beliefs now present in the United States, nor could they have envisioned the variety of conflicting demands that this religiously diverse population would make. In the rough and tumble of practical decision making, the abstract language of the First Amendment leaves its meaning open to a wide variety of plausible interpretations.

The great preponderance of religious liberty litigation to come before the Supreme Court has arisen out of the two religion clauses of the First Amendment—the establishment clause and the free exercise clause. In some instances, the amendment's two religion clauses support each other, but in other instances they seem to push in opposing directions. What appears from one angle to be support for the free exercise of religion may appear from a different vantage point to be a dangerous step toward religious establishment. Similarly, what seems from one perspective to be support for the separation of religion and government may appear to others to be an undue infringement on religious expression. These tensions will run through the discussion here and in Chapter 6, which takes up the free exercise clause. In addition,

Chapter 7 will show that these conflicting interpretations are mirrored in the general public's attitudes toward the proper mix of religion and politics.

Developments Since the First Amendment

Since the adoption of the First Amendment in 1791, American society has changed in many significant ways that dramatically affect its practical application. Following Weber (1990), one can identify five particularly important developments.

First, "incorporation" under the Fourteenth Amendment made the religion clauses applicable to the actions of state and local governments. The First Amendment provisions dealing with religious liberty, like all of the Bill of Rights, curtail the powers of Congress. These protections were added to the Constitution to prevent encroachment on individual rights by the *national* government. Beginning around 1900, however, the Supreme Court began what came to be called "selective incorporation." This process gradually ensured that the freedoms granted at the federal level would also be guaranteed against encroachment by state and local governments. These protections were extended under the Fourteenth Amendment's due process clause, which forbids state governments from depriving "any person of life, liberty, or property without due process of law," and its privileges and immunities clause, which states that "no state shall make or enforce any law which shall abridge the privileges or immunities of citizens of the United States." Incorporation of the First Amendment's two specific provisions concerning religious liberty came in the 1940s. In 1940, the decision in *Cantwell* v. *Connecticut* incorporated free exercise of religion at the state level. In 1947, non-establishment was incorporated in *Everson* v. *Board of Education*.

Second, both federal and state governments have become much more active and expansive over time, spawning large bureaucracies with extensive taxing, spending, and regulatory power. One example is government regulation of schooling (which was minimal in the founding era), with accompanying issues concerning the state's relationship with religiously-sponsored schools. Another example is the development of the welfare state, which has raised questions about the constitutionality of using government funds to support welfare programs administered by religious organizations. The expansion of taxation powers has led to questions regarding the taxing of income and property belonging to religious organizations. Finally, the recent move by government to guarantee and regulate health insurance has necessarily (and controversially) deepened its interaction with religious employers and health care providers.

Third, as government has expanded, so has religion, increasing the variety of its activities and organizations. Religious bodies now oversee extensive networks of educational institutions (from preschools to universities), hospitals, and charitable organizations. In addition, religious broadcasting on radio, television, and the internet is ubiquitous. Religious organizations themselves have become larger, more complex, and more bureaucratic, as well as more theologically and doctrinally diverse than the founders could have imagined. If faith were a purely private matter, there would be far less interaction between religion and government. But, as discussed in Chapter 1, virtually all religions have a significant social and institutional dimension as well.

Fourth, the advance of technology has inevitably affected the interactions between religion and government and raised difficult new issues. When utilized by religious groups, are communications technologies subject to the same regulations as when they are used by secular groups? Does the goal of protecting the public against fraud, for example, justify government surveillance of a religious organization's financial dealings? The government regulates what medical claims can be made by the manufacturers of nutritional supplements and therapeutic devices. Should it also oversee the claims made by faith healers?

Finally, the increased prominence and social voice of new religious groups over the last half century has challenged the accepted "rules of the game" on church–state relations that were developed over time by mainline Protestants. Evangelicals and many Catholics, for example, embrace a much less farreaching vision of church–state separation than the "wall of separation" metaphor implies. The Black Church, as Chapter 9 will show, sees religion and politics as inextricably and properly intertwined. Islam—a small but growing segment of the American religious mosaic—as it is practiced in most of the world sees the very idea of separation of religion from government as an absurdity. Finally, an increasingly vocal group of atheists, agnostics, and seculars has begun to challenge previously accepted accommodations of religion in public life.

In addition, as discussed in Chapter 4, recent decades have seen increasing demands for the accommodation of diverse religious practices in a variety of public institutions such as schools, the military, and prisons. Prisons and the armed services have traditionally provided chaplains at government expense. To what extent are they required to do so for a wide variety of faiths with small numbers of American adherents (Wicca, Buddhism, Hinduism, etc.)? What rights do incarcerated people have to follow the dietary, dress, and grooming restrictions of their religions? These issues will only become more prominent as American religious pluralism continues to expand well beyond what existed in the founding era.

Three Types of Cases

Constitutional issues dealing with the relationship between religion and government obviously arise in highly varied contexts, from school curricula to campaign finance to health care law. Nonetheless, cases involving the religion clauses of the First Amendment can generally be classified in one of three categories: pure establishment cases, pure free exercise cases, and mixed First Amendment cases (Drakeman 1991).

Pure establishment cases are those in which there is an alleged establishment of religion without any attempt at justification on the grounds that it is necessary to protect free exercise. An attempt by a state to declare an official religion would fall under this category. Pure free exercise cases are those in which it is claimed that certain activities are protected from government interference, without any accompanying establishment claim. The free exercise claims made for the use of peyote in Native American rituals exemplify this type, as do claims by Santeria practitioners of a right to practice animal sacrifice (both of which are discussed in the following chapter). Finally, the most complicated category is the mixed First Amendment cases, those that illustrate the tension between non-establishment and free exercise. An example is the provision of military and prison chaplains. Since they are paid by the government, they raise potential establishment issues. However, they are necessary in order to preserve the free exercise of soldiers and inmates who otherwise would be unable to practice their faith under the guidance of a religious leader.

Interpreting and Applying the Establishment Clause

Establishment clause cases have dealt mainly with two types of problems: support of church-related institutions (usually schools) with tax monies or other public funds, and support for religious activities, rituals, and displays by agencies of the government. Examples of the former include the provision of buses and textbooks for church-sponsored schools and, more recently, the controversy over the use of state-issued payment vouchers by the parents of children attending religiously affiliated primary and secondary schools. Examples of the latter include mandated prayers and other devotional activities in public schools, student-led prayers at graduation ceremonies, and religious holiday displays on public property.

Three Approaches to Establishment Clause Cases

The precise intent of the establishment clause is far from clear, and the Court's interpretation of it over the years has not been consistent. What is the exact meaning of the term "establishment"? What does "religion" mean in this context? What type and degree of interaction between church and state violates the provision? Different courts and different justices have answered these questions in varying ways. There have, however, been three distinct, identifiable approaches that have guided the U.S. Supreme Court in its decisions in establishment clause cases over the years: strict separation, strict neutrality, and accommodation (Abraham 1989; O'Brien 2011).

Strict Separation

The strict separation view in the context of establishment clause cases holds that the government can offer no support whatsoever to religion. Justice Hugo Black wrote the majority opinion in *Everson* v. *Board of Education of Ewing Township* (330 U.S. 1, 1947), a case considering the use of tax monies to provide transportation for children to parochial as well as to public schools. In it, he provided a clear articulation of the strict separationist position:

> The "establishment of religion" clause of the First Amendment means at least this: Neither a state nor the Federal Government can set up a church. Neither can pass laws which aid one religion, aid all religions, or prefer one religion over another. Neither can force nor influence a person to go or to remain away from church against his will, or force him to profess a belief or disbelief in any religion. No person can be punished for entertaining or professing religious beliefs or disbeliefs, for church attendance or non-attendance. No tax in any amount, large or small, can be levied to support any religious activities or institutions, whatever they may be called, or whatever form they may adopt to teach or practice religion. Neither a state nor the Federal Government can, openly or secretly, participate in the affairs of any religious organizations or groups and vice versa.

Many of the principles articulated by Justice Black would find agreement among people advocating other approaches to church–state jurisprudence as well. Some, however, are distinct hallmarks of the strict separation position, particularly the injunction against aid to all religions and the absolute prohibition against government financial support of *any* religious activities or institutions.

Strict Neutrality

Strict neutrality is in some ways similar to strict separation, but allows for greater flexibility. In upholding property tax exemptions for buildings owned by religious organizations and used only for religious purposes in *Walz* v. *Tax Commission* (397 U.S. 664, 1970), Chief Justice Warren E. Burger offered a frequently cited endorsement of the neutrality principle:

> Rigidity could well defeat the basic purpose of these provisions [the religion clauses], which is to insure that no religion is sponsored or favored, none commanded, and none inhibited. The general principle deducible from the First Amendment and all that has been said by the Court is this: that we will not tolerate either governmentally established religion or governmental interference with religion. Short of these expressly proscribed governmental acts, there is room for play in the joints

productive of a benevolent neutrality which will permit religious exercise to exist without sponsorship and without interference.

In many ways, the neutrality position is the most ambiguous of the three approaches, often frustrating both separationists and accommodationists who are unsure what result the "play in the joints" will produce in any given establishment case. It has, however, very often been the position of those who have held the balance of power on the Court, so it has been disproportionately influential in deciding the outcomes of cases.

Accommodation

Accommodation, or non-preferentialism, takes a limited view of the establishment clause, permitting government support for all religions so long as it does not discriminate among them. This view is reflected in the quote from Attorney General Edwin Meese that begins this chapter, and also in Justice William Rehnquist's dissent in the *Wallace* v. *Jaffree* (472 U.S. 38, 1985) moment of silence case. Going back to the record of deliberations in Congress over the First Amendment by James Madison and others, Justice Rehnquist wrote:

> It seems indisputable from these glimpses of Madison's thinking . . . that he saw the amendment as designed to prohibit the establishment of a national religion, and perhaps to prevent discrimination among sects. He did not see it as requiring neutrality on the part of government between religion and irreligion . . . The evil to be aimed at, so far as those who spoke were concerned, appears to have been the establishment of a national church, or perhaps the preference of one religious sect over another; but it was definitely not concern about whether the Government might aid all religions evenhandedly.

For the accommodationists, the key questions in any establishment clause case are whether the governmental action in question sets up an official religion, and whether it is designed to favor one sect at the expense of others. If not, they are inclined to allow government support for religion to stand.

Major Establishment Cases

Most establishment cases have concerned activities in schools, both public and parochial. The largest number of these since 1970 have dealt with government aid to religiously affiliated private schools. The analysis here will first consider those cases, followed by a discussion of cases involving religious activities in public schools (elementary, secondary, and post-secondary). The chapter will then conclude with a brief discussion of establishment jurisprudence outside the educational arena.

Two points are worth noting before examining specific cases. First, while there was considerable discussion of church–state issues during the founding era, there were very few establishment clause cases prior to the mid-twentieth century. Virtually all of the important judicial precedents in this area come from the period after World War II (and most since the 1960s). It is no coincidence that establishment clause conflicts heated up as the mainline Protestant cultural hegemony began to crumble in the face of growing secularism, evangelicalism, and religious diversity. Second, while the decisions of the Supreme Court are occasionally unanimous, they are more often closely contested—particularly when they deal with religion. Many of the most important cases in this area, especially since the 1980s, have been decided by 5–4 or 6–3 majorities. The focus here will be principally on the majority opinions in the various cases, since these are the ones that establish binding guidelines for constitutional interpretation. The fact that there are so often dissenting opinions, however, demonstrates that these are issues upon which even constitutional experts can be expected to disagree.

Everson *v*. Board of Education

Modern establishment clause jurisprudence can really be said to begin with the 1947 case of *Everson v. Board of Education of Ewing Township*. *Everson* was the first among the Court's major efforts at interpreting the establishment clause in regard to government aid to religiously affiliated schools. The case concerned a New Jersey law that provided for tax reimbursement to parents for money spent on bus transportation of their children to schools, whether public or private. The reimbursements to parents of children in religiously affiliated schools were challenged as an unconstitutional establishment of religion. The Court held, in a 5–4 decision, that the program simply did "no more than provide a general program to help parents get their children, regardless of their religion, safely and expeditiously to and from accredited schools." Thus, it was permissible under the First Amendment.

There are two important elements in this case, as far as the precedent set is concerned. First, the aid was provided without regard to religion, since the reimbursement was available to parents whose children attended public, non-sectarian private, and parochial schools. Second, the assistance went directly to the parents, not to the school. These features were critical in convincing a strict separationist such as Justice Black, who wrote the majority opinion in the case, to approve the program.

Lemon *v*. Kurtzman *and the "Three-Pronged Test"*

The Supreme Court has dealt with the question of the extent to which governments may constitutionally assist the instructional efforts of religiously affiliated schools repeatedly in the last fifty years. *Lemon v. Kurtzman* (403 U.S. 602, 1971) is in many ways the definitive case with respect to establishment clause jurisprudence in this area. Here, the Court was asked to evaluate the constitutionality of a Pennsylvania program that paid the salaries of teachers who taught secular subjects in religiously affiliated schools. Chief Justice Warren E. Burger, writing for the majority, pointed out that the Court had, since *Everson*, "permitted the states to provide church-related schools with secular, neutral, or nonideological services, facilities, or materials . . . [such as bus] transportation, school lunches, public health services, and secular textbooks." The *Lemon* case, however, was different in that it required much closer state monitoring of religious schools' activities to insure that the classes taught by funded teachers were sufficiently secular. This level of "entanglement" between the state and religious institutions was deemed by the majority to be unconstitutional. Justice William O. Douglas, with Justice Hugo T. Black joining, concurred with Burger's opinion and added:

> The surveillance or supervision of the States needed to police grants involved in these . . . cases, if performed, puts a public investigator into every classroom and entails a pervasive monitoring of these church agencies by the secular authorities. Yet if that surveillance or supervision does not occur, the zeal of religious proselytizers promises to carry the day and make a shambles of the Establishment Clause.

Lemon resulted in the clear enumeration of a three-pronged test of constitutionality in cases of this type. After noting that "we can only dimly perceive the line of demarcation in this extraordinarily sensitive area of constitutional law," Justice Burger nonetheless outlined the three criteria:

- A statute must have a secular purpose.
- Its principal or primary effect must neither be to inhibit nor to advance religion.
- It must not lead to "excessive entanglement" between governmental and religious institutions.

None of the three requirements of the *Lemon* test is always easy to apply. In cases of this type, the secular and religious intentions of legislators may be hard to differentiate. Exactly what constitutes a secular purpose? Not everyone agrees on the answer to this question, particularly in a country where religion has been so thoroughly woven into the fabric of public life. Even if a statute has a secular purpose, its end result might be to either advance or inhibit religion (see the discussion of the peyote cases in Chapter 6, for example). The question of what constitutes a "principal or primary effect" is relevant— and not always easily decided—as well. Just exactly when government entanglement with religion becomes "excessive" is another inherent subjectivity in the application of the *Lemon* test. For this reason, the Court's use of the *Lemon* test has not been consistent, and some justices (particularly the accommodationist ones) have rejected it entirely. However, it remains the most commonly applied standard (explicitly or implicitly) in establishment cases, as the Court has not replaced it with anything else similarly definitive.

Refining the Differences

Tilton v. *Richardson* (403 U.S. 672, 1971), decided the same day as *Lemon*, illustrates other significant elements of the Court's approach to these issues. While *Lemon* dealt with elementary and secondary schools, *Tilton* concerned state support for facilities construction at a Catholic college. In this case, the Court approved of the state support for a religious institution. From this decision, one can draw two significant lessons. First, as a general rule, the Court has held that college and university students are less subject to undue influence by teachers and schools than are those in the lower grades. As a result, assistance to religiously affiliated post-secondary schools is not seen as posing the same threat to the establishment clause that state assistance to religious primary schools would. Second, buildings clearly exert far less influence on student beliefs than do teachers and curricula. Thus, aid for construction has frequently been judged more favorably than aid for instruction.

Government Aid to Religious Primary and Secondary Schools

Several "working principles" have emerged in the last fifty years of Supreme Court decisions on what the establishment clause allows in terms of government aid to religious primary and secondary schools:

- The same aid must be available to all students.
- The aid should not be paid directly to the school, but to the students or their parents.
- Excessive government entanglement with religious institutions must be avoided.
- There must be no direct government subsidy of religious content.

The Aid Must Be Available to All Students

The first of these principles can be stated as follows: State aid for religiously sponsored education is permissible if the same aid is available to all, without regard to the type of school they attend.

Board of Education v. *Allen* (392 U.S. 236, 1968) firmly established this principle when the Court ruled that the provision of textbooks at no charge to students in religiously sponsored primary and secondary schools was constitutional because books were also provided free of charge to students in public schools. In *Wolman* v. *Walter* (433 U.S. 229, 1977), the Court held that supplying standardized tests and scoring services to religiously sponsored schools was constitutional because identical assistance was provided to public schools. Similarly, in *Committee for Public Education and Religious Liberty* v. *Regan* (446 U.S. 646, 1980), the Court held that reimbursement of both religiously affiliated and secular private schools for state-mandated testing and record-keeping concerning non-religious subjects was constitutional because it served the secular purpose of quality education for all children. Finally, the ruling in *Mueller* v. *Allen* (463 U.S. 388, 1983) established the constitutionality of a Minnesota state income tax deduction for educational expenses, since it was allowed for parents of children in all types of schools, religious and secular, public and private.

The Aid Should Not Be Paid Directly to Religious Schools

A second principle runs through many of these cases, as well as others: Aid is more likely to pass constitutional muster if it goes directly to the students and/or their parents, rather than being paid directly by the state to the school itself. *Lemon* v. *Kurtzman* dealt with the use of tax money to provide a salary supplement for teachers who taught secular subjects in religiously sponsored schools and with the practice of state reimbursements to religious schools for the cost of textbooks. Both were ruled unconstitutional, in part because the assistance went to the schools and thus amounted to direct state aid to religion. In *Committee for Public Education and Religious Liberty* v. *Nyquist* (413 U.S. 756, 1973), the Court held that subsidies for maintenance and repair of religiously sponsored primary and secondary schools did not survive establishment clause scrutiny for the same reason.

On the other hand, in *Zobrest* v. *Catalina Foothills School District* (509 U.S. 1, 1993) the use of public funds through the Individuals with Disabilities Education Act to pay for a sign language interpreter for a student in a religiously affiliated school was deemed constitutional. The Court approved this practice on the grounds that, although it took place in a sectarian school, it provided a religion-neutral service available to all students. In addition, the provision of an interpreter was a subsidy provided to the child's family wherever they chose to send him to school, rather than a direct subsidy to the parochial school per se.

The most significant Court ruling relying on this principle was the decision in *Zelman* v. *Simmons-Harris* (536 U.S. 639, 2002), which upheld the constitutionality of an Ohio program where parents of children in failing urban public schools were given a voucher that they could use to send their children, if they chose, to private schools, including religious ones. In fact, more than 90 percent of the parents receiving vouchers did ultimately choose religious school options. The Court applied stringent constitutional criteria to the program, but a 5–4 majority in the end ruled that the program had a legitimate secular purpose, that its primary effect was religion-neutral, that it covered a broad class of beneficiaries, that it included sufficient non-religious options (even if few parents chose them), and, crucially, that the state subsidy went to the parents, not directly to the schools. These five standards, clearly building on the ruling in *Lemon*, comprise what has come to be known as the "Private Choice Test."

The majority's holding in *Zelman* provoked some particularly sharp dissents. As Justice John Paul Stevens argued, "the private choice to prefer a parochial education over an education in the public school system . . . [is] quite irrelevant to the question of whether the government's choice to pay for religious indoctrination is constitutionally permissible." Justice David Souter went so far as to suggest that the Court's ruling in *Zelman* effectively overturned the Court's reasoning in *Everson*, though the majority did not explicitly say so. These reservations by dissenting justices notwithstanding, the *Zelman* ruling has opened the door for a variety of pilot school voucher programs in jurisdictions around the country.

The Aid Must Not Require Excessive Entanglement

In addition to the issue of direct state payments to religious schools, *Lemon* v. *Kurtzman* also asserted the principle that state support for religious schools must not entail "excessive entanglement" between governmental and religious institutions. The content of textbooks is fixed and can easily be evaluated. There is a substantially greater risk, however, that a classroom teacher, even of a secular subject, in the atmosphere of a religiously sponsored school, might inject religion into the course content. This has led to the further distinction that assistance in paying for personnel is less acceptable than assistance with textbooks and such. The intrusive state monitoring required to insure that subsidized teachers do not veer into unacceptably sectarian subject matter is not good, in the Court's view, for either the schools or the state. As Chief Justice Warren E. Burger wrote in the majority opinion in *Lemon*:

> Although the District Court found that concern for religious values did not inevitably or necessarily intrude into the content of secular subjects, the considerable religious activity of these schools led the legislature to provide for careful government controls and surveillance by state authorities in order to ensure that state aid supports only secular education . . . [T]eachers have a substantially different ideological character from books. In terms of involving some aspect of faith or morals in secular subjects, a textbook's content is ascertainable, but a teacher's handling of a subject is not.

Wolman v. *Walter* (1977) provides interesting insight into the Court's very nuanced perspective on the question of publicly funded school personnel and possible religious instruction. The Court held that the possibility that state-supported professionals providing speech, hearing, and psychological services in religiously affiliated schools might engage in conversation with students about religious topics was not problematic enough to make that support unconstitutional. Neither, the Court held, is state provision of therapeutic guidance and remedial services to religious-school students a violation of the establishment clause.

Later, however, in *Aguilar* v. *Felton* (473 U.S. 402, 1985), a 5–4 Court majority held that state personnel going into religiously sponsored schools to provide remedial and guidance services violated the establishment clause, and specifically the excessive entanglement provision of the *Lemon* test. The activity was said to take place in a pervasively sectarian atmosphere, thus requiring ongoing monitoring to ensure that the teachers did not become involved in religious counseling or instruction.

Twelve years later, the Court reversed itself yet again, over-ruling in *Agostini* v. *Felton* (521 U.S. 203, 1997) the decision it had handed down in *Aguilar*. In essence, the Court held that decisions in its more recent cases had undermined the four assumptions on which the *Aguilar* decision rested: (1) that any teacher teaching in a parochial school inevitably inculcates religion; (2) that public employees working on religious school grounds create a symbolic union between church and state; (3) that public aid to a religious school necessarily finances religious education; and (4) that such employment creates excessive entanglement between governmental and religious institutions. The program at issue in *Agostini* (a New York City Title initiative that allowed public school teachers to give remedial instruction to parochial school students on parochial school grounds) was held to violate none of the currently operative constitutional criteria: it did not result in religious indoctrination, select recipients on the basis of religion, or create excessive entanglement. The decision was 5–4, and dissenting justices expressed strong opposition based on concerns about breaching the division between religion and government called for, in their view at least, by the establishment clause.

The Aid Must Not Subsidize Religious Content

In order for the provision of services to religiously affiliated schools to pass establishment clause muster, there must be a high degree of certainty that no religious content is involved. In *Levitt* v. *Committee for Public Education and Religious Liberty* (413 U.S. 472, 1973), state reimbursement of religiously sponsored primary and secondary schools for expenses incurred in administering, grading, compiling, and reporting test scores when there was no means to ensure that the internally prepared tests were free of religious content was held to be unconstitutional. On the other hand, in *Wolman* v. *Walter*, the Court held that it was acceptable for the state to supply standardized tests and scoring services to religiously affiliated schools if the tests were clearly free of religious content—in this case, the same ones used in the public schools.

Religious Activities in Public Schools

To this point, the analysis in this chapter has focused primarily on private religious schools, and what relationship they might constitutionally have with the state. Another important category of establishment clause jurisprudence, however, concerns *public* schools, and what place, if any, religion might have within them. Cases of this type have, for the most part, concerned one of three things: prayer or devotional activity in schools, the teaching of creation and/or evolution, and the use of school facilities by religious groups.

Devotional Activities

Perhaps the most high-profile area of church–state law in recent decades has centered on the question of prayer in public schools. A range of Supreme Court decisions have wrestled with the idea of prayer in the classroom or in connection with other school-sponsored activities. Perhaps the best known is *Engel v. Vitale* (370 U.S. 421, 1962), sometimes referred to as the "New York Board of Regents prayer case." The New York State Board of Regents composed a non-denominational prayer and mandated its use at the beginning of every school day. School officials maintained that doing so was an aspect of the students' moral and spiritual training. The prayer was simple: "Almighty God, we acknowledge our dependence upon Thee, and we beg Thy blessings upon us, our parents, our teachers and our country." Students did not have to recite the prayer, but peer pressure to do so was obviously strong. The Court ruled the prayer to be a violation of the establishment clause. Justice Hugo L. Black's opinion was strongly worded and direct:

> [We] think that the constitutional prohibition against laws respecting an establishment of religion must at least mean that in this country it is no part of the business of government to compose official prayers for any group of the American people to recite as part of a religious program carried on by government.

In a similar case a year later, *Abington School District v. Schempp* (347 U.S. 203, 1963), the Court held that school board sponsorship of Bible reading and the recitation of the Lord's Prayer are clearly unconstitutional devotional exercises. Again, students whose parents wished it could ask to be excused from participation, but the Court viewed this opt-out as insufficient for compliance with the establishment clause.

Two important principles came out of this case. In his majority opinion, Justice Tom C. Clark noted that some people insisted that the prohibition of such devotional exercises would constitute the imposition of a "religion of secularism" in the schools. This same claim continues to be advanced today in a variety of cases dealing with religion in public education. Justice Clark stated firmly that the Court's ruling in *Abington* did not have the effect of "affirmatively opposing or showing hostility to religion."

A second key point is the distinction between devotional exercises and the teaching of religious doctrine, on the one hand, and teaching about religion on the other. Clark's opinion addressed this issue as well:

In addition, it might well be said that one's education is not complete without a study of comparative religion or the history of religion in its relationship to the advancement of civilization. It certainly may be said that the Bible is worthy of study for its literary and historic qualities. Nothing we have said here indicates that such study of the Bible or of religion, when presented objectively as part of a secular program of education, may not be effected consistently with the First Amendment.

This distinction made possible the teaching of religious studies courses in secondary schools and the development of religious studies programs in state-supported colleges and universities.

The Court has also heard other important cases involving devotional activities. Requiring the posting of the Ten Commandments in public school classrooms was held to violate the establishment clause in *Stone* v. *Graham* (449 U.S. 39, 1980), a judgment reaffirmed in *Van Orden* v. *Perry* (545 U.S. 677, 2005) even as the Court was approving a Ten Commandments monument on the Texas state capitol grounds. The Court has also held, in *Lee* v. *Weisman* (505 U.S. 577, 1992), that the practice of asking clergy to offer prayers of invocation and benediction at the beginning and end of public high school graduation ceremonies is unconstitutional, as is the practice of offering prayers before public school sporting events (*Santa Fe* v. *Doe*; 530 U.S. 290, 2000). On the question of state "moment of silence" statutes, the Court's guidance has been less clear. In *Wallace* v. *Jaffree* (472 U.S. 38, 1985), a 6–3 majority ruled Alabama's moment of silence law unconstitutional, on the grounds that the legislature had advanced no secular rationale for the law and that teachers were to explicitly encourage use of the time for "prayer or meditation." Some justices in the majority, however, made clear that they did not object to the idea of a moment of silence in principle, and as recently as 2011, the Court declined to hear a challenge to an Illinois moment of silence law (Stanley 2011), effectively leaving the practice in Illinois and twenty other states in place.

As Chapter 7 will show, the American public generally favors prayer and other devotional activities in public schools. This is reflected in movements for voluntary student prayers at graduation ceremonies, for example, and in things such as the "see you at the pole" movement, in which students gather around the school's flagpole in the morning for prayer. Generally speaking, the Court has taken a much more favorable view of such student-initiated, non-coercive devotions than of any institutionally mandated acknowledgements of religion.

Creation and Evolution

Since the time of the Scopes trial in the 1920s, American courts have wrestled with the question of what public schools must, may, and must not teach about human origins. In 1968, the Court's ruling in *Epperson* v. *Arkansas* (393 U.S.

97, 1968) struck down a law that made it illegal "to teach the theory or doctrine that mankind ascended or descended from a lower order of animals" or to use textbooks that taught the theory of evolution. Following this ruling, Arkansas attempted to establish a "balanced treatment" plan, under which both evolution and the Genesis account of divine creation would be taught. A federal district court ruled this "balanced treatment" approach unconstitutional on the grounds that "creationism" is a religious rather than a scientific doctrine, and that requiring it to be taught thus violated the establishment clause (and higher courts allowed this ruling to stand). Nearly two decades after *Epperson*, the Supreme Court in *Edwards* v. *Aguillard* (482 U.S. 578, 1987) struck down the Louisiana Balanced Treatment for Creation-Science and Evolution-Science in Public Instruction Act. The Act required the teaching of both perspectives. Thus, over the last fifty years, the law on this question has moved from a situation where the Genesis creation account could be taught as the *only* theory of human origins to one where it cannot be taught *at all* in public school classrooms.

A more recent manifestation of this controversy developed over the teaching of "intelligent design" in the context of human origins. Unlike the Genesis creation account, intelligent design is not specific to the Judeo-Christian tradition, and indeed is not rooted in any sacred text. It simply argues that the "irreducible complexity" of organisms and other features of the natural world point to the existence of an intelligent, purposive Creator. A requirement by a Pennsylvania school district that intelligent design be taught alongside Darwinian Evolution, however, was struck down by a federal judge in 2005 in the case of *Kitzmiller* v. *Dover Area School District* (400 F. Supp. 2d 707), with the judge ruling that intelligent design was a philosophical or religious rather than a scientific theory, and thus constitutionally inappropriate for a public school science classroom. As the case was not appealed to higher courts (because of turnover on the local school board in question), *Kitzmiller* remains the only real guidance from the federal courts on the intelligent design question.

Equal Access

Two key cases have defined the Court's approach to the use of public school facilities by religious groups. In each case, some were concerned that allowing the use of these government facilities by religious groups constituted an establishment, or at least an endorsement, of religion. In both cases, however, the Court ruled that such use did not violate the establishment clause. In fact, not only *could* school districts allow such use, but they were constitutionally *required* to do so. To prohibit use of a "limited public forum," such as a school building, to religious groups, is in itself not permissible. In 1984, the federal government passed the Equal Access Act, which required that public secondary schools that maintain a "limited public forum" and allow extracurricular student groups to meet on school property must allow equal access to such groups without regard to the "religious, philosophical, or other" content of their meetings. The constitutionality of the Act was upheld in *Board of Education* v. *Mergens* (496 U.S. 226, 1990). In this case, which began in Nebraska, a student had asked permission to form a student Christian club that would meet in school facilities after classes to read and discuss the Bible and pray together. The school claimed that such a club would violate the establishment clause, but a federal Appeals Court held that the school did maintain a "limited public forum" and thus could not discriminate against a particular club because of its ideological content. On appeal, the Supreme Court upheld the decision, and thus the constitutionality of the Equal Access Act. Similarly, in *Lamb's Chapel* v. *Center Moriches Union Free School District* (508 U.S. 384, 1993), the Court held that a church using public school facilities to show a religiously oriented film did not violate the establishment clause, and fell under the auspices of the Equal Access Act.

The Equal Access Act and the Court's upholding of its constitutionality has ramifications beyond access for religious groups to school facilities. It also requires equal access for student groups that come together around social issues over which people are deeply divided, frequently along religious lines. It means, for example, that public schools that permit extracurricular groups to meet on school premises must allow both the "Students for Traditional Family Values" and the "Student Gay Alliance," if such groups exist and request access to their facilities. It means that "Students for Reproductive Choice" and "Students for Life" must receive equal consideration.

Religious Activities and Post-Secondary Education

As mentioned previously, the Court has generally been less zealous in guarding public college students against potential exposure to religious content than it has about those in elementary and secondary schools. Those at the college and university level, the Court has reasonably concluded, are better able to evaluate a range of messages both consistent and inconsistent with their values, and to accept or reject them as they see fit. Still, however, public institutions of higher education are agents of the state, so establishment clause issues do arise. Typically, these concern questions of funding and access.

Monetary Aid

In *Tilton* v. *Richardson*, the Court upheld the 1963 Higher Education Facilities Act that provided grant money to religiously affiliated colleges for the construction of buildings that would be used for secular purposes. Although the religious school did benefit, the Court held that the principal or primary effect of the Act was to advance education, not religion. Two years later, in *Hunt* v. *McNair* (413 U.S. 734, 1973) the use of state-issued revenue bonds to help a religiously sponsored college borrow money was upheld, since the benefit was available to all institutions of higher education, regardless of affiliation. In 1976, the Court ruled that annual general purpose grants to religiously affiliated colleges do not violate the establishment clause, since post-secondary schools are not as "permeated by religion" as religiously affiliated primary and secondary schools (*Roemer* v. *Board of Public Works*; 426 U.S. 736, 1976). Finally, in a case in some ways similar to *Zobrest*, the Court found that the establishment clause does not prohibit the provision of state assistance (under a vocational rehabilitation program) to a blind student who was studying in a Christian college to become a full-time religious worker (*Witters* v. *Washington Department of Services for the Blind*; 474 U.S. 481, 1986). In this case, it was an important consideration that the money was paid directly to the student, rather than to the school.

The most interesting and controversial case concerning public funding of religious activity in the university context is *Rosenberger* v. *University of Virginia* (515 U.S. 819, 1995). The University of Virginia routinely authorized payments from the Student Activities Fund to outside contractors for printing costs for the publications of a range of student groups. All of the materials included a disclaimer that they were independent of the university and that the school did not necessarily endorse their content. It withheld, however, payment for the printing costs of an organization called Wide Awake: A Christian Perspective at the University of Virginia on the grounds that it "primarily promotes or manifests a particular belief in or about a deity or ultimate reality" and was therefore barred from funding by the university's guidelines. The student members of Wide Awake then sued, claiming that the university had violated their free speech rights and engaged in illegal viewpoint discrimination.

The Fourth Circuit Court of Appeals held that the university's action did indeed infringe the students' freedom of speech, but that the infringement was justified because funding of the religious publication by a state university would have violated the establishment clause. When the case reached the Supreme Court, however, the lower court's findings were overturned and the university was ordered to fund the publication. The majority opinion, written by Justice Anthony Kennedy, noted that the money was to be paid directly to a third-party printer, not to the religious organization itself. The Court also distinguished between the student activities fee money that was at issue in the case and tax monies, holding that the activity fees were not "public funds" in the same sense as tax revenues. More importantly, to fund secular student publications but not religious ones was found to violate both the students' free speech and free exercise rights, and was not excused by attempted compliance with the establishment clause. In addition, the Court held that funding all activities, without attempting to decide which were religious and which were not, required less government entanglement with religion than if the university had to monitor funded publications for impermissible religious content. Finally, it was noted that the funding regime could and should be administered in a way that was essentially neutral toward religion. That neutrality would not be violated if the university—as an agency of the government—followed uniform criteria for funding that neither favored nor disfavored religious organizations as such.

Not all on the high court agreed; the decision was 5–4. Justice David Souter, a strong advocate of the strict separation view during his time on the Court, noted the strongly evangelistic nature of Wide Awake, and was sharp in his dissent:

> Using public funds for the direct subsidization of preaching the word is categorically forbidden under the Establishment Clause . . . The Court is ordering an instrumentality of the State to support religious evangelism with direct funding. This is a flat violation of the Establishment Clause.

Equal Access

The case of *Widmar v. Vincent* (454 U.S. 263, 1981) parallels the high school equal access cases, but at the university level. In this case, a state statute that prohibited the use of public university buildings "for purposes of religious worship" was ruled unconstitutional. Since the university did maintain an "open forum," in which various groups used its facilities, it could not legally exclude a group based simply on the religious nature of its activities (and this was even before the passage of the Equal Access Act). No state endorsement of any faith would be implied by allowing religious use of the facilities, so long as a wide variety of religious and secular groups had the same access privileges.

Other Establishment Clause Cases

While the bulk of establishment clause jurisprudence has focused on educational settings, there are a number of other situations in which questions regarding the possible establishment of religion are involved. Some of the most controversial involve taxation, holiday displays, and government support for religious charities.

Taxation and Entanglement

One of the most far-reaching cases in its effects is *Walz v. Tax Commission* (397 U.S. 664, 1970). In *Walz*, the Court upheld the practice of allowing real estate tax exemptions for religious buildings against a challenge that such exemptions constituted an establishment of religion. The exemption was available to a wide range of not-for-profit groups, and this proved key to the Court's decision. Chief Justice Warren E. Burger wrote for the Court:

> The legislative purpose of a property tax exemption is neither the advancement nor the inhibition of religion; it is neither sponsorship nor hostility. New York, in common with the other states, has determined

that certain entities that exist in a harmonious relationship to the community at large, and that foster its "moral or mental improvement," should not be inhibited in their activities by property taxation or the hazard of loss of those properties for nonpayment of taxes. It has not singled out one particular church or religious group, or even churches as such; rather, it has granted exemption to all houses of religious worship within a broad class of property owned by non-profit, quasi-public corporations which include hospitals, libraries, playgrounds, scientific, professional, historical, and patriotic groups.

The other key in this case was the Court's decision that the elimination of tax exemptions would lead to much greater government entanglement with religion than did the exemptions themselves. The principle that a statute or practice must not lead to excessive government entanglement with religion, a key prong of the *Lemon* test, was first articulated in *Walz*. While providing the exemption required a one-time declaration of an organization's not-for-profit standing, doing away with it would "give rise to tax valuation of church property, tax liens, tax foreclosures, and the direct confrontations and conflicts that follow in the train of those legal processes." This would create, in the majority's view, an undesirable level of entanglement.

As have many separationists since, Justice William O. Douglas disagreed with the ruling. He rejected the majority opinion's distinction between a subsidy, which grants funds, and an exemption, which refrains from collecting funds. In his dissent, he stated succinctly: "Indeed I would suppose that in common understanding one of the best ways to 'establish' one or more religions is to subsidize them, which a tax exemption does . . . A tax exemption is a subsidy."

The Court's support for religious tax exemptions is not unlimited, however. In *Texas Monthly, Inc.* v. *Bullock* (489 U.S. 1, 1989), the Court struck down a sales tax exemption for periodicals published or distributed by religious groups solely for the purpose of promoting their faith as having insufficient breadth to avoid violating the establishment clause. The Court has decided other religion and taxation questions as well, but these have been seen largely as free exercise cases, and thus will be considered in the next chapter.

Holiday Displays

One of the most popular government interactions with religion that raises establishment questions is the creation of holiday displays with religious elements on public property. Two significant decisions have laid out the Court's guiding approach to this question. In *Lynch* v. *Donnelly* (465 U.S. 668, 1984), the Court upheld the display of a nativity scene on city property as one part of a Christmas installation that also included secular elements. Justice Sandra Day O'Connor (the swing vote in the case) concurred with the majority opinion, but also discussed at length the framework in which the governmental use of religious symbols was to be analyzed. Such use must not imply a government endorsement of any religion. Such an endorsement, she argued, "sends a message to nonadherents that they are outsiders, not full members of the political community, and an accompanying message to adherents that they are insiders, favored members of the political community." Whether the display is a government "endorsement," then, depends upon the effect and context of the display more than on the particular symbols it contains. Specifically, O'Connor stated that the decision turns on "what viewers may fairly understand to be the purpose of the display." In this case, the display contained an array of holiday symbols, both religious and secular. In a context that included such a diversity of items, O'Connor held that the setting "negates any message of endorsement" of the Christian belief about the nativity. While the four dissenting justices agreed with O'Connor in principle, they reached the opposite conclusion about this instance, seeing the inclusion of the nativity scene as setting the "government's imprimatur of approval on the particular religious beliefs exemplified by the crèche." The principle articulated in *Lynch* is important: governmental use of religious symbols is unconstitutional if it appears to endorse a specific religious belief, but acceptable if it does not, and the decision depends largely upon the context in which the religious symbols are displayed.

The second major case on this issue is *County of Allegheny v. American Civil Liberties Union* (492 U.S. 573, 1989). The case dealt with two recurring holiday displays. For many years there had been a nativity scene placed on the staircase of the country courthouse. There had also been a Hanukkah menorah (the eight-branched candle holder used in Judaism) outside the city-county building, along with a Christmas tree and a sign honoring liberty. In a ruling that was puzzling to many, the Court ruled the first an unconstitutional endorsement of religion, but permitted the second.

Writing for the majority, Justice Harry Blackmun argued that, based on the context, there was nothing in the nativity scene display that detracted from its religious meaning, as there had been in the *Lynch* case. Further, its location increased the likelihood that a viewer would interpret it as a government endorsement of Christian belief:

> Furthermore, the crèche sits on the Grand Staircase, the "main" and "most beautiful part" of the building that is the seat of county government. No viewer could reasonably think that it occupies this location without the support and approval of the government. Thus, . . . the county sends an unmistakable message that it supports and promotes the Christian praise to God that is the crèche's religious message.

With regard to the menorah and the Christmas tree, Blackmun thought differently. The menorah is certainly a religious symbol. But, like the Christmas tree, it was held to be "the primary visual symbol for a holiday that, like Christmas, has both religious and secular dimensions." For

Blackmun, endorsing both Christmas and Hanukkah as religious holidays would violate the Constitution just as much as endorsing one or the other. His opinion holds that the city was well within constitutional limits by acknowledging both as secular cultural holidays. This particular display, he wrote, "simply recognizes that both Christmas and Chanukah are part of the same winter-holiday season, which has attained a secular status in our society."

Illustrative of the deeply divisive nature of establishment clause jurisprudence is the fact that only two of the nine justices (Blackmun himself and Sandra Day O'Connor) completely agreed with what became the majority ruling in this case. Justices Brennan, Stevens, and Marshall, strict separationists, would have prohibited display of both the nativity scene *and* the menorah. By contrast, Justices Kennedy, White, Scalia, and Rehnquist, all inclined toward accommodation, would have allowed both. This confused jumble of judicial perspectives has ensured that litigation in this area continues. As Masci et al. (2006: 1) explain:

> What is and is not allowed when it comes to religious displays is still, to a large degree, open to debate. Some legal experts blame this uncertainty on the Supreme Court. The high court, they argue, has crafted a standard for judging the constitutionality of displays that is too subjective and thus leads to inconsistencies when applied by the lower courts.

Support for Faith-Based Charities

Almost immediately upon taking office in 2001, President George W. Bush created within the executive branch the White House Office of Faith-Based and Community Initiatives, whose mission was to partner with religious institutions around the country in their efforts to combat hunger, illiteracy, drug abuse, domestic violence, etc. The idea had widespread public support, and the program has been continued by Bush's successor, President Barack Obama. Strict separationists, however, have strongly objected to the effort, and filed suit in *Hein v. Freedom From Religion Foundation* (551 U.S. 587, 2007) to challenge it.

The ruling in *Hein* is complicated, because the decision turned as much on the question of standing (whether the plaintiffs had in fact been harmed and had a right to sue) as on the establishment clause substance of the case. Nonetheless, the basic result was that, by a 5–4 margin, the Court rejected the challenge to the Office of Faith-Based and Community initiatives. Justice Samuel Alito, writing for the majority, expressed skepticism about the seriousness of the establishment clause issues raised in the case. The government–religious partnerships in question, he noted, were designed to address widely acknowledged community problems of secular relevance, and did not have proselytism as an objective. They were also open to religious institutions across the spectrum of belief. They were not analogous, as the plaintiffs claimed, to an executive branch decision to "use its discretionary funds to build a house of worship or to hire clergy of one denomination and send them out to spread their faith," or to "make bulk purchases of Stars of David, crucifixes, or depictions of the star and crescent for use in its offices or for distribution to the employees or the general public." Thus, the Court left open the ability of government to partner with religious organizations to address issues of general social concern.

Summary and Conclusions

This chapter has focused on interpretations of the establishment clause of the First Amendment to the U.S. Constitution. As has been noted, establishment clause cases have generally arisen around two primary issues:

- the use of tax monies or other public funds for support of religiously sponsored organizations and activities, usually educational in nature. In general, the Court has held that the same aid must be available to all students, and that it is best if the aid goes to the students or their parents, rather than directly to religious schools. Assistance in paying for personnel is more suspect than paying for textbooks and buildings. State support for religious content per se must be avoided;
- support for religious activities by agencies of the government. Many of these cases have concerned devotional activities such as prayer and Bible reading in public schools. Others have dealt with how human origins should be taught. Disputes over equal access by religious groups to public buildings have resulted in a number of cases. Still others have dealt with holiday displays on public property. Taxation cases have considered whether religiously owned property should be taxable, and the faith-based initiatives case examined the permissibility of government–religious partnerships to combat social ills.

In approaching all of these cases, three distinct perspectives on the part of jurists and legal scholars are apparent:

- Strict separation holds that the government should offer no support at all to religion.
- Strict neutrality allows for greater flexibility, and has neutrality rather than complete separation as its goal.
- Accommodation allows for government support for religion as long as there is no attempt to establish a national church or to discriminate among sects.

It is difficult to wrap up the Supreme Court's holdings in establishment clause cases into one neat package. Certainly there can be differences of opinion on the overall doctrines that emerge, just as there are differences about specific cases. Nevertheless, the following conclusions seem fair as general statements of judicial sentiment over the last fifty years:

- With respect to government aid to religion, direct subsidies for religion per se clearly violate the establishment clause. At the same time, the fact that some indirect benefit may accrue to a religious organization from a particular policy or practice is not in-and-of-itself grounds for holding that action to be unconstitutional. In addition, religious organizations should not be barred from benefiting from programs that are open to similarly situated secular groups.
- Organized devotional exercises in public schools fall outside the pale of what is constitutionally permissible. However, religious groups and individuals cannot be excluded from access to school facilities simply because they are religious. Further, the ban on religious exercises does not encompass a prohibition on teaching and studying about religion from an academic perspective.
- In general, the Supreme Court's decisions in establishment clause cases have maintained three basic underlying principles:

  1. Religion and government are to be kept largely separate, with government remaining neutral toward religion.
  2. Some degree of interaction between the two, however, is inevitable, and is not necessarily problematic.
  3. Within the boundaries laid out by the general framework of separation, the Court should recognize and respect the important roles of religion and religious organizations in the lives of individual Americans and in the public life of the nation.

As this chapter has demonstrated, application of the seemingly simple principle of non-establishment is anything but straightforward. Chapter 6 will consider the application of the free exercise clause and the working out of its meaning through Supreme Court decisions. The inclusion of both clauses in the First Amendment, and their interaction, make church–state jurisprudence even more complex.

6   The Free Exercise Clause

> It behooves us to recognize that protecting religious minorities will sometimes mean protecting and perpetuating practices we deem morally repugnant . . . But if we are committed to the proposition that the claims of God are not subject to the authority of civil government but commended to the consciences of believers, then we will be forced to tolerate some claims that seem to us very wrong.
>
> (Michael W. McConnell, "Taking Religious Freedom Seriously," 1993)

The analysis in this chapter is guided by one underlying question: Under what circumstances are people free to practice their faith and live according to their religious beliefs, and under what circumstances can government legitimately limit those freedoms? This question is at the heart of understanding the scope and meaning of the First Amendment's requirement that "Congress shall make no law . . . prohibiting the free exercise" of religion. As in the previous chapter's consideration of the establishment clause, the principal focus here will be on interpretations of the free exercise guarantee by the Supreme Court, but legislative efforts in this area (e.g., the Religious Freedom Restoration Act) also merit discussion. The major questions guiding this consideration of the free exercise clause are:

- How have approaches to interpreting the free exercise clause differed from approaches to interpreting the establishment clause?
- What distinctions has the Supreme Court made between religious beliefs and actions based on those beliefs? If people are free to believe as they wish, are they also free to act in accordance with those convictions?
- What happens when an action of the government inadvertently or incidentally restricts the religious freedom of some people? Is the action unconstitutional?
- How have the religious grounds for military draft exemption changed over time? And how is this related to what the Supreme Court defines as religion? For example, in the event of a draft, could someone be exempted from military service on philosophical rather than religious grounds?

- What important religious liberty issues have been brought to the Supreme Court by minority religious groups such as Jehovah's Witnesses, Sabbatarians, and Native Americans? What happens when their beliefs and practices conflict with prevailing laws and community norms?
- How did the Religious Freedom Restoration Act come about, and what is its significance? What is the significance of the Supreme Court's limitation of the Act's applicability? What efforts have its supporters made in the wake of its limitation?
- How do the free exercise clause and the establishment clause sometimes conflict with one another? How have these conflicts typically been resolved?

Perspectives on Interpretation of the Free Exercise Clause

As discussed in Chapter 5, establishment cases are about setting limits on allowable direct or indirect government support for faith-based institutions. In other words, to what extent and under what circumstances can government legitimately encourage religion? Free exercise cases, by contrast, deal with the opposite question: to what extent and under what circumstances can government legitimately impede expressions of religious faith?

Free exercise jurisprudence often concerns making exceptions to generally accepted standards and practices for smaller, less-understood, and sometimes unpopular religious groups whose beliefs are regarded by the majority as "unconventional" (Corbett-Hemeyer 2010). Examples include Jehovah's Witnesses, whose door-to-door evangelism and distribution of tracts sometimes conflict with local ordinances banning these activities, Native American Church members whose use of peyote runs afoul of narcotics laws, and practitioners of Santeria, whose animal sacrifices may offend community sensibilities.

Interpretation of the free exercise clause of the First Amendment has developed differently from interpretation of the establishment clause in at least three significant respects:

1. It has not led to "the somewhat tortuous devising of tests to which the Court had to resort for establishment clause purposes" (U.S. Commission on Civil Rights 1983: 21). While some standards (most notably the "compelling interest" and "rational basis" ones discussed below) have emerged from free exercise jurisprudence, they come nowhere near the profusion and complexity of Court-articulated establishment criteria.
2. Whereas the meaning of the establishment clause has been worked out almost entirely in the judicial arena, legislative bodies (both state and federal) have sought to weigh in on the proper meaning of "free exercise."
3. While the justices have frequently referred to and debated the intentions of the framers of the Bill of Rights in establishment clause cases, there have been many fewer such references in free exercise cases (Eastland 1993).

Analysts and commentators do not agree on how much free exercise of religion the clause has been construed to allow. Some characterize the Court's general view as "an expansive interpretation that encompasses all sorts of religious belief, including the constitutionally protected right to have no religion" (U.S. Commission on Civil Rights 1983: 21). From this perspective, people in the United States—followers of majority religions, minority religions, or no religion at all—have been given generous latitude to practice their religious beliefs, subject only to essential and minimal restrictions on action as described below.

Others, however, take a less sanguine view. Law professor and former Federal Appeals Court judge Michael W. McConnell notes that the religion clauses of the First Amendment were intended to protect those whose practices seemed strange to the majority. Despite this intention, the religious clauses have not always been interpreted this way, and the strong language of free exercise has not always translated into sufficient protection for unorthodox religious practices (McConnell 1993).

It is not the purpose of this chapter to adjudicate this difference of opinion. A plausible argument can clearly be made for either position. As a review of the relevant Supreme Court cases will show, the difference is partly one of time: the mood of the Court has varied at different periods in its history when it comes to evaluating free exercise claims. The difference is also undoubtedly one of perspective: what to one observer appears broadly tolerant may seem to another unduly restrictive. The United States clearly affords more religious freedom than most other nations of the world, but perhaps less than it could or should according to an ideal or theoretical standard.

In the Beginning: *Reynolds* v. *United States* and Its Legacy

The first clear-cut test of the free exercise clause to come before the Supreme Court was *Reynolds* v. *United States* (98 U.S. 145, 1878). George Reynolds was a member of the Church of Jesus Christ of Latter-day Saints (a Mormon). Early in its history, until the end of the nineteenth century, the Mormon Church supported the practice of polygamy (or more specifically polygyny—allowing a man to marry more than one wife). Because this practice was clearly at odds with the dominant ethos and cultural pattern in the United States, Congress exercised its power to make laws for the territories and banned polygamy in Utah (as it was uniformly prohibited elsewhere). Reynolds, who made no secret of the fact that he had two wives, claimed that his conviction under this statute was an unconstitutional infringement of his religious liberty, and eventually his case made its way to the U.S. Supreme Court.

Belief and Action

The justices' decision in Reynolds—in which they rejected Reynolds's free exercise claim and upheld the anti-polygamy statute—set two important precedents. One is the distinction between religious beliefs and the actions that flow from those beliefs. The former are inviolate and untouchable by government; the latter, however, are not. Chief Justice Morrison Waite crafted the majority opinion, very conscious that his would be the first major judicial interpretation of the free exercise clause. In that opinion, he wrote: "Congress was deprived of all legislative power over mere opinion, but was left free to reach actions which were in violation of social duties or subversive of good order." In the opinion of the Court, and clearly of Congress, the practice of multiple marriage was definitely "in violation of social duties and subversive of good order." Thus, the restriction of Reynolds' free exercise of his religion was justified, even mandated.

This core distinction between belief and action, first articulated in *Reynolds*, was restated in *Cantwell* v. *Connecticut* (310 U.S. 296, 1940), although that particular case was decided in favor of free exercise (as discussed below). Justice Owen J. Roberts wrote for the Court that "the First Amendment . . . embraces two concepts, freedom to believe and freedom to act. The first is absolute but, in the nature of things, the second cannot be. Conduct remains subject to regulation for the protection of society."

Secular Regulation Rule

The other doctrine solidified in *Reynolds* has come to be known as the "secular regulation rule." This line of reasoning has origins that date back even farther than *Reynolds*, but that case focused it and set it firmly as precedent. Simply, the secular regulation rule stipulates that if a governmental action serves a valid and predominantly secular purpose, it can be enforced against a free exercise claim, even if it imposes a particular burden on the practice of religion.

A refined and clarified version of the secular regulation rule was critical to the resolution of *Employment Division* v. *Smith* (494 U.S. 872, 1990), as discussed below. In that case, Justice Antonin Scalia wrote for the Court. After noting that the free exercise of religion inevitably includes actions as well as beliefs, Justice Scalia reasoned that the state would be violating the First Amendment if it banned religious acts for religious reasons. However, if interference with a particular religious practice were an incidental effect (not the intent) of an otherwise valid law, then the free exercise clause would not be violated. In his opinion, Justice Scalia asserted that "we have never held that an individual's religious beliefs excuse him from compliance with an otherwise valid law prohibiting conduct that the State is free to regulate."

Currently, the distinction between belief and action still stands in American law, in that virtually everyone agrees that belief is both practically and normatively beyond state regulation, while at least some religiously motivated actions (e.g., human sacrifice) must be proscribed by government. As the discussion to follow will make clear, however, the fate of the secular regulation rule has been more complex, and remains the subject of both political and legal dispute.

Conscientious Objection and Free Exercise

Throughout American history, whenever the government has deemed it necessary to draft young men for military service, it has made provision for those who, by reason of sincere belief, could not participate in hostilities. The evolution of what constitutes a sufficient basis for exemption reflects both the increasing religious pluralism of the United States and a dramatically broadening vision of which conscience rights merit constitutional protection. Moreover, it is a constitutionally interesting manifestation of free exercise, because it emphasizes that religious freedom can involve the right *not* to engage in otherwise required conduct that conflicts with one's beliefs, as opposed to simply an affirmative right to do something required by one's religion.

Selective Service and the Two World Wars

World War I necessitated the first conscription under the Selective Service Draft Act of 1917. This Act exempted those who were members of a "well-recognized sect or organization" that had strict pacifism as a part of its official doctrine. These were the "historic peace churches"—for example, the Quakers, Amish, Mennonites, and Seventh-day Adventists. Each held, as a central tenet of its faith, that Jesus' life and words as recorded in the New Testament prohibited Christians from fighting in wars for any reason. Because the churches themselves had clear standards for who was to be considered a member, deciding who was and who was not exempt seemed a relatively straightforward matter.

The ambiguity in this apparently clear situation was that there were members of other churches who were also pacifists, although their communities of faith did not mandate pacifism as an official tenet. Methodism, for example, had within it a pacifist minority. The Selective Service Administration thus enlarged the interpretation of the 1917 Act so that it permitted exemption for members of any recognized church whose objections to participation in war were religiously grounded.

The Selective Service Act of 1940 incorporated that administrative decision. This Act exempted persons who "by reason of religious training and belief" were opposed to participation in war. Other reasons that were not clearly religious—personal moral grounds and philosophical objections, for example—were explicitly disallowed. Individual draft boards applied the exemption rules inconsistently during the Second World War, resulting in a flurry of cases in federal district and circuit courts.

The Universal Military Training and Service Act

Mostly because of the uncertain interpretation and uneven application of the 1940 Act, Congress passed a much more comprehensive measure in 1948. This Universal Military Training and Service Act extended the exemption to "anyone who, because of religious training and belief . . . is conscientiously opposed to a combatant military service or to both combatant and non-combatant military service." Religious training and belief was further defined by Congress as "an individual's belief in relation to a Supreme Being involving duties superior to those arising from any human relation." It specifically excluded as a legitimate basis for objection "any essentially political, sociological, or philosophical views or merely a personal moral code" (O'Brien 2011: 740).

This law made it very clear that the right to conscientious objection was grounded in the free exercise of *religious* beliefs as protected by the First Amendment. Furthermore, belief in a Supreme Being was assumed to be a definitional hallmark of religion. However, some outside the nation's broad Judeo-Christian tradition who had ethical qualms about warfare questioned the Act and its underlying assumptions as unduly narrow, setting the stage for conflicts down the road.

Expanding the Definition of Conscientious Objection

The first serious challenge came in 1965, as opposition to the escalating war in Vietnam increased among those whose reasons did not necessarily fit the terms laid out in the 1948 Act. Daniel Seeger was convicted when he refused induction into the military after his application for conscientious objector status was denied. He had placed quotation marks around the word "religious" on the application, and acknowledged some degree of agnosticism regarding the existence of a Supreme Being. He was, he maintained, a believer in "goodness and virtue for their own sakes" (*United States* v. *Seeger*; 380 U.S. 163, 1965).

In its ruling in the *Seeger* case, the Supreme Court dramatically enlarged the scope of what constituted allowable grounds for exemption. The justices held that the interpretation of the Act should be broadened to include those whose objections to combat stem from a "given belief that is sincere and meaningful and occupies a place in the life of its possessor parallel to that filled by the orthodox belief in God of one who clearly qualifies for the exemption." Further, "religious belief" was held to include "all sincere beliefs which are based upon a power or being, or upon a faith, to which all else is subordinate or upon which all else is ultimately dependent." With the inclusion of the phrase "or upon a faith," the Court augmented the meaning of religion in this context to include sincere non-theists (those whose religious belief does not involve a Supreme Being) as well as theists; it also, critics charged, opened the door to conscientious objection on the basis of exactly the sorts of ideological and philosophical grounds that Congress had expressly sought to exclude.

Five years later, *Welsh* v. *United States* (398 U.S. 333, 1970) presented an even greater challenge to the Universal Military Training and Service Act. Whereas Seeger on his application had enclosed the word "religious" in quotation marks, Elliott Welsh crossed out the entire phrase "religious training and belief." His objection, he claimed, was based purely on his study of history and sociology. He was, as one commentator noted, "a considerably larger camel for the needle's eye" of the conscientious objection provisions (Morgan 1972: 169).

In *Welsh*, the Court cited the "great weight" that they had declared should be given to a registrant's description of his belief as "religious," even if they were not rooted in the teachings of a specific organized denomination. The justices were considerably less willing to take Welsh's statement that his beliefs were not religious at face value:

> The Court's statement in *Seeger* that a registrant's characterization of his own belief as "religious" should carry great weight . . . does not imply that his declaration that his views are nonreligious should be treated similarly . . . Very few registrants are fully aware of the broad scope of the word "religious" as used [in the Act], and, accordingly a registrant's statement that his beliefs are nonreligious is a highly unreliable guide for those charged with administering the exemption.

This further expansion of the admissible grounds for exemption had the effect of removing the distinction between religious and non-religious grounds altogether. The permissible basis for objection to military service became conscience rather than religion. Such a shift does avoid the potential establishment clause charge that religion is being preferred over irreligion. It also, however, effectively made avoidance of military service an option for anyone willing to declare a philosophical objection to war. It put the Court in the odd position of extending a right based on the free exercise of religion to someone who disavowed any religious belief. In an opinion that concurred in the result but relied on very different reasoning, Justice John Harlan described the Court as having "performed a lobotomy and completely transformed the statute by reading out of it any distinction between religiously acquired beliefs" and those arising from other sources.

The final important Supreme Court decision on this subject was issued in *Gillette* v. *United States* (401 U.S. 437, 1971). In all the cases discussed to this point, the issue was conscientious, principled objection to war in general. Gillette, however, raised a different issue, albeit one also rooted in religion. The question in this case was whether one could legitimately claim that a particular war, rather than war in general, was unjust.

Gillette, a Catholic, claimed exemption from participation in the Vietnam War on the grounds that it had not been declared by Congress, the agency of the government authorized to declare war, and thus failed to meet traditional Catholic just war criteria (see Chapter 3). Gillette's attorneys argued that the Act was unconstitutional as written, and that the only way to preserve its constitutionality was to extend its protection to "selective objectors" as well. Otherwise, it was questionable under both the establishment and free exercise clauses (because fighting in a particular conflict might violate both Catholic and Quaker belief, but only the Quaker's objection would be honored). The Court held otherwise, and the requirement that a conscientious objector object to all wars in principle stood. Since the government ended the draft in 1973 in favor of an all-volunteer military, there have been no conscientious objection cases for forty years. While the issue raises a host of interesting and difficult free exercise questions, it will in all likelihood rest until and unless military conscription is once again revived.

Jehovah's Witnesses, Evangelism, and Religious Freedom

The challenge that conscientious objectors raised to the secular regulation rule, while significant, paled in comparison to the series of issues presented by the Jehovah's Witnesses. As discussed in Chapter 3, the Witnesses—also known as the Watchtower Bible and Tract Society—are an American offshoot of Christianity that originated in the 1870s. A very aggressive program of missionary activity, based largely on door-to-door evangelism and the distribution of religious tracts, is central to their belief and practice. Jehovah's Witnesses also emphasize the importance of giving honor to God alone. In order to avoid placing loyalty to the nation above loyalty to God (to whom they refer as Jehovah), they do not participate in patriotic exercises that most Americans take for granted, such as saying the Pledge of Allegiance to the flag and singing the national anthem. Chapter 3 discussed the social ostracism and prejudice that they encountered as a result. The discussion here will focus on how the Supreme Court has evaluated their beliefs and practices in light of the free exercise clause.

The Gobitis Case

Two early Witnesses cases involve a practice customary in the first half of the twentieth century (and still relatively common today). Very often, the school day for both elementary and secondary school students began with the class standing, facing the flag, and repeating the Pledge of Allegiance together. In 1940, William and Lillian Gobitis, aged ten and twelve, were expelled from their school when they refused to participate in this exercise because they were Jehovah's Witnesses. Their father sued, and both the federal district court and the federal appeals court upheld his claim based on the free exercise of his children's religion. The Supreme Court, however, in *Minersville School District v. Gobitis* (310 U.S. 586, 1940) ruled against the children's freedom to abstain from what their faith told them was idolatry.

Justice Felix Frankfurter authored the opinion of the Court. He was well aware of the gravity of any situation in which claims of liberty and authority come into conflict. Further, as he wrote, "judicial conscience is put to its severest test" when "the liberty invoked is liberty of conscience, and the authority is the authority to safeguard the nation's fellowship." Justice Frankfurter's reasoning in the opinion is complicated. He acknowledged that government may not interfere with the expression of religious belief. He then, however, raised the question of whether "the constitutional guarantee compel[s] exemption from doing what society thinks necessary for the promotion of some great common end, or from a penalty for conduct which appears dangerous to the general good?" Citing both *Reynolds* and a later Mormon polygamy case, he restated the secular regulation rule:

> Conscientious scruples have not, in the course of the long struggle for religious toleration, relieved the individual from obedience to a general law not aimed at the promotion or restriction of religious beliefs. The mere possession of religious convictions which contradict the relevant concerns of a political society does not relieve the citizen from the discharge of political responsibility.

Frankfurter then argues that the flag salute is required "in the interest of promoting national cohesion," and that a vital national interest is at stake since "national unity is the basis of national security." He recognizes that some measures to promote national unity may appear harsh, and that "others, no doubt, are foolish." These judgments, however, are not for the Court to make.

Both Justice Harlan F. Stone's dissent from the Court's opinion and a *Christian Century* editorial on the case reflect considerable uneasiness with the decision. Justice Stone agreed that government may suppress religious practices that are dangerous to public health and safety, or are a threat to public morals. However, he simply did not see the Gobitis children's refusal to participate in the Pledge of Allegiance as such an activity. If the First Amendment guaranteed anything, Stone wrote, it was "freedom of the individual from compulsion as to what he shall think and what he shall say."

The Court's decision was greeted with considerable skepticism by important segments of American elite opinion. Both *The New Republic* and *Christian Century* went so far as to compare an inflexible requirement that children salute the flag regardless of conscience to the hyper-nationalism of Nazi Germany, where Jehovah's Witnesses were, in fact, being actively persecuted by the state (Graber 2005). The editors of *Christian Century* made clear their view that "the decision was not a wise one," distinguishing sharply between loyalty to the nation, which is obviously important, and the flag salute, which they described as "an arbitrary piece of ritual which is one way of expressing and teaching loyalty." They acknowledged that, to Jehovah's Witnesses, the flag salute might well seem tantamount to worshiping an image, even though in the judgment of the editors, this is "a foolish idea." After noting that there must be room for even foolish ideas, the editorial averred that "willingness to salute the flag is no criterion of loyalty" (*Christian Century*, June 19, 1940, quoted in Eastland 1993: 37–38).

The Barnette Case

In the wake of the backlash against the *Gobitis* decision, the Court had an opportunity to revisit the question of Jehovah's witnesses and the pledge just three years later, in *West Virginia Board of Education* v. *Barnette* (319 U.S. 624, 1943). Because the grounds in *Barnette* were broader, the Court could avoid the embarrassment of directly reversing itself so soon after having decided *Gobitis* by an 8–1 majority. In effect, however, this is exactly what it did.

Religion had provided the motivation for Barnette to assert his rights of non-compliance with the pledge requirement. The Court, however, held that the question of whether his religious views merited an exception to the law was relevant only if the law itself was constitutional. Largely on free speech grounds, the Court held that it was not. Justice Robert H. Jackson wrote for the Court:

> If there is any fixed star in our constitutional constellation, it is that no official, high or petty, can prescribe what shall be orthodox in politics, nationalism, religion, or other matters of opinion or force citizens to confess by word or act their faith therein. If there are any circumstances which permit an exception, they do not now occur to us.

The case did, however, have an obvious free exercise dimension, and three of the concurring justices understood it at least partly in those terms. Justices Hugo L. Black, William O. Douglas, and Frank Murphy each addressed the issue of whether religious refusal to participate in the Pledge of Allegiance to the flag was a threat to the nation, and concluded that it was not. Justice Frankfurter, who had written for the Court in *Gobitis*, predictably dissented in *Barnette*, citing similar grounds as he had previously. "Law is concerned with external behavior," he wrote, "and not with the inner life of man . . . One may have the right to practice one's religion and at the same time owe the duty of formal obedience to laws that run counter to one's beliefs." The free speech dimension notwithstanding, *Barnette* has been widely understood both as a reversal of the Court's *Gobitis* ruling and as a free exercise case.

Door-to-Door Evangelism and Literature Distribution

Jehovah's Witnesses were responsible for bringing several more cases before the Supreme Court between the 1940s and the 1970s. All had to do with the Witnesses' missionary activity, which has been unpopular with many non-Witnesses. The Witnesses believe that they are responsible for reaching as many people as they possibly can with their message. This leads many members to commit a great deal of time to door-to-door evangelism, as well as to other similar activities. At times, people put off by their approach have sought to have their activities curtailed by local laws. In those cases that have reached the Supreme Court, however, the Witnesses' right to evangelize has been upheld.

Perhaps the best known of the cases involving missionary activity is *Cantwell* v. *Connecticut* (1940), decided the same year as *Gobitis*. *Cantwell* was mentioned in the preceding chapter as the case in which the free exercise clause was first incorporated at the state level. Cantwell and his sons, all Witnesses, were arrested in New Haven, Connecticut, after they had solicited funds, an activity for which they had not obtained the required license. This particular case is important because it is the first in which the Supreme Court invalidated on the grounds of religious liberty a statute enacted by a state government. Justice Owen J. Roberts wrote the Court's opinion:

> We hold that the statute, as construed and applied to the appellants, deprives them of their liberty without due process of law in contravention of the Fourteenth Amendment. The fundamental concept of liberty embodied in that Amendment embraces the liberties guaranteed by the First Amendment. The First Amendment declares that Congress shall make no law respecting an establishment of religion or prohibiting the free exercise thereof. The Fourteenth Amendment has rendered the legislatures of the states as incompetent as Congress to enact such laws.

The Connecticut statute in question required that all persons obtain a license before soliciting funds. To do so, they had to apply to a state officer (the secretary of the public welfare council of the state), who was empowered to decide whether the cause for which funds would be solicited was indeed a religious one. If he determined that it was not, approval to solicit was withheld. This was held by the Court to be an impermissible restriction on religion. Justice Owen Roberts, writing for an unanimous Court, asserted that "such a censorship of religion as a means of determining its right to survive is a denial of liberty protected by the First Amendment and included in the liberty which is within the protection of the Fourteenth."

One more ironic dimension of this case is worth noting. In addition to soliciting funds, the Cantwells had played for those to whom they spoke a recording that was very derogatory toward Catholics. The recording angered many who heard it, and as a result, the Cantwells had also been charged with disturbing the peace. After noting that "the offense known as breach of the peace" covers a wide variety of conduct, the Court observed that the recording attacked the Catholic Church in a way "which naturally would offend not only persons of that persuasion, but all others who respect the honestly held religious faith of their fellows." This unfortunate intolerance notwithstanding, the Court held that Cantwell's communication, "considered in light of the constitutional guaranties, raised no such clear and present menace to public peace and order as to render him liable to conviction of the common law offense in question."

Other Jehovah's Witnesses Cases

Several other cases involving Jehovah's Witnesses dealt with variations of the same issue. *Murdock* v. *Pennsylvania* (319 U.S. 105, 1943) held that a license tax on canvassing and soliciting could not be applied to the Witnesses, and in the same year, in *Martin* v. *Struthers* (319 U.S. 141, 1943) and *Jamison* v. *Texas* (318 U.S. 413, 1943), the court overturned ordinances banning the distribution of handbills (door-to-door in one case, on street corners in the other). The right of the Witnesses to distribute their literature in a private company town was upheld in *Marsh* v. *Alabama* (326 U.S. 501, 1946), as was their right to use public parks for religious purposes in *Niemotko* v. *Maryland* (340 U.S. 268, 1951). In 1977, a Witness challenged New Hampshire's requirement that his car bear a license plate with the motto "Live Free or Die." His challenge was upheld and he was allowed to cover the offending slogan (*Wooley* v. *Maynard*; 430 U.S. 705, 1977).

The Court's decisions in these cases were hailed by many as an impressive and welcome enlargement of religious freedom, not only for the Witnesses but for all religious people, particularly those whose actions were motivated by their adherence to an unpopular or little-understood minority faith. Others, however, were not as enthusiastic. Writing even before the passage of the American Indian Religious Freedom Act (1978) and the Religious Freedom Restoration Act (1993), both of which are discussed below, constitutional scholar Richard Morgan (1972: 208) cautioned:

> The Court has done ill to retreat from the secular regulation rule . . . The free-exercise clause should not be expanded into a general protection of unorthodox (otherwise proscribable) behavior . . . In a period of decline in traditional religions and rise of a welter of "fad faiths" it is extremely unwise to begin admitting exceptions to otherwise popular health, welfare, and criminal regulations.

Sabbatarians, Work Exemptions, and Title VII

Sabbatarians are people who observe Saturday as their Sabbath or religious day of rest. This includes not only Jews, but certain Christians, such as Seventh-day Adventists and most congregations of the Worldwide Church of God. Because of the predominance of traditional forms of the Christian faith in the history of the United States, laws were enacted and customs developed that either required or encouraged the closing of businesses on Sunday. This practice causes hardship for Sabbatarians, whose religion stipulates that they do not work on Saturday, or who close their place of business on their Sabbath, as well as being required to close it on Sunday.

"Blue Laws"

Many jurisdictions in the United States have historically had laws that require businesses to be closed on Sundays, at least until noon. In *Braunfeld* v. *Brown*

(366 U.S. 599, 1961), Orthodox Jews challenged these "blue laws" in the Supreme Court on free exercise grounds. Other cases—*McGowan v. Maryland* (366 U.S. 420, 1961) and *Two Guys from Harrison-Allentown v. McGinley* (366 U.S. 582, 1961)—had raised similar issues from the perspective of the establishment clause. Basically, these cases asked, were state and local governments within their constitutional rights to mandate Sunday as a day of rest? In the two establishment clause challenges, the Supreme Court held that the setting aside of Sunday as a day of rest does not violate the First Amendment; while the origins of the practice were clearly religious, the custom served a valid secular purpose and was defended on plausible secular grounds.

The *Braunfeld* case was more complicated, however, because the plaintiff approached the issue from a free exercise perspective, alleging that the blue laws seriously impeded his ability to observe his religious requirements as a practical matter. A group of Orthodox Jewish businessmen charged that requiring them to close their establishments on Sunday imposed a financial hardship on them of such magnitude that it was a significant interference with the practice of their religion. Orthodox Judaism stipulates that no work be done on the Sabbath, from nightfall on Friday through nightfall on Saturday. Thus, the appellants had to close their businesses during that time, while businesses owned by their gentile competitors remained open. In essence, the Jewish businessmen had two days during which they had to close their businesses, while gentiles had only one. The appellants alleged that the resultant economic disadvantage was severe enough that they were compelled to choose between their livelihood and their faith.

In a 5–4 decision, the Court rejected Braunfeld's claims. Chief Justice Earl Warren, writing for the Court, cited *Reynolds* as a precedent for the secular regulation rule. He also distinguished the circumstances in *Braunfeld* from those in the various Jehovah's Witness cases. Warren noted that the laws struck down in those cases made specific religiously motivated practices illegal. The Sunday closing laws, by contrast, did not outlaw any religious behavior, but rather sought to "simply regulate a secular activity." Justice Warren noted that the nation was made up of people of almost every conceivable religious preference, and that:

Consequently, it cannot be expected, much less required, that legislators enact no law regulating conduct that may in some way result in an economic disadvantage to some religious sects and not to others because of the special practices of the various religions.

In essence, Warren's comments upheld the secular regulation rule in its specific application to economic activity.

Justice Potter Stewart dissented, arguing that the Court's ruling "compels an Orthodox Jew to choose between his religious faith and his economic survival." That "cruel choice" would be adjudicated again and again in subsequent cases dealing with Saturday employment, and later on in cases involving Native Americans, the use of peyote in religious rituals, and the Religious Freedom Restoration Act (discussed below).

While *Braunfeld* dealt with the effects of *not* working because of Sabbath observance, most other cases in this area have concerned the opposite: the right to work *despite* observance of a Saturday Sabbath. It is from this question that some of the most significant precedents in free exercise jurisprudence have arisen.

Sherbert *and the* Compelling Interest Test

Sherbert v. Verner (374 U.S. 398, 1963) is a crucial case, because in it the Supreme Court ruled for the first time that the free exercise clause of the First Amendment requires that persons be exempted from secular regulations that impinge significantly on the practice of their religion. It represents a real judicial rethinking of the secular regulation rule laid out in *Reynolds*, and it set a standard for judicial decision making in free exercise cases that is in some ways comparable to the *Lemon* test in establishment jurisprudence (see Chapter 5). Adell Sherbert was a Seventh-day Adventist who lost her job because she refused to work on Saturday, her Sabbath. When she could not find a job that would excuse her from Saturday work, she filed for unemployment compensation, which she was denied on the grounds that she refused to accept "suitable work." In what one analyst calls "a critical turning-point for free-exercise jurisprudence" (Eastland 1993: 169), the Supreme Court held, by a 7–2 margin, in favor of Sherbert. The Court declared that the government must have a "compelling interest" in order to burden the free exercise of religion, not just the "rational basis" required by *Reynolds*.

Justice William J. Brennan, Jr., writing for the Court, found that the government had not demonstrated a sufficiently compelling interest to justify the imposition of a burden on Sherbert's free exercise of her religion, a hardship that he compared to "a fine imposed against the appellant for her Saturday worship." Justice Brennan understood the issue in this case to be quite different from that presented in *Braunfeld*; he argued that the state's interest in "providing one uniform day of rest for all workers" was sufficiently compelling to justify blue laws, and that the secular end could reasonably be met in no other way.

The standards laid out in *Sherbert* can be summarized as follows. In order to determine whether a law or policy is constitutional under the free exercise clause, the Court must first decide whether it places a burden on a religious group or practice. If so, then the Court must decide whether the government has a compelling interest that would justify the infringement of religious liberty. If a compelling interest is indeed present, then the government must demonstrate that the interest can be served in no other way than by limiting religious freedom. This became the standard until 1990, when it was overturned in *Smith* (discussed below).

Justice John M. Harlan, joined by Justice Byron R. White, wrote a strong dissent, part of which prefigured later questions about the wisdom of the Court's ruling. The purpose of the unemployment benefit, he held, was to tide people over during times when work was unavailable, not to subsidize those who chose (for religious reasons or otherwise) to make themselves unemployable. To mandate an exception for those whose unavailability stemmed from religious convictions meant giving benefit to religion over irreligion.

Civil libertarians hailed the decision as a crucial step in protecting the interests of minority religions against a culturally-imposed "tyranny of the majority." One report, for example, pointed out that "it is not accidental" that workplace rules and customs "are generally compatible with majority practices and beliefs" even if those rules and customs are essentially secular in intent (U.S. Commission on Civil Rights 1983: 42).

Others have been less enthusiastic. Writing almost a decade later, one analyst of the role of religion in American law identified three potentially serious problem areas that result from the *Sherbert* decision: (1) There is an apparent conflict between this ruling and at least one reading of the establishment clause, which forbids favoring religion over irreligion. (2) The finding potentially involves the Court in deciding what is and what is not a religion, in order to determine who is eligible for the exemption, again risking running afoul of the establishment clause. (3) Finally, decisions might have to be made, as a practical matter, on the basis of how many people seek to avail themselves of a particular exemption, an awkward situation at best (Morgan 1972). Later events, discussed below, illustrate that the matter of religiously motivated exemptions from otherwise applicable secular laws was far from settled by the *Sherbert* case.

The Civil Rights Act of 1964 and Religious Discrimination in the Workplace

What is and is not permissible in workplace-related religion cases is not only a matter of case law. Title VII of the Civil Rights Act of 1964 makes discrimination against employees on the basis of religion unlawful, whether by an employer or by a labor union. The relevant section of the Act (701j) protects both religious belief and practice, but is silent on the issue of what makes something "religious." It has usually been understood in light of the very broad definition of religion worked out in dealing with conscientious objection to military service (described above). The Act requires that an employer accommodate employees' religious needs unless such accommodation would cause undue hardship to the employer.

This left room for confusion about what constituted "undue hardship," and the Equal Employment Opportunity Commission (EEOC), the federal agency responsible for enforcement of the Act, issued additional guidelines in 1978 that clarified requirements for both employers and employees. The Office of Federal Contract Compliance Programs in the Department of Labor has also issued guidelines on the application of Title VII in workplaces in which federal contracts are involved.

Of course, no such regulations could develop without litigation along the way. *Trans World Airlines* v. *Hardison* (432 U.S. 63, 1977) began the process of delineating the exact nature of the accommodations that an employer had to make. In *Thomas* v. *Review Board of Indiana Employment Security Division* (450 U.S. 707, 1981) the denial of unemployment benefits to a worker who terminated employment because of religious objections to working in the production of weapons was struck down. In *Hobbie* v. *Unemployment Appeals Commission of Florida* (480 U.S. 136, 1987), the Court held that it was irrelevant that the worker experienced a religious conversion after beginning work. Finally, in an expansion of the exemption that echoed *Seeger*, the Court held that the denial of unemployment compensation to a person who refused Sabbath work ,even though he was not a member of a recognized religious denomination violated the free exercise clause (*Frazee* v. *Illinois Department of Employment Security*; 489 U.S. 829, 1989).

Religious Discrimination Compared with Racial or Gender Discrimination

The issue of religious discrimination in the workplace has both similarities with and differences from discrimination based on race or gender. Overt, intentional acts of discrimination are treated similarly whether based on religion, race, or gender, and are equally unlawful. Similarly as well, discrimination that is unintentional may still be unlawful, since employers are responsible for anticipating what might reasonably occur as a result of policies that they adopt. This applies equally in all three situations. The particular religion of the claimant is irrelevant, as is the race or gender of the complainant in race and sex discrimination cases.

However, there are significant dissimilarities in these contexts as well. In race and sex discrimination cases, the objective is generally to ensure equal treatment regardless of the defining characteristic. In religious discrimination cases, however, the appellants usually seek special exemptions or accommodations based on their religious beliefs and practices. The elimination of discrimination based on race or gender seeks to enhance equality, whereas the removal of burdens on religious practice help to enhance diversity. Race and gender discrimination often stems from historical patterns of inequality in the educational process, whereas this is not necessarily the case with religious discrimination. Whereas legislation concerning race and gender discrimination deals with a finite, relatively small number of races and two genders, that dealing with religious discrimination must take into account an almost infinite variety of beliefs and practices. Finally, because the implementation of workplace policies to protect religious liberty must be done in a way that does not violate the establishment clause, it is constrained in ways that similar action to combat race and gender discrimination is not (U.S. Commission on Civil Rights 1983).

Religious Employers and the Law

To this point, the discussion here has focused on the free exercise claims of religious *employees*. There are also, however, significant religious freedom issues with regard to religious *employers*. Title VII forbids religious discrimination in employment. Does this mean that synagogues, churches, and seminaries (schools for the training of ministers and other church professionals) cannot limit their hiring to members of their own faith? No. Title VII was amended in 1972 to exclude religious organizations from the ban on religious discrimination in all phases of workplace operation. This general exemption applies only to the ban on discrimination based on religion; other provisions of Title VII that ban discrimination on the basis of race, sex, or national origin apply to religious employers as much as to secular ones. There is, however, a widely recognized "ministerial exception" that allows religious organizations to be exempt from Title VII requirements in the employment of personnel who perform specifically religious functions. Thus, a Catholic church cannot be required to employ female priests, and a mosque has no obligation to consider gay Imams.

The ministerial exception was affirmed and broadened in the recent case of *Hosanna-Tabor Evangelical Lutheran Church and School* v. *EEOC* (565 U.S., 2012). In this case, an employee who performed a combination of religious and secular duties left her employment and claimed disability because she had narcolepsy. When she sought to return to work, she was told that she had already been replaced; when she objected and threatened to sue, she was fired for "insubordination and disruptive behavior." In an unanimous decision, the Court ruled in favor of the Church, affirming that religious institutions have the right to hire and fire ministerial personnel as they see fit, and expanding the definition of such personnel to include not just clergy per se, but others who perform significant religious duties (which the employee in question did, leading student prayers and teaching a religion class).

The question of employers' conscience rights has become much more pressing with the passage of the Patient Protection and Affordable Care Act (commonly known as "Obamacare") in 2010. Under authority granted by the Act, the Department of Health and Human Services issued a mandate requiring employers to provide their employees with insurance coverage that includes contraception, abortifacient drugs, and sterilization, all of which violate the teachings of the Catholic Church (and some other religious groups as well). The only exceptions would be, essentially, for churches per se (organizations that predominantly employ and serve members of their own religious group). Religiously affiliated schools, hospitals, and charities, as well as other businesses run by believers, would be subject to the mandate (McGuire 2012). As a result, dozens of organizations (most, but not all, of them Catholic) have filed suit against the Obama administration and challenged the constitutionality of this mandate on free exercise grounds. These legal battles are ongoing, and have not yet been adjudicated by the Supreme Court. When they eventually are (as seems quite likely), the outcome will be critical in defining the free exercise rights of religious employers.

Native Americans, Sacred Lands, and Peyote

As a result of the complicated history of the United States government's dealing with Native Americans, there are unique dimensions to the constitutional questions surrounding the free exercise of their traditional religions. Native Americans (or at least those on reservations) remain, to a degree, under the jurisdiction of the government, and are not completely in control of their own affairs. This status necessitates a degree of government involvement in accommodating their religious free exercise that in other circumstances would likely be an impermissible establishment of religion. Only in recent decades has the government really begun to take the religions of native peoples seriously. For most of the history of the United States, Native American religions were regarded as "heathen" or "pagan," perhaps not even genuine religions, and often actively suppressed. Religiously, Native Americans were seen only as objects of conversion for Christian missionaries, a view actively supported by the government for many years.

Sam Gill, commenting on the treatment of Native Americans by the federal government, writes that the white-dominated government has always assumed that it knew better than the Native Americans what they themselves needed, even when they made their desires known. At best, it has followed a paternalistic policy. At worst, it has moved entire tribes and even killed people in the service of white American interests. Not until late in the twentieth century, with the passage of the American Indian Religious Freedom Act in 1978, were Native Americans guaranteed the same rights that others took for granted (Gill 1988). Even then, the guarantee was not always enforced.

The 1934 Indian Reorganization Act established the principle of governmental non-interference in Native American religious affairs, ending active persecution. Significant problems remained, however, with otherwise neutral laws that heavily burdened Native religious practices. Such laws included those establishing museums' rights to keep and display Native American artifacts and those concerning public access to and use of government lands that are sacred to Native Americans.

Many Native American religions hold that the land itself is sacred; rocks, rivers, trees, and specific locales occupy in their thought a place equivalent to that of churches, mosques, and synagogues in Christianity, Islam, and Judaism. This means that forbidding access to them, or allowing tourist access to them, has the same impact on Native American religion that forbidding access to a church, synagogue, or mosque, or allowing indiscriminate tourist access to it, would have on Christians, Jews, or Muslims.

The American Indian Religious Freedom Act

One could argue that existing legislation and case law should have been adequate to deal with the special situation of Native American religions, but many felt that it was not. As a result, in 1978, Congress passed and President Jimmy Carter signed the American Indian Religious Freedom Act. In part, the Act states that:

> It shall be the policy of the United States to protect and preserve for American Indians their inherent right of freedom to believe, express, and exercise the traditional religions of the American Indian, Eskimo, Aleut, and Native Hawaiians, including but not limited to access to sites, use and possession of sacred objects, and the freedom of worship through ceremonials and traditional rites.

The wording of the Act seems clear enough, but its application proved otherwise. For example, in *Lyng v. Northwest Indian Cemetery Protective Association* (485 U.S. 439, 1988), the Supreme Court held that roads could be constructed and timber harvested in areas under the jurisdiction of the National Park Service that had traditionally been used by several Native American tribes for religious ceremonies. From the Native American point of view, commercial use of the land was a desecration of it. The Court did not dispute that logging activity "could have devastating effects on traditional Indian religious practices." It did, however, hold that the government's carrying out of public policy simply could not be contingent on "measuring the effects of a governmental action on a religious objector's spiritual development." The Native American groups involved here were not asking for a religious exemption from some policy; they were asking for the whole policy to be scrapped (or radically changed) on religious grounds. "Construction of the proposed road," Justice Sandra Day O'Connor wrote for the 5–3 majority, "does not violate the First Amendment regardless of its effect on the religious practices of the respondents because it compels no behavior contrary to their belief." Essentially, the ruling in *Lyng* was that the governmental interests involved simply outweighed the Native Americans' free exercise claims, particularly since they were neither being prevented from engaging in acts of worship nor required to do anything that violated the tenets of their faith. *Lyng* made clear that the American Indian Religious Freedom Act is not an absolute guarantee of Native American religious rights, even in cases where public health and safety interests are not at stake.

Native Americans, Peyote, and Woody

Traditional Native American religious practices come into play again in a landmark case that led directly to the passage of the Religious Freedom Restoration Act in 1993. The background is provided by a California State

Supreme Court case from the 1960s involving the Native American Church. The Native American Church blends elements of Christianity with traditional Native American spiritual practices, including the use of peyote. Peyote is a cactus that has psychotropic (consciousness-altering) properties, and is central to the rituals of the Native American Church. Peyote is also an illegal drug under both federal and California law.

In cases involving peyote and the Native American Church, members have often been charged with illegal use, transportation, or simply possession of the drug. Native Americans then argue that the drug is essential to the practice of their religion, and thus protected by the First Amendment. The issue becomes one of balancing the government's interest in regulating drug traffic and use against this free exercise claim. Several cases have been heard in lower courts in various states, with inconsistent results. The California case, however, had particular notoriety and influence.

In *People* v. *Woody* (1964), a California court convicted members of the Native American Church who were using peyote in a ritual context on narcotics possession charges. The Native Americans appealed to the California Supreme Court, which reversed the decision. The issue was whether the state government's legitimate interest in restricting the use of illegal drugs was sufficiently compelling to justify abridging the Native Americans' religious liberty. The Court rejected the state's assertion that it needed to be able to regulate the ritual use of peyote because of peyote's "deleterious effects upon the Indian community and . . . the infringement such practice would place upon the enforcement of narcotics laws." Justice Tobriner wrote for the majority:

> We have weighed the competing values represented in the case on the symbolic scale of constitutionality. On one side we have placed the weight of freedom of religion as it is protected by the First Amendment; on the other, the weight of the state's "compelling interest." Since the use of peyote incorporates the essence of the religious expression, the first weight is heavy. Yet the use of peyote represents only slight danger to the state and to the enforcement of its laws; the second weight is relatively light. The scale tips in favor of the constitutional protection.

Oregon *v.* Smith and the Reversal of the Compelling Interest Test

While the *Woody* case was a victory for the Native American Church, it was a state-level one, and applied only within California. The United States Supreme Court would not wrestle with the same issue until much later, in *Department of Human Resources of Oregon v. Smith* (494 U.S. 872, 1990). The case was similar to *Woody* in that it involved the ritual use of peyote by members of the Native American Church. Two members of the church were denied unemployment compensation after they were fired from their jobs because of their ritual use of peyote. What makes this case more complex is that the jobs from which the two church members were fired were as drug rehabilitation counselors. Citing a number of the earlier Sabbatarian cases, the two men claimed that the state could not make the availability of unemployment benefits contingent on their abstaining from a central element of their religious worship. When the case made its way to the Oregon Supreme Court, that body held that the petitioners were indeed entitled to benefits. The state of Oregon, however, appealed the case to the United States Supreme Court. The Court first sent the case back to Oregon, so that the state could decide whether the ceremonial use of peyote did in fact violate the state's controlled substance laws (on which the two parties had not agreed).

The Oregon court found that the petitioners' religious use of peyote did violate the law, which explicitly made "no exception for the sacramental use" of narcotics and hallucinogens. This, the state court concluded, made the law itself unconstitutional because it violated the free exercise clause. Thus, the petitioners were clearly entitled to benefits. Once again, the state of Oregon appealed.

Ultimately, the United States Supreme Court held that the denial was justified, and that Oregon's drug laws could be applied to Native American Church members. In doing so, the Court significantly reshaped the standards applied to free exercise jurisprudence. As a result, a close examination of the various opinions is justified, beginning with Justice Antonin Scalia's majority opinion, continuing with Justice Sandra Day O'Connor's concurrence, and concluding with Justice Harry A. Blackmun's strongly worded dissent.

Justice Scalia for the Court

Alfred Smith and Galen Black—the two Native Americans involved in this case—contended that requiring them to obey an otherwise constitutional law as a condition of receiving unemployment benefits interfered with the free exercise of their religion in a constitutionally unacceptable way. Justice Scalia, writing for the majority, held that the Court had "never held that an individual's religious beliefs excuse him from compliance with an otherwise valid law prohibiting conduct that the State is free to regulate." He cited jurisprudence to support his point, including references to both *Reynolds* and *Gobitis*, discussed above. Smith and Black had based a part of their argument on three Sabbatarian employment benefit cases: *Sherbert*, *Thomas*, and *Hobbie*. In these cases, it was held that the government had to show a "compelling government interest" if it sought to limit freedom of religion. Even then, it had to act in a way that restricted religious freedom as little as reasonably possible—the "least restrictive means" test.

Scalia argued that these two tests were not applicable in the *Smith* case. To apply them would result in the "constitutional anomaly" of a private right to ignore generally applicable laws. He noted that the states were free to enact exemptions from drug laws for the benefit of the Native American

Church, and that several states had done so. This, however, is not the same as saying that such exemptions are constitutionally *required*.

In the *Gobitis* case, the test of the constitutionality of the government's action in requiring participation in the flag salute ceremony was that it be a "reasonable exercise" of the state's power. In effect, Scalia held that this was what was required in *Smith* as well, rather than the more stringent "compelling interest" and "least restrictive means" tests used in *Sherbert*.

A Concurring Opinion

Justice Sandra Day O'Connor concurred in the outcome, but followed a different line of reasoning. In her opinion, the compelling interest test used in *Sherbert* should apply equally in *Smith*. There was no question that the criminal prohibition of the use of peyote imposed a severe hardship on the respondents' free exercise of religion. There was also no dispute that the state of Oregon had a significant interest in prohibiting the possession and use of controlled substances. The question was whether or not the state's interest was "compelling." In O'Connor's view, it was. She held that uniform application of the statute was essential to accomplish its goal:

> Because the health effects caused by the use of controlled substances exist regardless of the motivation of the user, the use of such substances, even for religious purposes, violates the very purpose of the laws that prohibit them . . . Under such circumstances, the free exercise clause does not require the State to accommodate respondents' religiously motivated conduct.

Dissent and Response

Justices Blackmun, Brennan, and Marshall dissented. In their view, the religious use of peyote by members of the Native American Church was a vastly different matter than its use by the general public. "The carefully circumscribed ritual context in which respondents use peyote is far removed from the irresponsible and unrestricted recreational use of unlawful drugs," they argued. "Far from promoting the lawless and irresponsible use of drugs, Native American Church members' spiritual code exemplifies the values that Oregon's drug laws are presumably intended to foster." Clearly, the dissenters did not believe that Oregon had a compelling interest at stake in preventing the ritual use of peyote.

The response to the decision in *Smith* was immediate and intense. The Court had eliminated the rigorous compelling interest test and replaced it with the much less exacting rational basis standard. A broad-based coalition quickly formed to begin work toward the passage of a bill that would strengthen protections for religious freedom. This coalition included people representing nearly every religious and political viewpoint. They sought to restore what had been taken away by judicial decision through an act of Congress. The coalition's membership ranged from large, "mainstream" denominations to small, unconventional religions. Never in the course of American religious history had such a widely disparate group come together around a single issue. Mainstream religious leaders were as concerned about the long-term effects of *Smith* as were leaders of "fringe" religions that were more likely to bear the brunt of future similar decisions. The general feeling was that infringement of the religious rights of any group meant the potential loss of freedom for all.

The Religious Freedom Restoration Act

In response to the outcry over the *Smith* decision, and to the more general sense that religious liberty in America needed additional protection (from majority faiths, from secular government, or both—the perceived source of the threat depended on one's perspective), Congress passed and President Bill Clinton signed the Religious Freedom Restoration Act (RFRA) in 1993. It recognized that otherwise neutral laws may interfere with the free exercise of religion as surely as laws specifically intended to do so. It recognized the compelling interest standard established in *Sherbert* as "a workable test for striking sensible balances between religious liberty and competing government interests," and restored it as the test to be used in all free exercise cases. Specifically, it required that government meet two conditions if an otherwise neutral law infringes on religious liberty. Section 3, which spells out the core of the Act, requires that:

> Government shall not substantially burden a person's exercise of religion, even if the burden results from a rule of general applicability, except as provided in subsection (b) . . . (b) . . . Government may substantially burden a person's exercise of religion only if it demonstrates the application of the burden to the person—(1) is in furtherance of a compelling governmental interest; and (2) is the least restrictive means of furthering that compelling governmental interest.

In other words, if the government acts in a way that impedes the free exercise of religion, it must have a very good reason for doing so, and then must proceed in a way that has the least possible impact on religious freedom.

The passage of the Act was hailed by many civil libertarians and religious liberty advocates as an essential restoration of an indispensable freedom (e.g., Wood 1993; Boston 1994). Religious people—even those whose faiths were not widely known and understood—could, in their view, now feel safe again, confident that their religious freedoms were secure. Others, however, were more skeptical. Some analysts contended that the compelling interest test was too rigorous and too absolute, without sufficient flexibility to work in the variety of cases that the Court might have to decide (Saison 1995). Others charged that the Act itself was an unconstitutional establishment of religion, because it protected religiously motivated conduct in situations where the same conduct would not be protected if it had secular motivations (Eisgruber 1994).

The Court and the Religious Freedom Restoration Act

The first free exercise case to come to the Court after the passage of the Religious Freedom Restoration Act was *Church of the Lukumi Babalu Aye v. Hialeah* (580 U.S. 520, 1993). As it turned out, however, the case didn't really test the Court's approach to the Act. In the case, the city of Hialeah, Florida, had enacted a law prohibiting animal sacrifice, which is a central part of worship in the Santeria religion. The law was struck down as unconstitutional because it was clearly directed specifically at the Santeria practitioners. Since the law was not one of general applicability, it did not come under the provisions of RFRA.

The Court finally addressed the Act in the case of *City of Boerne v. Flores* (521 U.S. 507, 1997). The congregation of Saint Peter Catholic Church in Boerne, Texas had become too large to worship comfortably in its existing sanctuary. The church thus requested permission from the city to expand its building. The request was denied, however, because Saint Peter is located in a historic landmark district of the city. As a result, the church sued the city under the RFRA.

The city's response charged that the RFRA itself was unconstitutional, and thus not binding. Lawyers for the city alleged that by allowing an action or exemption based on religion that would not be permissible on other grounds, the Act violated the non-establishment provision of the First Amendment. As in the original passage of the RFRA, a broad coalition of supporters came together and filed a friend-of-the-court brief arguing that Congress did act with proper authority in passing the Act and urging the Court to uphold its constitutionality.

Justice Anthony Kennedy wrote the opinion of the Court's 5–4 majority, which held that in enacting the legislation, Congress had overstepped its constitutional bounds. Although Congress does have the power, under the Fourteenth Amendment, to enforce guarantees of due process by legislation, the Act was held to have exceeded the limits of that power. Kennedy wrote that the "RFRA is so out of proportion to a supposed remedial or preventive object that it cannot be understood as responsive to, or designed to prevent, unconstitutional behavior. It appears, instead, to attempt a substantive change in constitutional protections." Such a "substantive change" goes beyond the power of Congress to enact by statute. Kennedy also dismissed the argument that the application of otherwise neutral laws imposes an unfair burden on religion:

It is a reality of the modern regulatory state that numerous state laws . . . impose a substantial burden on a large class of individuals. When the exercise of religion has been burdened in an incidental way by a law of general application, it does not follow that the persons affected have been burdened more than other citizens, let alone burdened because of their religious beliefs.

He was very clear in his statement that the precedent of the Court, not legislation enacted by Congress, must control the understanding and application of the Constitution.

Justice Stevens' concurring opinion argues that the RFRA, in its effort to enhance the protections provided by the free exercise clause, violated the establishment clause:

If the historic landmark on the hill in Boerne happened to be a museum or an art gallery owned by an atheist, it would not be eligible for an exemption . . . [The] statute has provided the Church with a legal weapon that no atheist or agnostic can obtain. This governmental preference for religion, as opposed to irreligion, is forbidden by the First Amendment.

Dissenting opinions focused primarily on doubts about the soundness of the *Smith* decision itself, and called on the Court to re-examine that case rather than invalidating the RFRA. Since it was *Smith* that, in large part, led to the passage of the Act, the dissenters argued that Court scrutiny should focus on the shortcomings of that decision rather than the legislative response to it.

On one level, *Flores* must be understood as a case not primarily about freedom of religion, but about the separation of powers in government. On this point, the majority of justices seemed to have no trouble agreeing that Congress had exceeded its authority in seeking to dictate the criteria by which the Court should evaluate the constitutionality of state and local statutes. On another level, however, it was clearly about freedom of religion. Kennedy's majority opinion devoted quite a lot of space to a discussion of the differences between the RFRA and the Voting Rights Act. Unlike the situation the Voting Rights Act was intended to remedy (persistent, widespread, and intentional disenfranchisement of racial minorities), Kennedy argued that the historical evidence does not indicate that there have been "modern instances of generally applicable laws passed because of religious bigotry." Burdens to religion from the enforcement of generally applicable laws have been incidental and unintentional, rather than deliberate. Kennedy's statement about the realities of the modern regulatory state, quoted above, appears to dismiss the constitutional significance of these unintentional burdens because they are not deliberately imposed. Basically, the decision appeared to leave the situation where it was in 1990 following *Smith*. The government must demonstrate that its interference with religious freedom has a rational basis;

it need not, however, demonstrate a compelling interest, nor satisfy the "least restrictive means" test.

Responses to Flores

Civil libertarians, a range of religious leaders, and members of Congress were predictably incensed by the *Flores* decision. In the years that followed, Congress passed the Religious Land Use and Institutionalized Persons Act (2000), which required localities to apply the "compelling interest" standard in dealing with religious properties if they received federal funding (which most do). In addition, Congress in 2003 revised the RFRA to limit its applicability to federal statutes, bringing the Act's requirements within the sphere of legitimate legislative authority. In *Gonzales* v. *O Centro Espirita Beneficente Uniao do Vegetal* (546 U.S. 418, 2006), the Supreme Court unanimously affirmed the constitutionality of this revised Act, asserting the right of a Brazilian church in New Mexico to use hallucinogenic tea in its rituals despite federal drug laws. Thus, under the terms of the amended RFRA, *federal* laws remain subject to the "compelling interest" and "least restrictive means" standards. This is significant, as it means that the various curtailments of religious freedom alleged under the Affordable Care and Patient Protection Act (discussed above) will be examined with this heightened degree of scrutiny.

There have also been significant responses to *Flores* at the state level. While the Court's ruling meant that state and local governments did not have to meet the compelling interest standard in their interactions with religion, many sought to impose this standard on themselves. In the decade and a half since the *Flores* decision, sixteen states have passed their own religious freedom restoration acts (Lund 2010). This has created an unusual situation in which federal courts evaluating federal laws, and state courts in these sixteen states, are to apply the "compelling interest" and "least restrictive means" tests originally articulated in *Sherbert*, while federal courts interpreting state laws, and state courts in the other thirty-four states, will apply the less stringent "rational basis" test from *Reynolds*, *Gobitis*, and *Smith*. Needless to say, jurisprudence in this area promises to remain inconsistent and unsettled.

The Establishment and Free Exercise Clauses: In Conflict?

As was pointed out in Chapter 5, the establishment clause and the free exercise clause of the First Amendment sometimes seem to conflict with one another. This issue was raised by Justice Potter Stewart in his dissent from the Court's holding in *Sherbert*. As he argued, "there are many situations where legitimate claims under the free exercise clause will run into head-on collision with the Court's sterile and insensitive construction of the establishment clause."

The conflict is most acute concerning the issue of exempting religiously motivated action from otherwise applicable laws (as in *Sherbert* and *Smith*, for example). The establishment clause, at least as many construe it, prohibits the government from preferring religious motivations over others, while the *Sherbert* interpretation of the free exercise clause appears to require special exemptions for religiously motivated actions. The conundrum is this: "If the government applies its laws neutrally, it will prohibit some people from practicing their religion. If the government exempts those with religious objections, it will discriminate against those with non-religious objections" (Sherry 1992: 124).

While some legal scholars see this tension as a problem, others regard it as part of the genius of the system. Some believe that the Court cannot, and perhaps should not, definitively reconcile the two clauses. Doing so, in this view, would defeat their purpose. Decisions should be based very narrowly on the facts of each case, and should seek to preserve the value of the clause that is the most applicable (Neuborne 1996). The dynamic tension between the clauses must, according to these scholars, be left intact.

Others, however, call for a harmonization of the two clauses. Free exercise is held to protect freedom of belief and practice by the prevention of penalties. The establishment clause likewise protects religious liberty by preventing individual choices from being circumscribed or pressured by governmental endorsement of a sectarian worldview (McConnell 1990; Marshall 1991). These two protections can work in tandem, some argue, and need not be at odds with one another. According to at least one scholar, however, all attempts at reconciling the conflict either simply recreate the paradox or devalue one of the two clauses. Which clause one would rather see de-emphasized is a matter of personal preference, but one or the other will have to be, if a true reconciliation is to happen (Sherry 1992).

Other analysts do hold out hope for an interpretation that devalues neither clause yet resolves the seeming paradox. The establishment clause and the free exercise clause together are "a single religion clause whose establishment and free-exercise provisions serve one central value—the freedom of religion" (Glendon 1993: 477). The job of the Court is thus to find an interpretation that allows the clauses to function together. It must "develop an interpretation of the two religious clauses that makes the free-exercise clause and the establishment clause consistent and complementary rather than antagonistic toward each other" (McConnell 1993: 506).

One proposal for doing so comes from Michael McConnell, a former Federal Appeals Court judge and currently professor of law at Stanford University. He advances three criteria: (1) A law or policy is unconstitutional if its purpose or likely effect is to increase religious uniformity, either by inhibiting the religious practice of the person or group challenging the law (free exercise clause) or by forcing or inducing a contrary religious practice (establishment clause); (2) A law or policy is unconstitutional if its enforcement interferes with the independence of a religious body in matters of religious significance to that body; (3) Violation of either of these principles should be permitted only if it is the least restrictive means for (a) protecting the private rights of others, or (b) ensuring that the benefits and burdens of public life are equitably shared (McConnell 1993). The ultimate test of the workability of this or any standard, of course, would be its actual application by the Supreme Court in religious freedom cases. For now, it remains just one proposal to reconcile the seemingly competing imperatives of non-establishment and free exercise.

An Illustrative Case

The case of *Board of Education of the Kiryas Joel Village School District* v. *Grumet* (512 U.S. 687, 1994) provides a good illustration of the complexity inherent in reconciling free exercise and non-establishment. The Satmar are a Hasidic Jewish group that is distinctive from the great majority of American Jews in that they try to remain as isolated as possible. All of their children attend private, religious schools except those for whom special education is necessary (recall that the Court ruled in *Aguilar* v. *Felton* that public school teachers could not teach in religious schools). When these children were forced to attend public schools in order to meet their special education needs, they were ridiculed by other children because they were "different" in dress, manners, and customs. The village then received permission from the state to form a school district of its own, so that public school teachers could provide the necessary special education to an exclusively Hasidic class. Learning-disabled Hasidic children from outside the district also attended this school. The New York State Supreme Court then ruled that creating a public school district whose boundaries were the same as those of the Hasidic enclave was unconstitutional because it created a symbolic union of government and religion, thus violating the establishment clause. The United States Supreme Court later held that the state law that had created the special school district was, indeed, unconstitutional, by a vote of 6 to 3.

If the question is framed in terms of the state's creating a special school district for a religious group, in effect "religiously gerrymandering" a district (Levy 1994: 252), then the action is clearly unconstitutional. However, if the question is seen as one of whether a state may create a school district whose boundaries happen to coincide with those of a particular village, in order to most effectively teach the learning-disabled children of that village (who happen to be Satmar), then the school district looks more like an accommodation of a minority religion, particularly since cultural isolation is itself a major tenet of Satmar belief. The outcome of the case will turn largely on whether it is viewed through the lens of establishment or free exercise.

Summary and Conclusion

The overall question that has guided this chapter is: Under what circumstances are people free to practice and live according to their religion, and under what circumstances can government prevent them from doing so? This issue has been the subject of considerable judicial and legislative wrangling for well over a century.

In the late nineteenth century, the *Reynolds* case led to a distinction between religious belief and action based on that belief. Beliefs are beyond the reach of any government intervention, but religiously motivated actions are potentially subject to state control. The "secular regulation rule" meant that a government action that serves a valid secular purpose is constitutional even if it burdens the free exercise of religion.

In the early and mid-twentieth century, many free exercise disputes surrounded religion and refusal to participate in war. The definition of "conscientious objection" was gradually broadened (and the impact of the secular regulation rule lessened) until it ultimately became a matter of freedom of conscience rather than freedom of religion per se.

Much of the case law on the free exercise clause developed in response to the claims of Jehovah's Witnesses. Both their refusal to salute the flag and their door-to-door evangelistic activities forced the Court to consider the meaning and application of the First Amendment guarantees. Court decisions in these cases have expanded freedom of religious practice, not only for the Witnesses but for members of all religious groups.

Religious issues in the workplace, including the "blue laws" that restrict Sunday business hours and Sabbatarians who refuse to work on Saturday, ultimately gave rise to the important "compelling interest" test. With this test, the Court held that a valid secular regulation that burdens free exercise is unconstitutional unless the government has a compelling interest in the regulation, strong enough to justify the free exercise burden (*Sherbert*, 1963). This test became the standard until it was set aside in *Smith* in 1990.

Unlike the situation with respect to the establishment clause, legislation, as well as jurisprudence, has played and continues to play a significant role in the development of free exercise law. This is apparent in the special case of Native American religious freedom, and one outcome of the *Smith* case was the passage of the Religious Freedom Restoration Act in 1993.

Finally, this chapter examined the tension between the two religious liberty clauses themselves. Compliance with the apparent requirements of one clause may lead to violation of the other. While some scholars see this as a dynamic balance that should be maintained, others see it as a problem to be resolved.

What conclusions can be drawn from all of this? The answer to the chapter's central question is far from clear; indeed, it cannot truly have a final, definitive answer. Religious liberty jurisprudence and legislation arise out of changing circumstances and, therefore, will themselves continue to evolve.

The same question that was raised in the *Sherbert* case—whether allowing for Sherbert's free exercise violated the establishment clause—was raised repeatedly about the Religious Freedom Restoration Act. Legislative bids to enhance the role of religion in public life and to extend protections for conscience rights are held by their supporters to be necessary guarantees of religious freedom. Their opponents, however, charge that they amount to an establishment of religion. As discussed in Part I, the issue of the role of religion in public life has been a part of American national discourse since before the nation was founded. It is a controversy that will be a lively part of the American political scene for the foreseeable future.

The growth of individual religious liberty is part of a larger expansion of individualism that began, as discussed in Chapter 4, in the decade of the 1960s. The nation's increased religious diversity, along with the growth of both evangelicalism and secularism, have only made these pressures more acute. All in all, the courts, like the American people as a whole, are committed in principle to non-establishment, to equal treatment under the law, and to the right to live according to the tenets of one's faith. When these principles conflict with one another, well-intentioned people differ on how to balance the competing goals. As Chapter 7 will show, this is just as true among ordinary citizens as it is among Supreme Court justices.

Part III

Religion and
Public Opinion

7 Public Opinion about Religion and Politics

Should the separation of church and state be absolute?
41% Yes   34% No   25% Not Sure
                    (*The Economist*/YouGov poll of American adults, March 2012)

The previous chapters have examined the positions of the courts and legal elites on the difficult issues involving religion in American public life. Where, however, do ordinary Americans come down on these questions? The division reflected in the survey results above, along with the high degree of uncertainty expressed, is a preview of the ambivalence that characterizes public attitudes about church–state relations and the proper role of religion in politics. The two preceding chapters documented the considerable inconsistency in the Supreme Court's interpretations of appropriate connections between church and state over time. As this chapter will show, the American public also holds a mix of ambiguous and sometimes contradictory views about the proper role for religion in public life. Here, we will examine public attitudes relevant to the establishment and free exercise clauses of the First Amendment. We will also explore the views on such questions of various elites in American society, both secular and religious. The analysis in this chapter will be guided by several key questions:

- What are the public's views on general, abstract principles concerning religious establishment and free exercise issues? For example, do people support the principle of complete separation of church and state, or do they believe that government should aid religion in some way?
- What are the public's views on more specific, concrete situations involving religious establishment and free exercise issues? For example, should the government provide financial aid to religious schools? Do religious groups have a right to get involved in the political process? Where does the public stand concerning religious freedom for the non-religious?
- In what ways can establishment issues and religious free exercise issues become intertwined in popular attitudes? For example, is school prayer seen by some as an establishment issue and by others as a free exercise issue? What about religious exemptions from the "Obamacare" contraception

coverage mandate? Should they be prohibited on non-establishment grounds, or required on free exercise grounds?

- What kinds of views do people hold in the specific area of religion in the public schools? If there is a widespread belief that the schools are too secularized, why have legal and constitutional efforts to address this failed?
- What kinds of views do political and religious elites in the United States hold toward religion and politics and the proper mix of the two?

The Public's Abstract Views on Church–State Relations

Very few public opinion surveys ask people, simply and directly, whether they favor or oppose the separation of church and state. When they do, they typically find widespread support for the general principle. Almost all Americans believe in some version of church–state separation; virtually none would support the idea of a single, official, governmentally administered church. Where ordinary Americans (just like Supreme Court justices) differ significantly, however, is on what, if anything, "separation of church and state" should imply beyond that. As data in this chapter will show, strong majorities typically favor government-sanctioned expressions of religion, at the same time that they endorse church–state separation as an ideal.

By far the most extensive extant research on American attitudes toward church–state relations is embodied in a series of surveys commissioned by the Williamsburg Charter Foundation in 1987. The Williamsburg Charter Foundation study (reported and described extensively in Wilcox et al. 1992, Wilcox 1993, and Jelen and Wilcox 1995) includes a mass public sample of 1,889 adults and an elite sample of 863 leaders in various areas of national life. Some of the elites are drawn from secular groups: 155 academics, 202 business leaders, 106 government leaders, and 100 members of the national media. Others are religious officials: 101 Protestant ministers, 100 Catholic priests, and 99 Jewish rabbis. The most comprehensive report of results from these surveys is Ted Jelen and Clyde Wilcox's *Public Attitudes Toward Church and State* (1995), which supplements the Williamsburg Charter data with in-depth interviews and focus groups. These sources, while they are not as recent as we would ideally like, remain the definitive treatments of American public opinion on the role of religion in public life. Moreover, the more recent survey data that do exist (and on which we report in this chapter) tend to confirm the enduring validity of the patterns found in the Williamsburg Charter Foundation surveys. Thus, the discussion to follow relies extensively on those data, and on Jelen and Wilcox's (1995) analysis of them.

The Public's Abstract Attitudes Toward Religious Establishment

The Williamsburg Charter surveys contain two abstract, general questions concerning religious establishment. These two questions and the percentages of respondents selecting each option are as follows:

Which of these statements comes closest to your opinion?

46% "The government should not provide any support to any religions."
54% "The government should support all religions equally."

Which of these statements comes closest to your opinion?

38% "The government should take special steps to protect the Judeo-Christian heritage."
62% "There should be a high wall of separation between church and state."

Each of these two questions articulates a *separationist* position (seeking to minimize any government involvement with religion) and an *accommodationist* one (supporting a non-denominational government endorsement of religion in public life). When responses to the two questions are combined, one can place respondents into one of four possible groups (Wilcox et al. 1992; Jelen and Wilcox 1995).

- The *separationists* are the 36 percent who took the separationist view on both questions—that government should provide no support for religion and that there should be a high wall of separation between church and state.
- The *accommodationists* are the 33 percent who took the accommodationist view on both questions—that government should help all religions equally while also protecting the nation's Judeo-Christian heritage.
- The *non-preferentialists* are the 21 percent who took the view that the government should help all religions equally while rejecting special protections for the Judeo-Christian heritage.
- The *Christian preferentialists* are the 9 percent who said that the government should not support religion generally but should take special steps to protect America's Judeo-Christian heritage.

There are, to be sure, some potential inconsistencies in these positions. How can one say, for example, that the government should not provide any support for religion, yet also believe that it should take special steps to protect the nation's Judeo-Christian heritage? Similarly, it seems at first blush contradictory to argue that government can truly help all religions *equally* if it is singling out Judaism and Christianity for special recognition. There are, however, several possibilities that could explain these apparent inconsistencies. First, the questions themselves present limited, binary choices. For example, the first question requires the respondent to choose between no government help for religion and the government helping all religions equally. This question does not allow for other possibilities, such as the person who wants the government to help some religions but not others (limiting support, perhaps, to those within the broad Judeo-Christian tradition, or excluding potentially objectionable "fringe" beliefs such as paganism, scientology, or Satanism). Second, some people are simply inconsistent in their attitudes, perhaps because they have some ambivalence on the issue and responded to the questions separately without thinking about the implications that one answer has for another. Most of us have at least some degree of ambivalence and inconsistency in our political and religious views, and this is frequently reflected in our survey responses (Zaller 1992). Third, Jelen and Wilcox (1995) suggest that some respondents might interpret the word "support" in the first question in terms of *financial* subsidies, which they might oppose while still favoring other forms of state recognition for religious belief. Finally, some respondents may simply be expressing "non-attitudes," a phenomenon where people have no real opinion on the question but answer nonetheless—essentially at random—so as to avoid appearing uninformed (Asher 2010).

Thus, in terms of abstract principles regarding the religious establishment issue, there is substantial ambiguity and inconsistency in public attitudes. Clearly, nothing approaching a national consensus exists.

The Public's Abstract Attitudes Toward Religious Free Exercise

The Williamsburg Charter survey does not include questions dealing with abstract principles regarding the free exercise of religion. However, other treatments of the question suggest that support for that general notion in America is virtually unanimous. What philosopher Robert Audi terms "the libertarian principle"—that people should generally be able to practice whatever religion they choose without governmental persecution or interference—is essentially uncontroversial in this country (Audi and Wolterstorff 1997). Moreover, Jelen and Wilcox (1995) did include two abstract free exercise questions in a survey that they did of Washington residents. The first question asked whether "people have the right to practice their religion as they see fit, even if their practices seem strange to most Americans." Since support for free exercise in this context was almost universal (96 percent), we can safely assume that a national sample would likewise have reflected very strong majority support for such a broad articulation of religious freedom.

Of course, as Audi and others recognize, there are *some* limits to this public support for religious free exercise. Jelen and Wilcox's second question asked whether "it is important for people to obey the law, even if it means limiting their religious freedom." Only 21 percent of respondents disagreed. We can thus speculate that a substantial majority of the American public would agree with the idea that respect for basic principles of law trumps religious freedom— respect for religious free exercise does not extend to human sacrifice or, as discussed in Chapter 3, to polygamy. However, in the abstract at least, the American understanding of and commitment to religious free exercise seems much more consensual and broadly shared than the approach to establishment questions.

The Public's Concrete Views on Church–State Relations

The American public's general attitudes toward church–state issues seem relatively clear from the data reported above: very broad support for the principle of religious free exercise, combined with seemingly paradoxical majority endorsement of both a "wall of separation" *and* general government support for religion. An examination of abstract endorsements, however, only takes us so far. A great many people who agreed in theory that "all men are created equal" nonetheless owned slaves (including the author of those very words); moreover, classic work in political science shows significant disparities between support for general constitutional and democratic ideals and willingness to implement those principles in specific, practical situations (Prothro and Grigg 1960; McClosky 1964). Thus, to really understand the American public's approach to the role of religion in public life, one must examine how they balance their support for religious free exercise, church–state separation, and religious accommodation in tangible, real-world situations.

Establishment Issues

While 62 percent of the respondents in the Williamsburg Charter survey said that they supported a "wall of separation between church and state," surveys also consistently show that majorities take an accommodationist position on many specific, concrete issues such as public religious displays and prayer in schools. Various studies (e.g., Green and Guth 1989; Servin-Gonzalez and Torres-Reyna 1999; Wilcox et al. 2002; Jelen 2009) show that most Americans favor an accommodationist approach in a wide range of areas. While this is especially true among conservative Christians, a generally accommodationist stance often extends even to those who are not particularly devout (Jelen and Wilcox 1995). Thus, while many Americans are attracted by the metaphor of a "wall of separation," they apparently want that wall to be relatively low and fairly porous.

The Williamsburg Charter survey contains a number of questions about specific, concrete matters related to religious establishment. Analysis by Wilcox (1993) and Jelen and Wilcox (1995) shows that respondents' attitudes on church–state relations—as indicated by their answers to thirteen specific questions—cluster into three attitude dimensions:

- public displays of Judeo-Christian religious symbols (e.g., manger scenes and menorahs during the holidays);
- religious activity in the public schools (e.g., school prayer and support for religious student groups); and
- using tax dollars to support religion (e.g., tax exemptions for churches and vouchers for religious schools).

Generally speaking, there is strong support in the Williamsburg Charter survey data for accommodationist positions. For example, 93 percent of respondents support the government's paying for military chaplains, 86 percent approve of city governments putting up manger scenes at Christmas, and 72 percent support Congress beginning its sessions with a public prayer.

On the other hand, there does appear to be significant separationist sentiment on at least a few issues. A clear majority of respondents reject a government requirement that Judeo-Christian values be emphasized in public schools, and the sample is closely divided on whether church property should be taxed and on whether the government should provide financial assistance to religious schools (with a small majority taking the separationist position on both of these questions).

Clearly, a large majority of the public supports church–state accommodation in many concrete situations—especially when the state support of religion in question is primarily symbolic. At the same time, however, most Americans do appear to reject accommodation under some circumstances. Such rejection is most likely to occur when the issue in question involves substantial financial support for religious institutions, when religious observance would be required as opposed to simply permitted, and/or when accommodation clearly favors one religious group over another.

While these results are illuminating, they come with the caveat that they are based on data from the late 1980s. Since that time, American society has become somewhat more religiously diverse, with a growth in religions outside the Judeo-Christian tradition and an increase in those who report no specific religious identification. It is possible that these trends may have contributed to an increase in separationist sentiment among the American public.

More recent data, however, suggest that this is not the case. While no survey as comprehensive as the Williamsburg Charter study has been done since that time, a series of church–state questions appearing in a variety of surveys over the last ten years provides some insight into contemporary attitudes. A sampling of such items is presented in Table 7.1.

The items reported in Table 7.1 indicate continued widespread public endorsement of broadly non-denominational government support for religion. A 2010 Gallup poll, for example, found that only 5 percent of Americans opposed the idea of a congressionally designated National Day of Prayer (though another 38 percent were indifferent). In the 2004 and 2005 State of the First Amendment Surveys commissioned by the First Amendment Center at Vanderbilt University, large majorities ranging from 61 percent to 77 percent supported posting of the Ten Commandments in government buildings, vouchers usable at faith-based schools, public school distribution of informational materials about religious youth programs, and government partnerships with churches in anti-drug efforts. Clearly, the weight of American public opinion remains on the side of broad religious accommodation as opposed to strict separation.

It is important to note that support for religious accommodation in many of these concrete situations is relatively high even among people who are not especially religious themselves, and/or who take separationist positions in the

Table 7.1 Public Attitudes Toward Religious Accommodation

Questions and Responses

As you may know, Congress in 1952 designated a National Day of Prayer . . . Do you favor or oppose having a National Day of Prayer, or doesn't it matter to you either way? (May 2010 Gallup Survey)

    Favor: 57%   Oppose: 5%   Doesn't Matter: 38%

Please tell me whether you agree or disagree with the following statement: Government officials should be allowed to post the Ten Commandments inside government buildings. (2005 State of the First Amendment Survey)

    Strongly/Mildly Agree: 70%   Strongly/Mildly Disagree: 29%

As you may know, public schools send home information with students periodically from various community groups. Please tell me whether you agree or disagree with the following: Schools should be allowed to send home information about youth programs sponsored by religious groups. (2005 State of the First Amendment Survey)

    Strongly/Mildly Agree: 77%   Strongly/Mildly Disagree: 21%

Please tell me whether you agree or disagree with the following statement: Parents should have the option of sending their children to non-public schools, including those with a religious affiliation, using vouchers or credits provided by the government that would pay for some or all of the costs. (2004 State of the First Amendment Survey)

    Strongly/Mildly Agree: 61%   Strongly/Mildly Disagree: 35%

Do you favor or oppose allowing the government to give money to religious institutions or churches to help them run drug-abuse prevention programs, even if the religious institutions would be allowed to include a religious message as part of their program? (2004 State of the First Amendment Survey)

    Strongly/Mildly Favor: 66%   Strongly/Mildly Oppose: 31%

Sources: www.gallup.com/poll/127721/few-americans-oppose-national-day-prayer.aspx; www.thearda.com/Archive/Files/Descriptions/SOFA04.asp; www.thearda.com/Archive/Files/Descriptions/SOFA05.asp.

abstract. Recall that, in the Williamsburg Charter survey, 36 percent of respondents (the plurality) were classified as separationists based on their answers to abstract questions; these are people who responded that government should provide no support for religion and that there should be a high wall of separation between church and state. Among this group, however, 92 percent did not object to the government paying for military chaplains, 81 percent did not object to a nativity scene on city property at Christmas, and 81 percent did not object to the after-school use of public school classrooms by student religious groups. It would certainly appear that the "high wall" envisioned by these separationists is relatively permeable.

Thus, on many concrete establishment issues, a majority of abstract separationists take an accommodationist position. What accounts for this discrepancy? The inconsistency might be due to the same types of factors discussed earlier (respondents simply don't think of the issues together, there are limitations on available response alternatives, etc.). However, Jelen and Wilcox (1995) also point out that in many cases, the survey respondents might be interpreting the situations as ones involving the free exercise of religion rather than as establishment issues. Thus, the mix of public attitudes may reflect the tension between the free exercise and establishment clauses discussed in Chapter 6.

Accommodationists—those who took the accommodationist position on both abstract issues—are also not completely consistent when it comes to concrete situations. Significant numbers of abstract accommodationists took the separationist position on some of the concrete issues. Among the accommodationists, for example, 45 percent rejected the idea that the government should require teaching of Judeo-Christian values in public schools, and 48 percent would tax all church property. Oddly enough, on the question concerning use of school classrooms by student religious groups, there were slightly more accommodationists (21 percent) than separationists (19 percent) who objected (though the difference falls short of statistical significance).

While such results imply inconsistencies in people's approach to establishment issues, they also highlight the difficulty of capturing complex, nuanced social attitudes with simple survey questions. The focus groups used by Jelen and Wilcox (1995) help to provide more insight. The discussions in these focus groups indicated that many people took the accommodationist position on concrete establishment issues (such as prayer in public schools) because they saw them as consensual government accommodations of religion that would not be objectionable to people outside the religious majority. Jelen (2005) reports that support for religious accommodation in specific circumstances is highly sensitive to perceptions of whether the practice in question would be offensive to "reasonable" members of minority religious traditions. Thus, at least some of the inconsistency between people's abstract and concrete establishment views is rooted in judgments about which specific accommodations are understandably objectionable to those outside the religious majority.

Free Exercise Issues

While scholars generally discuss establishment issues using a separationist/accommodationist axis, Reichley (2002) argues that a communitarian/libertarian distinction is more useful for understanding views about religious free exercise. Both views would allow people to hold whatever religious beliefs they wish, but communitarians and libertarians differ in terms of the scope of behavior that they would allow on the basis of these religious beliefs.

- The communitarian view would permit people to act on the basis of their religious beliefs so long as the behavior in question does not offend the majority's moral or cultural sensibilities. It is acceptable, in this view, for public policy to limit the behavior of religious minorities whose unconventional practices run counter to community norms (e.g. animal sacrifice in Santeria, drug use in some Native American religions, etc.).

• The libertarian view would permit a much broader range of behavior based on religious beliefs. Essentially, unless a religious practice violated fundamental human rights (e.g. human sacrifice), it should be permitted, even if it is distasteful or reflects a worldview out of step with community norms.

Levels of Support for Religious Free Exercise

The Williamsburg Charter study, in addition to a few more recent surveys, contains questions tapping support for religious free exercise. A sampling of these is reported in Table 7.2. Based on these results (and on others not included here), one can discern two distinct levels of support for religious free exercise.

Table 7.2 Public Support for Religious Freedom

Questions and Responses
Would you strongly favor, favor, oppose, or strongly oppose allowing Muslims in New York to build an Islamic community center and mosque two blocks from the site of the World Trade Center? (2010 Religion News Survey)   Strongly Favor/Favor: 31%   Strongly Oppose/Oppose: 57%
Should religiously affiliated institutions that object to the use of contraceptives be given an exemption from this rule [requiring them to subsidize insurance that covers contraceptives], or should they be required to cover contraceptives like other employers? (2012 Pew Survey)   Should Be Exempt: 48%   Should Have to Cover: 44%
Do you mostly agree or mostly disagree with the following statement: It should be against the law for preachers to use television to raise money? (1987 Williamsburg Charter Survey)   Agree: 34%   Disagree: 56%
Do you mostly agree or mostly disagree with the following statement: There should be laws to prevent groups such as Hare Krishna from asking people for money at airports? (1987 Williamsburg Charter Survey)   Agree: 49%   Disagree: 41%
Do you mostly agree or mostly disagree with the following statement: There should be laws against the practice of Satan Worship? (1987 Williamsburg Charter Survey)   Agree: 47%   Disagree: 42%
Do you mostly agree or mostly disagree with the following statement: The FBI should keep a close watch on new religious cults? (1987 Williamsburg Charter Survey)   Agree: 49%   Disagree: 41%

Sources: www.thearda.com/Archive/Files/Descriptions/PRRIRNSA.asp;
www.people-press.org/2012/02/14/public-divided-over-birth-control-insurance-mandate/2/;
www.thearda.com/Archive/Files/Descriptions/WMSBURG.asp.

First, in some situations a strong majority clearly supports the free exercise of religion. When respondents are asked about the right of religious people and leaders to get involved in politics, or about whether there is "a place in America" for Islam, most (though not all) respond in ways consistent with religious freedom. Thus, there does seem to be support for the general idea that people ought to be able to practice their faith in America, and that they ought to be free to bring their faith-based convictions to bear in the political process.

In more specific instances, however, when they are confronted with controversial actions or objectionable "fringe" groups, Americans' support for religious freedom begins to wane. For example, fewer than one third in a 2010 Religion News survey supported the right of Muslims to build an Islamic center in the vicinity of the World Trade Center site. Likewise, Americans in a 2012 Pew survey were sharply divided on whether religious groups that object to artificial contraception should nevertheless be required to subsidize it for their employees. Finally, pluralities in the Williamsburg Charter survey supported various forms of government surveillance and/or regulation of Hare Krishnas, Satanists, and members of "new religious cults."

While it is impossible to make a single generalization about all of the circumstances in which support for religious free exercise is low, it is apparent that many involve groups widely considered to be harmful. Jelen and Wilcox (1995) suggest that the public supports free exercise for those groups it does not consider dangerous, but is much more skeptical about the rights of groups that it deems potentially harmful. In addition, it is clear from the survey results reported in Table 7.2 that many Americans are willing to restrict the rights even of larger, more established religions if they deem the actions or stances of those groups somehow "inappropriate." For example, while most Americans believe that there is "a place in America" for Islam, that place is apparently not in the general vicinity of "Ground Zero." Likewise, many Americans appear willing to subordinate the conscience rights of Catholic employers to their conviction that contraception is morally unproblematic. In this view, Jelen and Wilcox argue, religious freedom is regarded in terms of its instrumental value in increasing social cohesion and general content- ment; if the religious freedom of certain groups promotes, by contrast, discord and controversy, then it is not especially worthy of protection.

The point here is not to suggest that one cannot make a reasonable case against the "Ground Zero Mosque," or for the Obamacare contraception mandate, or for suspicion of cultists and Satanists. All of these stances, however, require something closer to the limited, communitarian view of religious free exercise than to the more absolutist libertarian one. On this overarching question, the American public would appear to be deeply divided.

Attitudes Toward the Rights of the Non-religious

To this point, we have focused on public support for the rights of those whose religious views are outside the mainstream. What about those, however, with no religious faith at all? While clearly a minority of the American population, they are not a trivial one, and their ranks have grown somewhat in recent years. Table 7.3 reports results from several recent survey questions, three of which concern a hypothetical person who is against all churches and religion. While there was little support for the rights of such people in the 1950s (Stouffer 1955), these results show that tolerance for those who hold anti-religious views has increased dramatically. For example, as of 2012, only 22 percent of Americans would not allow such a person to give a speech in their community, and only 24 percent would favor removing his or her book from the public library. While people express somewhat more reservations about allowing such a person to teach, about two thirds would still support his or her right to do so.

On the question of whether a politician who did not believe in God would be fit for the presidency, there is considerably more division. In 2012, however, a small majority (54 percent) of those responding to a Gallup survey indicated that they would be willing to support a well-qualified nominee of their party if he or she were an atheist. While these results indicate that professed atheism would still be a major liability for a presidential candidate, the 2012 survey marked the first time that a majority of respondents indicated a willingness to consider voting for a non-believer (in the 1987 Williamsburg Charter survey, by comparison, the figure was 33 percent). Overall, these results suggest a higher level of acceptance for atheists than one might have expected in a generally religious society.

Table 7.3 Public Attitudes Toward the Rights of the Non-Religious

Questions and Responses
There are always some people whose ideas are considered bad or dangerous by other people. For instance, somebody who is against all churches and religion. If such a person wanted to make a speech in your community against churches and religion, should he be allowed to speak, or not? (2012 NORC GSS) 　　　Yes: 78%　　　　　　　　　　No: 22%
Should such a person be allowed to teach in a college or university, or not? (2012 NORC GSS) 　　　Yes: 65%　　　　　　　　　　No: 35%
If some people in your community suggested that a book he wrote against churches and religion should be taken out of your public library, would you favor removing this book, or not? (2012 NORC GSS) 　　　No: 76%　　　　　　　　　　Yes: 24%
If your party nominated a generally well-qualified person for president who happened to be an atheist, would you vote for that person? (June 2012 Gallup Survey) 　　　Yes: 54%　　　　　　　　　　No: 43%

Source: www.gallup.com/poll/155285/Atheists-Muslims-Bias-Presidential-Candidates.aspx.

Free Exercise Views and Establishment Views

While free exercise and religious establishment are clearly separate concepts, they are often intertwined in practice. On many issues of religion in public life, a person's response might depend largely on whether he or she tends to see the question principally through the lens of free exercise or the lens of establishment. Some would argue, for example, that to allow a public high school valedictorian to give a graduation speech about her faith in Jesus would verge too close to establishment, while others would argue that not to do so would infringe on her rights to free exercise (not to mention free speech).

In order to understand the complex interactions of Americans' views about religious establishment and free exercise, Jelen and Wilcox (1995) propose a fourfold typology produced by interacting the two primary positions on establishment issues (separation versus accommodation) with the two primary stances on free exercise questions (communitarian versus libertarian). Respondents in their Washington, DC sample divided fairly evenly into the resultant four groups: religious non-preferentialists, Christian preferentialists, religious minimalists, and religious free-marketeers.

Religious Non-preferentialists

Religious non-preferentialists are those who are both accommodationist and libertarian. They "favor allowing religion a place in the public square and favor allowing all religious groups to participate" (Jelen and Wilcox 1995: 150). They supported religious free exercise for groups both inside and outside the broad Judeo-Christian tradition—including such practices as Hare Krishnas soliciting money at airports, conscientious objection to military service, the refusal of children to pledge allegiance to the flag if such a practice violates their religious beliefs, and Christian Scientists withholding medical treatment from their children. This group also gave strong support to the abstract right to freely practice religion.

Religious non-preferentialists also gave broad support to religious accommodation. For example, they supported public displays of religious symbols, funding for military chaplains, and allowing student religious organizations to use public school property for meetings.

In terms of religious composition, this group consisted primarily of well-educated white Catholics and liberal black Protestants. Thus, Jelen and Wilcox (1995: 151) note that the "group of respondents who most clearly regarded religious accommodation as a component of religious free exercise were not evangelical Protestants but rather those who have been the historical victims of discrimination."

Christian Preferentialists

Christian preferentialists are those who are accommodationist but communitarian. Thus, they strongly favor a prominent role for religion in public life, but prefer that the public recognition of religion be confined to mainstream Judeo-Christian practices. In the Jelen and Wilcox study, they supported government help for religion, government protection of the Judeo-Christian heritage, school prayer, requiring that schools teach biblical values and creationism, and public displays of religious symbols. However, they opposed non-mainstream religious practices such as conscientious objection to military service, allowing children not to pledge allegiance to the flag, allowing Native Americans to use peyote in religious ceremonies, and civil disobedience based on religious values. They also tended to believe that non-Christian immigrants should convert to Christianity.

This group consisted primarily of conservative Protestants (both white and black) who held orthodox religious views, said they were "born again," and favored literalist readings of the Bible. Members of this group appear to believe that religious accommodation and free exercise are important values, but should be understood within the context of the nation's predominant and valuable Judeo-Christian religious heritage.

Religious Minimalists

Religious minimalists are both separationist and communitarian. They are strong proponents of non-establishment, and are skeptical of public free exercise by all kinds of religious groups. For example, they opposed allowing student religious groups to use school property for meetings. They also opposed fundamentalist ministers preaching on college campuses, Jews missing work on Jewish holidays, cults recruiting teenage members, and Hare Krishnas soliciting money at airports (Jelen and Wilcox 1995).

One might expect this group to be overwhelmingly secular, but that is not really the case. In fact, religious minimalists ranked second among the four groups in terms of frequency of attendance at religious services, in orthodox religious identification, and in belief that the Bible is literally true (Jelen and Wilcox 1995). They were also somewhat more likely than those in other groups to be Baptist and Pentecostal. Many in this group apparently believe that Christians should keep their distance from the sinfulness of the secular world (Jelen 1987), and that the mixing of church and state will have a corrupting influence on religion. Thus, in the tradition of Roger Williams, strong opposition to mixing church and state can come from people who are themselves very religious.

Religious Free-Marketeers

Religious free-marketeers believe in strict separation of church and state, but they are very supportive of religious free exercise when it does not appear to them to verge on establishment—in other words, they are separationist libertarians. This group would allow all kinds of sects to compete freely and openly for adherents. Their abstract separationist views are indicated by their opposition to government aid to religion, their opposition to government support for the Judeo-Christian heritage, and their support for a high wall of separation between church and state (Jelen and Wilcox 1995). Their concrete separationist views are reflected in their opposition to public displays of religious symbols, funding for military chaplains, teaching creationism in public schools, and public school prayer. Their support for religious free exercise, however, is reflected in their support for allowing Native Americans to use peyote in religious ceremonies, their support for allowing fundamentalist ministers to preach on college campuses, and their opposition to laws against cults and Satanism.

Jelen and Wilcox (1995) describe this group as generally well educated, disproportionately Jewish, and quite secular. They report low church attendance and low doctrinal orthodoxy. While some have suggested that secular Americans are hostile to religion, the results here tell a more complicated story. Religious free-marketeers, a relatively secular group, are very supportive of religious free exercise in situations that do not seem to impinge on strict church–state separation. This secular group extends its support for religious free exercise to conservative Christians as well. Thus, a bit of an irony is apparent in the data. The generally secular religious free-marketeers are quite supportive of religious free exercise (at least as they define it), whereas the relatively devout religious minimalists are much less supportive of public religious expression. Based on their analysis of these attitudes, Jelen and Wilcox (1995: 154) argue that we must "reject firmly the hypothesis that people who seek to minimize the public role of religion are either irreligious or antireligious and that those who are secular are hostile to religion." In reality, the relationship between personal religious devotion and attitudes toward religion in public life is more complicated and nuanced than one might expect.

A Case in Point: Public Attitudes on Religion in Public Schools

In no area of American life do the competing claims of non-establishment and free exercise clash more frequently than in the public schools. For most Americans, questions about Ten Commandments monuments, military chaplains, and the like are basically abstractions; such issues are unlikely to touch their own families in any meaningful way. The public schools, however, are a basic and ubiquitous institution of American society, in which 90 percent of the nation's children spend an enormous portion of their formative years. Thus, people are especially interested that their views of God, society, and the state be reflected, or at least respected, in the educational establishment.

Public opinion surveys ask people about religion in the public schools more frequently than they do about any other establishment or free exercise issues (though still less often than students of public attitudes toward religion and the state might like). A selection of responses to such questions in recent surveys is reported in Table 7.4. Unambiguously, these studies reveal a strong public disposition toward accommodation, rather than separation, in American education. In 2012, a majority of 59 percent disapproved of the Supreme Court's decision banning recitation of the Lord's Prayer and the reading of Bible verses in public schools—a figure that has remained stable for decades. In addition, in 2005 surveys, 76 percent of respondents expressed support for a constitutional amendment to allow voluntary school prayer, while 56 percent supported equal curricular treatment for biblical creationism and Darwinian evolution. Finally, when asked in general terms, 60 percent of respondents expressed the view that there is too little religious presence in public schools, while only 11 percent believed that there is too much. Clearly, most Americans feel that the public schools have moved further in the direction of secularism than they would like. Moreover, this sentiment is apparently shared by many who are not especially devout themselves; since only about 30–40 percent of Americans are regular churchgoers, the accommodationist majorities reflected in Table 7.4 necessarily include large numbers of people who are personally less observant.

While there is no doubt that the public would generally like to see a greater space for religion in public education, there are important limits to this desire.

Table 7.4 Public Attitudes Toward Religion in the Classroom

Questions and Responses
The United States Supreme Court has ruled that no state or local government may require the reading of the Lord's Prayer or Bible verses in public schools. What are your views on this—do you approve or disapprove of the court ruling? (2012 NORC GSS) Disapprove: 59%   Approve: 41%
Please tell me whether you favor or oppose a constitutional amendment to allow voluntary prayer in public schools. (August 2005 Gallup Survey) Favor: 76%   Oppose: 23%
If you had a choice, which would you prefer in the local public schools: spoken prayer, or a moment of silence for contemplation or silent prayer? (August 2005 Gallup Survey) Spoken Prayer: 23%   Silent Prayer: 69%   Both/Neither: 8%
Do you favor or oppose teaching the biblical story of creation alongside the theory of evolution in public schools—as equally valid explanations for the origins of human life? (2005 Anti-Defamation League Survey) Favor: 56%   Oppose: 39%
Thinking about the presence that religion currently has in public schools in this country, do you think religion has too much of a presence in public schools, about the right amount, or too little of a presence in public schools? (August 2005 Gallup Survey) Too Little: 60%   Right Amount: 27%   Too Much: 11%

Sources: www.gallup.com/poll/18136/Public-Favors-Voluntary-Prayer-Public-Schools.aspx; http://archive.adl.org/religious_freedom/poll_files/frame.htm.

Very few Americans are interested in a *coercive* religious presence in the schools. This is reflected in the fact that, as reported in Table 7.4, 69 percent of respondents would prefer that school prayer be silent rather than spoken, presumably to allow for varied forms of religious expression among the students. Moreover, surveys and (especially) focus groups frequently show that Americans broadly support the rights of non-Christian children to opt out of any religious exercises, and that support for school prayer declines in the hypothetical case where a significant portion of the class is offended or objects (Jelen 2005).

Opponents of school prayer and other religious accommodations in public education generally base their arguments on the establishment clause of the First Amendment, and view school prayer as an imposition on the religious freedom of those whose religious (or non-religious) views run counter to the particular beliefs expressed. The survey results presented here, however, clearly suggest that most Americans don't look at the issues this way. They tend to view religious expressions in the public schools in terms of exercising religious freedom rather than establishing or imposing any particular views on an unwilling audience. Most Americans, as surveys and focus groups consistently show, have a difficult time understanding why reasonable people would object to the sort of voluntary, non-sectarian religious exercises that they typically support (Jelen 2005).

If support for school prayer is so strong, and so many people favor a constitutional amendment to allow it, why has no such amendment ever been passed by Congress? Amending the Constitution requires a two-thirds vote of both the House and the Senate, and efforts on behalf of a school prayer amendment have always fallen short of this threshold in one or both houses. The reasons for this have more to do with elite views than with mass opinion, suggesting that elite attitudes on establishment and free exercise issues warrant examination.

Elite Views on Church and State

There are many kinds of elites in society—political elites, religious elites, business elites, social elites, media elites, and so on. It is harder to generalize about the attitudes of elites, however, than about the attitudes of the mass public, because there are many fewer systematic, representative studies of their preferences. It is well established, however, that elite cues are hugely influential in shaping public opinion (Zaller 1992), and that elites have disproportionate influence over law and policy. Thus, it makes sense to explore the insights that do exist into elite opinion on church–state issues in order to understand governmental stances in this area.

Beginning primarily with Samuel Stouffer's (1955) study of the general public and a sample of community leaders during the 1950s, research has shown that political elites and the mass public often differ significantly in their outlook on the world, in terms of both specific issues and broader values.

In general, political elites tend to support basic democratic principles more strongly and consistently than does the general public (Stouffer 1955; McClosky 1964; McClosky and Brill 1983). On this basis, one might expect that political elites would be more supportive of separation of church and state, and especially of religious free exercise, than the public at large. Thus, in terms of Jelen and Wilcox's typology, political elites might be found disproportionately in the religious free-marketeer (and, to a lesser extent, religious non-preferentialist) camps.

Much—if not all—of the difference between political elites and the general public stems simply from the fact that elites have higher levels of education. More educated individuals consistently show higher levels of support for both separation of church and state and for religious free exercise (Wilcox et al. 2002; Jelen 2005). On this basis, one might expect that other types of elites would also differ from the general public in the same ways that political elites do. On the other hand, religious elites, because of the specific nature of their training and calling, might differ from other kinds of elites on questions of religion in public life.

Elite Attitudes Toward Prayer in Public Schools

Table 7.4 demonstrated that a substantial majority of the American public favors prayer in public schools, and that over 70 percent support a constitutional amendment to bring it about. At the same time, however, as noted above, there has not been sufficient support (two thirds of each house) in Congress to send a school prayer amendment to the states for ratification. There are several reasons for this. First, many who favor such a constitutional amendment do not see it as a core voting issue, and some who initially favor a prayer amendment retreat from that position when asked whether this is an issue that merits changing the Constitution. Second, there are different ideas for how to bring prayer back into public schools, and it is difficult for supporters to agree on one particular proposal. Third, the demographic characteristics of those most likely to favor school prayer (racial minorities, those who did not graduate from college, and those with lower incomes) might blunt their ability to influence members of Congress. Finally, as we shall see, elites are far from unified in support of prayer in public schools.

Political Elites and School Prayer

Support for school prayer, while generally high, varies significantly among religious groups. For example, as reported in Table 7.4, the 2012 National Opinion Research Center General Social Survey (NORC GSS) asked people whether they approved or disapproved of the Supreme Court decision banning organized prayer and Bible reading in public schools. In a different question, people were asked their religious preference, allowing them to be grouped into "nones" (people with no professed religious affiliation), Jews, Catholics, mainline Protestants, and evangelical Protestants—a classification that will be elaborated more fully in Chapter 8. Disapproval of the Court's decision was expressed by:

- 31 percent of those who indicated no religion;
- 16 percent of Jews;
- 60 percent of Catholics;
- 62 percent of mainline Protestants;
- 82 percent of evangelical Protestants.

Overall, while 82 percent of evangelical Protestants objected to the prohibition on school prayer, only 52 percent of other respondents did. This divide is very relevant if political elites are less likely to be evangelical Protestants than the general public.

Table 7.5 shows the religious affiliations of U.S. senators and representatives of the 113th Congress that convened in 2013. The table is set up so that the largest group (Roman Catholics) is listed first, the second largest group is second, and so on. With 30 percent of the senators and representatives, Catholics are the largest religious group in Congress, but this is only a bit higher than the percentage of Catholics in the general population. Baptists (14 percent) are the second largest group, but they are actually under-represented in Congress, as about 20 percent of the American public is Baptist of one sort or another. Methodists constitute 8 percent of Congress, and this is close to their percentage of the overall population. Episcopalians, Presbyterians, and Jews are over-represented in Congress, relative to their share of the population. While 8 percent of Congress is Presbyterian, less than 5 percent of the public is; similarly, while 7 percent of Congress is Episcopalian, only 2 percent of the public is. Finally, Jews, who comprise only 2 percent of the U.S. population, make up 6 percent of Congress—including 10 of the 100 U.S. Senators.

In general, the religious composition of Congress is not drastically different from that of the general public, but the deviations that do exist are meaningful. Most notably, the group most likely to support school prayer—evangelical Protestants—is under-represented in Congress, while the group most likely to oppose it—Jews—is over-represented. This, in turn, means that baseline levels of support in Congress for school prayer are likely lower than in the general public.

In addition, some influential groups within political parties differ from the public consensus on school prayer. Big donors to political action committees (PACs) are much more closely divided on the school prayer issue than is the public at large, and very few of them outside of a handful of culturally conservative PACs see it as an important priority—a situation that dates back at least to the 1980s (Green and Guth 1989). Likewise, delegates, donors, and elites within the Democratic Party are much more strongly separationist on these sorts of questions than are rank-and-file Democrats (Layman 2001; Bolce and De Maio 2007), creating real pressure on Democratic legislators

Table 7.5 Religious Affiliations of U.S. Senators and Representatives, 113th Congress (2013)

Religious Affiliation	Senators	Represen- tatives	Total	Percentage (%)
Roman Catholic	27	136	163	30
Baptist	9	65	74	14
Protestant—Unspecified	9	58	67	13
Methodist	9	35	44	8
Presbyterian	16	27	43	8
Episcopalian	4	31	35	7
Jewish	10	22	32	6
Lutheran	5	17	22	4
Mormon	7	9	16	3
Unspecified/Unaffiliated	2	8	10	2
UCC/Congregationalist	1	4	5	1
Eastern Orthodox	0	5	5	1
Buddhist	1	2	3	1
African Methodist Episcopal	0	3	3	1
Christian Scientist	0	2	2	<1
Muslim	0	2	2	<1
Seventh-day Adventist	0	2	2	<1
Christian Reformed	0	1	1	<1
Hindu	0	1	1	<1
Moravian	0	1	1	<1
Pentecostal	0	1	1	<1
Quaker	0	1	1	<1

Source: CQ/Roll Call *Guide to the New Congress* (November 8, 2012), p. 16.

to "hold the line." All of these factors combine to make school prayer one of those quintessential moral issues on which both parties in Congress dig in their heels, and on which a move to the center of public opinion by the party in the minority is exceedingly unlikely (Oldmixon 2005).

Religious Elites and School Prayer

Clearly, members of Congress and other political elites do not match the general public's level of support for school prayer. This division among political elites on the question is also reflected in the views of religious elites. For example, while some religiously conservative Protestant leaders have supported a school prayer amendment, the National Council of Churches has opposed it. Such divisions, it turns out, are not uncommon. Studies of the political attitudes of American clergy have typically shown major variations by denomination on a wide range of political, social, and moral questions (Smidt 2004).

In a landmark study, Guth et al. (1997) surveyed almost 5,000 ministers from a range of traditions representing both mainline and evangelical

Protestantism. Their work revealed substantial theological and political divisions among the clergy. For a theological example, 97 percent of Assemblies of God ministers strongly agreed that Jesus is the only way to salvation, compared to only 22 percent of Disciples of Christ ministers. Politically, 58 percent of the Assemblies of God ministers were Republicans, compared to only 15 percent of the Disciples of Christ ministers. Other studies (Quinley 1974; Jelen 1993; Smidt 2004) have found similarly substantial differences among Protestant clergy.

Given both the theological and the political cleavages among the Protestant clergy, it is no surprise that there is no consensus among them on the question of school prayer. Ministers from some denominations (e.g., Assemblies of God and Southern Baptist Convention) were mostly in favor of school prayer, whereas those from others (e.g., Disciples of Christ and Presbyterian Church) were generally opposed (Guth et al. 1997).

Elite Views on Abstract Establishment Issues

The Williamsburg Charter Foundation study, in addition to surveying the mass public, also posed its questions about religion and public life to seven types of social elites. Four were secular: academic elites, business leaders, government officials, and media members. The other three were religious: Protestant ministers, Catholic priests, and Jewish rabbis. Recall that, in the study, two questions were used to measure abstract views on accommodation versus separation. In the first question, respondents selected either the "no help" position (the government should not provide any support to any religions) or the "help all" position (the government should support all religions equally). In the second question, respondents selected either the "protect" position (the government should take special steps to protect the Judeo-Christian heritage) or the "high wall" position (there should be a high wall of separation between church and state). These two items were then combined to form a typology ranging from the most separationist position (no help/high wall) to the most accommodationist position (help all/protect). To be sure, these questions do not capture the full range of possibly nuanced approaches to these questions (especially among elites), but they do provide good insight into generally accommodationist or separationist inclinations.

Based on data reported by Wilcox et al. (1992), Figure 7.1 presents the percentages of the public and each of the seven types of elites who took the most separationist abstract position (the government should not provide any support to religion and there should be a high wall of separation between church and state). While only 36 percent of the public took this separationist position, a majority of all secular elites were abstract separationists. Among academic elites, an overwhelming 86 percent took the separationist position. Approximately two-thirds of the other secular elites did likewise. Media elites were the least separationist (63 percent), although elite journalists remain much more secular than the general public (Covert and Wasburn 2009). Thus,

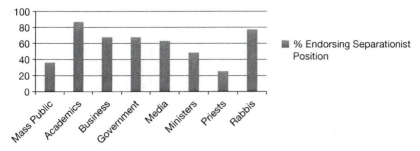

Figure 7.1 The Public and the Elites on Church–State Separation.
Source: Williamsburg Charter Survey, as presented in Wilcox et al. (1992: 271).

secular elites of all sorts are much more separationist in the abstract than is the general public.

Among the religious elites, there is considerably more variation. Jewish rabbis are strongly (77 percent) separationist, perhaps because they would expect that any religious accommodation would favor the culturally predominant Christian views. Approximately half (48 percent) of the Protestant ministers took the separationist position, and only 22 percent of them took the most accommodationist position (help all religions equally/protect the Judeo-Christian heritage). More revealingly, when Jelen and Wilcox (1995) separate Protestant ministers into mainline and evangelical groups, they find that a majority (60 percent) of mainline ministers take the most separationist position, as compared with only 37 percent of the evangelical ministers. Thus, we see again that there is deep division among Protestant ministers along denominational lines on issues of church–state relations.

Catholic priests are the only elite group that is more accommodationist than the general public. Only 25 percent of Catholic priests took the strong separationist position, whereas nearly half of them took the most accommodationist stance (help all religions equally/protect the Judeo-Christian heritage). In sum, among religious elites, Jewish rabbis overwhelmingly favor strict separation of church and state, Protestant ministers lean towards separationism but are sharply divided along denominational lines, and Catholic priests are more supportive of religious accommodation than any of the other elite groups, and even a bit more so than the public at large.

Elite Views on Concrete Establishment Issues

Recall that, in addition to the abstract items, the Williamsburg Charter Foundation surveys contained a number of questions that concerned more specific, concrete establishment issues (e.g., school prayer, allowing nativity scenes on public property at Christmas, etc.). Many in the general public who endorsed a "high wall of separation" in the abstract were nonetheless supportive of many specific accommodations of religion. As it turns out, the same pattern generally obtains with elites as well.

Among secular elites, academics were distinctively separationist, even on most concrete issues (Jelen and Wilcox 1995). They were more likely than the general public or any of the other elite groups (although Jewish rabbis were a close second) to support separationism in specific situations. For example, at least three out of four academics opposed each of the following: prayer in Congress, prayer at high school sports events, government funds for religious schools, a moment of silence in public schools, and the government requiring the teaching of Judeo-Christian values. These results are consistent with other studies finding an American professoriate dramatically more secular than the public at large, and than most other groups of social elites (Gross and Simmons 2009). On the other hand, even academics took accommodationist positions on a few of the concrete establishment issues—they favored, for example, government funding of military chaplains (both Christian and Buddhist), opposed taxing church property, and favored allowing student religious groups to use school property for meetings. Many academics likely saw these issues more as free exercise questions than as establishment ones.

Jelen and Wilcox (1995) show that the other secular elites (business, government, and media) were fairly similar in their approach to concrete establishment issues. A majority of these elites took the separationist position only on four issues; they were especially opposed to accommodationism in funding for religious schools and in the government requiring the teaching of Judeo-Christian values. Unlike the academics, a majority of business and government elites took the accommodationist position on nine of the thirteen concrete issues (or eight for the media elites). In sum, while these business, media, and government elites are much more supportive of separation of church and state in the abstract than the general public, they are not much more separationist than the public on these concrete establishment questions. Only academics maintain consistently and distinctively secularist stances.

Looking at religious elites, Jewish rabbis were very similar to the academics in their strong support for separation of church and state on most of the thirteen concrete establishment issues. They took the accommodationist position on only a few issues, such as favoring government funding for military chaplains (Christian and Buddhist) and opposing taxing church property (Jelen and Wilcox 1995). Interestingly, rabbis were more opposed than any other group, including academics, to the display of menorahs on public property during Hanukah, with 83 percent of them objecting to the practice. Clearly, elite Jewish opposition to public religious accommodation extends even to acknowledgments of their own faith.

By contrast, a majority of both Catholic priests and Protestant ministers expressed accommodationist sentiments on most concrete establishment issues. Catholic priests took the accommodationist position on all but one of the thirteen questions, and Protestant ministers did so on all but three. Jelen and Wilcox (1995) also compared mainline with evangelical Protestant ministers, just as they did on the abstract questions, and found that evangelical ministers were more accommodationist than mainline ones on every issue.

Elite Views on Religious Free Exercise

As discussed earlier, the public generally supports religious free exercise when it does not consider the groups involved to be potentially harmful, and when the practices in question are not too offensive to mainstream sensibilities. On seventeen questions from the Williamsburg Charter Foundation survey used to measure support for religious free exercise, a majority of the public supported free exercise on nine issues and opposed it on eight. For the seventeen issues, the average percentage of the public supporting religious freedom was 49 percent. Thus, on average, about half of the public took the free exercise position on each issue. Based on information reported by Jelen and Wilcox (1995), one can compute similar figures for each of the seven types of elites in order to facilitate comparisons.

While a majority of the public supported religious free exercise on only nine of the seventeen issues, the number of issues on which elite groups gave majority support to free exercise ranged from fourteen to seventeen. Business elites were the least supportive of religious free exercise, but a majority of them opposed it on only three of the seventeen questions (opposition to Hare Krishnas soliciting money at airports, agreement that religious groups should stay out of politics, and disagreement with the idea that religious groups should be able to hide illegal immigrants). Thus, even the least supportive of the elite groups is much more consistently in favor of religious free exercise than is the general public.

The extent to which elites supported religious free exercise varied by group and by issue. For example, 100 percent of the academic and media elites rejected the notion that there is no place in America for Islam. Conversely, only a bare majority of Catholic priests (51 percent) supported the right of Hare Krishnas to solicit money at airports.

Figure 7.2 shows the average percentage of the public and each elite group supporting religious free exercise on the seventeen questions. As indicated previously, on average 49 percent of the public took the free exercise position across the questions. Figure 7.2 makes it clear that all the elite groups are much more consistently supportive of religious free exercise than is the general public. Again, the elite group that is least supportive of free exercise is the business group, yet even it significantly exceeds general public levels of support for religious freedom. The most supportive group on these free exercise questions is the academic elite group, which averaged 80 percent support across the seventeen questions.

In sum, academic elites are the most consistently supportive of religious free exercise (at least as measured by the Williamsburg Charter survey), business elites are the least supportive (but not by much), and there is little difference among government elites, media elites, ministers, priests, and rabbis.

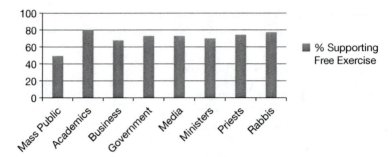

Figure 7.2 The Public and the Elites on Religious Free Exercise.
Source: Williamsburg Charter Survey, as presented in Jelen and Wilcox (1995: 133–134).

Given that elites have disproportionate power in society, this suggests that religious free exercise will in practice probably hew closer to the more expansive vision of the elites than to the more restricted one of the general public.

Summary and Conclusions

American public attitudes toward religious establishment and free exercise are complex, ambivalent, and at times contradictory. Nevertheless, an analysis of available survey data does reveal some clear patterns.

- About a third of Americans are religious separationists, about a third are religious accommodationists, about a fifth are religious non-preferentialists who believe the government should help all religions equally but also believe in a high wall of separation between church and state, and about a tenth are Christian preferentialists who want the government to focus predominantly on preservation of the nation's Judeo-Christian heritage.
- People hold apparently conflicting views on establishment issues; such contradictions might be explained in various ways (e.g., by survey question inadequacies, people thinking of different issues in isolation from one another, particular interpretations of the principles at stake in a given situation).
- At least in the abstract, public support for religious free exercise appears very high. Analysis of the public's views on more concrete, specific establishment issues allows for a fleshing out of these general observations.
- A majority of the public takes an accommodationist view on many specific, concrete establishment issues (especially when state support of religion is primarily symbolic rather than financial).
- At the same time, a majority takes the separationist view in some situations—especially when the issue concerns financial aid to religion,

requiring religious teaching or observances in public institutions, or favoring one mainstream religious group over another.

- People's views on religious free exercise can usefully be characterized as either communitarian (people can act on their religious beliefs, but only as long as their actions don't offend community standards) or libertarian (people can act on their religious beliefs so long as they do not violate the fundamental rights of other people).

- In many situations, small to strong majorities support the free exercise of religion. This includes such matters as allowing religious groups to take part in politics, using religious themes in political discourse in some situations, and tolerance of at least some degree of religious diversity.

- In other situations, a majority does not support religious free exercise. This is especially true in cases involving groups that the general public considers to be harmful in some way (e.g., "cults"). It appears that public attitudes in such situations tend to be communitarian rather than libertarian.

- Most Americans support the rights of those who are not religious (or even anti-religious), but a substantial minority of the public does not.

- When establishment views are combined with religious free exercise views, four major combinations result: religious non-preferentialists (accommodationists who support religious free exercise); Christian preferentialists (accommodationists who limit the accommodation to Christian groups—or perhaps just orthodox Christian groups—and take a communitarian view on religious free exercise); religious minimalists (those who support separation of church and state and oppose religious free exercise); and religious free-marketeers (those who advocate separation of church and state but also generally support religious free exercise). They form roughly equally sized segments of the American public.

A particularly contentious area of debate over the role of religion in public life involves the public school system. In this arena, school prayer seems to be the most salient issue.

- A strong majority of the American public favors prayer in public schools, and a constitutional amendment if necessary to insure that it is permitted.

- Most people, however, would not *require* that school children take part in prayer, and would allow non-believers and members of religious minorities to opt out.

- It appears that most supporters of school prayer think of it as a religious free exercise question more than an establishment issue, whereas most opponents tend to view it through the prism of establishment.

Finally, this chapter has considered the views not only of the mass public, but also of both secular and religious elites. The elite approach to establishment and free exercise questions, while similar to that of the public in some respects, also differs in important ways.

- The kinds of people in the general public who most support school prayer tend to be somewhat under-represented in Congress, among PAC contributors to political candidates, and among delegates to political party conventions; thus, support for school prayer is lower among political elites than it is in America as a whole.
- Religious elites are not unified in terms of their political views, and they are sharply divided on the issue of school prayer.
- Both secular and religious elites are more separationist than the public is on the abstract question of religious establishment.
- With the exception of academics, the secular elites are not much more separationist than the general public on concrete establishment issues.
- While Jewish rabbis gave high support to separation of church and state, Protestant ministers (especially evangelicals) and Catholic priests took the accommodationist position on most concrete establishment issues.
- Although academic elites were the most supportive of religious free exercise and business elites were the least supportive, all elite groups—both religious and secular—gave higher support to religious free exercise than did the public as a whole.

Overall, it is apparent that the American public has a complex mix of attitudes toward church–state relations. While they definitely do not want narrow, sectarian impositions, they are clearly comfortable with a presence of religion in public life. Americans support separationism more in the abstract than in specific situations, and their level of support for religious free exercise depends to a great extent on the nature of the group and practice involved. Generally speaking, Americans are communitarian: they will support religious freedom for various viewpoints provided that this doesn't conflict substantially with community norms and values. At the same time, elites are usually more likely than the public to support separation of church and state, and they are much more likely to support religious free exercise for groups outside the religious mainstream.

   This chapter has demonstrated that Americans vary significantly in their views of church–state relations. The next chapter will examine the ways in which differences in religious attitudes are linked to differences in the political views that people hold concerning such matters as political tolerance, racism, social welfare programs, pornography, capital punishment, and other issues.

8 Religious Orientations and Political Behavior among White Americans

> The presidential election revealed that the "God gap" in electoral politics remains as large as ever—and is much larger than the gender gap that was often touted during the campaign ... How fervently one practices one's religion is—apart from race—still the best predictor of how one votes.
> (David Heim, "The Persistent God Gap," 2012)

Religion has always been an important factor in shaping Americans' attitudes toward major political issues. Positions on questions ranging from slavery to prohibition to the teaching of evolution have historically broken down to a significant degree along religious lines. Since the 1980s, religion has become an increasingly important determinant of party identification and vote choice as well, eclipsing other factors such as gender, income, education, and region as a predictor of presidential voting among white Americans. This chapter will explore the various ways in which people's religious orientations influence their views of parties, candidates, and issues.

This analysis will focus on links between religious values and political behavior among white Americans, while Chapter 9 will examine religion's effects on the politics of racial minorities. The distinctive nature of the black and, to a lesser extent, Latino religious and political experiences in America merit separate consideration. Religion shapes political life in these communities in very different ways than it does among America's white majority (Savage 2008; Wilson 2008).

It is impossible to consider in a single chapter all of the different manifestations of religious identity, belief, and practice that might shape political behavior. Instead, the analysis here will center on three manifestations of religious orientation: denominational identity, biblical literalism, and religious commitment. Through the prism of these measures, the chapter will explore three key questions:

- Why are people's political views often related to their religious views?
- Why aren't the links between religious and political views even stronger than they are?

- In what ways are denominational identity, biblical literalism, and religious commitment related to party identification, ideology, vote choice, and positions on a range of issues?

Why Are Religious and Political Orientations Linked?

For a variety of reasons, it ought not come as a surprise to anyone that Americans' religious values and affiliations are important predictors of their political attitudes and behaviors. There are three main theoretical explanations for such linkages, any or all of which might operate in the life of a given individual to link religion and politics. These are the *substantive* explanation, the *compositional* explanation, and the *subcultural* explanation.

The Substantive Explanation

The substantive explanation refers to a direct translation of religious values or teachings into political beliefs. For example, religious prescriptions against the intentional taking of another human life might translate directly into positions on issues such as capital punishment, abortion, or euthanasia. Similarly, religious beliefs about human dignity and the equality of persons before God might result in opposition to slavery and segregation, and support for various other forms of social egalitarianism. Finally, the pacifist religious teachings of some sects might result in opposition to all military conflicts. Clearly, the substantive explanation is the most intuitive and direct route by which religious convictions become relevant for politics.

The Compositional Explanation

The compositional explanation refers to the ways in which differences in socio-economic characteristics between religious groups can affect their political views. In this case, the connection between religious affiliation and political orientation is more about correlation than causation, since the political differences do not spring from religious belief per se, but from other characteristics that adherents of particular faiths tend to share. Demographic composition—in terms of such characteristics as education, income, region, and race—can vary significantly from one religious group to another, and these variations can in-and-of-themselves lead to important political differences. For example, Jews tend to be more politically tolerant than either Protestants or Catholics. This difference, however, likely stems more from Jews' higher average levels of education than from theology, since the faiths do not have obviously different teachings with regard to political tolerance. To take another example, Presbyterians and Episcopalians are somewhat less supportive of social welfare programs than are many other groups of Protestants; to some extent, this conservatism on economic matters might be a function of the higher-than-average incomes in these denominations. Thus,

the socio-economic composition of religious groups likely affects some of their
political stances, an important reality to keep in mind when examining links
between religious and political orientations.

Given the compositional explanation, one must be cautious when interpreting apparent relationships between religious affiliations and political
preferences: if a religious orientation is correlated with a political one, this
does not necessarily mean that the political orientation stems from the group's
distinctive theology or religious practice. It is possible that the real causal
factor(s) might be some other characteristics that just happen to be correlated
with the religious orientation. For example, African American Protestants
tend to be very supportive of government programs designed to help the poor.
While this support might stem in part from the strong social justice orientation
in black theology, it might also simply be a result of the fact that African
Americans are disproportionately poor and, thus, disproportionate beneficiaries of such programs. Moreover, to make matters even more complicated, it
may be that the social justice theology of the black church is itself partly
shaped by the historical economic disadvantage of African Americans. The
analyses in this chapter will try, where possible, to disentangle these knotty
issues of causation, but it is important to keep in mind that the mere existence
of a correlation between a religious orientation and a political one does not
automatically imply that one caused the other.

The Subcultural Explanation

The subcultural explanation is based on the idea that members of a particular
religious group often share common cultural patterns that go beyond their
explicitly religious beliefs. Such patterns could result from the particular
historical circumstances in which a religious group existed at some time (either
past or present), as well as from distinctive patterns of education, media
consumption, entertainment preferences, and even commercial activity within
the group. The cultural patterns of a religious group could lead to distinctive
political preferences. For example, during an earlier time in the United States,
the Democratic Party recruited many Catholic immigrants due largely to its
appeal to relatively poor immigrants—an example of the compositional
explanation discussed above. However, elements of this preference for the
Democratic Party persisted among many Catholics—especially older ones—
long after they had achieved economic parity with Protestants (Mockabee
2007; Wilson 2007). Similarly, the high level of political tolerance among
Jews can only partly be explained by their higher education levels discussed
above; it likely also stems from their history as a persecuted minority and
resultant subcultural wariness of any discrimination by the state. Finally,
evangelical Protestants have frequently been said to have their own subculture
in America, which reinforces a distinctive, politically relevant worldview
(Balmer 2000; Reimer 2000). Thus, some links between religion and politics
might arise neither from religious belief nor from compositional differences

(or at least not entirely), but instead from either past or present cultural circumstance.

Why Aren't Religious–Political Links Stronger?

To many people, the most puzzling question is likely not why religious and political orientations are connected, but why the link between the two is not even stronger and more consistent than it is. At times, the relationship between certain religious orientations and particular political attitudes and behaviors is weaker than one might expect, or even non-existent. There are four main explanations for this attenuation of religious–political ties: belief superficiality, compartmentalization, belief translation difficulties, and cross-pressures.

Belief Superficiality

When people are deeply committed to a value or belief, it will almost certainly shape the other beliefs that they hold. Conversely, when people hold a value or belief in a shallow, superficial way, it is unlikely to color their approach to other questions. Intuitively, the more superficial a particular political or religious belief is to a person, the less likely it is to be strongly related to other beliefs.

Abundant evidence suggests that some people's religious and political orientations are fairly superficial. One reason is that people sometimes "inherit" religious and/or political orientations within a particular family or cultural environment, and orientations attained in this way might not have great depth or substantive meaning to the individual. As an example, consider any specific religious denomination. While some members chose that denomination because of its distinctive teachings or practices, others chose it because their parents, spouses, or friends were members, or for various other reasons apart from theology. For these people, we would not necessarily expect their denominational affiliation to have an especially strong effect on the political beliefs that they hold.

Similarly, people can hold political orientations superficially. For example, when people are asked to identify themselves as liberals, moderates, or conservatives, most will classify themselves. However, these self-identifications are not consistently related to views on specific issues, and many people seem to use the labels without much understanding of what they actually mean (Luttbeg and Gant 1985; Erikson and Tedin 2010). Similarly, many of the issue positions that people express in surveys do not reflect deeply held preferences, but instead mask considerable ignorance, ambivalence, indifference, and "non-attitudes," or opinions formulated essentially at random, on the spot (Zaller 1992; Asher 2010). Consequently, it is not surprising that links between these expressed political preferences and religious orientations are not particularly strong.

Compartmentalization

Even if individuals hold strong and sincere beliefs about both religion and politics, they might keep them mentally separate, and rarely if ever think of them in tandem with one another. In some ways, such a compartmentalization is encouraged in America by all the talk about a "wall of separation" between church and state, and by elements of the Protestant religious tradition dating back to Martin Luther. For some people, whether consciously or unconsciously, religion exists in one realm and politics exists in another, and they have little to say to one another. Religion, in their view, speaks to eternal questions and/or to issues of personal morality, not to competing visions of good government or the good society. Thus, for these people, religious beliefs have very limited influence on political ones, and vice versa.

Belief Translation Difficulties

Even if someone has deeply held religious views and believes, in general, that moral convictions are relevant for politics, he or she might still have difficulty "translating" some of those beliefs into specific policy prescriptions. There might be ambiguity about whether a particular moral doctrine applies in a given circumstance, or competing moral values might push someone in different directions on a given issue, party, or candidate. For example, should a Baptist's (or a Mormon's, or a Muslim's) belief that gambling and drinking alcohol are wrong compel him or her to support laws against those practices? Does a general religious inclination to help the poor necessarily translate into unlimited acceptance of welfare-state programs? There can also be significant variations in doctrinal interpretation, even within a religious tradition. For example, what exactly does Islam prescribe with regard to the social and political role of women? Muslims disagree sharply among themselves on this question. As a result, people who share a particular religious belief might in some cases draw different political implications from it, resulting in weaker overall links between religious and political orientations.

Cross-Pressures

In the United States, a host of different factors influence political attitudes and behaviors. For many people, religious orientations are simply one influence among a number of factors, such as educational background, economic situation, regional subculture, racial identity, psychological traits, and so forth. Some influences might push a person in one political direction, while other influences might push the other way. In this case, the person is "cross-pressured." An African American Baptist, for example, might believe strongly in traditional marriage and oppose President Obama's endorsement of same-sex unions, but feel a strong pull of racial solidarity to support the nation's first black president. Likewise, a Jewish voter might strongly support the state of Israel (and prefer Republicans to Democrats on this score), but prefer liberal policies on a variety of other questions. For some people, religious beliefs are the primary influence on political behavior; for others, religious beliefs have little or no influence; for still others, it depends on the context and situation.

Measuring Political and Religious Orientations

This chapter will present research findings concerning political and religious linkages among white Americans, using data from the National Opinion Research Center General Social Survey (NORC GSS). Almost every year since 1972, the NORC GSS has surveyed adults in the United States on a broad range of topics, including political and religious matters. The analyses here combine the 2006–2012 NORC GSS surveys to create a large database containing information from 7,870 white survey respondents.

Unless otherwise noted, all differences between groups discussed in the text are statistically significant at the .05 level or better. In other words, one can be at least 95 percent confident that the relationships found in these NORC GSS samples do apply to the general population in the United States, and are not an artifact of sampling variation.

Political Orientations

The GSS data provide a variety of measures to capture different aspects of respondents' political attitudes and behavior. They are briefly outlined here, with fuller descriptions of all survey questions provided in Appendix B.

Political Identifications and Vote Choice

The GSS data allow for an examination of political party identification, liberal–moderate–conservative self-classification, and reported presidential vote in the 2004 and 2008 elections. These are the attitudinal and behavioral variables most commonly studied by political scientists.

One caveat, however, is in order with regard to reported presidential vote— the well-documented "winner's bias," in which respondents tend to over-report voting for the winning candidate (Wright 1990; Atkeson 1999). This pattern is clearly evident in the GSS data, where support for Bush in 2004 and (especially) Obama in 2008 is exaggerated. In the GSS sample, 53.2 percent report having voted for Bush in 2004 (his real percentage was 50.7 percent), and a whopping 61 percent report having voted for Obama in 2008 (his real percentage was 52.9 percent). Thus, one should pay more attention to the relative rates of partisan voting among religious groups than to their absolute values, and apply significant discounting to apparent partisan shifts within a group between 2004 and 2008.

Support for Social Welfare

The NORC GSS contains, during the 2006–2012 time period, two questions that tap public attitudes toward government social welfare policy. One asks whether the government is spending too little, about the right amount, or too much on welfare programs, while the other asks how actively the government should seek to reduce income differences in society. Responses to these two items are combined and normalized on a 0–100 scale, such that 100 indicates maximum support for welfare spending and redistribution, while 0 indicates maximum opposition.

Gender Equality

In recent years, the number of GSS items tapping support for the general principle of gender equality has dropped off considerably, largely because support for such equality (at least in the abstract) has become almost universal in American society. There are, however, two remaining questions that measure attitudes towards women's roles in public life (or at least in political life). One asks whether the respondent would support a qualified female nominee of his or her party for president, while the other asks whether respondents agree or disagree that women are "not suited for politics." These two items combine to form a gender equality scale, once again normalized to run from 0 to 100.

Racial Liberalism

A generally liberal orientation on racial questions is captured through a combination of three GSS items: support for government spending to improve the condition of blacks, support for a federal open housing law, and support for race-based affirmative action in hiring. For the purposes of these analyses, the heated debate over the extent to which responses to such items reflect racial prejudice (Kinder and Sanders 1996; Sniderman and Carmines 1999) is beside the point; clearly, they represent some of the central race-related policy questions in contemporary American political life. Once again, the items have been combined to form a scale running from 0 (most racially conservative) to 100 (most racially liberal).

Political Tolerance

Following a long tradition of social science research dating back to Samuel Stouffer (1955), political tolerance here is measured on the basis of willingness to allow members of unpopular groups to give public speeches, teach in colleges, and have their books in public libraries. The specific groups used to form the tolerance index are atheists, communists, homosexuals, militarists, racists, and anti-American Muslim clerics. The scale runs from 0 (minimally tolerant—would not allow members of any of these groups to do any of the three things) to 100 (maximally tolerant—would allow members of all of the groups to do all three things).

Issue Positions

In addition to partisanship, ideology, and candidate preference, the GSS surveys ask respondents about their positions on a range of social and political issues. Since the indices described above already capture attitudes toward the welfare state, race and gender equality, and political tolerance, the focus here is on social and moral issues that touch on traditional norms and values. With just two exceptions (defense spending and, arguably, gun control), the individual issues that we examine all fall into this category. They include homosexuality, access to birth control for young teens, abortion, the death penalty, marijuana legalization, pornography, and euthanasia. Together, these provide a comprehensive overview of the sort of "hot button" social issues on which religious values are generally thought to play a prominent role.

Religious Orientations

In addition to its range of political items, the GSS also contains a varied battery of questions about religion. They allow for an examination of three different dimensions of religious orientation: *belonging* (identification or affiliation with a specific religious tradition), *believing* (the actual substance of an individual's religious views), and *behaving* (performing specific religious acts, such as prayer and church attendance). All three are increasingly regarded as essential and distinct elements in understanding the relationship between religion and American political behavior (Kohut et al. 2000; Olson and Warber 2008).

Religious Identifications

The GSS asks people: "What is your religious preference? Is it Protestant, Catholic, Jewish, some other religion, or no religion?" The analyses here exclude those who indicated "some other religion," because this category is small (only 2 percent of white respondents) and it includes a disparate mixture of religious preferences (Hindus, Muslims, Buddhists, Eastern Orthodox, etc.).

A wide body of research suggests that it is not especially meaningful to analyze all Protestants (or even all white Protestants) as a single group; there are great variations in both doctrine and religious practice under the broad umbrella of Protestantism. Thus, one might examine differences among specific Protestant denominations. However, a detailed comparison of political differences among many specific denominations would be unwieldy. As a result, researchers have developed various methods of grouping Protestants into broad but cohesive and analytically useful categories. In political science, the "industry standard" is a division, based largely on denomination, into "mainline" and "evangelical" Protestant religious traditions (Green et al. 1996). Each of these groups "is composed of particular congregations and denominations that are socially and organizationally linked together and whose members share beliefs that constitute a distinct worldview" (Smidt 2007: 32).

The analysis here classifies white Protestants as either mainline or evangelical using the criteria outlined by Green et al. (1996). The evangelical category includes such groups as Southern Baptists, members of the Missouri Synod Lutheran Church, and various Pentecostal denominations. The mainline category includes such groups as United Methodists, Episcopalians, and most Presbyterians.

Using this classification scheme for Protestants allows for a comparison of the political views of five religious identification groups: "nones" (18 percent of white survey respondents), Jews (2 percent), Catholics (25 percent), mainline Protestants (24 percent), and evangelical Protestants (29 percent).

Biblical Literalism

While there are obviously many different potential measures and dimensions of religious belief, one that has relevance across the boundaries of Protestantism, Catholicism, and Judaism is attitudes toward the Bible. Moreover, one's approach to scripture has been shown by a variety of scholars to be a significant determinant of various political attitudes and behaviors (Kohut et al. 2000; Layman 2001; Olson and Warber 2008). A NORC GSS question asks respondents which of three statements comes closest to their view of the Bible. Based on their responses, they can be divided into three groups as follows:

- *biblical literalist* if they chose "The Bible is the actual word of God and is to be taken literally, word for word";
- *biblical conservative* if they chose "The Bible is the inspired word of God, but not everything in it should be taken literally, word for word";
- *biblical liberal* if they chose "The Bible is an ancient book of fables, legends, history, and moral precepts recorded by men."

Religious Commitment

Religious commitment, or the seriousness and intensity of a person's faith, is now widely regarded as more important than religious affiliation in shaping many aspects of political behavior (Wuthnow 1988; Olson and Green 2006; Green 2007). Religiously committed Catholics and Presbyterians, for example, are likely to have more in common with each other politically than they do with nominal members of their own churches. The GSS contains three questions that indicate the extent to which people are committed to religion, at least in the traditional sense. These items concern frequency of attendance at religious services, frequency of prayer, and strength of religious preference (all self-reported). Using responses to these questions, we construct a composite religious commitment measure, and then categorize people into roughly the highest third in religious commitment (33 percent), the middle third (34 percent), and the lowest third (32 percent).

Religious Identifications and Political Orientations

Using the denominational classification scheme discussed above permits a comparison of the five major religious groupings among white Americans: "nones," Jews, Catholics, mainline Protestants, and evangelical Protestants. We will analyze them here in terms of presidential vote choice, political party identification, and ideological self-description, then turn to an analysis of their views on specific social and political issues.

"Nones"

The category "nones" consists of those who selected the "no religion" response when asked whether they were Protestant, Catholic, Jewish, some other religion, or no religion. It is important to note, however, that by no means all of these people are atheists or agnostics; indeed, those who would embrace such labels actually comprise a minority of the group (Boorstein 2012; Hunter 2012). This is reinforced by an examination of the nones' responses to various other items in the GSS survey. On the biblical belief question, for example, 37 percent of nones report that they regard the Bible as either the literal or the inspired word of God. Moreover, many report that they pray with some regularity, and some even attend religious services. Thus, it appears that many people selected the "no religion" category even though they do have religious beliefs of some sort—perhaps unorthodox ones that don't quite fit into any of the other categories, or ones that are more individualistically "spiritual" than institutionally religious. At the same time, however, it is clear that among the "nones," religion does generally play a lesser role in life than in any of the other groups. They also tend to score quite low (not surprisingly) on both religious commitment and doctrinal orthodoxy. So, while "nones" should by no means be conflated with atheists, they are clearly different in their approach to spiritual questions than those who identify with a religious tradition.

However varied their beliefs may be, the "nones" are a rapidly growing segment of American society. In 1972, when the NORC GSS was first done, 5 percent of respondents selected the "no religion" category. By 1994, that percentage had grown to 9 percent. In the most recent iteration in 2012, the figure was nearly 20 percent, a number large enough to approach the Catholic, mainline Protestant, and evangelical Protestant segments of the population.

Political Identifications and Voting Behavior of Nones

Of the five religious groupings of white respondents, the nones provided the highest level of support for Democratic presidential candidates in 2004

(67 percent for Kerry) and 2008 (81 percent for Obama). Table 8.1 shows that nones voted Democratic at rates equal to or a bit higher than Jews, and much higher than any of the Christian groups. On the other hand, perhaps in line with their religious non-affiliation, more than half (56 percent) of nones are independents rather than Democrats (31 percent) or Republicans (13 percent). While nones are not strongly committed to the Democratic Party label, they are more likely than any other group except Jews to call themselves liberals (46 percent).

Nones' Views on Political Issues

Table 8.2 shows that nones, along with Jews, score most liberal of the groups on all four of the previously described indices (support for social welfare, gender equality, racial liberalism, and political tolerance). It should be noted, however, that there is relatively little variation among the groups on some of these indices. There is significantly more divergence on the individual issues. Nones are the most liberal of all the groups on defense spending, birth control for teens, pornography, euthanasia, and marijuana legalization (tied with Jews). They are the second most liberal group (to Jews) on homosexuality, abortion, and the death penalty. On only one issue are they more conservative than most other groups—gun control, perhaps reflecting something of a libertarian bent. Overall, though, the pattern is clear: nones are significantly to the left of the American political center on most questions.

Table 8.1 Political Orientations by Religious Identification

	"Nones" (%)	Jews (%)	Catholics (%)	Mainline Protestants (%)	Evangelical Protestants (%)
2004 Presidential Vote					
Kerry	67	67	40	35	21
Bush	33	33	60	65	79
2008 Presidential Vote					
Obama	81	75	54	45	34
McCain	19	25	46	55	66
Party Identification					
Democrat	31	54	31	24	20
Independent	56	26	42	36	36
Republican	13	20	28	40	44
Ideological Identification					
Liberal	46	52	24	21	11
Moderate	36	29	42	35	36
Conservative	19	20	34	44	53

Source: NORC GSS, 2006–2012.

Table 8.2 Issue Positions by Religious Identification

	"Nones"	Jews	Catholics	Mainline Protestants	Evangelical Protestants
Social Welfare Index	52	53	43	45	42
Gender Equality Index	93	92	88	87	78
Racial Liberalism Index	54	56	50	48	42
Political Tolerance Index	78	73	64	71	53
	(%)	(%)	(%)	(%)	(%)
Support cuts in government spending on defense	51	45	37	29	23
Believe homosexuality is "not wrong at all"	70	75	44	40	15
Support allowing young teens access to birth control	76	70	53	53	42
Believe abortion should be allowed "for any reason"	66	74	39	46	21
Oppose death penalty for murder	34	39	33	25	18
Support permit requirements for gun ownership	73	96	80	76	70
Support marijuana legalization	67	67	40	42	29
Oppose banning pornography	88	83	69	62	43
Approve suicide by the terminally ill	87	80	62	66	45

Source: NORC GSS, 2006–2012.

Why are nones so liberal? The possible answers are varied. Perhaps the lack of commitment to orthodox or institutional religion reflects a more general aversion to "the establishment" and to prevailing cultural norms. Nones may react politically against those who make religiously based political appeals, which in recent years has been disproportionately Republicans and conservatives. In addition, nones' disproportionate youthfulness may incline them in the direction of "lifestyle liberalism." Whatever the reason, nones' liberalism has made them an increasingly important part of the Democratic coalition (Layman 2001; Bolce and De Maio 2007).

Jews

Jews are by far the smallest religious group examined here, comprising just over one in fifty white Americans. They are, however, disproportionately affluent and well educated, and are significantly over-represented among the nation's cultural and financial elites, as well as in Congress (see Chapter 7).

Thus, their political views and preferences are more significant than their numbers alone would suggest.

Jewish Political Identifications and Voting Behavior

Of the five religious groups considered here, Jews are by far the most Democratic in terms of party identification (54 percent), they are the most likely to call themselves liberals (52 percent), and they rival nones in their reported level of support for recent Democratic presidential candidates (67 percent for Kerry in 2004 and 75 percent for Obama in 2008). This strong Democratic loyalty dates back a century (Menendez 1977) and, unlike many other elements of Roosevelt's "New Deal coalition," Jews have wavered very little in their commitment to the party.

Jewish Views on Political Issues

Jewish GSS respondents score similar to religious "nones" on the social welfare, gender equality, racial liberalism, and political tolerance indices, a bit to the left of the three Christian groups on all four scales. On the specific issues measured, they are the most liberal group on homosexuality, abortion, the death penalty, gun control, and marijuana legalization (tied with nones), and the second most liberal on defense spending, teen birth control, pornography, and euthanasia. On not a single one of these issues or indices are they to the right of any Christian group.

Obviously, not all Jews are liberal (indeed, it should be noted, none of these groups is politically monolithic). Sigelman (1991) and Djupe (2007) argue that there are significant ideological differences among American Jews, and that they are often responsive to conservative appeals on some fiscal and foreign policy questions. On the kinds of social and moral issues that are our primary focus here, however, Jewish liberalism is unmistakable—at least for the great majority of American Jews who are not Orthodox (Cohen 1989). The historical experience of being a persecuted minority, combined with relatively low average levels of religious commitment (to be discussed later), make for a distinctly libertarian outlook on questions of personal morality (Lerner et al. 1989).

Catholics

As discussed in Chapter 4, the social teaching of the Catholic Church does not fit neatly with the platform of either the Democratic or the Republican Party in the United States. While Church views on life, family, and the role of religion in the public square align better with Republicans, Catholic approaches to social welfare, immigration, and war and peace issues have more in common with those typically taken by Democrats. As a result, white Catholics are often regarded as a critical swing constituency in American politics. Hispanic Catholics, on the other hand, incline more heavily toward the Democratic Party—a pattern to be discussed in Chapter 9.

Catholic Political Identifications and Voting Behavior

Unlike in previous eras, when white Catholics—predominantly immigrants and the children of immigrants—were heavily Democratic, they are now very much up for grabs for both parties, leaning a bit, if anything, in the Republican direction. This movement of Catholics away from the Democratic Party began in the 1970s, and it was Catholic voters who formed the core of the "Reagan Democrats" (Prendergast 1999). As Table 8.1 reflects, John Kerry (himself, ironically, a Catholic) in 2004 became the first Democratic presidential candidate to lose the Catholic vote, though Barack Obama in 2008 rebounded to roughly split the white Catholic vote with John McCain (recall that the reported Obama support reflected in Table 8.1 reflects some exaggeration due to "winner's bias"). While white Catholics still vote more Democratic than do white Protestants, they are substantially less Democratic than "nones" and Jews. Moreover, as other work has noted (Mockabee 2007; Wilson 2007), young, observant Catholics have become especially likely to vote Republican.

In terms of political party identifications, white Catholics have become much more independent (42 percent) than they are Democratic (31 percent) or Republican (28 percent). This represents a significant change compared to several decades ago, when Catholics were heavily Democratic. In the 1972 GSS survey, for example, 54 percent of white Catholics were Democrats, 30 percent were independents, and only 16 percent were Republicans.

With regard to ideological identification, Catholics are in the middle of the five groups. They are less likely to classify themselves as conservative than are Protestants, but more likely to do so than are nones or Jews. Catholics are more likely to classify themselves as moderate (42 percent do so) than members of any other group; indeed, they are the only group for whom "moderate" is the plurality identification.

Catholic Views on Political Issues

Turning to the specific issue positions reported in Table 8.2, a general pattern is apparent. On virtually every issue, Catholics are more liberal than evangelical Protestants, and more conservative than Jews and those with no religious affiliation. Their mean positions are typically very close to those of mainline Protestants, with just a few interesting exceptions. Catholics are appreciably more liberal than mainline Protestants on defense spending, the death penalty, and pornography, and appreciably more conservative on abortion—all deviations (with the exception of tolerance for pornography) in the direction of the teachings of their Church. Second, Catholics take their most conservative stance on abortion. Thus, on specific issues just as on general partisan and ideological orientations, Catholics occupy a middle ground between the Protestant groups on their right and the non-Christian groups on their left.

Mainline Protestants

Of all the religious groups considered here, mainline Protestants are the most doctrinally and politically eclectic. The broad grouping of mainline Protestantism includes individual congregations that range from Anglo-Catholic to essentially evangelical to virtually Unitarian. It is also a group that has seen a significant change in its place in American life over the last fifty years. Once by far the dominant religious group in America, mainline Protestants now have smaller numbers than Catholics or evangelicals, as they have lost members to both of those groups and to the ranks of the unaffiliated in recent decades.

Mainline Protestant Political Identifications and Voting Behavior

Table 8.1 reveals that the political leanings of white mainline Protestants are generally Republican. They report having given 65 percent of their votes to George W. Bush in 2004, and 55 percent to John McCain in 2008. Moreover, Republicanism is the plurality party identification in the group, at 40 percent, compared with only 24 percent who identify as Democrats. Similarly, 44 percent of mainline Protestants call themselves conservatives, as opposed to only 21 percent who call themselves liberals.

In historical context, however, these figures actually reveal an appreciable erosion of Republican strength with this group over time. More than any other religious group, white mainline Protestants have traditionally been the backbone of the GOP since the nineteenth century. As recently as 1988, fully 74 percent of white mainline Protestants voted Republican for president, but Barack Obama approached parity with John McCain among these voters in 2008. As evangelical Protestants have become more and more influential within the GOP, some mainliners may have begun to feel less enthusiastic about the party. In addition, as noted in Chapter 4, mainline clergy have actually become quite liberal in recent decades, which may have had a "trickle-down" effect in some congregations. Finally, the exodus of many doctrinally conservative mainline Protestants into evangelical churches has likely had political effects as well—a phenomenon noted by Kellstedt et al. (1994) as far back as the Clinton era.

Mainline Protestant Views on Political Issues

Mainline Protestant scores on the four indices—social welfare, gender equality, racial liberalism, and political tolerance—are generally more liberal than those of evangelicals, more conservative than those of Jews and nones, and similar to those of Catholics (with the exception of political tolerance, where they score closer to Jews). As discussed above, on the specific issues, mainline Protestants look very similar to Catholics, with a bit more liberal approach to abortion and a bit more conservative approach on defense spending and the death penalty. Together with Catholics, they clearly constitute the broad center of the American political spectrum.

Evangelical Protestants

As discussed in Chapter 4, evangelical Protestants have emerged over the last several decades as perhaps the most significant religious group in American political life. As their share of the American religious "market" has increased (they are now the largest religious grouping among white Americans), so too has their level of political engagement and their centrality in the Republican electoral coalition. While not entirely synonymous with it, white evangelicals have indisputably been the driving force behind the "New Christian Right," and have more recently been an important component of the Tea Party movement.

Evangelical Political Identifications and Voting Behavior

Table 8.1 shows that evangelical Protestants have become by far the strongest base of support for Republican presidential candidates. In 2004, 79 percent of white evangelicals report having voted for George W. Bush, and two thirds report having voted for John McCain in 2008. In addition, they have in recent years surpassed mainline Protestants in terms of Republican Party identification, with 44 percent now calling themselves Republicans. In terms of ideological identifications, evangelical Protestants have by a healthy margin the highest percentage of self-described conservatives of any of the groups (53 percent), and the lowest percentage of liberal identifiers (11 percent).

Evangelical Views on Political Issues

As Table 8.2 shows, evangelical Protestants are more conservative than any other group on every single index and issue examined here, by margins of varying degrees. While they score lower than other groups on the social welfare, gender equality, and racial liberalism indices, the differences are not large; they are, however, significantly less inclined toward political tolerance for unpopular outgroups than members of other religious traditions. Turning to the individual issue positions, evangelical conservatism is especially pronounced on the most obviously "moral" issues. They are dramatically less likely than any other group to approve of homosexuality, to support legal abortion "for any reason," to oppose a ban on pornography, and to approve of suicide by the terminally ill. On the other issues, evangelical distinctiveness from other groups is less dramatic, but it is uniformly in a conservative direction. Where once evangelical conservatism was largely confined to social and moral questions, recent studies (Guth 2009; Jelen 2009; Wilson 2009) have found that it now extends across the issue spectrum to include support for conservative stances on economic policy, foreign affairs, and the environment as well. This tendency is certainly confirmed in the data presented here.

Biblical Attitudes and Political Orientations

The analyses to this point have focused on the relationship between professed denominational affiliations and political orientations. While these are undoubtedly important, it is also useful to examine what people actually believe when it comes to religion. Some denominations (especially, but not exclusively, many mainline Protestant ones) contain within them considerable theological diversity. While it undoubtedly represents a fairly crude simplification of a range of complex doctrinal beliefs, an individual's professed attitude toward the Bible has been shown to be a reasonably good proxy for general religious orthodoxy and theological approach (Tamney et al. 1989; Jelen 1991; Kellstedt and Smidt 1993). Recall, as discussed above, that the GSS allows a classification of individuals as *literalists*, *conservatives*, or *liberals* with regard to their views of scripture. In the 2006–2012 GSS pooled data set, this produces a distribution among white respondents in which 29 percent are biblical literalists, 50 percent are biblical conservatives, and 21 percent are biblical liberals.

The clear majority (64 percent) of literalists are evangelical Protestants, but 18 percent are Catholic and 14 percent are mainline Protestants. Most mainline Protestants are biblical conservatives (71 percent), with roughly equal minorities of literalists (15 percent) and liberals (14 percent). Evangelicals are predominantly literalists (73 percent), with a conservative minority (24 percent) and very few biblical liberals (3 percent). About two thirds of Catholics are biblical conservatives, with the remaining third split between literalists (19 percent) and liberals (15 percent). Jews are split between the conservative (44 percent) and liberal (43 percent) groups, with a small minority (13 percent) of literalists—presumably predominantly Orthodox. Among "nones," 63 percent are biblical liberals, 31 percent are conservatives, and 7 percent are literalists. Some of these results indicate a bit of slack in the way that people answer survey questions about religion—for example, one wonders exactly who the 7 percent of "no religion" biblical literalists are, or the 3 percent of evangelicals who regard the Bible as an exclusively human creation. Nonetheless, expressed attitudes toward the Bible do tend to match up with respondent religious tradition in roughly the way that one would expect.

Biblical Attitudes, Political Identifications, and Voting

Table 8.3 shows the relationship between attitudes toward the Bible and presidential voting, party identification, and ideology. As one would expect, biblical literalists and biblical liberals are mirror images of one another. Literalists gave 80 percent of their votes in 2004 to George W. Bush, and 67 percent in 2008 to John McCain. Biblical liberals, by contrast, gave 66 percent in 2004 to John Kerry and 80 percent in 2008 to Barack Obama. Literalists are twice as likely to be Republicans as to be Democrats, while the reverse is true among liberals. Similarly, a majority (53 percent) of biblical literalists call themselves conservatives, while only 20 percent biblical liberals do so. Not surprisingly, biblical conservatives, the largest group of respondents, fall somewhere in between the literalist and liberal camps. They gave Bush a clear, but not overwhelming, majority in 2004, and split between Obama and McCain in 2008. They are more likely to identify as Republicans than Democrats and more likely to be conservatives than liberals, but the plurality identifications in the group are independent and moderate. Overall, then, biblical conservatives look politically more like literalists than they do like liberals, but they are clearly distinguishable from both. The most striking pattern in these data is the obvious political distinctiveness of biblical liberals. The roughly one fifth of white Americans who regard the Bible as just a human book of fables and legends really stand out as dramatically more liberal and Democratic than other white voters in the GSS sample.

While the differences in political orientations according to views of the Bible are illustrative, one problem that muddies the relationship is a failure to distinguish among the different religious identification groups (nones, Jews, Catholics, mainline Protestants, and evangelical Protestants). The relationship between views of the Bible and political orientations may not be equally

Table 8.3 Political Orientations by Views of the Bible

	Biblical Literalists (%)	Biblical Conservatives (%)	Biblical Liberals (%)
2004 Presidential Vote			
Kerry	20	39	66
Bush	80	61	34
2008 Presidential Vote			
Obama	33	50	80
McCain	67	50	20
Party Identification			
Democrat	22	28	35
Independent	36	39	49
Republican	43	33	15
Ideological Identification			
Liberal	12	24	46
Moderate	35	39	34
Conservative	53	37	20

Source: NORC GSS, 2006–2012.

strong in all groups, in part because biblical literalism is not doctrinally normative in all traditions. Another problem is that the bivariate data in Table 8.3 do not take into account demographic variables (education, region, etc.) that are related to both biblical attitudes and political orientations. Kellstedt and Smidt (1993) do an extensive analysis of the relationship between biblical literalism and these political orientations (and views on abortion) within the Catholic group, the mainline Protestant group, and the evangelical Protestant group while statistically controlling for the effects of education, age, gender, and region. They find that view of the Bible is an important predictor of presidential vote choice among Protestants, but less so among Catholics (perhaps because even doctrinally conservative Catholics do not typically take a literalist view of the Bible). Views of the Bible were, however, strongly related to abortion attitudes in all groups. While the relationship between biblical attitudes and political ones exists to some degree for all groups examined here, it is most analytically useful in differentiating among Protestants.

In addition to the results presented in tables in this chapter, we have also performed all the analyses while controlling for respondents' education levels. In general, this does not result in any major alterations to the patterns reported here, so we have not complicated the discussion by reporting these results. However, there is a general pattern worth noting when one controls for the effects of education: overall, relationships between religious variables and political ones are stronger among those with higher levels of education. At all education levels, biblical literalists differ substantially from biblical liberals (and, to a lesser degree, from biblical conservatives) in vote choice, partisanship, and ideology. These differences are especially pronounced, however, among college-educated respondents. In part, this is likely due to the greater precision and understanding with which more educated respondents answer survey questions. It is also likely the case, however, that education tends to sharpen and clarify relationships between respondents' religious and political worldviews.

Biblical Attitudes and Political Issue Positions

Turning to the attitudinal indices reported in Table 8.4, approach to the Bible appears to have little impact on approaches to social welfare or racial liberalism, a modest effect on support for gender equality (which, it should be noted, is quite high in all groups), and a substantial correlation with political tolerance. Biblical literalists are substantially less politically tolerant than biblical conservatives, who are in turn somewhat less politically tolerant than biblical liberals.

The most significant effects, however, are evident on the individual issues. With only one exception (support for a gun permit requirement), attitudes toward the Bible are strongly correlated with respondents' issue stances. On

Table 8.4 Issue Positions by Views of the Bible

	Biblical Literalists	Biblical Conservatives	Biblical Liberals
Social Welfare Index	45	43	49
Gender Equality Index	80	88	92
Racial Liberalism Index	46	48	53
Political Tolerance Index	53	68	78
	(%)	(%)	(%)
Support cuts in government spending on defense	25	33	50
Believe homosexuality is "not wrong at all"	12	47	70
Support allowing young teens access to birth control	38	58	7
Believe abortion should be allowed "for any reason"	16	45	71
Oppose death penalty for murder	22	26	36
Support permit requirements for gun ownership	70	78	75
Support marijuana legalization	26	44	69
Oppose banning pornography	42	69	84
Approve suicide by the terminally ill	40	68	89

Source: NORC GSS, 2006–2012.

some (the death penalty, for example), the relationship is modest. On others, however, it is overwhelmingly strong. Only 12 percent of biblical literalists, for example, believe that homosexuality is "not wrong at all"—the position taken by 70 percent of biblical liberals and about half of biblical conservatives. Similarly, only 16 percent of biblical literalists support the most pro-choice position (that abortion should be allowed "for any reason"), as compared to 71 percent of biblical liberals and 45 percent of biblical conservatives. Biblical liberals are more than twice as likely to support marijuana legalization, the availability of pornography, and suicide by the terminally ill as are literalists. In addition, research elsewhere (Guth et al. 1995a: 367) shows that biblical literalists are more conservative on environmental issues as well, and that they "take seriously the anthropocentric view of Creation in the Genesis account—that the world was created for humans to use, or even exploit." Clearly, one's approach to the Bible is powerfully associated with a wide and diverse range of specific political preferences.

To be sure, some of these large differences on issues between biblical literalists and others are driven by demographic factors (the compositional explanation discussed above). Those who interpret the Bible literally are, on average, less educated, older, more likely to be female, and more likely to be from the South than are biblical liberals and conservatives (though one must always keep in mind that these are demographic tendencies, not absolutes—there are biblical literalists of all ages and both genders, at all education levels and in all parts of the country). Many of these characteristics can be important predictors of political conservatism, especially on social issues. In general, however, the relationships between biblical attitudes and issue positions described here hold even after controlling for these demographic factors. They are a bit stronger in the South than elsewhere, but they clearly exist in the rest of the United States as well. The relationships generally do not vary significantly by gender, age, and education.

To say that these demographic characteristics do not greatly affect the relationships between biblical literalism and political conservatism is not to say that the overall results are the same regardless of education level, region, etc. Rather, the relationship, the pattern of association between biblical attitudes and political ones, is similar even when controlling for the effects of demographic characteristics. The relationship might be more pronounced for certain groups (e.g., southerners, women, college graduates, etc.) on a particular issue, but the fundamental pattern is the same.

Take, for example, the relationship between biblical attitudes and political tolerance, controlling for the effects of education. For illustrative purposes, the sample can be divided into two groups: those who completed twelve or fewer years of schooling, and those who completed more than twelve years (presumably, at least some college). Figure 8.1 shows that all three religious groups with more than twelve years of school are more politically tolerant than their less educated counterparts. Biblical literalists with at least some college education score 21 points higher on the tolerance scale than literalists with no college, and similar (though somewhat smaller) upward shifts with education are evident among biblical conservatives and biblical liberals. Significantly, however, at both education levels, the relationship between biblical attitudes and political tolerance is the same: biblical literalists are the least tolerant, conservatives are in the middle, and liberals are the most tolerant. In this case, the relationship between biblical attitudes and political tolerance is a bit stronger among less educated respondents, but it is clearly present in the more educated group as well.

It is important here to emphasize a point: the relationships between religious orientations and political ones are generalizations—they are not iron-clad, absolute patterns. For example, the data presented here reveal that evangelical Protestants and biblical literalists tend to be conservative on social issues, and that biblical liberals, Jews, and those with no religion tend to be liberal. There are always significant exceptions, however. As the data here show, one out of every eight biblical literalists believes that homosexuality is "not wrong at all," and about a third of those with no religion favor restrictions on abortion. Thus, while examining group tendencies is very useful for understanding the relationship between religion and politics in America, they are just that—

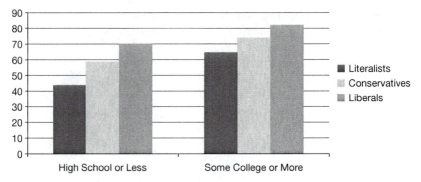

Figure 8.1 Political Tolerance Index Scores by Education and Views of the Bible.
Source: NORC GSS, 2006–2012.

tendencies. There is considerable variation and nuance in the political and religious attitudes of all groups of Americans.

Religious Commitment and Political Orientations

The analyses presented to this point have focused on the relationships between people's professed religious affiliations and biblical views and their political attitudes and behaviors. These capture the "belonging" and "believing" dimensions of religion, but they say little directly about "behaving." To what extent do people make a commitment to their particular religion? Is their religion important to their daily lives? These might be important political questions as well. In their classic work, Stark and Glock (1968) identified four dimensions of religious commitment: belief, practice, knowledge, and experience. Operationally, scholars doing research in this area have usually used several indicators of religious commitment, such as frequency of praying, church attendance, Bible reading, or measures of subjective salience that more directly question respondents about how important religion is to them.

Existing research has shown that certain aspects of religious commitment are important either as predictors of political attitudes or as factors that accentuate relationships between other religious variables (e.g., religious identifications) and political attitudes (Guth and Green 1993; Mockabee et al. 2001). Wilcox (1987: 274) argues that religious variables "may exert strong influence on the attitudes and behaviors of those for whom religious beliefs are highly salient." The question of salience here means: How important is religion to the person? Mockabee et al. (2001) suggest that salience might be the core concept on which we should focus our efforts in looking for linkages between religious and political orientations. Similarly, a number of studies have found that relationships between religious and political variables are affected by another aspect of religious commitment—frequency of attendance at religious services. Catholicism, for example, is a predictor of Republican vote choice and pro-life attitudes, but only if one confines the analysis to religiously observant Catholics (Mockabee 2007; Wilson 2007). Churches can serve as political communities that give members cues about political issues (Jelen 1992; Wald et al. 1993; Welch et al. 1993). Members are much more likely to receive these cues, of course, if they actually attend religious services. Thus, regular church attenders will presumably be more in tune with the social and political messages flowing from their religious leadership, and thus be more influenced in their worldview by their religious tradition's distinctive doctrines and emphases. Another aspect of religious commitment, devotionalism (as indicated by such things as frequency of praying and Bible reading) has also been shown to affect political attitudes (Leege et al. 1993)—generally in a politically conservative direction.

Given the questions available in the NORC GSS, religious commitment can be measured using a scale combining frequency of praying, frequency of attendance at religious services, and strength of religious preference. Based on their scores on this scale, respondents can be divided almost exactly into thirds and classified as low, medium, or high religious commitment. While more complex, denomination-specific measures of commitment are certainly possible, Mockabee et al. (2001) maintain that these common measures actually do quite a good job of capturing religious commitment across denominational lines. The only caveat would be that this scale does tap religious commitment in a traditional sense. People who hold non-traditional spiritualities might conceivably be very committed to their religious views while scoring low on traditional indicators such as prayer or attendance at religious services.

Since the commitment scale measure captures traditional religious devotion, it is probably related both to evangelical Protestantism and to biblical literalism. At the same time, if biblical literalism, religious commitment, and evangelical Protestantism are too closely linked, then examining all three would be redundant. Figures 8.2 and 8.3 show that, while high religious commitment is clearly correlated with both evangelical Protestantism and biblical literalism, the relationships are nowhere near so strong as to suggest that we are dealing with the same concept under different names. For example, among those who score high in religious commitment, 52 percent are biblical literalists, but nearly half are not. Similarly, while evangelicals are clearly the most religiously committed group in the sample, 15 percent of them actually score low on religious commitment; conversely, about a fifth of Jews (the most secular religious group in the sample overall) score in the top third on religious commitment. Catholics and mainline Protestants have significant representation (at least 25 percent) in all three commitment groups.

Two other points make it necessary to analyze biblical literalism and religious commitment separately. First, the two concepts are related in different ways to certain other important political variables. For example, biblical literalists are less likely to vote than those with other attitudes toward

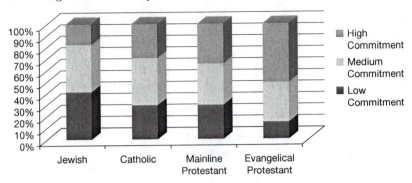

Figure 8.2 Religious Tradition and Religious Commitment.
Source: NORC GSS, 2006–2012.

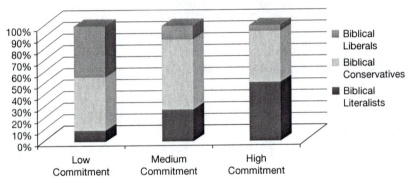

Figure 8.3 Religious Commitment and Views of the Bible.
Source: NORC GSS, 2006–2012.

the Bible; however, individuals with high religious commitment are more likely to vote than those who score lower. Second, biblical literalism and religious commitment are related to various demographic characteristics in different ways, and this can make a difference in how each is related to political orientations. Biblical literalism is strongly related to income, education, gender, age, and region. While biblical literalism and religious commitment share a link to age and gender (older people and women are more likely to be both biblical literalists and religiously committed), religious commitment is not related at all to income, and is only weakly correlated with education and region.

Religious Commitment, Political Identifications, and Voting Preferences

As Table 8.5 shows, religious commitment was strongly related to presidential vote choice in both 2004 and 2008. In both years, only whites scoring in the lowest third on religious commitment gave a majority of their votes to the

Table 8.5 Political Orientations by Religious Commitment

	Low Commitment (%)	Medium Commitment (%)	High Commitment (%)
2004 Presidential Vote			
Kerry	54	39	24
Bush	46	61	76
2008 Presidential Vote			
Obama	69	50	37
McCain	31	50	63
Party Identification			
Democrat	30	29	22
Independent	49	40	31
Republican	21	31	47
Ideological Identification			
Liberal	35	23	14
Moderate	40	40	30
Conservative	25	37	56

Source: NORC GSS, 2006–2012.

Democratic candidate. The results are similar with regard to partisan and ideological identification. High-commitment whites are more than twice as likely as those with low religious commitment to identify as Republicans and conservatives. On all three measures, those with medium levels of religious commitment are roughly equidistant between those in the high and low categories.

Religious Commitment and Issue Positions

Turning to the issue items and indices (Table 8.6), religious commitment appears unrelated to racial liberalism, and modestly predictive of attitudes toward social welfare, gender equality, and political tolerance. On the individual issues, religious commitment has little effect on attitudes toward gun control and the death penalty (though, interestingly, those with high commitment are the most likely to oppose capital punishment); otherwise, higher levels of religious commitment are associated with more conservative stances across the board, most dramatically on homosexuality and abortion. While, as we have shown, high religious commitment and biblical literalism are by no means interchangeable concepts, their effects on political attitudes are quite similar.

Summary and Conclusions

This chapter has explored relationships between religious orientations and political attitudes and behavior among white Americans. While there are

Table 8.6 Issue Positions by Religious Commitment

	Low Commitment	Medium Commitment	High Commitment
Social Welfare Index	48	44	40
Gender Equality Index	91	86	81
Racial Liberalism Index	51	47	47
Political Tolerance Index	72	67	58
	(%)	(%)	(%)
Support cuts in government spending on defense	42	32	27
Believe homosexuality is "not wrong at all"	60	43	18
Support allowing young teens access to birth control	69	59	34
Believe abortion should be allowed "for any reason"	59	43	21
Oppose death penalty for murder	26	25	30
Support permit requirements for gun ownership	75	75	75
Support marijuana legalization	59	42	26
Oppose banning pornography	82	67	41
Approve suicide by the terminally ill	81	64	42

Source: NORC GSS, 2006–2012.

multiple reasons to expect such relationships (most notably the substantive explanation, the compositional explanation, and the subcultural explanation), there are also several factors (including belief superficiality, compartmentalization of beliefs, belief translation difficulties, and cross-pressures) that might prevent these relationships from being universally strong and consistent. An analysis of pooled data from the 2006–2012 NORC GSS surveys reveals that religious identifications, attitudes toward the Bible, and religious commitment are all important predictors of vote choice, ideology, party identification, and issue preferences.

In comparing the political orientations of five major religious identification groups among white Americans ("nones," Jews, Catholics, mainline Protestants, and evangelical Protestants), certain patterns are apparent:

- Nones and Jews clearly occupy the liberal end of the political spectrum.
- Nones and Jews are by far the groups most likely to support Democratic presidential candidates and to call themselves liberals. However, in line with their religious non-affiliation, nones are much more likely to be independents, whereas most Jews identify as Democrats.

- Nones are a bit more liberal than the other groups on economic issues while Jews are about average now, but differences among the five groups on economic issues are not great.
- Nones and Jews are much more liberal than other groups on virtually all political issues. Both groups are especially liberal on social/moral questions (homosexuality, abortion, pornography, drug legalization, etc.).
- In contrast to their past as staunch Democrats, Catholics are now in the political middle and can best be thought of as a swing constituency in elections. White Catholics are now plurality independent, and about equally likely to identify as Republicans and Democrats.
- In ideology, a plurality of Catholics are moderates, though there are more conservatives than liberals.
- On specific issues, Catholics are generally near the middle of the group spectrum, though they do show some evidence of conservative inclinations on abortion and liberal ones on the death penalty.
- Mainline and (especially) evangelical Protestants occupy the conservative end of the political spectrum.
- Evangelical Protestants have replaced mainline Protestants as the strongest and biggest core of the Republican Party. Both groups, however, are more likely to identify themselves as Republicans and conservatives than anything else.
- While both groups of Protestants tend to be conservative on individual issues, evangelicals are especially so—particularly on social issues such as abortion, homosexuality, pornography, and euthanasia.

It is also clear that there are significant relationships between attitudes toward the Bible and political orientations.

- Biblical literalists were the most Republican and biblical liberals the most Democratic in presidential voting in both 2004 and 2008. Biblical liberals are also the most likely to be Democrats, followed by biblical conservatives.
- There is also a clear tendency for ideological self-classification as liberal, moderate, or conservative to correspond with the biblical liberal, conservative, and literalist categories, respectively.
- Biblical attitudes are also clearly correlated with party identification, with literalists three times as likely to be Republicans as liberals.
- On most political issues, biblical literalists are the most politically conservative, biblical conservatives are in the middle, and biblical liberals are the most politically liberal. The relationship is especially strong on social/moral issues.
- While compositional factors (especially related to education and region) help to explain some political conservatism among biblical literalists, they do not account for anywhere near all of the rightward tilt.

Finally, levels of religious commitment are also important predictors of political orientations, though the strength of the relationships varies somewhat by religious tradition.

- While high religious commitment is correlated with both biblical literalism and evangelical Protestantism, the correlation is by no means overwhelming, suggesting that they are three distinct dimensions.
- Whites with high religious commitment were more likely to vote Republican in both 2004 and 2008.
- Level of religious commitment is clearly associated with both partisan and ideological self-classification.
- Stronger religious commitment predicts more conservative stances on most issues, especially social/moral ones.

Overall, the patterns of association between religious and political orientations among white Americans have become unmistakable. These patterns are strongest for the non-economic issue areas (political tolerance, moral issues, and cultural questions). On these matters, it is clear that, for whites at least, political conservatism and religious conservatism often go hand in hand. Because these issues have gained increased importance in American politics since the late 1960s, religion has become an increasingly important determinant of both vote choice and partisan and ideological self-definition. These relationships show no sign of abating.

The next chapter will show that religion and politics have also been very much intertwined among black Americans, especially since the civil rights movement. However, the role of religion in politics among African Americans (and, to a lesser extent, among Hispanics) differs sharply from what one finds among whites.

9 Religion and Politics in Racial Minority Communities

> Like other predominantly black churches across the country, Trinity embodies the black community in its entirety—the doctor and the welfare mom, the model student and the former gang-banger . . . The church contains in full the kindness and cruelty, the fierce intelligence and the shocking ignorance, the struggles and successes, the love and yes, the bitterness and bias that make up the black experience in America.
>
> (Barack Obama, "A More Perfect Union" speech, March 18, 2008)

The Black Church has historically played a powerful and unique role in the lives of African Americans. The distinctiveness of the black experience in America—and the crucial fact of slavery—has shaped the theology, worship, and community role of black churches in ways that have survived in large part to the present day. The combination of historical memory and the lingering effects of history (e.g., lower levels of income and education among black Americans) has led to important differences between black and white Americans in terms of religious emphases, political views, and the ways in which religious and political orientations connect to one another.

This chapter will examine the historical development of the Black Church, showing how it became the central institution in the black community from its beginnings, through the civil rights period, and on up to the present. It will then explore patterns of religious and political difference between black and white Americans, and examine the ways in which religious views shape political orientations in the black community.

Of course, African Americans are not the nation's only large racial minority community. The growing presence of Latinos as part of American society (and, by extension, as part of the electorate) has prompted increased examination of Latino religious faith and practice, and of links between religion and politics in Hispanic communities. While there is not a cohesive, distinctive, ethnically insular Hispanic analogue to the Black Church, Latino religious experiences do differ in some important ways from those of Anglos in America, meriting at least a brief exploration here as well.

The analyses in this chapter are guided by a series of key questions:

- What does the term "Black Church" mean?
- How did Christianity develop among slaves in the United States, and what purposes did it serve for both slavemasters and slaves themselves?
- How did the church become the central institution in the black community, and how did churches serve as training grounds for political activities?
- What role did the Black Church play in the civil rights movement?
- What role does the Black Church play in politics in the black community today, and what factors might be decreasing this role?
- Does religion among African Americans serve as an inspiration for political involvement or an opiate that undercuts motivation to improve the situation of the community?
- What differences exist between black and white Americans in religious and political views?
- Among black Americans, how are religious identifications, biblical literalism, and religious commitment related to political attitudes and behavior?
- What has been the religious experience of Hispanics in America? Has it contributed to a distinctive outlook on politics?
- How does religion shape political orientations among Latinos in the United States? Do its effects more closely resemble those found among white or black Americans?

Historical Development of the Black Church

In order to understand religion and politics among African Americans, it is crucial to understand the role and history of the Black Church. As Lincoln and Mamiya (1990: 1) argue in their landmark work *The Black Church in the African American Experience*, the term "Black Church" serves "as a kind of sociological and theological shorthand reference to the pluralism of black Christian churches in the United States." It does not suggest that all predominantly black congregations are doctrinally identical or institutionally connected; it does, however, acknowledge a general commonality of theological emphasis, worship style, and historical experience that crosses denominational lines within African American Protestantism.

The Black Church has historically been the central institution in most African American communities. Scholars generally estimate that about 80 percent of black Christians are in seven predominantly black denominations: the African Methodist Episcopal Church; the African Methodist Episcopal Zion Church; the Christian Methodist Episcopal Church; the National Baptist Convention, U.S.A., Incorporated; the National Baptist Convention of America, Unincorporated; the Progressive National Baptist Convention; and the Church of God in Christ (Lincoln and Mamiya 1990; Baer and Singer 2002). Black Christians are primarily Baptists and Methodists, with a significant minority of Pentecostals.

Although there are obviously religious differences among individual African Americans and among black churches, there is an underlying pattern that describes the development of the Black Church and gives it its unique character. Thus, it merits examination as a cohesive entity with a common story of historical development. The presentation of that story here will draw significantly on the aforementioned definitive treatment by Lincoln and Mamiya (1990), as well as on Floyd-Thomas et al.'s (2007) *Black Church Studies: An Introduction.*

Black Religion During Slavery

When black people were brought to America as slaves, they brought their African culture with them. However, there is debate over how much of this culture, especially in terms of religion, survived the slave experience and white efforts to convert slaves to Christianity. Whites were at first ambivalent about converting slaves, particularly since English common law tradition maintained that Christians could not be held in bondage, in essence making slave baptism tantamount to emancipation. In reaction, many colonies passed laws that permitted slaves to be converted and baptized without freeing them (Scherer 1975). By the time of the Civil War, most slaves had been converted to Christianity, primarily by Baptist and Methodist missionaries. However, many whites viewed slave conversion in instrumental terms: Christian slaves, they hoped, would be better slaves. Religion was often used to teach slaves to be respectful and obedient not only to God, but also to their masters in this world (Raboteau 2004).

While it might appear that this "slave religion" was an oppressive force that only served the purposes of the slavemasters, Lincoln and Mamiya (1990) make several points that provide a more positive slant to antebellum African American religious experience. First, slaves developed over time their own vision of Christianity that reflected elements of their African past and responded to the circumstances in which they found themselves. While whites may have introduced Christianity to the slaves, they did not completely control its development. Slaves ordinarily attended white churches (though they sat in a separate section). However, they also exercised some freedom in their religious lives and met secretly to develop their own songs, religious rituals, and spiritual leaders. This underground slave religion is referred to by scholars as the "invisible institution" (Frazier and Lincoln 1974; Raboteau 2004).

Second, Lincoln and Mamiya (1990) point out that religion was the only institutional area that was allowed to develop among slaves to any substantial degree. Aside from religion and (to some extent) the family, slaves were generally not allowed to develop political, economic, educational, or cultural institutions. As a result, the Black Church took on many roles that its white counterpart did not, and over time became the primary focus for dealing with social, economic, and political problems in the black community. As Lincoln and Mamiya (1990: 8) argue, "the Black Church has no challenger as the cultural womb of the black community." Thus, the multiple needs served by religion during slavery had lasting effects on the role of the Black Church in later periods.

Third, slave religion clearly performed a survival function for African Americans in bondage. There is a debate—to be discussed later in this chapter—about whether black religion focuses too much on otherworldly themes and undercuts efforts to improve social conditions in the here-and-now. This kind of criticism might be applied to Christianity among the slaves—it promised them rewards in the next life while requiring that they serve their masters in this one. However, Floyd-Thomas et al. (2007) and some other scholars (Berry and Blassingame 1982; Wilmore 1998) have argued that in the face of oppression, religion helped slaves to survive by preventing their total dehumanization and by giving them some feeling of hope and self-worth. Further, survival itself became a political act, because it kept open the possibility that future leaders would be able to overcome oppression—an attitude that has become known as the "survival tradition."

Fourth, even during slavery, black religion developed a liberation tradition that would grow stronger in later periods. Floyd-Thomas et al. (2007) argue that this emphasis on freedom has persisted in the religion of black Americans from slavery to the present, but that freedom has meant different things at different times. During slavery, freedom clearly meant liberation from bondage; the three largest slave revolts in American history were led by black ministers (Lincoln and Mamiya 1990). After emancipation, freedom meant the freedom to be educated, the freedom to be employed, and the freedom to move from one place to another in search of a better life. In the civil rights era, freedom became synonymous with enfranchisement and the end of segregation. Today, it has come to be defined more broadly, in terms of political equality and economic justice. The origins of all of this, however, can be traced back to the liberation tradition developed in slave religion.

Black Religion from Reconstruction to the Great Urban Migration

After the Civil War, the Civil Rights Act of 1867 allowed black Americans to participate in the political process for about ten years—until the end of Reconstruction. During that brief time, a number of blacks were elected to public office in the southern states. Many who were elected were members of the clergy, and many black ministers were active in state and local political activities. The Black Church began to function as a political organization, and was so influential that political factions frequently attempted to persuade black voters through the church—especially by working through black religious leaders.

This brief era of political empowerment ended along with Reconstruction in 1876. A range of factors combined to produce a general disenfranchisement of black voters in the South: the removal of protections provided by federal troops, increased Ku Klux Klan activity, economic discrimination, restrictive black codes, electoral obstacles such as poll taxes and "grandfather clauses," and the legitimation of Jim Crow segregation by the Supreme Court in the *Plessy* v. *Ferguson* decision of 1896.

From the end of Reconstruction to the passage of the Voting Rights Act in 1965, the Black Church necessarily became the primary arena for black political activity. While blacks were excluded from mainstream politics, they engaged in "surrogate politics" within the church by electing pastors, trustees, deacons, and so on. These intra-church contests "became an intensive training ground of political experience with all of the triumphs and disappointments of which the political process is capable" (Lincoln and Mamiya 1990: 206). In addition, the political skills developed in church politics could be transferred to the broader public arena if and when opportunities presented themselves.

The church became, in the late nineteenth and early twentieth centuries, a place where talented black men could achieve some degree of success and respect. In order to achieve a prominent position in the Black Church, a minister generally had to have great political ability and strong bureaucratic and leadership skills (in addition, of course, to pastoral gifts). Black ministers were typically the most educated people in the black community, and they often served as liaisons between African Americans and the dominant white culture. The black clergy who derived their livelihoods from the church were not as economically vulnerable as others in the community, and they were thus expected to speak out about political and social issues, including racial discrimination.

Black Religion from the Great Urban Migration to the Civil Rights Period

In the twentieth century, with the decline of family farms, millions of black Americans moved from the rural South to take jobs in urban, industrial areas of the North and West. This led to the growth of established churches in northern and California cities, and also to a proliferation of "storefront churches"—small religious congregations that often met in a rented commercial space. However, despite these changes, the Black Church continued to be the central institution in the African American community, both in the South and outside.

During the early part of the twentieth century, political organization among blacks took a new turn with the development of secular, broad-based civil rights organizations such as the National Association for the Advancement of Colored People (NAACP, established in 1909) and the Urban League (established in 1911). However, while these political organizations were not inherently religious, they drew their primary support from the Black Church and black clergy. Thus, while organizations such as the Urban League and the NAACP provided non-religious loci for social activism and community advancement, they did not significantly diminish the role of the church as the central political institution in black America.

During the Great Depression, "the devastating economic conditions which gripped black communities pushed many black churches into a conservative political stance, and many of the new storefront churches withdrew into a revivalistic sectarianism" (Lincoln and Mamiya 1990: 209). While much political activity was centered on the church during the Depression, it was also a time when many black clergy emphasized otherworldly themes rather than pushing for political action to alleviate the poverty of blacks in this world.

Up until the beginning of the major thrust of the civil rights movement in the 1950s, many black clergy who tried to improve the conditions of blacks did so in a low-key, behind-the-scenes, non-confrontational way (Floyd-Thomas et al. 2007), although there were exceptions, such as Adam Clayton Powell's civil rights protests in Harlem. They attempted, for example, to negotiate with white employers to secure jobs for black workers. The retreat of some black clergy into an otherworldly stance and the relatively low-key approach of many others made the interwar period a relatively quietistic time for black church leadership. That changed dramatically with the coming of the civil rights movement.

The Black Church and the Civil Rights Movement

While some important milestones in racial equality (for example, President Truman's integration of the armed forces) occurred earlier, many scholars mark the 1954 decision of the Supreme Court in *Brown* v. *Board of Education of Topeka, Kansas* as the beginning of the core "civil rights era." In this famous case, the Supreme Court rejected the "separate but equal" formulation of the 1896 *Plessy* v. *Ferguson* decision, ruled that racial segregation in educational institutions was unconstitutional, and ordered that schools desegregate "with all deliberate speed."

Another critical event sparking the civil rights movement took place the following year in Montgomery, Alabama. Rosa Parks, a black domestic worker returning home from her job, took a seat on a public bus near the front—a section reserved for white patrons, if there were any. When the bus driver later asked her to surrender her seat to a white rider and move to the back, she refused. For this, Rosa Parks was arrested. In response, black leaders in Montgomery—most of whom were ministers—organized the famous Montgomery bus boycott. Blacks (the predominant users of public transportation in the city) refused to ride the city buses and, after about a year, were successful in desegregating the city's transportation system. This basic scenario was repeated in several other southern cities as well. Further, this successful boycott provided a model and an inspiration for many civil rights protests (marches, boycotts, sit-ins, freedom rides, etc.) that came later, especially during the early 1960s.

Black churches were the centers for coordinating the boycott activities, and the black clergy involved in the Montgomery boycott selected a young Baptist minister, Dr. Martin Luther King, Jr., to be their leader and spokesman. King's success in uniting black clergy, strengthening black resolve, negotiating with white leaders, and addressing the national media during the Montgomery bus boycott ultimately led to his leadership of the civil rights movement in general. In 1957, King led a group of black ministers in founding the Southern Christian Leadership Conference (SCLC), which became one of the nation's leading civil rights organizations during the 1960s. Lincoln and Mamiya (1990: 211) refer to the SCLC as the "political arm of the Black Church." Black churches also provided help for other, more secular civil rights organizations such as the Student Nonviolent Coordinating Committee (SNCC) and the Congress of Racial Equality (CORE).

Based on his faith in Jesus Christ and his study of Mohandas Gandhi, King advocated non-violent resistance to racial injustice. This included civil disobedience, or deliberate defiance of laws that were unjust. In the 1940s, sociologist Gunnar Myrdal (1944) had famously argued that the issue of race was truly "an American dilemma." White Americans, Myrdal argued, gave strong support to democratic ideals such as equality, but did not apply these ideals to black Americans. Myrdal predicted that white Americans would ultimately have to resolve this dilemma one way or another—they would either abandon the ideals, or they would begin to apply them to blacks. Building on this insight, King's strategy was to confront the conscience of white America—to force whites to see the contradiction between the high ideals that they professed on one hand and the oppressive reality of Jim Crow segregation and black poverty on the other. King wanted reconciliation with whites, but only on terms of true racial equality.

While imprisoned for participating in protest activities, King (1963) wrote his famous "Letter from Birmingham Jail," which provided the moral rationale for the civil rights movement and for civil disobedience. Drawing on Augustine and Thomas Aquinas, King distinguished between a just law (which people had a moral responsibility to obey) and an unjust law (which had no moral force). A just law is in accord with the natural law or the law of God, and an unjust law undermines the basic principle of human dignity inherent in the natural law. Laws that institutionalize racial inequality are unjust, especially when a minority was not allowed to vote or to have any say about the passage of such laws. The civil rights movement openly defied laws that legitimized racial discrimination and segregation—laws that came tumbling down during the 1960s as new laws (e.g., the 1964 Civil Rights Act and the 1965 Voting Rights Act) created a changed racial reality in America.

Black and white Americans of many different religious backgrounds supported the push for racial equality. However, the Black Church was indisputably the heart of the civil rights movement (Morris 1984). Hundreds of black clergy and their congregations formed the backbone of the effort, throughout the South and beyond. Black churches provided meeting places, information centers, and the activists for civil rights demonstrations. From their pulpits, black clergy provided the inspiration and guidance. Many black churches paid a heavy price for this work. White racists opposed to civil rights also understood the importance of religion in supporting the movement, and several hundred black churches were attacked, bombed, or burned during the civil rights years (Lincoln and Mamiya 1990).

The Black Church Since the Civil Rights Era

After the end of the classic "civil rights era" (generally marked by the assassination of Martin Luther King in 1968), the national prominence of African American churches and religious leaders receded somewhat. While the role of the Black Church today does not match its centrality during the civil rights era, however, it has continued to be very important in black politics and remains a core institution of the black community. The centrality of the Black Church in politics—but also some important shifts—is demonstrated very well by its role in the presidential campaigns of two prominent black politicians: Jesse Jackson in 1984 and 1988, and Barack Obama in 2008 and 2012.

Jesse Jackson was one of the talented black ministers who attracted national attention for his work with Martin Luther King during the civil rights movement. Additionally, Jackson gained recognition for creating Operation Push (People United to Save Humanity), a program designed primarily to motivate black teenagers to get an education and to succeed economically. In his 1984 campaign for the Democratic presidential nomination, Jackson advanced the idea of a "Rainbow Coalition" of different races and groups working together to solve various social problems (e.g., racial inequality and poverty).

Black churches and black ministers played a crucial role in Jackson's campaigns. Jackson told ABC's *Nightline* program that Mondale had big labor, Reagan had big business, but he had "Big Church" (Castelli 1988: 58). Jackson frequently spoke in black churches, obtained support and endorsements from many black ministers, and raised a great deal of money for his campaign from black congregations. In the 1984 campaign, Jackson was more controversial among blacks than he would be later; some viewed him as a publicity-seeker with no real chance to get elected. However, Hertzke (1991: 12) argues that by 1988, "Jackson was the undisputed leader of black America." In this role, Jackson continued to use black churches and ministers as crucial resources in his 1988 campaign. Although black support for Jackson's bid was strong across the board, those who attended churches where ministers preached politics and endorsed candidates were even more likely to support Jackson and (most significantly) to actually vote in the primaries (Wilcox 1991).

Barack Obama's successful pursuit of the Democratic nomination and, ultimately, the presidency in 2008 was obviously a watershed for African Americans. Not surprisingly, Obama attracted overwhelming black support, and African American religious leaders and congregations mobilized behind his candidacy with great enthusiasm. In several important respects, however, Obama's campaign differed markedly from those of Jesse Jackson twenty years before. To begin with, Obama was much less obviously tied into the African American community and the Black Church. As the mixed-race son of a white mother and a Kenyan father, raised in Kansas, Hawaii, and Indonesia, Obama's background differed markedly from that of Jackson, who actually grew up in segregated South Carolina and marched with Martin Luther King. Perhaps as a result, the Obama campaign sought from the outset to transcend race in a way that was never really possible for Jackson (and, in doing so, became more than a niche or protest candidacy). Moreover, Obama's relationship with the Black Church was markedly different from Jackson's. Obama, unlike Jackson, is not a clergyman, and he came to the Black Church (and, indeed, to Christianity) as an adult (Obama 2006). During the campaign, Obama's connection to African American Christianity became more a liability than an asset, as his association with the racially vitriolic Reverend Jeremiah Wright became one of the biggest obstacles during his primary bid (and prompted a speech in which he distanced himself from his former pastor). Thus, Obama's two elections were much less a triumph for the Black Church per se than a successful bid by Jesse Jackson would have been.

This is not to suggest by any means that the Black Church has become politically irrelevant. It was indisputably an integral part of the Obama electoral coalition. In addition, the continuing importance of the Black Church in the post-civil rights era is indicated by several factors. First, black churches continue to serve as forums for candidates (overwhelmingly Democratic ones), and ministers continue to give endorsements to candidates. Second, though less common than it once was, some black ministers still hold elected or appointed public offices. Third, black Americans still overwhelmingly endorse the role of their churches and ministers in politics. Most black Americans in a study by Walton (1985) indicated that black churches and black ministers were the major influences in their thinking. Another study found that 82 percent of blacks believed that the church had helped the condition of blacks in America, 12 percent believed the church had made no difference, and only 5 percent believed that the church had hurt blacks (Taylor et al. 1987). Political scientists continue to find that black churches are critical agents of political mobilization in the African American community (Pinn 2002; McDaniel 2008).

At the same time, certain factors are decreasing cultural unity within the black community and, thus, the influence of the Black Church as a dominant institution. First, increasing secularization in the black community, while not as pronounced as among whites, reduces the influence of religion and the black churches to some degree. Second, with the breakdown of segregation and the expansion of opportunities for black Americans, black society is becoming more differentiated and pluralistic, reducing cultural unity. The role of the minister in the black community has been diminished by the

development of competing, secular elites such as lawyers and other professionals. Black ministers were once the most educated and prosperous members
of their communities, but this is no longer necessarily the case. Third, the
increasing separation of the black community into two primary class divisions
(a "coping sector" of middle-class people and a "crisis sector" of the working
and dependent poor—see Lincoln and Mamiya 1990) has reduced cultural
unity. Finally, while the traditional Black Church has been the predominant
institution in terms of both religion and politics in the black community,
it has faced some significant challenges from competing viewpoints in the
post-civil rights era.

Religious Challenges to the Traditional Black Church

Chidester (1988) argues that black leaders pursued three major religious–
political strategies to deal with racial inequality: separation, integration, and
liberation. The integration strategy was clearly the one favored by Martin
Luther King, Jr., and became the predominant focus of the mainstream Black
Church and the civil rights movement. It is important to remember, however,
that not everyone in the Black Church supported a political integration focus;
some wanted the church to tend to people's religious needs and avoid social
and political activism. Second, the kind of integration strategy pursued by
Martin Luther King, Jr. lost influence in the latter part of the 1960s as more
militant (and more secular) leaders such as Stokely Carmichael rejected King's
non-violent, moderate, inter-racial approach and substituted a more aggressive
strategy with the slogan "Black Power."

While traditional African American Protestantism is by far the predominant religious perspective in the black community (claiming the allegiance
of more than 80 percent of black Americans), meaningful challenges to its
typical approach to religion and politics have arisen both inside and outside
African American Christianity. The two most significant of these are black
liberation theology and Islam.

Black Liberation Theology

The theme of liberation has permeated black Christianity since slaves were
first converted. However, black liberation theology takes a different approach
to the concept. Whereas the traditional liberation theme was based on
mainstream Christian theology (developed primarily by whites), black
liberation theology is an approach to Christianity developed systematically
from an African American perspective. For example, some black liberation
theologians argue that Jesus was black—either metaphorically (e.g., Cone
1969) or literally so (e.g., Cleage 1968).

There are many different black liberation theologians, and they do not
agree on everything, either theologically or politically. However, there
are several themes on which most black liberation theologians agree. The

controlling theme of black liberation theology is the idea that Jesus is the liberator of the poor and oppressed (Corbett-Hemeyer 2010). While this liberation orientation might contain some otherworldly elements and might offer some hope for a future in which oppression and pain no longer exist, the crucial focus of this liberation is the here and now, liberation in this world, defined in terms of sociopolitical and economic justice.

In black liberation theology, God is on the side of the oppressed and opposes oppressors. God wants justice and equality in this world, and black people can help bring this about. Instead of focusing on transcendent concerns, black liberation theology emphasizes determined, aggressive political action to bring about social change in this world.

The best-known proponent of black liberation theology is James Cone, whose first major work in this area was *Black Theology and Black Power* (1969). Cone argued that religious authority arises out of resistance to oppression, and that people come to know Christ through their experience of oppression. Because Jesus is the liberator of the oppressed and blacks in America are the oppressed, then God must be black (at least ontologically). Any theology that does not stand for the liberation of oppressed people is simply wrong— or even anti-Christian. Christianity, Cone argues, must be viewed and interpreted through the lens of black liberation. White people, he contends, had Christianity all wrong or else they could not have oppressed others. Whites, however, can free themselves from their own oppressive structures by joining in the liberation of blacks.

Cone (1969) charged that black churches were corrupted by adoption of the otherworldly orientation of white Christianity. White missionaries taught blacks to be obedient and compliant in this world and promised them rewards in the next. His theological orientation is very tangible, he advocates direct action by blacks to achieve racial goals in this life, and (unlike Martin Luther King, Jr.) he does not in principle reject violence as a tool to achieve liberation and social equality.

There are significant differences among black liberation theologians on important questions such as the ultimate goal in the relationship between white oppressors and the black oppressed. Some (e.g., Cleage 1972) advocate black nationalism—a black nation within the United States. Others (e.g., Roberts 1974) advocate reconciliation between whites and blacks. Still others (e.g., Johnson 1993) have little to say about white people at all.

How much influence has black liberation theology had among black ministers? It is difficult to answer such a question definitively, but it appears that the Black Church has not changed dramatically as a result of black liberation theology. Lincoln and Mamiya (1990) indicate that black liberation theology has only a limited influence on those in their national survey of black ministers. They asked black clergy: "Have you been influenced by any of the authors and thinkers of black liberation theology (e.g., James Cone, Gayraud Wilmore . . .)"? Only about one third of the black ministers interviewed indicated any influence from black liberation theology. This is consistent with work by Pinn (2002) and Harris-Lacewell (2007), both of whom suggest that black liberation theology has been much more influential among intellectuals and in seminaries than in most actual black churches. There are obviously exceptions—younger and more educated black ministers were more likely to say that they had been influenced by black liberation theology, and President Obama's Chicago church was clearly steeped in a liberation theology outlook. Overall, however, black liberation theology has remained a minority perspective within African American Christianity.

Islam

Based on their sample of more than 100,000 Americans, Kosmin and Lachman (1993) estimate that up to 2 percent of the African American population (as distinct from the African immigrant population) is Muslim. This makes Islam the largest non-Christian faith among American blacks. Overall, African Americans comprise about 20 percent of the total Muslim population in the United States—a smaller share than in decades past, because of an influx of Asian Muslim immigrants (Djupe and Green 2007).

In general, Islam has attracted black men more than black women. In black Christian churches, the majority of active members are female, but the reverse is true in mosques. Islam is a patriarchal religion, and this is probably part of its appeal to black males, Kosmin and Lachman (1993) suggest, because it increases their self-respect. Lincoln and Mamiya (1990) suggest that black Muslims project a more "macho" image. At the same time, however, it is important to remember that Islam requires people to live a self-disciplined, modest life and to avoid evils such as drinking, gambling, and illicit sex. Lincoln and Mamiya also contend that black males are more involved in Islam because Muslims have worked actively with black males in prisons and on the streets in order to convert them.

The Nation of Islam

In terms of the religious–political linkage, the most important strand of Muslim development in the United States is the Nation of Islam group— widely known as the "Black Muslims." The Nation of Islam was founded in 1933 in Detroit by Wali Fard, who advocated an unusual version of Islam that was often in conflict with traditional Muslim teaching. The movement was led by Elijah Muhammad (born Elijah Poole) from 1934 until his death in 1975. Elijah Muhammad taught that Christianity was a slave religion designed by white masters to exploit blacks. Islam was the true religion for blacks, who should separate themselves from whites rather than integrating with white society and consorting with "white devils."

The Black Muslims advocated a separate nation for blacks within the United States. At the personal level, the group emphasized self-help and self-discipline for blacks. It demanded changes in self-defeating ghetto lifestyles and greater stability in work habits and family life. The Black Muslims prohibited drinking alcohol, gambling, illegal drugs, and sexual license, and required respect for women (within a patriarchal family structure). While these values were in accord with mainstream Islam (and, indeed, with much of traditional African American Christianity), many of the Nation of Islam's teachings were not (e.g., the emphasis on racial solidarity and separation from whites).

Malcolm X

The Nation of Islam was small and obscure until Malcolm X became Elijah Muhammad's national representative in the 1950s and established mosques in many major cities. Born Malcolm Little, the son of a Baptist minister who was killed by a white mob, Malcolm later rejected the name Little and took the X as his last name to stand for his missing African name. Malcolm Little became a criminal during his teenage years, and he was in prison when he converted to Islam (Black Muslims had been and still are very active in converting and working with black prisoners). After his conversion, Malcolm X began a program of educating himself in prison. When he was released in 1952, he began working with the Black Muslims and quickly gained prominence in the movement.

By the early 1960s, the Black Muslims had gained some national prominence and Malcolm X had become the most recognized figure in the movement, although Elijah Muhammad was still the group's leader. It was during this time that the Black Muslims made "black power" a term known in every household. Malcolm X continued to advance the themes of black self-help, self-discipline, integrity, and separation from whites. He wanted blacks to be unified, to have control over their own institutions, and, ultimately, to have their own separate nation. He famously called for African Americans to assert their rights "by any means necessary."

Conflict between Malcolm X and Elijah Muhammad developed in 1963 when the leader chastised Malcolm for publicly asserting that President Kennedy's assassination was "the chickens coming home to roost." In 1964, Malcolm X formed his own organization, Muslim Mosque, Incorporated. Later that year, he traveled to the Islamic holy city of Mecca on a pilgrimage, and returned with a different perspective. The new Malcolm X adopted a much more traditional Islamic view (rather than the unorthodox theology that Black Muslims had developed), and this entailed a softening of his views on the inherent evil of whites. While Malcolm X still condemned white racism, he began to emphasize the need to humanize all people. In addition to his religious organization (Muslim Mosque), Malcolm X formed a secular, non-sectarian organization (the Organization of Afro-American Unity) that welcomed people of any race or creed. However, before he could develop his new views very much, Malcolm X was murdered in 1965 by men who were alleged to be Black Muslims.

The American Society of Muslims

After the departure of Malcolm X, the Nation of Islam continued its course until 1975 when Elijah Muhammad died. After that, the group ultimately went in two directions. The larger part of the group followed Elijah Muhammad's son Wallace (later changed to Warith) Deen Muhammad, who steered his followers away from the Nation of Islam into a new group that was eventually called the American Muslim Mission, then the American Society of Muslims. This group embraced traditional Islamic beliefs, abandoning many tenets that had been peculiar to Black Muslims, and rejected racial separatism and hatred. In the American Society of Muslims, a racially integrated organization, there were no black, white, or Asian Muslims—just Muslims.

These Muslims who followed Warith Deen Muhammad were politically different in many ways from the Black Church, and the differences are apparent in their weekly newspaper, *The Muslim Journal*. This newspaper advocated conservative ideas such as the free market, self-discipline, and hard work to get ahead, and at times even endorsed Republican candidates (Kosmin and Lachman 1993). Thus, this Muslim group among black Americans represents a substantial departure from the Black Church in terms of both religion and politics.

Louis Farrakhan and the Nation of Islam

While many Black Muslims beginning in the 1970s moved away from the Nation of Islam and its racially radical views, some did not. Thus, the Nation of Islam survived, albeit in much reduced form. It has been led since 1979 by Minister Louis Farrakhan, and estimates of the group's size range from 10,000 to 70,000 (Hallowell 2013). Farrakhan has continued to advocate the views of Elijah Muhammad—including the view of whites as the devil and the ideal of racial separation. However, he has probably gained the most public attention for his anti-Semitism, exemplified by his assertion that Jews were members of a "gutter religion."

In his 1984 campaign for president, Jesse Jackson came into conflict with American Jews in large part because of his close association with Louis Farrakhan (though his reference to New York as "Hymietown" did not help). Farrakhan created a very disciplined security organization and supplied bodyguards for Jackson during the campaign. While he initially embraced Barack Obama and his candidacy in 2008, Obama disavowed him and his support. Later, Farrakhan turned on Obama over his decision to intervene militarily in Libya and his failure to support the Palestinians, disparagingly calling him "the first Jewish president" (Davis 2011). Farrakhan's following has never been very large, but he has wielded disproportionate influence and garnered significant media attention because of his controversial and outspoken style. His potential influence was best reflected in his success in organizing the Million Man March in Washington, D.C., in 1995, an effort that drew significant participation from African American Christians. Since 2007, however, Farrakhan's failing health has significantly limited his public presence, raising serious questions about the Nation of Islam's future when he is no longer able to lead the group.

Black Religion: Opiate or Inspiration?

As the long-standing central institution in African American community life, the Black Church will inevitably be influential in shaping African Americans' approach to politics. While the Church's role in the civil rights movement is well documented, some have actually argued that religion, on balance, serves—in Karl Marx's words—as an "opiate" for black Americans. When religion has an otherworldly focus, it emphasizes heaven and eternal life after death; this is sometimes called a "pie-in-the-sky" approach to religion. Such an approach tends to de-emphasize, or even discourage, political involvement. When religion has a thisworldly focus, it stresses political and social action to improve conditions here and now; this is basically the social gospel orientation. This take on politics naturally lends itself to political engagement. Of course, these two approaches to religion represent poles, and are not mutually exclusive; most churches emphasize some combination of the social and the personal, the tangible and the transcendent. Nonetheless, a particular church or denomination's tendency in one direction or the other can be consequential for its adherents' level of political activity.

Some critics have argued that the otherworldly focus of religion gives black Americans comfort in this life by promising them a better life in the next, and thus undercuts any motivation to undertake political and social actions to remedy inequalities. By contrast, other analysts have concluded that religious involvement among black Americans stokes a sense of social justice and inspires political activism on behalf of change. These two conflicting takes on religion among African Americans can be labeled the "opiate" view and the "inspiration" view, and each merits examination.

The Opiate View

One of the best-known statements of the opiate view of the effects of religion among black Americans is offered by E. Franklin Frazier (1963), although versions of this critique have been advanced by others in the post-civil rights era as well (e.g., Reed 1986; Davis 2010). Frazier argued that the authoritarian control of the church over African Americans inhibited their development and kept them from learning democratic processes. In fact, he argued that the Black Church and black religion were in many ways responsible for the "backwardness" of American blacks. The Black Church, he contended, kept African Americans subservient, meek, and ignorant. With increasing secularization—especially in urban areas—some blacks were able to escape the influence of the church and take action to improve the situation of their community. The otherworldly focus of black churches, Frazier argued, had historically kept most blacks from taking that sort of direct political and social action.

The first significant social scientific research to test this opiate view was Gary Marx's (1967, 1969) survey of over a thousand black Americans in urban areas. Marx developed a measure of religiosity by combining items concerning religious orthodoxy, attendance at religious services, and the subjective importance of religion in one's life. He measured civil rights militancy by asking respondents several questions about their attitudes toward civil rights demonstrations, the pace of civil rights progress, and willingness to take part in direct actions for civil rights. His findings showed that, in general, blacks who scored higher on religiosity were less militant in terms of civil rights—and this was true even when controlling for demographic variables (e.g., age, region, education) that might affect the linkage between religiosity and militancy. However, some blacks who were very religious were also militant, and Marx (1969) analyzed the types of religious orientations within this group. In general, his study supported the idea that an otherworldly religious orientation inhibited civil rights activism, while a religious focus on the here and now increased it.

Subsequent studies have tended to reinforce Marx's basic insight that the relationship between black religion and political activism is highly dependent on the theology and dynamics of the individual church congregation (Calhoun-Brown 1996; Harris-Lacewell 2007; McDaniel 2008). Different black churches have had different views on political involvement, and several studies have shown substantial variation among black clergy. For example, Johnstone's (1969) study of fifty-nine black ministers in Detroit classified them as militants (organizers and activists in the civil rights movement), traditionalists (those who wanted the church to focus on the gospel and stay out of politics), and moderates (who were in between the other two groups). While Johnstone studied clergy only, the views of these ministers about political involvement can be reflected by entire congregations—either because the members of the congregation are influenced by the ministers, or because members originally chose the church at least in part because they agreed with its political orientation. Thus, religious commitment among blacks in a church with a non-political focus might very well inhibit political involvement. Indeed, this is exactly what Harris-Lacewell (2007) finds with regard to the growing number of "prosperity gospel" black churches, or those that emphasize the link between personal righteousness and material well-being more than the imperative for group solidarity and struggle against social injustice.

The Inspiration View

The inspiration view sees black churches and religion as providing strong motivation for political involvement among African Americans. Religion is seen as a resource to spur and facilitate political involvement. For example, religious commitment such as manifested by church attendance might foster group identity and black consciousness, and this could motivate black Americans to take part in political activities that would improve their collective situation. Church attendance also might expose members of the congregation to the liberation theme emphasized by some black ministers. Wilcox and Gomez (1990) argue that black churches mold black pride and black identification; this comes about in large part through exposure to sermons by preachers seeking to build black consciousness. It is also possible that religious commitment might enhance self-esteem, and this in turn can provide the confidence and sense of efficacy needed for political involvement.

Lincoln and Mamiya's (1990) study of 1,894 black clergy showed very high support for political involvement. For example, 91 percent supported protest marches on civil rights issues, and 92 percent said that churches should express their views on day-to-day social and political questions. They further argue that black churches actually help to overcome African American alienation from electoral politics, and thus increase political participation among their members.

The inspiration view is generally supported by the bulk of modern social scientific data and analysis. Many scholars have found that blacks with higher levels of religious commitment and church involvement are more likely to vote than their less religious counterparts (Wilcox 1991; Peterson 1992; Harris 1999). This pattern is born out in NORC GSS data from recent elections. Figure 9.1 shows self-reported voter turnout among African Americans in the low, medium, and high religious commitment groups for the 2004 and 2008 presidential elections. In both years, religious commitment had a clear and dramatic mobilizing effect. In 2004, only 40 percent of the least religious African Americans report having voted, as compared with 70 percent of the most religious. In 2008, with Barack Obama as the Democratic nominee, turnout was, not surprisingly, higher among all groups of black voters. Still, religious

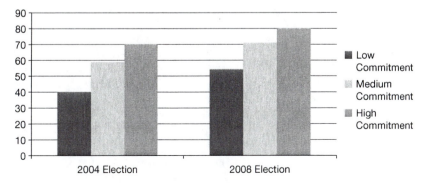

Figure 9.1 Religious Commitment and Voter Turnout among African Americans.
Source: NORC GSS, 2006–2012.

commitment made a major difference, as 80 percent of high-commitment African Americans report having voted, as compared with only 54 percent of the low-commitment cohort. Clearly, religious commitment and political participation among African Americans are strongly correlated.

On balance, there is more evidence to support the inspiration view of black religion and politics than the opiate view. To be sure, there is variation from congregation to congregation; "politicized" churches mobilize much more than apolitical ones (Calhoun-Brown 1996), and liberation theology spurs political involvement much more than the "prosperity gospel" (Harris-Lacewell 2007). In addition, there is a difference between simple voting and true "militancy"; it is possible that Black churches tend to foster the former while discouraging the latter (and one might legitimately question whether militancy ought, in fact, to be the goal). In any event, it is clear that, taken as a whole, one can hardly call the contemporary Black Church apolitical.

Racial Differences in Religious and Political Attitudes

The historical experience of black Americans and the unique role of the Black Church as the center of the African American community (including its politics) have no doubt had important effects on the ways in which their religious and political attitudes are linked. Before examining these relationships, however, it is important to demonstrate the substantial differences in both religious and political attitudes between African Americans and their white fellow citizens. These differences are likely due in large part to the divergent historical experiences of black and white Americans. Because of these religious and political variances, the patterns of religious/political linkages among whites discussed in the previous chapter will likely not entirely apply in the black community—although some of the patterns will no doubt be similar. This examination of differences between whites and blacks in their religious and political orientations will provide context for the subsequent discussion of how these two types of views are linked among black Americans.

Religious Differences

Table 9.1 (based on the 2006–2012 combined NORC GSS data described in Chapter 8) shows that there are substantial disparities between whites and blacks in terms of all three religious variables examined in the previous chapter: religious identifications, views of the Bible, and religious commitment. In terms of religious tradition, blacks are overwhelmingly (77 percent) Protestant, and a clear majority (59 percent) are evangelical Protestants. African Americans are significantly less likely than whites to be "nones" (11 percent), Jews (less than 1 percent), or Catholics (8 percent). In addition, blacks differ significantly from whites in their approach to the Bible. While the majority position among whites is biblical conservatism (the view that the Bible is the inspired, but not literal, word of God), a clear majority of

Table 9.1 Religious Differences between Whites and Blacks

	White Respondents (%)	Black Respondents (%)
Religious Group Identifications		
None	17	11
Jewish	2	<1
Catholic	25	7
Mainline Protestant	23	16
Evangelical Protestant	26	57
Biblical Views		
Biblical Literalist	29	57
Biblical Conservative	50	33
Biblical Liberal	21	9
Religious Commitment		
Low	38	20
Medium	32	31
High	30	49

Source: NORC GSS, 2006–2012.

African Americans (57 percent) are biblical literalists. Moreover, while an appreciable minority of whites (21 percent) regard the Bible as a purely human collection of legends, fables, etc., this view is held by fewer than one in ten blacks.

Finally, blacks score much higher on religious commitment than do whites. The previous chapter described a religious commitment score based on frequency of attendance at religious services, frequency of prayer, and reported strength of religious preference. White respondents were then divided into thirds based on their scores on this index. For Table 9.1, the same scores were re-computed, this time using both black and white respondents. When the two are measured together, Table 9.1 shows that 49 percent of blacks are in the high religious commitment category, as opposed to only 30 percent of whites. Conversely, while the plurality (38 percent) of whites are classified as low-commitment, only 20 percent of blacks merit this classification—the smallest group. Clearly, religion on average plays a larger role in the lives of American blacks than of American whites. This is in accord with much research (e.g., Gallup and Castelli 1989; Wilcox 1991; Corbett-Hemeyer 2010) showing blacks to be highly religious in a variety of ways: attending religious services, praying, participating in other church activities, Bible reading, strength of religious preference, church membership, ranking God as important in their lives, and ranking religion as an important part of life. Alluding to the Gallup International organization surveys on religious beliefs in twenty-three nations, Gallup and Castelli (1989: 122) conclude that "American blacks are, by some measures, the most religious people in the world." This observation is as valid today as it was two decades ago.

Political Differences

Even the most casual observer of American politics knows that there are significant differences in political loyalties and priorities between whites and blacks in the United States. Since emancipation, African Americans have tended to be very strong and unified in their partisan attachments, first to the Republican Party, and later to the Democrats.

Democratic Identification and Voting among Black Americans

As one would expect, Table 9.2 demonstrates that there are persistent and dramatic political differences between black and white Americans. First, blacks vote overwhelmingly Democratic in presidential elections. While George W. Bush was able to make some minor inroads among black voters in 2004, winning about one eighth of their votes, black support for Barack Obama four years later was monolithic. Fully 97 percent of African Americans in the GSS sample report having voted for Obama in 2008 and, while this survey (as discussed previously) exaggerates Obama's support somewhat, the true figure among blacks was not far short of that. While clearly this overwhelming percentage reflects the special circumstance of the first viable African American candidate for President, it is in keeping with longstanding black support for Democratic candidates. Before the 1930s, most black voters supported Republicans—because Abraham Lincoln has freed the slaves, and because the Democratic Party in the South supported African American disenfranchisement long after Reconstruction ended. However, because of

Table 9.2 Political Differences between Whites and Blacks

	White Respondents (%)	Black Respondents (%)
2004 Presidential Vote		
Kerry	39	88
Bush	61	12
2008 Presidential Vote		
Obama	53	97
McCain	47	3
Party Identification		
Democrat	27	66
Independent	41	30
Republican	32	4
Ideological Identification		
Liberal	25	33
Moderate	38	44
Conservative	38	24

Source: NORC GSS, 2006–2012.

the appeal of Democratic economic programs to help the poor during the Great Depression, black voters have been predominantly Democratic since Franklin Roosevelt's New Deal coalition was formed.

The attraction of black voters to the Democratic Party was strengthened by the success of a Democratic president, Lyndon Johnson, in obtaining passage of the 1964 Civil Rights Act—a major step in outlawing racial discrimination. While many Republicans in Congress supported this legislation, the key point is that the Democratic president pushed for its passage while the Republican presidential candidate in 1964, Barry Goldwater, opposed it. Other legislation passed during the 1960s (e.g., the Voting Rights Act and various affirmative action and "Great Society" anti-poverty programs) further cemented Democratic loyalties among African Americans. Today, blacks are by far the most loyal group of Democratic voters.

Table 9.2 shows that about two thirds (66 percent) of black Americans identify themselves as Democrats—as compared to only 27 percent of whites—and only 4 percent identify with the Republican Party. Moreover, even among the 30 percent who call themselves independents, a strong Democratic lean is evident, as three times as many report an inclination toward the Democrats as toward the GOP.

Political Liberalism and Conservatism among Black Americans

In terms of ideological identifications, Table 9.2 shows that blacks are more likely than whites to call themselves liberals (33 percent vs. 25 percent) and less likely than whites to call themselves conservatives (24 percent vs. 38 percent). It is not clear, however, how much these self-classifications mean in terms of specific political issues and behaviors. As some scholars (e.g., Harris-Lacewell 2004) have pointed out, conservatism in the black community often means something different than it does to white Americans, emphasizing personal responsibility and respect for traditional values more than an embrace of libertarian economic doctrines or the Republican Party. Indeed, the vast majority of black "conservatives" supported Barack Obama's bids for the presidency. Overall, when one examines black and white positions on specific issues, several patterns are apparent.

First, blacks are more liberal on economic questions than whites—even when one controls for racial income differences. Blacks are more supportive of social welfare programs to help the poor and disadvantaged because they are more likely to be poor; even for those who are not, however, the African American historical experience has created a spirit of racial solidarity that inclines blacks to look at economic questions through a group, rather than individual, lens (Dawson 1994; Wilson 2012).

Second, while blacks are (not surprisingly) more supportive of racial equality than whites, there is no substantial pattern of differences between whites and blacks concerning gender equality. In addition, African Americans are somewhat less politically tolerant (as measured by the scale discussed in

Chapter 8) than whites. This lower tolerance among blacks is likely due in large part to their lower average education levels and to less exposure to social and religious diversity.

Finally, blacks tend to be more conservative than whites on a range of social and moral issues. Traditionally, African Americans have been less supportive of legal abortion than whites (Combs and Welch 1982; Secret 1987), though this divergence has declined somewhat over time (Carter et al. 2009). In addition, blacks tend to be less supportive than whites of gay marriage (Bruni 2011). Finally, blacks in the 2006–2012 GSS data are more conservative than whites on the Supreme Court's school prayer decision and on the euthanasia issue.

Overall, blacks are more politically liberal than whites on many issues, especially economic ones. At the same time, blacks are often more conservative on questions with an obviously religious component. Kosmin and Lachman (1993: 205) refer to this situation among African Americans as "the apparent paradox of theological conservatism and political liberalism." Blacks and whites also differ in their attitudes toward church–state relations; African Americans are less supportive of the separation of church and state, both in abstract terms and in many concrete applications (Jelen and Wilcox 1995). In the 2006–2012 NORC GSS data, for example, black respondents are significantly more likely than others to say that there should be daily prayer in public schools.

Links between Black Religious and Political Attitudes

In examining the relationship between African American religious and political orientations, it makes sense, for the sake of comparison, to explore the three dimensions of religious orientation that structured the analysis of white Americans in Chapter 8: religious identification, views of the Bible, and religious commitment. Jews are excluded from these analyses, because there are too few black Jews in the GSS sample to permit reliable generalization. Otherwise, all of the analytical categories are identical to those described in the previous chapter.

Religious Group Identification

Analysis of the 2006–2012 NORC GSS data reveals no significant differences in presidential voting among blacks by religious tradition. In 2008, there is simply no variation to explain—African Americans of all denominations and of none gave near-unanimous support to Barack Obama. Even in 2004, where there was at least a bit more variance in African American vote choice, religious identification is not significantly associated with the likelihood of voting for George W. Bush. The small group of blacks (roughly 12 percent in the GSS sample) who report supporting the Republican are distributed roughly proportionately across the evangelical, mainline, Catholic, and no religion categories.

Religious identification also has very limited effects on African American partisanship. Those with no religious affiliation are more likely than others to call themselves independents as opposed to Democrats (echoing a pattern found among white voters as well), but more than two thirds of those in every other religious identification category identify with the Democratic Party. Republican identification is in the single digits in every religious group. Similarly, religious identification appears to have no major effect on the likelihood that African Americans will call themselves liberals, moderates, or conservatives.

In terms of specific issues, the effects of religious identification among African Americans are modest and sporadic. Blacks in the "none" category of religious identification score a bit higher than others on political tolerance, while evangelicals score a bit lower. Mainline Protestants are somewhat more likely to oppose capital punishment than are blacks in other traditions, and "nones" are less likely to favor prayer in public schools. Overall, though, the general pattern is one of little to no effect of religious identification, on issues ranging from gender equality to euthanasia to defense spending to pornography.

Overall, these results are consistent with older studies (Wilcox and Gomez 1990; Kellstedt and Noll 1990) arguing that denominational affiliation means very little among African Americans when it comes to politics. To the extent that religion matters in differentiating black political attitudes and behavior, denomination appears not to be the key variable.

Attitudes Toward the Bible

Biblical literalism had no discernible impact on presidential voting patterns among African Americans in either 2004 or 2008; as mentioned previously, there is simply too little variance to explain. Attitudes toward the Bible are, however, associated with both partisan and ideological identification. While fewer than 10 percent of those in each biblical category (literalists, conservatives, and liberals) are Republicans, Democratic and independent identification vary appreciably according to biblical view. Biblical literalists are more likely (71 percent) to be Democrats than are biblical conservatives (65 percent) or biblical liberals (52 percent). Thus, the more literalist black Americans are in their interpretation of the Bible, the more Democratic they are, and vice versa. On the other hand, biblical literalism is negatively related to liberal self-identification: 43 percent of biblical liberals identify as political liberals, compared with 35 percent of biblical conservatives and 27 percent of biblical literalists.

Thus, among blacks, biblical literalists are more likely to be Democrats but less likely to be liberals. This seeming paradox can probably be explained by the tendency of blacks who are more orthodox in religion to also be more "orthodox" politically, in the sense of remaining loyal to the group's traditional Democratic identification. On the other hand, blacks who are more orthodox religiously are probably also more conservative on many social issues, and therefore would be reluctant to call themselves liberals. If this is in fact the case, one would expect to see a link between biblical literalism and African American positions on a range of specific issues.

Turning to Figure 9.2, this is exactly the pattern that emerges. Figure 9.2 reports the percentage of African American respondents to the 2006–2012 NORC GSS surveys in each biblical category who believe that abortion should be allowed "for any reason," who believe that homosexuality is "not wrong at all," who support marijuana legalization, and who approve of suicide by the terminally ill. On all four issues, there are dramatic differences between biblical literalists (the majority, one should keep in mind, of African Americans) and other blacks in the sample. Biblical liberals, for example, are twice as likely as literalists to take the most pro-choice position on abortion (53 percent versus 27 percent), and are three times as likely to approve of homosexuality (43 percent versus 14 percent). To be sure, biblical attitudes are not universally important—as one moves away from obviously moral issues, to questions such as defense spending and gun control, the differences according to biblical view diminish to the point of insignificance. Clearly, though, attitudes toward the Bible are an important factor in shaping African American approaches to a range of hot-button social issues.

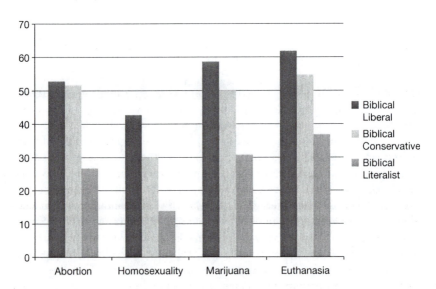

Figure 9.2 Biblical Views and Issue Positions among African Americans.
Source: NORC GSS, 2006–2012.

Religious Commitment

An analysis of the political effects of religious commitment among African Americans produces results very similar to the analysis of biblical attitudes. This is in large part because the two are more closely correlated among blacks than they are among whites; biblical literalism is clearly predominant among blacks with high levels of religious commitment (over 70 percent). In any event, religious commitment is not associated with any significant differences in African American vote choice in either 2004 or 2008. It is, however, related to identification with the Democratic Party; while more than 70 percent of high-commitment blacks call themselves Democrats, only about half of those with low religious commitment do so (with the difference accruing overwhelmingly to the independent, rather than the Republican, category). Clearly, among blacks, commitment to the Church and commitment to the Democratic Party go hand-in-hand. As is the case with biblical literalism, however, that Democratic identification does not generally translate into a self-conception as "liberal." While about half of low-commitment African Americans call themselves liberals, fewer than 30 percent of those with high religious commitment identify this way—probably because of their more conservative positions on many social issues.

Among whites, as Chapter 8 showed, high religious commitment is associated with political conservatism more or less across the board. Among blacks, by contrast, the effect is more clearly confined to social issues. Degree of religious commitment is not significantly related to African American attitudes on such issues as gender equality, political tolerance, gun control, capital punishment, and defense spending. However, more religiously committed blacks are clearly more conservative on many questions with obviously moral dimensions. As Figure 9.3 demonstrates, the relationship between black religious commitment and attitudes toward abortion, homosexuality, drug legalization, and euthanasia looks very similar to the pattern observed with biblical attitudes: the most religiously committed African Americans (about half the sample) differ sharply from other blacks in their distinctively conservative approaches to these questions.

Overall, then, it is clear that religious differences do shape African American approaches to politics, but in limited ways. Unlike the pattern among white Americans, religious orthodoxy and commitment among blacks do not translate into conservative economic positions or support for Republican candidates. A long history of slavery, oppression, and economic disadvantage have largely closed the door to those attitudes, at least for the time being. Just like religiously observant whites, however, religious African Americans do embrace conservative positions on a range of individual social and moral issues. Thus, while they have not generally proven responsive to appeals by conservative candidates, Black churches are often receptive partners for white conservatives in referenda on gay issues, gambling, drug legalization, etc.

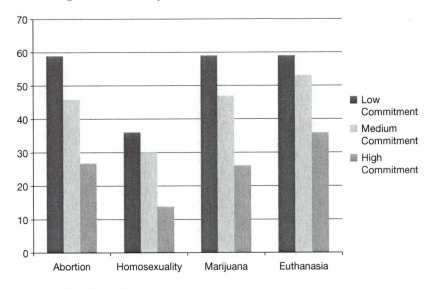

Figure 9.3 Religious Commitment and Issue Positions among African Americans.
Source: NORC GSS, 2006–2012.

Religion and Politics among Latinos

While at one time in America the term "minority" was roughly synonymous with "black," immigration and birth patterns over the last several decades have made this equation (which was always an oversimplification that marginalized Hispanics, Asians, and Native Americans) completely untenable. One of the most significant demographic changes in recent years has been the dramatic growth in America's Latino population, and its diffusion beyond the traditional areas of concentration (in the Southwest, South Florida, and New York City) to become a visible presence in all regions of the country. Latinos now outnumber African Americans in the overall population (17 percent as opposed to 12 percent), and will likely surpass them as a share of the electorate by 2030 (Taylor et al. 2012). Moreover, Latino voting patterns are not as monolithic as those of African Americans, and have shown much more fluctuation from election to election and region to region. Thus, Latino political behavior has been the subject of much recent discussion and analysis, by strategists, pundits, and scholars alike.

The study of the relationship between religion and politics in the Latino community is not nearly as well developed as the voluminous literature on the political effects of African American religion. This is true for several reasons. First, prior to the 1990s, Latinos did not comprise a major share of the national electorate; as recently as 1988, they cast less than 4 percent of the nation's presidential ballots (Taylor et al. 2012). Second, the Latino population is more internally diverse than the African American population, with significant variations in culture, socioeconomic status, and political outlook according to country of origin; these variations can make generalization difficult. Finally, and perhaps most significantly, there is no Latino analog for the Black Church, no religious institution that served as the primary locus of community political organization for generations. Thus, scholarly analysis of Latino religion and politics, if no longer in its infancy, is still in its adolescence.

Latino Religion and Politics in Historical Perspective

Historically, the most obvious difference between black and Latino religion in America is a denominational one. Until relatively recently, Latinos in the United States were overwhelmingly Catholic. One early study, based on data from the mid-1960s, estimated that only about 5 percent of American Hispanics were Protestant (Grebler et al. 1970). Because Latinos were part of a global church with a uniform liturgy and doctrine, they had less opportunity than did African Americans to develop their own ethnically based theologies and indigenous ecclesiastical leadership. Because the priests in Latino churches, unlike black ministers, were often not from the Latino community, they had less inclination and ability to become local political leaders (Sanchez 1993; DeSipio 2007). While the Catholic Church was clearly central to Latinos' *cultural* identity, it generally did not seek to shape their *political* identity. Thus, traditionally, the basic pattern among American Latinos was one of pervasive, but generally apolitical, Catholicism.

In recent decades, this traditional reality has begun to shift in several important ways. First, there is significantly more religious diversity among Latinos than there once was. As a result of aggressive Protestant missionary efforts, both in Latin America and in the United States, only about 70 percent of Hispanics in America now identify as Catholic—still the clear majority, but down appreciably from a few decades ago (DeSipio 2007). Like blacks, Latinos remain more religious, on average, than white Americans (Gibson and Hare 2012), but a significant minority now express that religiosity in Protestant churches. Second, the Catholic Church has begun to be more active in facilitating Latino political organization (Warren 2001), and to speak out more forcefully on issues of concern to Hispanics, such as immigration policy (e.g., the U.S. Conference of Catholic Bishops' 2003 statement *Strangers No More*). Finally, beginning in the early 2000s, Republicans sought to attract Latino voters on the basis of shared culturally conservative values, particularly on human life and family issues. This effort bore fruit for George W. Bush in 2004, when he captured somewhere between 37 and 44 percent of the Latino vote, depending on how one estimates (Leal et al. 2005; Suro et al. 2005). In more recent elections, however, these overtures have been overwhelmed by the politics of immigration, in which Republican positions have alienated many Latino voters. In 2012,

Republican nominee Mitt Romney won only 27 percent of the Latino vote (Cillizza 2013).

Latino Religion and Politics Today

In examining the connections between religion and politics among Hispanics in America today, the central question is whether the patterns look more like those observed among white Americans or black Americans. In other words, do liberal positions on economic and racial solidarity issues over-whelm generally conservative attitudes on moral questions to produce strong Democratic loyalties regardless of religious orientations (the pattern among blacks)? Or, alternatively, does a "culture wars" model prevail, in which religiously orthodox and observant Latinos are much more conserva-tive and Republican than their less religious co-ethnics (the pattern among whites)?

The emerging data on Latino voting behavior and partisanship over the last decade suggest a complex and evolving answer to the question. It is clearly true that, on average, Latino attitudes on most moral issues are more conservative than those of whites, though this social conservatism is more pronounced among Latino Protestants than among Catholics (DeSipio 2007). The extent to which these conservative attitudes drive vote choice, how-ever, varies significantly according to religious tradition. Among Protestant Latinos, Republicans have made significant inroads on the basis of social issues, actually capturing a majority of their votes in 2004 (Suro et al. 2005). Even today, after several years of divisive immigration politics, Protestant Latinos are just as likely to identify as Republicans as Democrats, while Democrats hold a two-to-one or better identification edge among Catholic and secular Latinos (Gibson and Hare 2012). While Republicans have had some success in attracting Latino Protestants, they have not been especially successful in mobilizing those voters; several studies indicate that Latino Protestants vote at even lower rates than do Latino Catholics (Jones-Correa and Leal 2001; DeSipio 2007; Lee and Pachon 2007).

Essentially, it appears that the effects of religion on politics among Latino Catholics look more like those in the black community, with faith fostering economic liberalism and community solidarity and fueling Democratic loyalty despite social conservatism. While Latino Catholics are not as monolithically Democratic as blacks, the basic pattern is similar. Among Latino Protestants, by contrast, religious commitment does seem to drive receptivity to Repub-lican values-based appeals, much as it does among whites. Of course, these patterns are by no means static. The Latino community in America is continually evolving, and increasing religious diversity, social and economic assimilation, and the trajectory of the immigration question in American politics will all be important in shaping the relationship between Hispanic religion and politics in the years to come.

Summary and Conclusions

Religion has played a crucial role in African American political life since before the birth of the United States. During slavery, blacks were converted to Christianity, but they infused it with their own perspective that emphasized liberation. Religion and liberation became inextricably intertwined in slave religion, and this connection has continued, although the meaning of liberation has changed over time. Religion also served a survival function for slaves by preventing their complete dehumanization and by giving them a sense of self-worth. The church was the only African American institution that was allowed to develop in the antebellum era, and it took on many different roles as a result.

After the Civil War, black Americans in the South were allowed to participate in politics for a while during Reconstruction. During this time, the Black Church continued to be the central institution in the black community, and it became the center of political activity as well. After Reconstruction was abandoned, blacks were largely disenfranchised, but the church became an arena for surrogate politics. By taking part in church governance, black leaders developed skills that could be transferred to the broader political arena when the opportunity arose. Black ministers became the leaders of the community, and those who were in a position to do so were expected to speak out about political and social issues, particularly racial injustices.

The 1950s saw the coming of the civil rights movement, and the Black Church took on a central role which it maintained throughout the civil rights era. The Reverend Martin Luther King, Jr., the movement's most prominent leader, pursued a strategy of non-violent confrontation in order to convince white Americans to extend to blacks the same freedoms they claimed for themselves. Black churches were at the center of the civil rights movement, providing resources and activists. While the Black Church has remained at the center of African American politics in the post-civil rights era, certain factors are decreasing cultural unity within the black community, and hence the influence of the church.

The post-civil rights era has also seen the rise of religious challenges to the traditional Black Church. One of these, Black Liberation Theology, is a Christian theology developed systematically from an African American perspective. Its controlling theme is the idea of Jesus as the liberator of the poor and oppressed. Since blacks are the oppressed and God is on their side, and since Jesus' earthly life was marked by suffering, black liberation theologians argue that Jesus is black (either metaphorically or literally). Black liberation theology emphasizes aggressive political and social action in this world to bring about racial justice and equality.

Another challenge to the Black Church has come from Islam. The most notable strand of distinctively African American Muslim development is the Nation of Islam—the Black Muslims—which adopted a modified version of traditional Islamic religion. The Black Muslims emphasized self-help and self-discipline for blacks, rejected whites as the devil, and pushed for a separate black nation within the United States. This group was inconspicuous until Malcolm X took a prominent role in it during the 1950s. In the 1960s, however, Malcolm X left the Nation of Islam and formed his own organizations. Further, after a pilgrimage to Mecca, his views moved in the direction of traditional Islam, and he softened his stand toward whites and integration. After the death of Elijah Muhammad in 1975, his son led almost all of the members of the Nation of Islam into a new, racially integrated organization that followed traditional Muslim teaching and rejected views of the Black Muslims that were not in accord with mainstream Islam. The remnants of the Nation of Islam still exist, however, led by Louis Farrakhan, who has maintained a prominent and controversial profile, and still advocates the basic ideas of Elijah Muhammad.

Scholars in recent decades have advanced two competing views of the Black Church's role in political mobilization. The "opiate view" says that the otherworldly view of religion (as opposed to a present-oriented one) leads blacks to focus on heaven and eternal life after death and to ignore activities on this earth that could advance racial and economic justice. The "inspiration view," by contrast, says that religion serves as a resource that helps to motivate blacks to involve themselves in political activities to improve the condition of their communities. Religious involvement among blacks does generally serve to increase political involvement, but the otherworldly orientation of some ministers and churches can lead to an acceptance of the status quo.

Divergent historical experiences and present circumstances have led to substantial differences between black and white Americans in religious orientations, political orientations, and the kinds of linkages that exist between the two. Blacks are overwhelmingly Protestant (mostly evangelical), are more likely to be biblical literalists, and have higher average religious commitment than whites. Black Americans vote overwhelmingly Democratic and identify themselves as Democrats much more than whites do. Blacks are more likely than whites to be liberals, and this is reflected in many political issues, especially economic ones. However, on some social issues (e.g., gay marriage and prayer in public schools), blacks are more conservative than whites.

Unlike among whites, religious group identifications have little impact on the political orientations of blacks except for the greater political conservatism of black evangelical Protestants on some social issues. Among blacks, biblical literalism has no impact on presidential voting. However, biblical literalists are more likely to be Democrats, but less likely to call themselves liberals. As it is among whites, biblical literalism among blacks is linked to political conservatism on many social issues. Voting behavior is not linked to religious commitment among blacks, but blacks with high religious commitment are more likely to be Democrats (though less likely to call themselves liberals). Among blacks, religious commitment is not related to many political attitudes, but it is associated with conservatism on certain social issues such as abortion, prayer in public schools, euthanasia, and pornography.

The relationship between religion and politics among Latinos, now America's largest ethnic minority, does not entirely follow the patterns observed among either blacks or whites. Hispanics are distinctive from both Anglos and African Americans in that they are predominantly Catholic, though religious diversity in the Latino community has been increasing in recent decades. While Hispanic Catholic churches have historically been largely apolitical, they have lately entered the political fray much more directly, particularly on the question of immigration policy. Republicans have sought since at least 2000 to woo Latino voters on the basis of their social conservatism, but this effort has been much more successful among the minority of Hispanics who are Protestant than among the Catholic majority. For Catholic Latinos, social conservatism seems generally trumped by liberal positions on economic questions and immigration.

Overall, religion has played a critical role in structuring cultural identity for America's racial minorities, though its political dimension has been much more pronounced among blacks than among Latinos. The historical experiences of black and Hispanic Americans have led to certain patterns of religious and political views that differ sharply from those observed among white Americans. For blacks unquestionably, and for Latinos increasingly, religion plays a central role in shaping political life.

Part IV

Effects of Religious Influences in Politics

10 Religion and Interest Group Activity

> When the vast majority of interest groups are advocating public policies which will benefit them, it is important that we have strong groups that advocate on behalf of others. Furthermore, amid the self-interest of policymaking and the battles over legislative and regulatory details, it is important that we have groups articulating a political program founded on ethical and religious convictions.
>
> (Robert Zwier, "An Organizational Perspective on Religious Interest Groups," 1994)

Organized religious interest groups seek to influence public policy in Washington and at the state and local levels in much the same way as other pressure groups. At the same time, however, there are some important unique features of religious lobbying. This chapter will examine the various types of religious interest groups in America today, along with their goals, strategies, and levels of effectiveness—primarily, but not exclusively, at the national political level. As one would expect given the religious pluralism in the United States, there is substantial diversity in the objectives of religious interest groups and in the means by which they seek to achieve them. The major questions guiding the examination of this diversity are:

- With what kinds of issues have religious interest groups in America been involved?
- What strategies do interest groups generally use to pursue their goals, and to what extent do religious interest groups use these same strategies?
- What types of religious interest groups exist, and what are the relative strengths and limitations of the different types?
- How do religious interest groups lobby politicians, and how successful are they at it?
- To what extent are the leaders of and lobbyists for religious groups representative of the views of their members? Do some religious interest groups have more of a problem in this regard than others?
- As the largest and most high-profile religious interest in recent decades, how have the lobbying efforts of the New Christian Right shaped public

policy? How has the movement's political influence strategy evolved over the years?

Increasing Diversity of Religious Interest Groups

Basically defined, an interest group is "a group of people who share some interest or set of interests and pursue their interests through the political system" (Corbett 1991: 292). They may pursue private interests (policies that are of direct, tangible benefit to themselves) or public ones (policies that advance their vision of the good society—see Schattschneider 1960). As previous chapters have discussed, religious interest groups have historically been involved in a diverse array of American political issues, including civil rights, abortion, pornography, public religious observances, international human rights efforts, foreign policy (with regard to Israel, South Africa, China, etc.), homelessness, defense issues, aid to religious schools, tax policies, same-sex marriage, and health care reform. At times, different religious interests have opposed each other on many of these questions.

Perhaps because of the increasing emphasis on social issues (prayer in public schools, abortion, gay rights, pornography, euthanasia, etc.) in the United States in recent decades, the number of religious lobbying groups has increased tremendously. Hertzke (1988) noted that in 1950 there were only sixteen religious lobbying groups in Washington. By 2005, however, that number had increased to a whopping 413 (Hertzke 2009)—and that doesn't even count state and local-level lobbying efforts. Further, as a reflection of the increasing religious pluralism in the United States, the diversity of religious lobbying groups has increased and their issue agendas have become much broader.

Hertzke (2009) sees great ideological and theological diversity among the religious lobbyists, but highlights the two identifiable poles. The liberal end consists of what Hertzke calls the "peace and justice" cluster: liberal mainline Protestants (Methodists, Presbyterians, Lutherans, Episcopalians, the United Church of Christ), the peace churches (Mennonites, Friends, Brethren), the black churches, some Catholic groups (Network, Maryknoll), and Jewish groups. On the conservative end are those groups emphasizing traditional moral values (e.g., the National Organization for Marriage, Concerned Women for America, and Focus on the Family), most evangelical Protestant groups, and Catholic anti-abortion groups. In between the liberal and conservative poles are groups such as the U.S. Catholic Conference and Evangelicals for Social Action that combine conservative views on abortion, family issues, and the role of religion in public life with liberal views on most economic and foreign policy questions. Hofrenning (1995) provides a slightly different classification, but is in essential agreement with Hertzke's (1988, 2009) analysis.

Interest Group Strategies

Religious interest groups employ many of the same strategies as other kinds of interest groups. However, they are also unique in certain ways. The basic goal of any interest group is to move public policy in the direction of their preferences. This might involve supporting or preventing the passage of laws, pushing for the enforcement, non-enforcement, or reinterpretation of existing statutes, proposing constitutional amendments, or any other attempt to influence the formulation, interpretation, or execution of policy. How do interest groups pursue their goals? Depending on the nature of the interest group (its size, resources, goals, etc.), it might seek to pursue one or more of several avenues to shape policy, as outlined below.

Referendum Voting

In recent decades, many states have presented voters with ballot propositions on issues of concern to different religious groups: state lotteries, capital punishment, gay rights, tax issues, abortion, liquor sales, and so on. In such situations, a religious interest group might try to mobilize those who share their views and persuade those who are undecided—both inside and outside their own faith. For example, in gay marriage referenda in a variety of states over the last decade, religious interest groups (representing Catholicism, evangelical Protestantism, Mormonism, and African American churches) have actively sought to mobilize support for traditional marriage norms (Camp 2008). Interest groups can be successful in referendum voting (and have been in most of these gay marriage votes), but Magleby (1989) argues that those who oppose any ballot proposition have an advantage over supporters because they can raise doubts about the need for, implementation of, and unintended consequences of the proposed policy.

Shaping Public Opinion

Even outside the context of a referendum, a religious interest group might try to persuade the general public to support its views in order to achieve its public policy goals, both by bringing pressure to bear on legislators and by voluntary behavioral change. The interest group might try to shape public opinion through media campaigns (including, recently, social media), letters to the editors of newspapers or magazines, calls to radio call-in shows, and mass mailings or emailings. If public opinion moves in the group's direction, then public officials will presumably be more amenable to the group's policy goals. While this sounds good in theory, there are at least two significant drawbacks to this strategy.

The first problem is that it is extremely difficult for any interest group to shape public opinion. Most interest groups lack the resources to carry on a sustained multimedia campaign. Even when such campaigns are undertaken, people—especially those who aren't predisposed to agree with the group—often ignore them, creating a "preaching to the choir" effect. Also, the effort might even backfire and make people more negative toward the interest group and its agenda (Key 1961; Page et al. 1987). This is demonstrated by the fact that political candidates often try to distance themselves from public support by "extreme" interest groups—including religious ones—on their side of the ideological spectrum, and by the fact that many school board candidates supported by New Christian Right groups have run as "stealth candidates" who do not advertise their ties to these interests (Deckman 2004).

The second problem is that even when there is popular support for a particular measure, this does not guarantee that public officials will act in accord with public opinion. For example, as discussed in Chapter 7, a substantial majority of the public supports prayer in the public schools, but school prayer amendments have consistently failed in Congress. This issue is particularly problematic for religious interest groups, because many of the issues that they care about (abortion, gay rights, school prayer, religious free exercise, etc.) are decided largely in the judicial rather than the legislative domain, and are thus less influenced by the currents of public opinion.

It is clearly true, however, that the religious values within a society (and resultant public opinion) affect the policies that are enacted. For example, several studies have shown an empirical connection between state-level policies and the religious composition and culture of the state electorates, both on morality issues generally (Hutcheson and Taylor 1973; Fairbanks 1977) and on abortion more specifically (Segers and Byrnes 1995; Norrander and Wilcox 2001).

Grassroots Efforts

Grassroots efforts are attempts by interest groups to generate a large number of communications from a public official's constituents to persuade him or her to take some action (such as voting for or against a particular bill). These communications can include personal visits, letters, telephone calls, faxes, and (most commonly today) emails. Some religious interest groups have become extremely adept at generating quick and massive grassroots pressure on public officials, while others have little or no capability in this area.

In earlier periods, most religious interest groups did not feel a need to generate grassroots pressure on policymakers. However, especially since the political thrusts of New Christian Right groups beginning in the 1970s, grassroots efforts have become more important. Hofrenning (1995) argues that grassroots, "outsider" lobbying strategies are generally favored by religious groups, and recent research suggests that grassroots strategies can be quite effective in persuading legislators (Bergan 2009). Grassroots lobbying in state legislatures around the country was especially important in laying the groundwork for the surge in Christian homeschooling over the last twenty years (Bates 1991).

Grassroots efforts are also important in raising money for religious interest groups. Direct-mail appeals to supporters raise money for the group to use in achieving its political goals. Berry and Wilcox (2008) argue that the key to success in direct-mail solicitation is to demonize the opposition and make the reader angry. This is true of interest groups in general (both liberal and conservative), including many religious ones. In an early direct-mail fundraising appeal for his Moral Majority organization, Jerry Falwell wrote:

> We have been silent too long. We have let the liberals and the socialists and the gay rights advocates and the left-wing politicians run our nation. If you will stand with me . . . I'll go right into the Halls of Congress and fight for decent, God-fearing laws.

The tenor of such fundraising has not changed much over the years. What *has* changed, however, is the method of distribution. In addition to direct mail, grassroots fundraising by religious (and other) interest groups is done using email and, increasingly, social media.

Seeking Public Office

Members of a religious interest group might choose to seek elective or appointed public offices in order to further their policy goals. African American clergy have at times doubled as interest group activists and local officeholders in black communities, and Jesse Jackson and Al Sharpton (both ministers) sought the Democratic presidential nomination. Robert F. Drinan, a Jesuit priest, served for ten years (1971–1981) as a congressman from Massachusetts, until Pope John Paul II declared that Catholic clergy should not seek elective office. The Reverend Pat Robertson, founder of The 700 Club, and Gary Bauer, president of the Family Research Council, both sought the Republican presidential nomination. Mike Huckabee, former governor of Arkansas and Republican presidential candidate, is a Baptist minister.

Generally speaking, however, seeking public elective office is seldom a good strategy for an interest group. In order to win elections, candidates must usually have a broad base of support, and those who are viewed as representatives of a narrow interest group will have difficulty in getting elected. Members of religious interest groups will have special problems in seeking public office because of the American public's leeriness about mixing religion and politics. As a result, in their presidential bids, Al Sharpton and Mike Huckabee seldom mentioned their ministerial credentials, and most high-profile bids for office by religious interest-group representatives (including Jackson's, Sharpton's, Robertson's, Bauer's, and Huckabee's) have been unsuccessful.

Electoral Campaign Efforts

While it is not usually very fruitful for members of an interest group— particularly a religious one—to run for public office, it does make sense for them to put substantial effort and resources into the campaigns of other candidates. Ideally, an interest group would like for its favored candidate to win the election, have everyone perceive the efforts of the interest group as crucial in the victory, and create the impression that the efforts of the interest group will prevail in future elections as well.

In practice, elections can be a tricky business for interest groups. First, a single interest group is seldom in a position to determine the outcome of a race. Second, the participation of an interest group might backfire (e.g., "My opponent is a puppet of special interest groups"). Third, many interest groups concentrate their resources on candidates who are already favored to win or who have at least a moderately good chance of winning, and give only token help to candidates they are fairly sure will lose. For this reason, incumbents usually have an advantage in obtaining campaign contributions from interest groups (Jacobson 2012). Sometimes interest groups will even give campaign contributions to strong candidates that don't support their views in order to soften their opposition—though these kinds of strategic compromises of principle can be problematic for religious interests.

While some interest groups try mightily to determine who wins an election, most interest groups realize that their efforts will only occasionally be decisive to the outcome. Instead, their electoral efforts are more focused on what happens after the race is over. One of the central goals of campaign contributions and other efforts by an interest group is to gain access to elected officials. That is, members of a group that contributes to an elected official's campaign—or their lobbyists—are more likely to be able to discuss their views directly with the official and receive a respectful and attentive hearing.

Langbein (1986) showed that the amount of time a U.S. representative spends in the office with interest group representatives is related to the value of PAC campaign contributions from the group to the member. Subsequent work (Lohmann 1995; Milyo et al. 2000) has confirmed that contributions do in fact gain a group access. There is no assurance that all viewpoints on an issue will be represented in the legislative process, and a public official who only hears one side of an issue is more likely to be moved in that direction.

Do campaign contributions influence the voting behavior of public officials? It is difficult to say conclusively. Of course, interest groups are most likely to support the campaigns of candidates who already agree with their viewpoint. If a pro-Israel candidate receives contributions from pro-Israel groups, gets elected, and takes a pro-Israel stand on foreign policy, this does not mean that campaign contributions influenced the representative's votes. Thus, studies of the effects of campaign contributions on the voting decisions of public officials have to take other factors into consideration, such as the political ideology and party affiliation of the representative. Several studies have done this, and their basic conclusion is that campaign contributions do seem to predispose representatives to vote favorably on the interests of a group, but only in situations where the issue is not very visible to the public and does not seem to be very important to the representative, the representative's party leadership, or the representative's constituency (Ginsberg 1982; Jones and Keiser 1987; Jacobson 2012).

However, religious interest groups seldom deal with the low-profile issues on which campaign contributions seem to have the most effect, and few of them form PAC organizations. The two primary sources of substantial religious financial support for candidates are black churches that raise campaign funds for favored candidates, and conservative Christian groups that campaign for favored candidates through devices such as very selective voter registration drives and the massive distribution of "scorecards" or other literature that shows some candidates in a favorable light and some in an unfavorable light (practices that cost the Christian Coalition their tax-exempt status in the late 1990s).

Leaving campaign contributions aside, the electoral efforts of Christian conservatives have been widely seen as decisive in several Republican victories in recent decades. In the 1980 elections, several New Christian Right groups (especially Jerry Falwell's Moral Majority) supported Ronald Reagan in his landslide victory; they also targeted a number of liberal U.S. senators for defeat, and most of them did in fact lose. Thus, the Moral Majority and other conservative groups appeared to be effective in this effort (though some argued that many of these Senators would likely have lost in such a strong Republican year anyway). In 1994, when Republicans took control of Congress for the first time in forty years, the grassroots electoral efforts of Christian right groups, though not universally successful, were widely credited with fueling the "Republican Revolution" (Green 1995; Regnerus et al. 1999). Finally, the mobilization of evangelical Christian "values voters," particularly surrounding gay marriage referenda in a variety of states, was widely seen as critical to George W. Bush's narrow re-election victory in 2004 (Campbell and Monson 2008). Thus, under the right circumstances, electoral efforts can be an important element of religious interest group influence.

Court Cases

Sometimes interest groups pursue goals through litigation. Some groups, such as the NAACP and the American Civil Liberties Union (ACLU), have used legal action or the threat of legal action as their primary influence strategy. Jehovah's Witnesses are not usually involved in politics at all, but they have instigated several important court cases (see Chapter 6) concerning the free exercise clause of the First Amendment. When groups resort to the courts to achieve their objectives, it is often because their policy goals are unpopular and have little chance of success in the legislative process.

Religious interest groups of various persuasions frequently do battle in the courts over religious issues, especially those involving religious observances in schools and other public fora. On the liberal side—favoring strict separation of church and state—one finds such groups as Americans United for the Separation of Church and State, the Baptist Joint Committee, and the

American Jewish Committee (along with several other liberal Jewish groups). On the conservative side—favoring greater accommodation of religion in the public square—one finds such groups as the Rutherford Institute, the Christian Legal Society, and the American Center for Law and Justice (Hoover and den Dulk 2004).

Protest

Interest groups might also engage in unconventional political activity, such as protests, in order to affect public policy. Chapter 9 described the role of churches and church-based groups in civil rights protests, which included marches, demonstrations, boycotts, freedom rides, and some acts of civil disobedience. In more recent times, religious organizations have staged many demonstrations against abortion clinics, have boycotted the sponsors of television shows that they find to be offensive, and have sometimes picketed stores that sell pornographic materials. Sometimes religious groups have held marches or demonstrations to protest violent crime, racial discrimination, nuclear weapons, hunger, or some other issue of concern. Indeed, one study found that religious interest groups were significantly more likely to engage in unconventional influence strategies, such as demonstrations and boycotts, than secular groups (Guth et al. 1995b).

Lobbying

Lobbying refers to direct personal efforts to persuade public officials to support a particular view on a policy issue. Lobbying by religious groups has gone on for some time in the United States, but in recent decades has increased substantially. This is the central method by which religious groups (and, indeed, most interest groups) attempt to influence the political process, and it will be considered at length below.

Types of Religious Interest Groups

In their analysis of faith-based lobbying activity, Paul Weber and his colleagues (Weber and Stanley 1984; Weber and Jones 1994) divide religious interest groups into three types: church-based groups (e.g., the Baptist Joint Committee or the U.S. Catholic Conference), individual membership groups (e.g., Bread for the World or Evangelicals for Social Action), and coalition groups (e.g., the Washington Interreligious Staff Council). In the spirit of this categorization, Zwier (1994) interviewed representatives of a number of religious interest groups in Washington in order to investigate differences between church-based and individual membership groups. Based on his interviews, he makes several important distinctions between the two:

1.   While church-based groups were usually established to monitor govern-
     ment actions affecting the churches (and took on legislative lobbying as

a secondary function), individual membership groups were generally focused from the outset on influencing policy through lobbying or mobilizing members to contact government officials.

2. For church-based groups, the Washington office is part of the denominational hierarchy, whereas individual membership groups are not usually subunits of larger organizations.

3. The Washington staff of church-based groups are often church bureaucrats, and over half come from pastorates or other church positions. For individual membership groups, the staffs have more diverse backgrounds, and generally less experience with institutional church organizations.

4. Political activity is not the primary goal of the churches, so church-based groups have to compete within their denominations for resources, attention, and legitimacy. By contrast, individual membership groups consist of people who usually joined the organization specifically because of its political goals, and therefore have no reservations about supporting political activities.

Strengths and Limitations of Each

Having identified differences between these two major types of religious interest groups, one might reasonably ask whether such distinctions lead to variations in activities and differential strengths and limitations. According to Zwier (1994), the Washington staffs of the two types of organizations have very different authority relationships. Church-based groups have greater organizational restrictions than do individual membership groups, as they have to clear their activities with leaders in their denominations. However, because they are funded by institutional appropriations rather than direct individual contributions, church-based groups in Washington do not have to pay as much attention to the views of church congregations back home. For mainline Protestant churches, this has often led to situations in which religious lobbyists took positions well to the left of the average member of their denomination (Adams 1970; Hertzke 1988; Reichley 2002).

On the other hand, while individual membership groups are less constrained by organizational authorities, they are more subject to the preferences of their members. Individual membership groups depend for their very existence on financial support from the membership, and they cannot afford to lose that following by deviating too far from the views of their supporters.

Zwier (1994) discusses the relative strengths and limitations of church-based groups versus individual membership groups. His major conclusions are summarized below.

Strengths of Church-Based Groups

1. Church-based groups have a generally positive public image and "brand name" that gives them legitimacy as political actors.

2. Churches often have large institutional resources to support their advocacy.
3. Churches represent relatively large numbers of voters (though this varies from denomination to denomination).
4. Churches have the "inside track" for access to public officials who are members of that church.
5. Churches have potential nationwide strength because of their many local organizations.
6. Church-based groups generally have longer experience in Washington than do individual membership groups

Limitations on Church-Based Groups

1. Many people—including some members of churches themselves—oppose the involvement of churches in political activities.
2. Most people did not join their churches for political reasons, so the political activities of the church might not be important to them, even if they are not opposed in principle.
3. The hierarchical organization of church-based groups reduces their reaction speed and flexibility.
4. The Washington representatives of church-based groups often have little training in policy analysis and lobbying.
5. Church-based groups tend to deal with too many issues rather than focusing on a few core concerns.
6. Because many church representatives see their role as witnessing to the faith as much as winning legislative battles, they are constrained in the political strategies and influence techniques that they can employ.

Strengths of Individual Membership Groups

1. Individual membership groups tend to have a more politically active constituency than do church-based groups.
2. Because of their organizational structure, individual membership groups can act more quickly and more flexibly than church groups.
3. Individual membership groups often focus on and specialize in a single issue or a small group of issues, allowing them to concentrate their resources and political capital.

Limitations on Individual Membership Groups

1. Individual membership groups have a greater need to achieve victories to sustain their donor base, and the need for victories in the present might detract from important long-term strategies and efforts.
2. Individual membership groups, depending on their geographic dispersal, might have difficulty in obtaining access to the most appropriate public officials if they have little or no presence in the relevant districts.

Lobbying by Religious Interest Groups

As mentioned previously, the most significant influence strategy for religious interest groups (or, indeed, any interest groups) is direct lobbying of governmental decision makers. Representatives of churches and other religious organizations are active in Washington and in all fifty state capitals trying to influence policy in a direction consistent with their faith convictions. They lobby not only the members of Congress and the state legislatures who make the laws, but also the various executive branch officials charged with implementing them. In their lobbying efforts, religious groups share much in common with others who seek to shape public policy. They also, however, have certain unique advantages and disadvantages that affect their level of influence.

Legal Limitations on the Political Activities of Religious Interest Groups

One past limitation on religious involvement in politics was a prohibition against members of the clergy holding public office. Two states, Maryland and Tennessee, still banned the clergy from holding office until the bans were ruled unconstitutional in the 1970s (Kelley 1991). Even though clerical office-holding can no longer be formally prohibited by government, there remain (as discussed previously) significant public reservations about electing clergy to political positions. Moreover, some denominations—most notably the Catholic Church—impose this prohibition on themselves.

Churches and religious organizations also have substantial legal limitations on their activities. Under section 501(c)(3) of the Internal Revenue Code, religious groups and other public service organizations are tax exempt. Further, such organizations can receive tax deductible contributions, which is critical for their support. In order for organizations to receive these benefits, they must be non-profit, and must meet two important additional requirements. First, the organization cannot devote a "substantial" part of its activities to attempts to influence legislation. Second, such organizations are prohibited from "participation" or "intervention" in political campaigns on behalf of any candidate for public office. These two requirements are called the lobbying clause and the electioneering clause.

These requirements and exemptions have resulted in both controversy and court cases (Davis 1991; Gaffney 1991; Pew Forum 2012). Some argue that such requirements ought to be ruled unconstitutional, and that religious organizations ought to be able to retain their tax-exempt status while saying whatever they want about politics, as an exercise of their prophetic mission. Others argue exactly the opposite—that religious groups ought to either surrender their tax exemption or face even more stringent restrictions on intervention in politics. While the existing requirements do limit the political activities of religious groups, their vagueness is sufficient to leave a fair amount of "wiggle room." The IRS and the courts have been relatively liberal in interpreting how much political activity religious organizations can carry out (Pew Forum 2012). In fact, O'Daniel (2001) argues that most violations of these requirements are overlooked entirely, and enforcement is especially lax with regard to African American churches (James 2007). Further, religious organizations have developed ways to work within the letter of the law and still achieve their political goals. For example, a religious organization might distribute "report cards" or "scorecards" about candidates in an election. Even though these reports are, strictly speaking, "informational" and do not explicitly endorse any candidate, they make it very obvious who the favored candidates are. In 1996, however, the government did bring charges against the Christian Coalition (who distributed such voter guides) for violating the provisions concerning political activities by religious groups, and the organization ultimately disbanded at the national level when it lost its tax-exempt status.

General Strategies of Lobbying

Hertzke (1988) groups the strategies of lobbyists into two categories: home district pressure (which does not depend on direct access to the legislator) and classic insider strategies (which *are* based on direct access). Although most religious lobbyists use both strategies to some degree, different groups have different advantages and disadvantages in the two areas, and those that have substantial capabilities in both strategies are the most likely to advance their policy objectives.

Home District Pressure

Home district pressures are designed to bring influence on the legislator from the constituents in the district. Hertzke (1988) describes four methods that religious interest groups use to bring such pressures to bear.

First, mass constituency mobilization consists of strategies aimed at generating a groundswell of constituent support (through letters, telephone calls, emails, etc.) for some policy and making it appear that there are many, many people in the legislator's district who are passionately concerned about the issue. Schlozman and Tierney (1986: 184) note that public officials are not particularly concerned with an amorphous perception of the views of the general public; rather, what influences them is "the understanding that there is a narrower group of citizens who care intensely about a policy matter and are likely to act on their views." The New Christian Right has become expert in mobilizing grassroots pressure, but this strategy is also used by liberal religious groups to a more limited extent.

Second, elite mobilization consists of efforts to bring pressure through especially powerful and influential constituents in the legislator's district. Lobbying organizations keep lists of well educated, influential, politically engaged individuals in the legislator's district who can be alerted to contact their representative quickly about policy issues. Whereas conservative religious groups have mastered mass mobilization better than others, liberal religious groups often have the advantage in elite mobilization.

Third, direct electoral mobilization (discussed previously) consists of attempts to influence who wins in elections. Religious interest groups can do this through registering voters, distributing materials on the candidates' views, making endorsements (to the extent allowed by tax law), contributing campaign money, providing campaign workers, and making sure that supportive voters get to the polls on election day.

Fourth, media strategies consist of attempts to use the media strategically by staging dramatic events. Hertzke (1988) uses the example of famous athletes testifying in favor of school prayer while, on the other side, religious leaders in full clerical garb hold a press conference on the Capitol steps to explain why they oppose prayer in public schools. Such tactics are designed to influence the media in order to arouse attentive constituents within the district so that they will put pressure on members of Congress.

Classic Insider Strategies: The Detail Work

Grassroots mobilization might mold the congressional agenda, create a favorable environment, or predispose legislators to respect the power of an interest group, but the "detail work" of lobbyists is necessary to forge the precise language or outcomes of bills. There is a big difference between insider lobbying and token lobbying. When a religious interest group focuses just on making its views known to legislators, this is not really insider lobbying. Insider lobbying requires activities designed to achieve very specific policy goals: drafting the language of bills, providing possible amendments, creating support coalitions, negotiating with opponents, and providing information and arguments to members of Congress.

Hofrenning (1995) argues that most religious lobbies are not particularly good at the insider strategy for several reasons. First, most religious lobbies have small staffs, limiting the hours that they can devote to tedious legislative detail work. Second, many religious groups lack focus; because of their broad-based moral calling, they are involved in so many issues that it is difficult for them to concentrate their efforts on the ones where they might be most effective. Third, some religious groups lack extensive lobbying experience, and many religious lobbyists are not very assertive in obtaining access to legislators and in using that access aggressively when they get it. Fourth, given the nature of religious issues and the deeply held views of religious lobbying groups, it might be difficult for them to think strategically and to compromise on questions of principle—qualities that are usually necessary in order to have an impact in the legislative process. Zwier (1989: 185) gives a description that is critical to understanding some of the behavior of religious interest groups:

[M]any of these groups are in Washington not so much to pass or defeat legislation but to make a statement. Their foremost concern is not with the results of the policy process (although they would rather win than lose) but with how the process is conducted and with the nature of the debate. Success is defined in terms of whether the moral aspects of public issues have been included in the discussion.

On the other hand, Hertzke (1988, 2009) notes that religious lobbying groups have had at least occasional effectiveness on the insider detail work, and suggests that religious lobbyists have done their best such work on church–state issues. Hertzke provides several examples of religious lobbyists' effective detail work: Jewish groups such as the American Jewish Committee have been very skillful at insider work in general, and particularly on issues concerning support for Israel; the Seventh-day Adventists helped write the Equal Employment Opportunity Commission guidelines in 1964 and 1972 because of their concern about their members losing jobs due to their Saturday worship; the National Association of Evangelicals has worked on matters relating to taxing the auxiliaries (such as nursing homes) of religious institutions; Concerned Women for America essentially wrote an anti-pornography bill; and Bread for the World has had an impact on the Food for Peace international aid program and famine relief bills.

Coalitions

In order to study the coalition strategies of religious interest groups, Zwier (1989) interviewed thirty-eight representatives of religious groups with offices in Washington. He found that religious interest groups frequently worked in coalitions because they tend to have small staffs and limited budgets, as well as similar values, cultures, and priorities. Hertzke (2004) echoes this theme, and emphasizes the importance and frequency of inter-denominational coalitions on human rights issues.

Zwier (1989) and Hofrenning (1995) both stress that religious interest groups don't fit traditional interest group theory well in some respects. One difference is that traditional interest group theory tends to focus on groups' material priorities. Although religious groups do at times get involved in material issues that affect them directly (such as tax policy or even seeking earmarks for specific projects—see Henriques and Lehren 2007), material benefits are not usually their primary consideration. Zwier (1989) also notes that, contrary to traditional interest group theory, many of these religious groups are concerned with the process of cooperation at least as much as the legislative results. Another interesting finding is that religious interest groups tend to form coalitions with other religious groups that hold similar *political* perspectives rather than (necessarily) similar *theological* views. Thus, for example, at the state level, Knutson (2013) provides examples of joint advocacy between Catholic, Jewish, Muslim, and mainline Protestant groups, but indicates that none of these groups has partnered on a consistent basis with evangelical Protestant lobbyists.

Overall, most religious interest groups appear ready to join in a coalition on a particular political issue with just about any other group that shares their views on that issue. There are, however, a few exceptions to this general pattern. Secular lobbyists realize that it is often advantageous for them to have religious groups in their coalition. The leaders of religious interest groups realize that they are sometimes used for purposes of adding legitimacy to a coalition, and they might thus be reluctant to join. Further, some religious groups such as the Seventh-day Adventists are particular about choosing coalition partners; for example, their representative indicated that they would be reluctant to form an alliance with the Church of Scientology or the ACLU even if they were in agreement on the political issue involved (Zwier 1989).

One example of a broad inter-faith coalition was the one involved in pushing for the Religious Freedom Restoration Act of 1993 (discussed in Chapter 6). Support ranged from secular groups such as the ACLU to very conservative Christians, and included mainline Protestants, evangelical Protestants, Jewish groups, Catholics, members of Native American religions, and Muslim groups. This united front across the theological and ideological spectrum gave added impetus and legitimacy to the coalition's position, and greatly facilitated the passage of RFRA.

While religious interest groups often form temporary coalitions around some particular issue, Zwier (1989) and Knutson (2013) note that there are some relatively permanent coalitions of religious interest groups, both in Washington and in state capitols. One example of such a standing coalition is WISC (Washington Interreligious Staff Council). When it was established in 1968, WISC included only denominations within the National Council of Churches, but it has since expanded to include about thirty-five religious groups. WISC includes liberal Protestants, Catholics, and Jews, but does not include the more religiously conservative Protestant groups. WISC utilizes task forces to combine and share their resources for political issues on which they share a common view. Rather than having a number of different religious groups working individually to pursue the same goal, these groups pool their resources in order to be more effective. However, Zwier also notes that, aside from any legislative goals, participants in religious interest group coalitions indicated that they benefited from the communal association itself, as they learned from each other and enjoyed each other's company—a finding echoed by Knutson (2013).

Distinctiveness of Religious Lobbying

What do religious lobbyists represent? Aside from the usual view that lobbyists represent the views of the members of their interest groups, Hertzke (1988) describes three kinds of representation that are relatively distinct for religious lobbyists.

First, most religious lobbyists represent church institutions. While they are concerned predominantly with values issues, church organizations do also have tangible institutional interests because they own property, employ people, have tax exemptions, and operate schools, hospitals, universities, and other enterprises. As institutions, church organizations have a variety of material interests to protect.

Second, religious lobbyists represent theological traditions and teachings on moral questions. While most religious interest groups avoid using overt "God talk" when they are lobbying policy makers, these religious values provide the motivation and parameters for the goals sought in the legislative process. By contrast, many other types of interest groups are focused overwhelmingly on securing tangible, material benefits for their members.

Third, some religious lobbyists represent world church (or parachurch) organizations rather than just U.S. entities. Many churches are international organizations that engage in such activities as running relief agencies, missionary efforts, and development programs. Church organizations that have international activities include the Catholic Church (obviously), the National Council of Churches, the Baptists, the Seventh-day Adventists, the National Association of Evangelicals, and others. International connections inevitably affect the perspectives and goals of a religious lobbying group, especially on issues involving foreign policy. For example, many religious lobbying groups have been actively involved in human rights and religious freedom issues involving the Middle East and China.

Lobbying Co-religionists in Public Office

Can religious lobbyists count on the support of public officials who share their religious views? Chapter 7 discussed the religious preferences of members of Congress and argued that the particular distribution of religious affiliations might partly account for the fact that Congress has never achieved sufficient support for the passage of a school prayer amendment. In general, scholars have found that religious affiliation, while not generally a major predictor of legislators' voting patterns, does matter to a degree in shaping positions on hot-button social issues such as abortion and gay rights (Haider-Markel 2001; Oldmixon 2005; Oldmixon and Calfano 2007).

For some time, however, scholars have realized that legislators' actual religious beliefs matter more than their nominal affiliations. Doctrinal orientations have been found to exert a significant influence on legislative voting on a range of issues, even after other predictors (party, district characteristics, etc.) are controlled for (Hanna 1979; Burden 2007; Oldmixon 2009). Members who identify with the same religious denomination might differ dramatically from one another in their levels of religious commitment and/or theological emphases. Though both Nancy Pelosi and Paul Ryan, for example, identify as Catholic, it is safe to say that they draw significantly different lessons from their faith as it relates to their legislative behavior.

Nonetheless, if religious lobbyists are sensitive to these variations and realize that religion is one factor among many shaping a legislator's voting decision, they can effectively use shared religious values as part of their appeal in certain instances.

Access

To what extent do religious interest groups achieve access to public officials? Hertzke (1989) observes that the extent to which congressional members grant serious access to religious lobbyists depends to a great extent on their own ideological and religious views, a pattern observed at the state level as well (Cleary and Hertzke 2006). Legislators tend to filter out the views of religious groups with whom they disagree. In reference to New Christian Right groups, for example, the congressional members interviewed by Hertzke appeared to be very biased for or against such groups and to base access on whether or not they agreed with their agenda. Groups whose agenda crosses partisan and ideological lines are more likely to have cordial relations with (and, thus, access to) a wide range of legislators—a phenomenon observed with regard to Catholic groups (Steinfels 2004; Cleary and Hertzke 2006). Most policymakers grant greater access to those with whom they agree. As a result, interest groups usually lobby policymakers who sympathize with their goals, and avoid those that they perceive to be hostile. When it comes to religious lobbying, however, this usual pattern might not hold. Berry (1977) finds that public interest groups (including religious ones) are more likely than others to lobby their legislative opponents.

Hertzke (1989) argues that Jewish groups have been very successful in achieving access in Congress and in the White House. Part of the reason for this is their ethnic and religious link to strategic foreign policy concerns. However, Hertzke also attributes this success to the quality of their leadership and the educated, politicized, and affluent nature of their constituents. Hertzke argues that the success of Jewish interest groups means that excellent lobbying on the part of other religious groups could, under the right conditions, overcome policymakers' filtering biases. With some notable exceptions, however, religious groups usually are not very aggressive; this may, at times, limit their access.

It is important to note that the degree of access for a particular religious interest group will ebb and flow depending on the political winds at any given time. For example, when Republicans gained control of Congress in 1994, access increased for conservative religious groups and decreased for liberal religious groups. The reverse, however, happened in 2006, when Democrats recaptured control. Conservative evangelical leader James Dobson expressed, in a message to supporters in 2009, the frustration and powerlessness of an interest group whose allies are out of power:

> I want to tell you up front that we're not going to ask you to do anything, to make a phone call or to write a letter or anything. There is nothing

you can do at this time about what is taking place because there is simply no limit to what the left can do at this time. Anything they want, they get and so we can't stop them. We tried with [Health and Human Services Secretary] Kathleen Sebelius and sent thousands of phone calls and emails to the Senate and they didn't pay any attention to it because they don't have to.

(Gilgoff 2009)

Similarly, access to the White House will depend to a great extent on who the president is. For example, Hertzke (1989) notes that the Reagan White House appointed a Protestant, a Catholic, and a Jew to establish and maintain contacts with religious constituencies. However, the Protestant coordinator was an evangelical sympathetic to the New Christian Right, the Catholic was strongly associated with the Right to Life movement, and the Jew was a neoconservative. Thus, access for all religious groups was funneled through a conservative filter. In the Obama administration, by contrast, religious outreach is channeled through the elements of the various faith communities that have a "social justice" orientation. In addition, African American church groups likely have an advantage in gaining a sympathetic hearing from Obama and his administration, on the basis of both racial and religious affinities.

Factors Shaping the Effectiveness of Religious Lobbying

In his study of religious lobbyists in Washington, Zwier (1994) investigated two models of what religious groups are supposed to do in the political arena. The *witnessing model* "calls for the group to be a faithful witness, speaking truth to power, regardless of the policy impact the group has" (Zwier 1994: 110). The "winning model," by contrast, calls for the group to have a substantial impact on the outcome of the policy process—perhaps necessitating the sordid tactics and compromises of insider politics.

Among the religious lobbyists in his study, 44 percent saw their role primarily in terms of witnessing, 28 percent saw their principal mission as winning, and the rest were unable to choose. Thus, winning on policy is not necessarily the paramount goal of religious interest groups. This focus is confirmed by Hofrenning (1995), who views religious lobbyists as serving a prophetic role that emphasizes the faithful articulation of religious values rather than necessarily achieving specific policy outcomes. Further, there is a very important pattern in Zwier's results: Almost three fourths of the witnessing-focused interests were church-based groups, while nearly two thirds of the winning-focused interests were individual membership groups. Thus, church-based groups are clearly more focused on faithfully articulating their values, while individual membership groups place more emphasis on achieving policy victories.

In assessing the requirements for effective lobbying, Berry and Wilcox (2008) identify several key rules. First and foremost, lobbyists must have credibility. Policymakers must be able to depend on the honesty and integrity of the lobbyist. It is likely that most religious lobbyists are seen by policymakers as scoring high on honesty and integrity—certainly relative to other lobbyists. Second, lobbyists must separate factual information from rhetoric and platitudes. Lobbyists must have a great deal of knowledge in their policy area, and they must be able to provide information and insight that policymakers need. Third, lobbyists shouldn't burn their bridges—if they don't have the support of a policymaker on a particular issue, they should not unduly antagonize that policymaker and cut off chances for cooperation in the future. Fourth, lobbyists must be able to compromise and accept "half a loaf"—which can be more difficult at times for religious interest groups dealing with moral values than it is for groups seeking material benefits. Finally, lobbyists should create a dependency on the part of the policymaker so that he or she comes to rely on them as a vital source of information.

Hertzke (1988) indicates that lobbyists will be most successful when their expertise and argument is backed up by constituency support. Thus, good lobbyists will be able to generate a groundswell of grassroots sentiment to back up their efforts. Some religious interest groups do this very well, some are less skillful, and some have virtually no capability in this area.

Hertzke (1988) also indicates that the level of cohesiveness within a religious interest group is important in determining its effectiveness. For example, when Jewish lobbying groups discuss issues of church–state separation with policymakers, the policymakers know that there is a relatively cohesive position among Jews on such questions. On the other hand, when liberal mainline Protestant church groups discuss social welfare issues with policymakers, the legislators are aware that there can be substantial differences between the views of church leaders and their followers on these questions. Similarly, Catholic interest group opposition to the Obamacare contraception mandate was undermined to some degree by divisions in American Catholic opinion on the issue. The level of cohesiveness among the members of a religious group will also, of course, affect the ability of the group's lobbyists to generate grassroots support for their positions.

The Representativeness of Religious Lobbyists

As with all interest groups, a perpetual issue with religious lobbies is the extent to which their positions reflect the preferences of those that they purport to represent. As far back as Ebersole's (1951) *Church Lobbying in the Nation's Capital*, scholars have found that church lobbyists in Washington generally promoted the views of church leaders rather than church members. This theme was emphasized in Hadden's (1969) *The Gathering Storm in the Churches*, in which he demonstrated that the enthusiasm for the civil rights movement and Great Society programs on the part of liberal mainline Protestant clergy was not shared by the more conservative majority of members in their churches. Using data from his own study of Protestant clergy and from Glock and Stark's (1965) study of laity, Hadden (1969: 68) concluded that "Protestantism is divided within and among denominations on the most basic issues of theological doctrine." Foreshadowing the exodus of many conservatives from mainline into evangelical churches, Hadden (1969: 5) warned that the "Protestant churches are involved in a deep and entangling crisis which in the years ahead may seriously disrupt or alter the very nature of the church."

This theme of a gap between the liberalism of mainline Protestant clergy and the moderate to conservative orientations of their congregations has been echoed in many later studies (Reichley 1985; Hertzke 1988; Guth et al. 1997; Wilson 2009). Overwhelmingly, mainline Protestant lobbies in Washington reflect the liberal views of clergy more than the positions of church members. Moreover, while this disconnect has been examined most extensively in the context of mainline Protestant churches, it exists in other traditions as well. American Catholics, for example, are neither as consistently conservative on life and family issues, nor as consistently liberal on welfare state questions, as their religious leaders and Washington lobbies (Leege and Mueller 2004). Similarly, American Jews as a whole are not as ardently Zionist or as supportive of Israeli government policies as are Jewish interest group leaders (Vitello 2010).

The Role of Church Leaders and Lobbies: Delegate versus Trustee

Scholars have long argued that the leaders of any organization seek to dominate it in order to achieve their own goals rather than those of the group; this is Michels's (1962) "iron law of oligarchy." Drawing upon Pitkin's (1967) work, Hertzke (1988) distinguishes between two types of roles that religious group representatives might play: the trustee role and the delegate role. The trustee view argues that a representative should use his or her own judgment and expertise to determine what policies are most in keeping with the group's interests and ideals. The delegate view, by contrast, holds that the representative must faithfully articulate and advocate the positions of group members, regardless of his or her own views.

One can make a plausible case for either of these two representation roles. It can be argued, for example, that the leaders of mainline Protestant, Catholic, or Jewish groups are actually taking the morally appropriate positions given the teachings of their faiths, and that the real problem is that they have not educated their congregations sufficiently on the issues. Key (1961) argues that attachment to group goals varies with the degree of involvement in the group: top leaders express the group's position in its purest, most thought-out form, a lower level of group activists basically support the official position, and below that members subscribe to the leaders' positions to varying degrees depending on their own level of commitment, understanding, and involvement. Elliott Corbett, chief Washington lobbyist for the United Methodist Church, argued to Reichley (1985) that where moral issues are involved, the church must exercise leadership and cannot afford to wait for its members to agree. However, in terms of effectiveness, Hertzke (1988) argues that "representative" lobbying (the delegate role) is likely to produce more impressive results than "oligarchic" lobbying (the trustee role).

Increased Representativeness of Religious Lobbyists

Hertzke (1988, 2009) notes two important trends that have increased the representativeness of religious interest groups. First, increases in the number and diversity of lobby groups have made them more representative of the pluralism of religious beliefs and practices in the general public. Second, religious lobbyists are now more likely to feel that they must generate constituent pressure on members of Congress, and this requires that religious leaders and their followers be more in accord with one another.

Following Weber and Stanley (1984), Hertzke (1988) distinguishes between two organizational types of religious interest groups: (1) the church denomination, in which lobbying is secondary to other activities, and (2) the direct-mail organization, in which members join for specifically political reasons. Drawing upon Hirschman's (1970) work, Hertzke argues that a key feature of the direct-mail organizations that distinguishes them from the denominational ones is the ease of exit. If, for example, a supporter of Focus on the Family becomes dissatisfied with what the leadership is doing and wants to "exit" the organization, it is quite easy to do so; the person simply doesn't send any more contributions. However, it is not as easy for a member of the Presbyterian Church to leave the local congregation because of disagreement with what Presbyterian leaders in Washington are doing (though such a move is not unheard of). Thus, direct-mail organizations must pay closer attention to the views of their members than the denominational organizations.

Hertzke's (1988) examination of the representativeness of religious interest groups leads him to three conclusions. First, for just about any religious group, there will sometimes be disparity between the views of the lobbying group and the views of the members. For example, the Lutheran Council is in accord with the views of its members on environmental spending (both support it), but not on school prayer (which the members support but the elites do not). Second, the emphases of religious lobbies and their effectiveness in mobilizing constituents are strongly linked to the degree of member support. For example, while various mainline Protestant church lobbies support legal abortion, the Episcopal Church leads the lobbying effort because it has stronger member consensus on the issue. Similarly, religiously conservative Protestant lobbying groups will tend to emphasize social issues, in part because this is where they have the greatest member consensus and intensity.

Third, the collective impact of religious lobbying works reasonably well to represent broader public sentiment. Collective representation concerns how well all representatives as a group represent all the constituencies taken together. Rather than asking how well each individual religious lobbyist represents his or her particular constituents, collective representation measures how well all the religious lobbyists in Washington as a group represent the religious and political views of the American public as a whole. Hertzke argues that while the religious lobbying representation in Washington is not perfectly reflective of the general public, it does work reasonably well in providing collective representation. There is great variation among religious lobbyists in terms of ideology, theology, and organization, and they represent diverse views on a wide variety of issues of broad public concern.

The Range of Religious Interest Groups

To this point, the discussion in this chapter has focused on general features of religious interest group activity, and the features that tend to promote and inhibit the effectiveness of religious lobbying as a whole. While they clearly do share important characteristics, however, the interest groups associated with different religious traditions also have distinctive strategies, emphases, strengths, and challenges. Thus, individual examination seems warranted, at least for the four most active and visible religious lobbying blocs in Washington: Jewish groups, mainline/liberal Protestant groups, Catholic groups, and conservative/evangelical Protestant groups.

Jewish Interest Groups

There are many different Jewish lobbying organizations in Washington, even though they agree for the most part on a wide range of issues. The major Jewish groups (including the American Jewish Committee, B'nai B'rith's Anti-Defamation League, the American Jewish Congress, and the Union of American Hebrew Congregations) all strongly support Israel, and all are liberal on most other policy questions. Altogether, the Jewish lobby is not large, but it is effective, especially with regard to issues concerning Israel and church–state separation. Each Jewish organization has its own lobbying staff, and they are generally regarded as quite effective. Also, while the American Civil Liberties Union is a secular organization, Jews comprise a substantial proportion of its membership.

Jews constitute less than 2 percent of the American population, but they have influence and access to policymakers disproportionate to their numbers for several reasons. First, Jews have higher than average levels of income and education, and this—coupled with impressive achievements in many areas of society—has led to enhanced influence. Second, Jews have been very active in American politics. They turn out to vote and, especially, contribute to campaigns at rates significantly higher than the American public as a whole (Ben Zion 2012). Third, the geographic concentration of many Jews in politically, economically, and culturally influential states (e.g., New York and Florida) has meant that the national political party organizations cannot ignore Jewish voters and opinion leaders. Finally, Hertzke (1989) has argued that Jewish groups have been successful in achieving access in Congress and the executive branch because of the quality of their leadership and their active and energetic pursuit of access.

Not all Jews or Jewish organizations are liberal. Chapter 8 discussed the emergence, beginning in the 1980s, of a small politically neoconservative movement among some Jewish intellectuals. These neoconservatives have argued, among other things, that the economic interests of Jews and society are not served well by liberalism (Lerner et al. 1989). In terms of non-economic issues, Orthodox and Hasidic Jews tend to share many of the views of conservative Catholics and Protestants. The Rabbinical Council is the national organization for Orthodox Jews, who constitute about 10–12 percent of the Jewish community. While Reform, Conservative, and especially secular Jews (who have a Jewish background but are not religiously observant) tend to be politically liberal, Orthodox Jews are more politically conservative on many issues and more open to supporting Republican candidates (Mellman et al. 2012). Moreover, Jewish lobbying organizations are not liberal on every question. Many, for example, have been critical of affirmative action programs because they see them as tantamount to quotas, which have been used in the past to limit Jewish occupational and educational opportunities.

Above all, Jewish organizations have been very dedicated to protecting Israel, although there have been differences of opinion on some specific policies. The pro-Israel lobby is spearheaded by AIPAC (the American Israel Public Affairs Committee), which is widely regarded as one of the most effective interest groups in Washington. Most Jewish lobbying organizations have a variety of political goals, but AIPAC's only focus is the security of Israel. The leaders of most other major Jewish lobbying organizations are on its executive committee. AIPAC lobbies policymakers, distributes records of how legislators vote on issues related to Israel, keeps its members informed on relevant policy matters, and influences campaign contributions to candidates. Through this range of activities over multiple decades, AIPAC and other Jewish groups have been very successful in maintaining robust U.S. support for Israel—to an extent that some critics allege has not served American interests (Mearsheimer and Walt 2007). Others, however, contend that the influence of "The Israel Lobby" has been exaggerated, and that U.S. support for the Jewish state stems at least as much from a commonality of culture and values as from lobbying efforts (Verbeeten 2006).

Domestically, Jewish organizations have strongly supported strict separation of church and state, liberal social and economic policies, and civil liberties. In coalitions with other groups, they have supported such liberal causes as legal abortion, racial equality, and assistance to the poor.

In terms of strategy, Jewish lobbying organizations seem to be especially effective at the detail work of insider lobbying. They are also good at inspiring key influential elites to contact the policymakers in a particular district, and they can generate substantial grassroots pressure—sometimes in cooperation with evangelical Christians (Spector 2008)—on issues concerning Israel.

Mainline Protestant Interest Groups

Most mainline Protestant denominations (e.g., Methodists, Episcopalians, Presbyterians, Lutherans, Disciples of Christ) have their own representatives in Washington. The National Council of Churches is the primary coalition of a number of liberal Protestant groups, though there are also some individual membership groups, such as Bread for the World (a religious coalition that works on global hunger issues), with heavy mainline Protestant representation. Most major mainline Protestant church lobbies are members of two coalition groups, Interfaith Impact (a coalition of Protestants, Catholics, Jews, Muslims, and others) and WISC. Through these coalitions, member groups are able to share some resources (e.g., mailing lists) and coordinate activities to achieve common goals. There are other coalition groups, such as the Religious Coalition for Abortion Rights (a coalition of liberal Protestant and Jewish groups), in which some mainline church lobbies participate. Mainline Protestant lobbies also form coalitions with other religious and secular groups (e.g., the American Civil Liberties Union) on an ad hoc basis, depending on the issue involved.

While, as Chapter 8 showed, the partisan and ideological orientations of mainline Protestants in America are actually quite diverse, the lobbying efforts of their representatives in Washington have been predominantly left-leaning. Taking their original impetus from the social reformist, ethics-oriented foundation of the Social Gospel movement, mainline Protestant leaders have been active in a variety of political issues and causes. Their participation in the civil rights movement in the 1950s and 1960s has been regarded by some as the high point of mainline political activism (Jelen 1993). Mainline Protestant leaders have also worked for abortion rights, gender equality, affirmative action, and separation of church and state on such issues as school prayer, against apartheid in South Africa and various aspects of U.S. Middle East policy, and for health care reform as well as programs for the hungry and the homeless. There has also been a substantial degree of pacifism (especially from the historic peace churches—Quakers, Mennonites, and Brethren) and opposition to nuclear weapons among many mainline Protestant leaders. Finally, many mainline groups have sought to root efforts to protect the environment in Christianity (Kearns 1996). In short, the theologically liberal mainline Protestant groups have generally supported liberal positions on a wide range of issues.

After their heyday of political and social activism during the civil rights and anti-war movements of the 1960s, mainline Protestant leaders retreated somewhat from political activity. The leadership had been criticized because of the gap between their own views and those of the church members that they purported to represent. Further, mainline churches began to lose many members to evangelical ones, and mainline Protestants are now significantly less numerous than evangelicals (see Appendix A).

Jelen (1993) notes three important characteristics of mainline Protestant political involvement. First, the Protestant mainline has emphasized the importance of structural or institutional factors—as opposed to individual behavior—in accounting for social problems. In their view, large, impersonal forces (e.g., the economic and educational systems) are predominantly responsible for human problems, and must be fixed in order to alleviate the root causes of crime, poverty, and familial breakdown. Second, mainline Protestant politics is associated with the liberal (and sometimes far left) side of the political spectrum. Third, mainline Protestant politics has been conducted almost completely at the level of religious elites. Mainline leaders have engaged in direct lobbying of lawmakers, but have seldom attempted to mobilize grassroots support for their positions. Similarly, they have not attempted to mobilize their members to vote for particular candidates in elections.

With a few exceptions, mainline Protestant church lobbying groups have simply not been very successful at mobilizing church members even when they have tried. Hertzke (1988) argues that the liberal church lobbies collectively have been able to mobilize respectable constituent opinion only on hunger and peace issues—and the term "collectively" here means the mainline Protestant churches in coalitions with Catholic, Jewish, and black church groups. Hertzke notes that the weakness of mainline Protestants at the constituency level is indicated by the small size of their mailing lists. At the time of his study, in the late 1980s, one of the mainline lobbying organizations would typically have a mailing list of about 2,000 names—tiny compared to the Christian Coalition, which claimed over 1.75 million members.

As Olson (2007) argues, these problems for mainline interest groups have persisted. In addition to the aforementioned problems of ideological disconnect between church leaders and members and shrinking congregations, she contends that the wariness of many liberal mainline Protestants about mixing religion and politics hamstrings denominational lobbying efforts. Thus, to a large extent, those church members who support religious engagement with politics don't agree with the leaders' agenda, and those who agree with the agenda are reluctant to support religiously based political activism. Clearly, this pattern poses a challenge for the effectiveness of mainline Protestant religious lobbies.

Overall, it seems clear that the political influence of mainline Protestant groups has declined from its heyday in the 1960s. In addition to the factors mentioned above, some (e.g., Hertzke 1991) have attributed this decline to religious leaders' concern with being principled and pure rather than thinking about tough choices and tradeoffs. Similarly, Zwier (1994) argues that many church representatives see their role as witnessing their beliefs rather than winning legislative battles—an attitude that will clearly limit tangible effectiveness.

Catholic Interest Groups

The Second Vatican Council, called by Pope John XXIII in 1962, transformed many aspects of the Church's approach to the world and to secular politics. Prior to Vatican II, the overwhelming focus of Catholic lobbying in the United States had been the defense of specific Church interests, such as Catholic religious freedom and the well-being of Catholic schools (Byrnes 1993). The council, however, provided the impetus for a more wide-ranging, outward-looking Catholic engagement with social and political issues, summarized by Hanna (1989: 76):

> The council stressed that the church as an institution and Catholics in general had a positive obligation to involve themselves in the problems of the world; it issued a series of documents that denounced various political, social, and economic ills—poverty, illiteracy, political repression —as morally wrong under Christian doctrine; and it urged Catholics to work to alleviate them.

The policy arm of the United States Conference of Catholic Bishops (USCCB) is the organization through which Catholic leaders in America attempt to shape public policy on issues ranging from immigration to abortion to nuclear weapons to health care. The USCCB's Washington office includes both lay and religious scholars and a staff of lobbyists. Since the National Conference of Catholic Bishops (precursor to the USCCB) was established in 1966, the bishops have issued more than 200 statements on public issues. The bishops also lobby members of Congress and sometimes file *amicus curiae* ("friend of the court") briefs in legal proceedings to present their views. The bishops have historically been especially active on issues and in court cases concerning abortion (Segers 1990).

With its extensive network of local churches, the Catholic lobbying group has a strong base for generating grassroots pressure on congressional members on a range of issues. For example, Libby (1986) reported that during the 1980s, the USCCB generated a large volume of mail from U.S. Catholics to congressional members opposing U.S. policy in Central America. Much more recently, the bishops' "Fortnight for Freedom" events in 2012 and 2013 drew widespread participation and sought to call attention to (and pressure lawmakers on) the religious freedom issues surrounding the Obamacare contraception mandate and same-sex marriage (Bunderson 2013).

On economic issues, the bishops have generally taken liberal positions and supported expanded government assistance for the poor. On foreign policy, they have advanced a peace-and-justice agenda. For example, the bishops opposed the U.S. invasion of Iraq, arguing that it did not meet Catholic just war criteria (Goodstein 2002), and have argued against nuclear weapons as a strategy of deterrence (USCCB 1983a). The bishops have also condemned capital punishment, urged amnesty for Vietnam draft resisters, and supported a grape boycott to help Cesar Chavez's efforts for farm workers (Hanna 1989). Thus, on many kinds of issues, the bishops have taken what are, at least in the American context, left-leaning positions. However, on the social issues (e.g., abortion, religious observances in public schools, homosexuality) the bishops have adopted conservative positions similar to those taken by evangelical Protestants. Further, it appears that increasingly over the last two decades, the bishops have given primacy to their conservative stances over their liberal ones, arguing that opposition to abortion, euthanasia, human cloning, embryonic stem cell research, and same-sex marriage are "non-negotiable" elements of an authentically Catholic political life (Nichols 2012).

While the bishops take liberal positions on some issues and conservative ones on others, the seeming contradiction is resolved through the metaphor of "the seamless garment" of concern for life (or "consistent life ethic") as put forth by Catholic intellectuals such as the late Cardinal Bernardin of Chicago. This seamless garment approach is pro-life in a comprehensive way. It opposes abortion, capital punishment, euthanasia, nuclear weapons, and war. At the same time, the seamless garment view also supports government efforts to better the lives of the poor and the downtrodden. From the Catholic standpoint, it is not the bishops who are inconsistent; rather, it is both American liberals and American conservatives who fail to adopt a consistent and coherent ethic of life and morality, creating a situation in which fidelity to Christian truth requires straddling the partisan divide.

In an attempt to assess the bishops' attitudes toward politics, Gelm (1994) surveyed 150 of the approximately 300 U.S. bishops (some active and some retired) and found that most believed that they should be politically active. However, at the same time, they were rather pessimistic about their ability to influence the views of Catholics in the general population. Gelm also found a high degree of political unity among the bishops, on both their liberal and their conservative positions. Overwhelming majorities (greater than 90 percent) favored intensified efforts to eliminate poverty, steady or decreased defense spending, stronger measures to control pollution, and stricter abortion restrictions. However, the bishops were less cohesive on some issues. For example, they were split 51 percent to 49 percent on the issue of tougher penalties for criminals.

Unlike the decentralized Protestant community, the Catholic bishops are publicly quite unified. Nevertheless, the Catholic lobbying effort is not completely hierarchical; there are actually many different Catholic organizations, not all of which are formally affiliated with the Church. For example, Network, the "nuns' lobby," was also spawned by Vatican II. Based on the idea that action on behalf of justice was the same as preaching the gospel, some nuns abandoned their habits and began serving as social workers among the poor. Because of the structural problems in society that lead to poverty, the nuns started their Washington lobby in order to work for policy changes that would reduce poverty. Network is also active on peace and foreign policy issues because of its association with the Maryknoll nuns who do mission work on behalf of the poor in Central America and in other parts of the world (Hertzke 1988). On all of these issues, their positions are very much in line with those of the bishops. They have drawn criticism, however, from some bishops and from the Vatican because of their exclusive focus on "social justice" issues and silence on the Church's life and family teachings. Moreover, the nuns garnered considerable attention for supporting President Obama's health care reform bill, despite opposition from the bishops (Landsberg 2010).

Other Catholic religious organizations who do at least some policy lobbying include the Campaign for Human Development, the Jesuit Social Ministries, the Catholic League for Religious and Civil Rights, the National Catholic Action Coalition, and other groups. O'Hara's (1990) analysis of Catholic-based lobbying organizations resulted in a list of thirty-one groups with a wide range of viewpoints, some of them explicitly rejecting aspects of Catholic teaching, and many others have sprung up since that time. These Catholic lobbying organizations range from the very conservative (e.g., The Catholic League) to the very liberal (e.g., DignityUSA, which argues for gay rights and ministry to homosexuals).

An important interest group that is disproportionately—but not entirely— Catholic is the National Right to Life Committee (NRLC), which opposes abortion. Although the NRLC (like the bishops) has an ultimate goal of ending all abortions, they have also fought smaller battles, at both the federal and state levels, to impose limits on abortion—such as working against public funding for abortions and supporting various restrictions (e.g., requiring a twenty-four-hour waiting period, mandatory counseling about alternatives to abortion, and requiring that teenage girls obtain a parent's consent). While the bishops and several Catholic or primarily Catholic organizations have been publicly unified in their opposition to abortion, Catholics in the general public (as Chapter 8 showed) are not especially unified or distinctive in their attitudes toward abortion—a reality that at times undercuts Catholic organizations' anti-abortion lobbying.

Overall, Catholic lobbying groups have employed various methods, including the detail work of insider lobbying and the strategy of generating grassroots pressures on legislators, at both the national and the state level (Yamane 2005). In their efforts, Catholic lobbyists have formed coalitions with Jewish and liberal Protestant groups on some issues (e.g., war and peace, economic justice), and they have worked with conservative Protestants and Mormons on others (e.g., right to life, marriage and family). All in all, this makes Catholic interest groups the most diverse, complex, and wide-ranging of all religious lobbies in America.

Evangelical Protestant Interest Groups

Contrary to some popular portrayals, evangelical Protestants are not a monolithic group in terms of either religion or politics. One way of looking at differences among theologically conservative Protestant groups is to classify them as either evangelicals or fundamentalists—although there are other groups, such as Pentecostals and charismatics, that do not fit neatly into this rough classification scheme. While fundamentalists are usually thought of as a subgroup of evangelicals, they are distinguished by their strong emphasis on biblical literalism and correct doctrinal belief—as distinguished from evangelicalism's predominant focus on communicating the Christian Gospel to everyone. The Reverend Billy Graham is perhaps the quintessential example of an evangelical, while the late Reverend Jerry Falwell was a nationally prominent exemplar of fundamentalism.

Beginning with Jerry Falwell's Moral Majority in the 1970s, a series of politically and religiously conservative groups has constituted what has variously been called the New Religious Right, the New Right, the New Religious and Political Right, or, most commonly, the New Christian Right (discussed in Chapter 4). In addition to fundamentalists, some non-fundamentalist evangelicals are members of New Christian Right organizations. Other evangelicals, conversely, have serious reservations about the movement. The analysis here will focus briefly on the activities of evangelical interest groups outside the New Christian Right, then turn greater attention to the dramatic emergence of the New Christian Right into the interest group landscape.

Evangelical Interest Groups

A variety of evangelical Protestant interest groups have been active for some time in Washington, including the National Association of Evangelicals, Evangelicals for Social Action, the Baptist Joint Committee for Public Affairs, the General Conference of Seventh-day Adventists, the Christian Legal Society, and Sojourners. Generally, much like the Catholic groups discussed above, these evangelical lobbying groups sometimes find themselves aligned with liberals and sometimes with conservatives, depending on the issue.

Several evangelical lobbying groups are concerned with religious establishment or religious free exercise issues. Some groups (e.g., the Seventh-day Adventists) have been more concerned with perceived threats to religious freedom from the right and have often aligned themselves with liberal religious groups. These groups favor strong separation of church and state, so one could say that they are mostly concerned with the religious establishment clause (although some groups, such as the Baptist Joint Committee, are equally concerned with establishment and free exercise issues). On the other hand, Hertzke (1988, 2009) notes that groups such as the Christian Legal Society and the National Association of Evangelicals have become more concerned with perceived threats to religious freedom from the left, from secular forces that they believe want to restrict religious expression (especially for evangelicals) through a misuse of the establishment clause. Thus, these groups are more concerned with the religious free exercise clause.

Evangelicals for Social Action, founded in 1973, is a membership group that combines generally conservative social positions (e.g., opposition to abortion and pornography) with a fairly liberal economic and foreign policy agenda (Hertzke 1988). As the group's website (www.evangelicalsforsocial action.org) proclaims, "We are pro-life and pro-poor, pro-family and pro-creation care." The group works with liberals on issues concerning hunger, poverty, peace, racism, and the environment, but they also support traditional social values. Their goal is "a holistic discipleship which actively pursues peace, justice, and liberty in society according to biblical principles" (Smidt et al. 1994: 138). While such evangelical efforts garner much less attention than those of the New Christian Right, they have been part of the religious lobbying scene in Washington for decades.

Evangelical religious interest groups outside the New Christian Right have used a variety of techniques ranging from endorsing candidates in elections to traditional lobbying methods. Like the Catholic bishops, their diverse and ideologically cross-cutting issue agenda has led them to develop contacts and partnerships across the political spectrum. Increasingly, they are playing an important role in leading a broad evangelical re-thinking of immigration issues and lobbying Congress accordingly (Preston 2013).

New Christian Right Interest Groups

While it is important to note the existence and activities of the kinds of ideologically diverse evangelical groups discussed above, the primary vehicle for evangelical engagement with politics over the last several decades has indisputably been the New Christian Right movement. The New Christian Right is not an exclusively evangelical phenomenon, and it has certainly drawn important support from conservative Catholics, mainline Protestants, and Mormons. Nonetheless, the movement was born in the evangelical churches, and they remain its core and bedrock. Their rise as a movement and their electoral activities have been discussed extensively elsewhere in the book, particularly in Chapter 4. Thus, the focus here will be more specifically on their lobbying and influence efforts.

The New Christian Right, in incarnations ranging from the Moral Majority in the 1970s and 1980s, to the Christian Coalition in the 1990s, to Focus on the Family, the Family Research Council, and even elements of the Tea Party movement today, has waged a variety of policy battles, at both the state and national levels. They have fought against abortion, pornography, communism, secular humanism, expansions of the welfare state, and various gay rights measures. They have strongly supported home schooling, school vouchers, the teaching of creationism and intelligent design, public religious observances, parental rights to discipline children, strong national defense, and support for Israel (in this respect making common cause with Jewish groups, with whom they disagree on almost everything else).

Although there are exceptions (such as the Christian Life Commission within the Southern Baptist Conference), the New Christian Right is characterized more by individual membership groups than by church-based organizations. Today, some of the biggest such groups are Focus on the Family (founded by James Dobson), the Family Research Council (headed by Tony Perkins), and Concerned Women for America (founded by Beverly LaHaye). These groups pursue similar objectives, and they have characterized their overall efforts in terms of support for traditional "family values." Additionally, there are other groups that pursue more limited objectives or have smaller memberships. For example, the American Family Association is a large group that focuses primarily on what it sees as anti-family values in the mass media and corporate America and uses boycotts to achieve its objectives. Another example is Phyllis Schlafly's Eagle Forum, a smaller group that focuses its efforts predominantly (though not exclusively) on education issues.

While the family values theme of New Christian Right groups might encompass their views on many social issues, their agenda has gradually expanded over the years to include many items rather far afield from their core moral values concerns. For example, the Eagle Forum website (www. eagleforum.org) in June, 2013, contained in its "topics" section positions on issues ranging from immigration to internet regulation to the United Nations (they oppose all three). At the same time, the website of Concerned Women for America (www.cwfa.org) asked "Are We Getting the Truth about Benghazi?"—perhaps a valid question, but one not obviously related to an agenda of faith and family. Moreover, this "mission creep" into more secular conservative and Republican concerns is not new. In the early days of the movement, Moral Majority founder Jerry Falwell called on his followers to evaluate political candidates using criteria that included not only opposition to abortion, homosexuality, drug legalization, prostitution, etc., but also support for lower taxes, a balanced budget, smaller government, and more state autonomy (Falwell 1980).

It is important to note that the New Christian Right has never been completely politically unified. This was demonstrated very visibly in 1988, when televangelist Pat Robertson sought the Republican nomination for president. While he had a strong evangelical base of support, he was not able to mobilize the entire New Christian Right movement, and Jerry Falwell pointedly chose to endorse George Bush. More recently, conservative evangelicals have failed to coalesce fully behind the candidacies of Mike Huckabee in 2008 and Rick Santorum in 2012, both of whom won plurality, but not overwhelming, support from this constituency (Moormann 2012). Further, there is not complete agreement within the movement about approaches to some issues. For example, leaders within the movement differ on how exactly to frame and pursue their support for traditional marriage (Wilcox and Robinson 2011), and even differ on the basic efficacy and limits of political engagement (Thomas and Dobson 2000; Lindsay 2007). Further, there are some theological differences among New Christian Right groups (between fundamentalists and Pentecostals, for example) that can make it difficult for them to achieve complete unity.

To a great extent, the New Christian Right had its roots in televangelism (televised religious programming). Jerry Falwell used his mailing list of donors from his Old Time Gospel Hour as an initial base from which to form the Moral Majority. Pat Robertson's 700 Club (an evangelical talk show), the flagship program of Robertson's Christian Broadcasting Network (CBN), provided the base for his 1988 bid for the Republican presidential nomination. In turn, the contacts from his 1988 campaign provided the initial mailing list for the formation of the Christian Coalition (Reed 1994). Note that for both the Moral Majority and the Christian Coalition, there is a common origin in televangelism, but this is not to say that televangelism itself produced the New Christian Right movement; in fact, Johnston's (1989) analysis indicated that televangelism per se had little impact on the political behavior of viewers. What religious programming did do (and continues to do), however, is to provide an invaluable communications network for the movement. In this vein, the New Christian Right has also been very active in radio programming, and the last several decades have seen a proliferation of evangelical Christian radio stations, often with social/political as opposed to simply religious programming.

It is somewhat ironic that a movement espousing traditional values is at the same time quite technologically adept. Focus on the Family, for example, uses massive mailing lists, fax and email facilities, various social media, and a very sophisticated website. In its 1990s heyday, the Christian Coalition was noted for its technological and communications sophistication (Wilcox and Robinson 2011). Given these capabilities and their mass membership base (collectively numbering in the millions), New Christian Right organizations have great ability to mobilize constituency opinion, and to generate a huge volume of mail, email, and faxes to policymakers.

Despite its size, however, the New Christian Right by itself is not big enough, either at the national level or in most states, to win the policy victories that it seeks. Therefore, beginning in the 1990s, New Christian Right groups began to actively seek partnerships with those outside the movement. The Christian Coalition in particular made a substantial effort to broaden its appeal. Rozell and Wilcox (1995) cite the Christian Coalition training manual as listing the following groups as potential allies: anti-tax, pro-business, educational reform, pro-family and pro-life, veterans, right-to-work, gun owners, home educators, anti-pornography, and others. On the basis of agreement on social issues such as abortion, pornography, and gay rights, the Christian Coalition reached out to make connections with Catholics, Orthodox Jews, and black Protestants. For example, in 1996 Ralph Reed, William Bennett, and Rabbi Yechiel Eckstein (an Orthodox Jewish leader who has worked to strengthen relations between evangelical Protestants and Jews) together established a Center for Judeo-Christian Values in America.

Around the same time, the Christian Coalition organized a branch called the Catholic Alliance, a group that attracted over 200,000 members despite opposition from some bishops (Schlumpf 1996). These coalitional efforts have continued after the demise of the Christian Coalition at the national level in the late 1990s, as the fight against same-sex marriage has been waged by organizations (such as the National Organization for Marriage) uniting evangelicals, Catholics, Mormons, and African American Protestants.

Of course, coalition building for the New Christian Right, as for any movement, is not without difficulties. As the movement reaches out beyond its core of evangelical supporters to build partnerships with secular Republicans and believers in other religious traditions, there is a risk that the commitment of the original members could wane. Oldfield (1996: 277) sees a fundamental dilemma in coalition building for the movement:

> To reach beyond its religious base, the Christian Right needs to present its arguments in broadly acceptable secular language, tolerate compromise, and move beyond a strict social-issue focus. Yet doing so could well undermine the movement's organizational resources that . . . have been the source of the movement's strength.

Similarly, Wilcox and Robinson (2011: 184) maintain that there is considerable public support for restrictions (though not a complete ban) on abortion, for a civil union (as opposed to marriage) approach to accommodating same-sex couples, and for multi-faith expressions of religion in public life. However, making a shift to this "softer" version of their issue agenda carries with it perils for the New Christian Right movement. "The danger of the moderation strategy," they argue, "is that the movement may win a larger audience but lose one of its key assets—the enthusiasm of its volunteers."

This difficult tradeoff between political effectiveness and purity of principle has confronted the New Christian Right movement throughout its history (as, indeed, it has faced other religious interest groups as well). It has also resulted in a legislative track record that is decidedly mixed. After forty years of engagement with American politics, the New Christian Right has won some battles (particularly at the state and local level), but has not been able to win significant policy changes on the issues it cares about most (abortion, religion in public life, and homosexuality—where policy movement has actually been steadily against them). As Wilcox and Robinson (2011: 199) argue, "The Christian Right has paradoxically been the most successful social movement in influencing elections and party politics over the past century and the least successful in influencing policy and culture." Whether that assessment continues to apply in the years to come will depend largely on how Christian Right groups define and articulate their issue agenda, and on the coalitions they are willing and able to form with interest groups outside their own movement.

Summary and Conclusions

Religious interest groups, like all interest groups, share a particular set of goals and pursue them by working within the political system in a variety of ways. The number of such groups has increased steadily since the 1950s and continues to do so. Religious interest groups are currently involved in a wide range of issues that they perceive as having important moral dimensions. Although there is considerable diversity among religious interest groups, they can be thought of along a continuum ranging from the "peace and justice" cluster on the liberal side to the "traditional values" advocates on the conservative side—with some taking positions at both ends.

Religious interest groups are like other interest groups in the techniques they use. They try to influence how people vote in elections, they try to shape public opinion, they engage in grassroots efforts to generate communications to public officials, they use the media to present their views, they sometimes seek public office for some of their members, they lobby public officials, they use the courts to pursue their goals, and they periodically engage in protest activities. However, they are different in what they represent: religious interest groups typically represent single religious institutions (such as the Southern Baptist Convention), theological traditions and values (for example, pacifism), and/or international religious bodies (such as the Catholic Church).

Some religious interest groups are church-based (e.g., those associated with the Methodist Church or the Presbyterian Church) and some, such as Focus on the Family, are individual membership groups that draw members from a variety of faith traditions. Each type has its relative strengths and limitations.

Religious interest groups lobby public officials through home district pressures and through insider strategies. In recent decades, it has become more important for a religious interest group to be competent in both types of strategies. Religious interest groups must often form coalitions with other interest groups in order to achieve their goals. In order to succeed, it is very important for religious interest groups to gain access to public officials and use that access aggressively to advocate for their agenda. There are rules that are important in order for lobbyists to be effective (e.g., they must be credible, they must have a great deal of knowledge in the issue area, and they must be able to compromise). Additionally, it is important that the skills of the lobbyist are backed up by constituency support, and that there is cohesiveness within the religious interest group.

Mainline Protestant religious interest groups in particular have had problems with regard to cohesiveness because the leaders of these denominations are more liberal than their members. However, it does appear that this gap has decreased somewhat over time. Generally speaking, church-based religious interest groups have greater difficulty in achieving cohesiveness than do individual membership groups.

The chapter examined in depth the goals and strategies of Jewish interest groups, mainline Protestant groups, Catholic groups, and conservative

Protestant groups. Jewish interest groups have generally supported liberal causes and security for Israel, and they have excelled at the insider strategy. Mainline Protestant groups have generally supported a variety of different liberal causes, but they have not been especially successful in some of these pursuits because they have often not had great support from their members. Catholic groups (and a few evangelical organizations) have supported liberal economic positions on most welfare state issues, but have taken conservative stances on social questions such as abortion and marriage. Most evangelical Protestant organizations have advocated conservative positions across the board. The most dramatic manifestation of evangelical interest group activity (and, indeed, of religious interest group activity in general) has been the New Christian Right, which has been remarkably successful in mobilizing supporters and in influencing elections, but less so in shaping policy, at least at the national level.

This examination of religious interest groups has demonstrated a great deal of diversity among them in terms of goals and strategies. Some religious groups support liberal views, some support conservative views, and some support a mixture of both. Although there are times when this diversity turns into unity (e.g., the wide support among many different religious groups for the Religious Freedom Restoration Act), the range of political positions espoused by religious interest groups certainly seems to match the diversity of political views found in the general public. What does unite them, though, almost by definition, is the conviction that religion ought to play a significant role in government and public life. Of course, not all Americans (nor all religious groups) are of one mind as to what this role should be. The next chapter considers a range of views on this score.

11 Religion in Public Life
The Contemporary Debate

[The] fundamental notions of democracy—of the dignity of the human person, therefore of the necessary limits of the state, of the discrete spheres of influence of economic, political, and cultural life—are rooted in Christianity.
(Richard John Neuhaus, "A Crisis of Faith," 1985)

[There] has been no correlation in our own century between Christian belief and liberal democracy ... Wherever liberal democracy has taken root and flourished, it has done so owing to the ideas and legacy of the Enlightenment—not to those of any particular faith.
(Aram Vartanian, "Democracy, Religion, and the Enlightenment," 1991)

A recurring question throughout American history has centered on what role, if any, religion should play in the nation's public life. Chapter 2 discussed how religion and politics were intertwined in the colonial beginnings of this country, and how the Founders held differing views on exactly what the relationship between the two should be. Chapters 3 and 4 demonstrated that religion in America has played a highly visible role in many significant public issues, both past and present. Chapters 5 and 6 examined significant Supreme Court cases, as well as laws, that have helped to shape religion's presence in the public sphere. Chapter 7 surveyed the attitudes of the public and of elites regarding this issue, while Chapters 8 and 9 examined the ways in which American religious and political attitudes are intertwined. Chapter 10 described the organized efforts of religious groups to shape public policy in a variety of ways.

With all of those discussions as backdrop, this chapter will discuss the contemporary debate concerning religion's proper influence in American political life. Should the United States become a more secular society, a more religious one, or neither? Would either a greater or a lesser role for religion in our public discussions—or perhaps just a different one—produce a healthier body politic? This chapter will present the different sides of this issue and demonstrate the complexities involved in answering the question. Individuals and organizations in the United States hold wide-ranging and divergent views on these issues. On one end of the continuum are those who assert that religion and politics should remain completely separate, often believing that this arrangement is best for both religious and political institutions. On the opposite end are those who see the ideal situation as one in which religion and politics work closely together in support of common goals. As Chapter 2 showed, these debates are not new; they were quite relevant during the founding era. The focus here, however, will be on perspectives that have emerged in the contemporary, post-1960s, "culture wars" era.

It should be noted that most discussions of the issue by scholars and most popular debates on the subject assume that the question concerns how Christianity should or should not influence American public life. Since Christianity is by far the dominant religious perspective in the United States, "religion" in the American context will necessarily mean, for the most part, "Christianity." Some of the logic and argument in this area is indeed specific to that religion; for the most part, however, the basic points can be applied to the discussion of more general religious roles and influences in public life. With that in mind, the major questions to guide this chapter are:

- Based on the two religious clauses of the First Amendment to the U.S. Constitution, what four basic positions are there on the proper role of religion in public life?
- What arguments have been made for the idea that the participation of organized religion in politics is bad for the political system? Conversely, what arguments have been made for the idea that mixing religion and politics is bad for religion?
- What arguments have been made for the proposition that religion is a necessary support for democracy? And what arguments have been made for the idea that religion is a necessary mediating structure between the individual and the government?
- What arguments have been made for the proposition that the government should be guided by and serve the goals of religion?
- What proposals have been made to involve religion in politics while respecting religious pluralism and individual conscience rights?
- What is the "culture war" and how does it concern religion and politics?

Religion and the Public Square: Four Competing Views

Chapter 7 introduced a typology of four views held by elements of the public on the proper role of religion in public life: Christian preferentialism, religious non-preferentialism, religious minimalism, and the religious free-marketeer view (Jelen and Wilcox 1995). These four types result from combining viewpoints on both religion clauses of the First Amendment. The discussion here returns to those viewpoints themselves without combining the two clauses. One can conceptualize the role of religion in the nation's public life along two vectors: (1) government support for religion, or the establishment vector, and (2) government non-interference with religion (including religious practice in public locales), or the free exercise vector.

The two points of view about the establishment clause both have implications for the role of religion in public life. The accommodationist position holds that the government should enact policies that favor religious belief and practice. This would not entail preferences for a specific sect, but would encourage religion in general over and against secularism. It is based on two assumptions: (1) Religion has generally beneficial consequences for human behavior, and may even be a necessary undergirding for democracy. (2) Most religions in the broad Judeo-Christian tradition affirm essentially the same moral values and have similar political effects, providing a "sacred canopy" that is the ethical basis for public life (Berger 1967).

The separationist position, by contrast, holds that religion should be kept in the private realm. It tends to emphasize the problems involved in the absolute nature of religion's claims over and against the compromises often required in democratic life. Religious claims, in this view, tend to divide the culture rather than to unite it. Religion is thus seen as introducing an especially dangerous element into public life, meaning that it should be kept in the private realm.

Reviewing Chapter 7, there are also two distinct approaches to the proper meaning of the free exercise clause. Those who favor a communitarian view believe that the scope of religious free exercise should be limited by the actions of state and local legislatures. Because they reflect the consensus of the majority of the citizens of an area, these bodies may legitimately impose limits on religious free exercise that seriously violates the communal norms and values. The view that commonly held standards of proper behavior and decency should constrain the free exercise of religion is reflected, for example, in the *Reynolds* (polygamy) case discussed in Chapter 6.

On the other hand, a libertarian interpretation of free exercise supports maximum religious freedom for all, as long as religious practices do not violate the basic human rights of, or cause serious harm to, unwilling participants. Thus, something such as human sacrifice would not be permissible, but polygamy likely would.

As Jelen and Wilcox point out, there is no necessary connection between the view that someone holds about one clause and his or her stance on the other. They can be combined in various ways, as this chapter will make clear.

A High Wall of Separation

As Chapter 7 showed, most Americans do want religion to have a significant place in public life. However, there are substantial arguments in favor of keeping public life wholly secular, and an appreciable minority of Americans support this view. Arguments for keeping religion—or at least any organized version of it—out of public life come from two starting points: (1) The presence of religion in public life, because of its absolute claims, often undercuts the rationality and civility of public discourse; and (2) religion and democracy are based on different and fundamentally incommensurable premises.

Religious Absolutism and the Civility of Public Discourse

One common argument by separationists is that religion's presence in the political arena adversely affects the style and tenor of political discourse. Religion, the argument goes, contributes to extremism, intolerance, fanaticism, and unwillingness to compromise, and generally undermines the calm and rationality that ought to characterize political debate and decision making. When religion enters the political arena, it may become, in the words of Judge Learned Hand, "too sure it is right." As one analyst of church–state relations in the United States writes, "No matter how deep your faith, the quality of being 'too sure' resides in the disposition to impose it on others" (Frankel 1994: 108).

When religious activists bring their deep moral convictions into the rough and tumble of politics, they may fail to exhibit the capacity for compromise and for treating political opponents with respect that is crucial for the democratic process. They may find themselves unable to resist translating their heartfelt belief that they know eternal truth into demagoguery (Wogaman 1988). The introduction of religion into the political realm may lead to a tendency for each side to demonize its opponents, as the rhetoric in the current conflicts over abortion and same-sex marriage illustrates.

Writing specifically about the political involvement of the New Christian Right, James E. Wood, Jr., former editor of the *Journal of Church and State*, observed that when moral absolutes are confused with public policy, anyone who disagrees with the policy is often seen as immoral and ungodly. Such religious grounding of public policy ignores the diversity of American religion and the safeguards essential in a democratic society (Wood 1987). Similarly, church–state analyst Ronald B. Flowers voices strong appreciation for the Christian Right's role in keeping moral issues before the public and in stimulating national discussion, but also notes that advocates on the side of the Christian Right "have often taken intractable positions that have tended to polarize society." He also notes as "more problematic" the movement's tendency to engage in "political efforts to remake the country in its own image" (Flowers 1994: 127). Of course, taking intractable positions and "demonizing" one's political opponents is hardly the exclusive province of the Christian Right, or even of religious groups; nonetheless, separationists argue that such practices are especially likely when religion enters the political discourse.

When religion becomes political, it may well end up acting contrary to its own best insights. As the Williamsburg Charter (1988: 15) states:

> Too often, ... religious believers have been uncharitable, liberals have been illiberal, conservatives have been insensitive to tradition, champions of tolerance have been intolerant, defenders of free speech have been

censorious, and citizens of a republic based on democratic accommodation have succumbed to a habit of relentless confrontation.

Incompatible Premises?

Another argument for the exclusion of organized religion from participation in organized politics is made on the basis that their underlying values and premises are not merely different, but incompatible (Vartanian 1991). While Vartanian restricts his discussion of religion in politics to conventional Christianity, the basic arguments that he makes are more broadly applicable— to Islam, for example.

Religion operates in the realm of dogmas that are "nondiscussable and nonnegotiable" (Vartanian 1991: 12). Democracy, by contrast, requires the readiness for give and take, and willingness to compromise. Effective democracy demands "rational discourse and the rules of evidence," whereas conventional religion, he argues, will often replace those principles with "obscurantism and willfulness" (Vartanian 1991: 12). Religion expects its adherents to surrender to an absolute power that Vartanian holds to be antithetical to the democratic "faith in freedom, rights and self-rule" (Vartanian 1991: 14). Thus, he contends, "democracy and conventional religiosity . . . have been not merely different but incompatible systems of thought and behavior" (Vartanian 1991: 9).

At the end of his discussion, Professor Vartanian expands his argument beyond conventional Christianity to assert the incompatibility of religion in general with democracy. He also affirms secular humanism or secularism as the only appropriate basis for a political system that respects individual liberties. He concludes that religion must remain outside public life and church and state must remain altogether separate, "not simply because the Bill of Rights so prescribes but because they do not in fact mix (Vartanian 1991: 45).

Vartanian's arguments are echoed by other theorists as well. Most notably, John Rawls (1993) argues that political discourse in a democracy must be based solely on "public reason," or arguments rooted in universally accessible and agreed-upon premises (essentially precluding religious contentions). Philosopher Robert Audi goes even further, arguing that proper argument in a pluralistic society must have not only "secular rationale," but also "secular motivation" (Audi and Wolterstorff 1997). In other words, religious people must not only offer secular justifications for their policy preferences, but must refrain from advocating any policies that they would not support absent any religious motivation. Clearly, a substantial body of scholarly opinion regards religious perceptions of truth and democratic processes as inherently at odds.

Humanist Manifesto II and A Secular Humanist Declaration

Vartanian, Rawls, and Audi all echo, to varying degrees, opinions articulated in the foundational documents of humanism in the United States. The American Humanist Association has held a consistently separationist viewpoint throughout its history. *Humanist Manifesto II* describes the "separation of church and state and the separation of ideology and state" (Kurtz 1973: 19) as imperatives. A *Secular Humanist Declaration* makes the point more sharply. It opposes "all varieties of belief that seek supernatural sanction for their values" (Kurtz 1981: 7). Its authors further hold that any imposition of an exclusive view of what constitutes "truth, piety, virtue, or justice" for a whole society violates liberty. No group should be permitted to make its own views, "whether moral, philosophic, political, educational, or social, the standard for all people" (Kurtz 1981: 12).

The *Declaration* goes on to make several concrete recommendations: tax monies should not be used to benefit or support religious institutions; properties owned by religious organizations should be taxed, as are other properties; and no organized prayers and religious oaths should be permitted in public institutions.

Atheist Challenges to Public Religion

Two organizations that have worked intensively to construct a complete wall of separation between church and state and to thoroughly secularize American public life are American Atheists and the Freedom from Religion Foundation. American Atheists was founded in 1963 by Dr. Madalyn Murray O'Hare for the purpose of advancing atheism and the "total, absolute separation of government and religion." The organization grew out of the Murray family's challenge to organized prayer and Bible reading in the public schools attended by their children (*Murray v. Curlett*, which was consolidated and decided along with *Abington*—see Chapter 5). Dr. O'Hare (who was murdered in 1995 by a member of her own organization) was perhaps best known for her opposition to the motto "In God We Trust" on coins. She held that the presence of a religious motto on the official "legal tender" of the nation violates the establishment clause (because it means that the government has selected belief in God as an official stance), the free exercise and free speech clauses (since non-believers have to use money), and the equal protection clause of the Fourteenth Amendment.

The Freedom from Religion Foundation (established in 1978) is an umbrella organization for "freethinkers" (atheists, agnostics, deists, spiritualists, etc.) of whatever persuasion. It was formed to "establish an ongoing and authoritative voice for separation of church and state." They believe that organized religion has no place in government and that the Constitution was purposefully written to be a godless document since the only references to religion in it are exclusionary.

In recent years, non-believers' objections to the presence of religion in public life have been reinvigorated by the work of the "New Atheists" (Harris 2004; Dawkins 2006; Hitchens 2007). Unlike previous generations of atheists, these writers have asked not merely for separation and toleration, but for an aggressive social effort to marginalize, denigrate, and, ultimately, exterminate religious belief in the human species. They argue not simply that religion (or irreligion) ought to be a private matter beyond the sphere of the state, but that its very existence is a detriment to society and to the political order. While their views are clearly extreme, even among humanists, the fact that their books collectively sold millions of copies speaks to an increasing appetite in some quarters for confrontational challenges to religion in public life.

Normative or Inevitable?

Secular humanism offers as a normative judgment—a prescription for the way things ought to be—what some theorists see simply as an inevitable progression of affairs. The secularization thesis, originally emerging from the work of social theorists including Karl Marx and Max Weber, argues that as modernization advances, religion's social role inevitably declines (Norris and Inglehart 2004). Modernization in this context includes the scientific way of thinking, modern technological advances and complex economic life, mass communication and entertainment, and the growth of government bureaucracies and public education. In addition to its basic articulation, the secularization thesis has two variants. The first says that, although religion may continue to be a strong force in the lives of the general public, cultural elites and the institutions associated with them have become highly secularized. The second variant says that religion does not actually decline in response to modernity; in fact, it may even grow stronger. It is, however, relegated to the private sphere of life, increasingly retreating from formal, institutional involvement in political life (Fowler et al. 2010).

All versions of the secularization thesis are controversial (Swatos and Olson 2000), and recent scholarship argues that it may ultimately be rendered inoperative by demography—specifically the tendency of more devout people in every religious tradition to have more children than their secular counterparts (Kaufmann 2010). Nonetheless, it provides at least a potentially viable framework for thinking about the shift away from public religion in America and other industrialized nations over the last century.

The Religious Case for Separation

The viewpoints described above focus predominantly on secularist attempts to protect the political order from religious influence. Others, however, have come to a separationist position from a desire to protect religion from being sullied by politics. Mingling the two, this perspective argues, can lead to idolatry, worldliness, and attempts to join things that are simply incommensurable.

A Baptist Voice

Throughout the history of the United States, Baptists have been a strong voice for religious liberty and church–state separation. While surveys show that this commitment (certainly in terms of separation) is not as strong as it once was among rank-and-file Baptists, it remains an important element of the denomination's approach to society, at least at the elite level. This view is reflected in the writings of J. Brent Walker (1997, 2008), long-time general counsel for the Baptist Joint Committee, who provides four major reasons why governmental support for religion often ends up doing more harm than good for religious bodies.

First, Walker writes, government support for religion often comes with strings attached. In accepting government aid, religious groups make themselves susceptible to government regulations that might interfere with their witness and mission. Second, the more a religious group becomes financially dependent on government largesse, the less willing they will be to exercise their prophetic voice and criticize government for immoral policies; any group will naturally be reluctant to "bite the hand that feeds them." Moreover, government support for the activities of a faith community can relieve members of the community themselves from stepping up to fund the religious mission, so that government support in effect crowds out (much more desirable) private support. Finally, government funding for religious activities can lead to denominational conflict because it can create perceptions (founded or not) of favoritism towards one group or set of groups over others.

For all of these reasons, Walker and many other Baptists actually opposed the Bush (and now Obama) administration's support for faith-based charitable initiatives. Some may find this stance on the part of an evangelical denomination surprising, but it is consistent with a long history of Baptist separationism, and with the rationale articulated above.

The Religious Free Market

Having religion function on its own, without governmental support or interference, means that all religious groups compete for followers on an equal footing, just as businesses do in a free-market economy. It has often been noted that religion flourishes better in the United States than it does in many of the countries where religion has direct government support and/or the "benefit" of establishment. One explanation given for this puzzling observation is that the free market economy of religion in America naturally encourages the development of a large and diverse number of faith groups and styles of worship. As a result, religion can appeal to a wide variety of people with different theological orientations and aesthetic sensibilities. It also means that less effective religious groups, those that do not meet people's perceived needs, will fail, just as commercial ventures that do not meet the needs of a constituency fail (Finke and Stark 1992).

This view diverges sharply from the communitarian one, which holds that a unified "sacred canopy" (Berger 1967) of faith is necessary for a flourishing society and that rampant religious pluralism weakens rather than strengthens religion. It is also disconcerting to many who are reluctant to conceptualize faith as a commodity subject to market forces. Nonetheless, the type of economic analysis advanced by Finke and Stark suggests that, far from weakening religion, intense and "market-driven" competition can actually strengthen the role of faith in the life of the nation.

The Danger of Idolatry

As is abundantly clear from any analysis of history, religion moves and motivates people in a way that secular concerns seldom can. Thus, politicians and political interest groups can be tempted to use its power in people's lives to help them achieve objectives that they might not be able to otherwise. By identifying the limited goals and perspectives of a nation or a political movement too closely with God, however, it is easy to make the movement into an idol. Thomas and Dobson (2000) are critical of the religious right for having done exactly this, at times slipping into a view of political victory as an end in itself rather than a means of furthering the Gospel. In a similar vein, former Oregon Senator Mark Hatfield, himself an evangelical Christian, expressed in an interview with Jim Wallis (1996a: 29) a suspicion of "Christian politics," whether from the right or the left. Arguing that the natural tendency for both liberal and conservative believers is to continuously expand the set of issues where their position is *the* normative Christian one, Hatfield says:

> I am basically suspicious of anyone who claims to speak for everyone within the Christian faith. And I get so uptight about those who purport to speak for the Lord for political reasons. That to me is saying, here is the political agenda that is, in effect, a substitute for the biblical gospel.

Even as passionate an advocate of the political involvement of Christians as Philip Wogaman (a prominent Methodist pastor and spiritual counselor to President Bill Clinton) recognizes the danger of idolatry and the seductions of power. While lobbying is, in his view, a legitimate activity for church groups, it brings with it danger because of the power it can have, power that can extend beyond the immediate issue at hand. It also necessarily involves compromise. For this reason, only those who are "thoroughly grounded in the faith and of unimpeachable integrity should ... be entrusted by the church with that responsibility" (Wogaman 1988: 203).

That Which God Hath Not Joined . . .

It is difficult to summarize succinctly the theological view that politics and true Christian life are simply incommensurable. It comes in several variants, but all essentially argue that to combine religion and politics is like trying to mix the proverbial oil and water. The work of French sociologist and lay Protestant theologian Jacques Ellul offers one approach to this perspective;

American theologian John Howard Yoder provides another. Both men's views have in common that they see the primary role of the Christian in politics as one of simply "being" rather than "doing." Neither advocates withdrawal from the political world, but both reject the idea of a specifically Christian political platform; authentically Christian politics should be distinguished more by its style than by its content. Both take the view that they do on the grounds that Christian faith and politics are two vastly different orders of being and do not properly mix. Individuals motivated by their Christian faith have a definite role within the public realm; organized religion, however, does not, and, if it is true to itself, cannot.

Jacques Ellul: Of Human Bondage and Radical Freedom

Ellul's starting point is that God makes freely available in Jesus the gift of radical freedom. That gift delivers human beings from entrapment in the "order of necessity," the state of bondage. However, all human institutions, especially politics, belong to that order of bondage and necessity. Thus, political activity can provide no ultimate answers, nor can it solve ultimate problems. When people make the mistake of thinking that it can, they mire themselves more deeply in their slavery to necessity. Therefore, trying to use the political order to infuse society with Christian values—or to limit non-Christian ones—is doomed to failure (Ellul 1967, 1972a, 1972b).

However, Ellul maintains that there is a crucial role for the Christian in politics: that of the witness. The state is necessary to see to it that relative freedoms are embodied and evil restrained, but beyond that, it has no use. Its moral impotence is seen clearly, for example, in the fact that all societies rely on violence to achieve and secure their ends. But violence, Ellul argues, is clearly one of the defining marks of the "order of necessity" and "unfreedom," a singular element of all that from which Christians have been freed by Christ. By definition, participation in violence cannot be a characteristic of authentic Christian freedom (Ellul 1972b).

Because politics exists in the realm of the relative, the best approach that one living under ultimate freedom can take is simply being there, a constant challenge to political "business as usual." Ellul (1976: 396) writes:

> [If] Christians are to be in political life to bear witness, if this is in truth their only motive . . . [others] will then look with astonishment at these odd people who instead of doing like others, i.e., hating one another for political reasons, are full of love for one another beyond these secondary barriers.

In Ellul's view, when Christians plunge into the rough-and-tumble of political compromise and power brokering, they lose their vital capacity to bear witness to the one thing that politics most desperately needs.

John Howard Yoder: The Politics of Inevitable Violence

American Mennonite theologian John Howard Yoder provides a different interpretation of this perspective on Christian participation in politics. Like Ellul, Yoder is deeply disturbed by the incompatibility of the use of violence with the Christian vision (Mennonites have historically been among the most consistent Christian advocates of pacifism and non-violence). With Ellul also, he is inclined to see the existence of the state as necessary only to control evil. Even its positive functions—the provision of education and welfare, for example—rely heavily on the use of compulsion to get people to pay the necessary taxes. As a result, they depend implicitly on the threat of violence (non-payment can and probably will result in incarceration). From his perspective, the state is thus something entirely alien to Christianity, to the Kingdom of God, which is founded on peace. He does not advocate disobedience to requirements such as paying taxes; insofar as they can in good conscience, Christians are to be subject to the state and its regulations. But, as with Ellul, the unique Christian way of participation in the processes of the state is by witnessing with one's life to a very different reality from the state.

According to Yoder, Christians are not called to "manage the world." That is God's business. Given the witness of Christians, God will in time transform the world in accordance with the Kingdom (Yoder 1972). Thus, there is no Christian imperative to fight perceived injustice or immorality through the use of law and politics.

Thus, while support for a "high wall of separation" between church and state can come from the conviction that anything less is a threat to liberty and civil public debate, it can also stem from the belief that the commingling of religion and government is bad for religion. Others hold that the two orders simply do not mix, and in principle cannot. The assertion that religion and politics need to work together, or that religion is necessary for democratic politics, can also be made from a variety of perspectives. It is to these views that the discussion now turns.

Religion as a Necessary Support for Democracy

Quite contrary to the strict separationist view, many theorists hold that modern democratic principles are rooted in Judeo-Christian religious values, and that liberty and democracy require this religious grounding if they are to survive over the long term. In terms of the fourfold distinction with which the chapter began, this is an example of an accommodationist view. Catholic scholar Michael Novak (2000: 178) has argued strongly that American democratic liberties are vitally and unmistakably rooted in religion:

> Judaism and Christianity . . . reinforced in men's minds the role of reason in human affairs; the idea of progress in history (as opposed to a wheel

of endless rotation); the centrality of personal dignity and personal liberty in human destiny; and the idea of a cosmic process conceived, created, and governed (even in its tiniest details) by a benevolent Deity: Lawgiver, Governor, Judge, gentle and caring Providence.

These assumptions, Novak argues, were critical in the creation of American democracy, and equally critical in its maintenance today. This point is also stressed by Lutheran pastor-turned Catholic priest Richard John Neuhaus, who further argues that the political realm necessarily derives its direction from shared cultural and moral sensibilities. In the United States, the vast majority of people make moral judgments within a framework deeply informed by Judeo-Christian principles (even if they are not especially religious). Thus, the Judeo-Christian ethic provides the binding thread that brings the nation closer to civility (Neuhaus 1984).

The Inadequacy of Secular Value Systems

Another proponent of this accommodationist viewpoint is A. James Reichley. Reichley understands the underlying issue in the discussion of religion in American public life to be whether or not "a free society depends ultimately on religious values for cohesion and vindication of human rights" (Reichley 1985: 8). He distinguishes among three kinds of secular (non-religious) value systems, and finds each one ultimately inadequate to fully support democratic values and practices.

The first of these non-religious value systems is egoism, or the pursuit of self-interest. Some people who hold that egoism is a sufficient undergirding for democracy believe that human nature is such that, when freed from oppression and repression, people naturally act in ways that support democracy. Others, the "tougher-minded" egoists, argue that even though human nature cannot be counted on to cause people to behave democratically, the free competition between them will ensure maximum benefits to all. Reichley, on the other hand, says that the historical record will support neither viewpoint. Neither human nature nor the results of free competition can be counted on to produce a free democratic society, and unfettered "egoism is practically guaranteed to cause social disaster" (Reichley 1985: 341).

The second secular system that Reichley reviews is authoritarianism, which he sees as "almost by definition hostile to democracy." Even the most benign authoritarian government, he argues, cannot possibly uphold anything approaching democratic standards of personal liberty (Reichley 1985: 343). Moreover, most authoritarian regimes, unfettered by democratic or religious restraints, will quickly become anything but benign.

Civil humanism is the third secular value system that Reichley considers. It claims to "legitimiz[e] both individual rights and social authority and establis[h] a balance between them." Reichley distinguishes several variants of this philosophy. *Libertarian* humanism holds that individuals voluntarily give up some of their freedom and civil liberties in order to enjoy the benefits of a civil society. The more *communitarian* version of civil humanism holds that civil liberties are products of the evolution of the social group, and hence are dependent on it. Reichley argues that both are unworkable from the outset. The libertarian version falls prey to "atomistic selfishness, obsessive materialism, and personal alienation," while the communitarian version tends "toward social indoctrination, state control, and group aggression" (Reichley 1985: 344–345).

Reichley also identifies a third type, which he calls *classical* civil humanism. Human nature, in this version, "depends for fulfillment on order, justice, and freedom." Since human beings naturally aspire to these goals, they provide adequate moral grounding for a "free and humane society" (Reichley 1985: 346–347). Reichley sees this approach as inadequate, as well, and not supported by historical evidence. The core of his critique of this approach, and indeed of all secular civil humanism, is that a balancing of self and society as dual ultimate sources of value simply cannot be held together in any widespread, sustainable way without there being a third value source upon which they both rely. Otherwise, one will always over-run the other, because the essential moral support for a free but orderly democratic society is lacking. Religion provides this third, independent value source, and therefore, "the health of republican government depends on moral values derived from religion" (Reichley 1985: 340).

Novak (2000: 176) echoes these points, arguing that religion is an indispensable support for true freedom and human rights. If religion were ever marginalized in society, he contends, there would be no check on political orthodoxy and the power of the state. He argues:

> Against these, there would remain no principled intellectual defense. If legitimate authority wills to put something into law, and does so, citizens can no longer argue that it is unjust (says who?) or in violation of the laws of nature and nature's God (so what?).

Absent an appeal to an independent standard of right and justice embodied in religious teachings and/or sacred texts, all objections to the exercise of state power become inherently subjective and arbitrary.

Christian Faith and Democratic Values

One listing of specific democratic values that are held to derive from the Judeo-Christian tradition and, ultimately, to depend on it, is provided by Ernest Griffith and his co-authors. Griffith et al. (1956: 101) are interested in the "cultural attitudes or mores which will sustain democracy." What sorts of attitudes will provide the necessary psychological undergirding for democracy, and further, will give democracy the "emotional content" that will make its adherents willing to fight for it?

They hypothesize that the Judeo-Christian tradition, and especially Christian faith, is the matrix that best grounds the values necessary for a functioning democracy. Only religious faith can give such attitudes the character of absolutes, a feature that they see as necessary for the survival of democracy. They then list seven specific democratic attitudes that they believe are best grounded in Christian faith:

- "Love for and belief in freedom" is supported by the Judeo-Christian belief in the sacredness of each person as a child of God.
- Commitment to active participation in the life of the community is based on a belief in the obligation to accept one's responsibility to work cooperatively with all humankind.
- Truthfulness in discussion can be based on belief in truth as the inner light of God's righteousness.
- The obligation of economic groups to serve society is an outgrowth of the Christian view of society as whole, in which each person has a responsibility for all the rest.
- Leadership and office-holding seen as public trusts reflect the biblical examples of prophetic service.
- Religious faiths lead to attitudes that promote a balancing of individualism and responsibility.
- Cooperation and goodwill among nations grows out of a vision of the world that says we are all children of the same God (Griffith et al. 1956: 113).

Of course, assertion of a necessary link between such values and Christianity is not without controversy. One of a more secular inclination might argue that civil humanism is just as capable of supporting the traits that Griffith et al. deem necessary for democracy, and without the risks posed by grounding such critical features of our common life in the tenets of one particular faith tradition. Moreover, from the standpoint of religions outside the Judeo-Christian tradition, it could also be argued that there is little if anything on the list that could not be gleaned from their teachings as well.

A Broad Consensus on Essential Values

Another variation on the theme of why politics and religion go hand-in-hand is the argument that the United States operates on the basis of a broad consensus on essential values and that religion is an integral part of that consensus. "In this view," argues Ted Jelen, "we as a people not only agree on a set of rules, but on a substantive set of moral and metaphysical principles with a transcendent basis." Such an arrangement, if it does in fact exist, does not require denominational uniformity; it does, however, establish certain broad parameters for socially acceptable values. Jelen explains that such a consensus would mean that "tolerance for diversity cannot and should not be unlimited." Although the boundaries may be both broad and somewhat vague, they do exist. Tolerance should, however, be extended to all those who are within the boundaries (Jelen 1995: 272–273).

This perspective is similar to the one articulated by Richard John Neuhaus (1984), and draws heavily on the "sacred canopy" idea of Peter Berger (1967). It entails an accommodationist interpretation of the establishment clause coupled with a communitarian view regarding religious free exercise. Organized religion has a definite role in public life, and it is legitimate for deeply held cultural values to set broad constraints on religious free exercise.

This view has definite implications for public policy issues and for the sorts of questions discussed in Chapters 5 and 6 on the First Amendment. "Religious symbols and imagery" certainly have an important place in those institutions that affirm and inculcate the common culture, such as "schools, public buildings, [and] national holidays" (Jelen 1995: 274). Prayer in the public schools and the public celebration of religious holidays are important for maintaining the consensus. While the government would not be permitted to assist particular religious denominations, aid to religion in general would be encouraged. The religious preferences of the majority, broadly defined, could well receive government support.

Religion as a Necessary Mediating Structure

Many religious thinkers take issue with the privatization of religion that has come about, at least to some extent, in the wake of modernization and the secularization of American life. Religion and the churches, they argue, are absolutely necessary for the health of a democracy, and the privatization of religion poses a substantial long-term threat to American liberty. While many thinkers have advanced arguments along these lines, the analysis here will focus on Robert Booth Fowler, Richard John Neuhaus, and Stephen L. Carter as representative examples.

The idea that religion and the liberal democratic order are "unconventional partners" goes back at least to Alexis de Tocqueville. In this analysis, American religion and democratic culture greatly assist each other. Religious institutions do not engage directly in politics, but are a source for meaning, moral values, and authentic community that the government simply cannot provide. As articulated by Tocqueville, however, the relationship remains at a pre-reflective level. The contemporary theorists in this vein, by contrast, articulate a vision in which that relationship moves from being incidental to consciously intentional, and in which religion's role in politics becomes more active.

Religion as an Alternative to the Liberal Democratic Order

According to Robert Booth Fowler (1988), there are two prevailing types of views about the relationship between religion and culture. "Integrationist" views emphasize the ways in which religion reinforces liberal culture, while "challenge" views emphasize the ways in which religion opposes that culture. Against both these views, Fowler proposes that religion presents an *alternative* and *corrective* to the liberal order. The liberal order is inherently very individualistic, and thus lacks the dimension of community that human beings need. By providing that community, religion sustains the liberal order by making it possible for people to live with the inevitable inadequacy of liberal individualism. By offering believers a sharply alternative reality, religion provides a counterweight to liberalism that allows believers to sustain and participate in the liberal order as the best way of organizing temporal affairs (Fowler 1988).

The Naked Public Square

Richard John Neuhaus describes the situation in modern America metaphorically in the title of his book, *The Naked Public Square* (1984). He believes that political practice and doctrine have operated to systematically exclude religion and religious values from the public arena, thus leaving the public square "naked." Such an absence of authoritative symbols and values is both temporary and very threatening to the survival of democracy, because it creates an ideological vacuum that will ultimately be filled. The only question is, "filled with what?".

Neuhaus's concern is that if religious values are excluded from the public square, public morality will be decided by cultural elites whose views do not coincide with those of the majority. This concern is consistent with survey demonstrations of the differences between the views of the mass public and the elites presented in Chapter 7. If religion is excluded from a position of influence in the public square, then the realm of public life will eventually be controlled by the secular government.

A key element of Neuhaus's argument is that the moral authority of the democratic state is rooted not so much in individual rights or a concept of "the people," but in those communities that comprise the society and through which "the people" interact with the state. The marginalizing of religion in the arena of public discourse has left the United States without "an effective and believable linkage between the vast institutions (megastructures) of the public sphere and the values by which people live day-by-day" (Neuhaus 1984: 259). Thus, despite demanding increasing government services from the growing welfare state, people do not have confidence in or affection for that government, creating problems with both legitimacy and alienation (Kerrine and Neuhaus 1979). Neuhaus writes with a sense of urgency born out of his belief that we face a real crisis of legitimacy that can only get worse unless a "transcendent moral purpose" can focus its judgment on the state and make it clear that the state is simply the servant of the law, not its source. Events during the twenty-five years between the publication of *The Naked Public Square* and Neuhaus's death in 2009 only served to deepen his conviction on this score.

He has a very specific prescription for fixing what he understands to be wrong with America: the values that we associate with democracy must not only be sustained, but revitalized. This can only be done, he argues, by grounding them in biblical faith. He believes that the basic concepts of democracy have their foundation in Christianity, and that only by acknowledging this foundation can democracy as we know it survive, since the actual religion of the American people is "overwhelmingly and explicitly Judeo-Christian" (Neuhaus 1985: 62). Unlike some religious conservatives, Neuhaus does not base his claim of the necessity of the Judeo-Christian tradition for democracy on divine revelation or the words of the Bible. Rather, he argues from the more generally accessible standpoint that Judeo-Christianity provides a necessary grounding for democratic values.

A Culture of Disbelief?

Stephen L. Carter, author of the influential book *The Culture of Disbelief: How American Law and Politics Trivialize Religious Devotion* (Carter 1993a), also sees an important role for religion as a bulwark against unfettered state power. By being an independent moral voice, religions make claims on their adherents that can be a balance to the competing claims of the government, thus limiting the subservience of religious people to the state and providing a reference point from which the state can be judged (Carter 1993b).

This makes it possible for religions to be "intermediary institutions" active in the space between the individual and the government, a space that the state might otherwise take over. Strong religious bodies that retain their independence are also able to fulfill their historic function as the transmitters of values and meaning from generation to generation. Religion is uniquely able to meet these needs, since it engages the faithful in thinking about ultimate questions and searching for ultimate answers.

According to Carter's thesis, modern America has constructed a "culture of disbelief," in which law and politics have joined forces to trivialize religion and relegate it to the private sphere, effectively silencing its public voice. Religious people are expected "to act publicly, and sometimes privately as well, as though their faith does not matter to them." He continues: "Aside from the ritual appeals to God that are expected of our politicians, for Americans to take their religions seriously, to treat them as ordained rather than chosen, is to risk assignment to the lunatic fringe" (Carter 1993a: 3–4).

Religions are "autonomous communities of resistance and . . . independent centers of meaning" (Carter 1993a: 40). This makes them "radically destabilizing." It is also what makes them able to stand up against state tyranny. One sees this destabilization and moral independence, says Carter, in the civil disobedience of Dr. Martin Luther King, Jr., Gandhi, and the anti-abortion group Operation Rescue. This point of Carter's is reinforced by Nicholas Wolterstorff, who argues:

[M]any of the social movements in the modern world that have moved societies in the direction of liberal democracy have been deeply and explicitly religious in their orientation: the abolition movement in nineteenth-century America, the civil rights movement in twentieth-century America, the resistance movements in fascist Germany, in communist Eastern Europe, in apartheid South Africa.

(Audi and Wolterstorff 1997: 80)

For believers, religion makes "claims that exist alongside, are not identical to, and will sometimes trump the claims to obedience that the state makes" (Carter 1993a: 35). It is this possibility of refusal to accept the will of the state on the grounds of conscience that "leads to America's suspicion toward religious belief" (Carter 1993a: 41).

Carter also addresses the issue of church–state separation. While he clearly does not advocate a national church, he sees the religion clauses of the First Amendment as intended to protect religion from governmental interference, not to insulate government from religious influence. To misinterpret it in the second manner will "carry us down the road to a new establishment, the establishment of religion as a hobby, trivial and unimportant for serious people, not to be mentioned in serious discourse" (Carter 1993a: 115).

This interpretation leads him to very definite views on the proper application of the two clauses. Regarding the establishment clause, he is an accommodationist. He believes that churches and programs run by religious organizations should be "able to compete on the same grounds as other groups for the largesse of the welfare state—they should not, on establishment clause grounds, be relegated to a second-class status" (Carter 1993a: 119). If, for example, a wholly secular drug-treatment program is fundable, so should be a religiously based program that relies heavily on prayer and Bible study. Both should be subject to the same criteria of effectiveness. This is essentially the view embraced by the Supreme Court majority in *Rosenberger* v. *University of Virginia*, and that underlies the Office of Faith-Based and Community Initiatives (see Chapter 5).

A libertarian regarding the free exercise clause, Carter also argues for a very broad set of exemptions from otherwise applicable laws for religious groups and individuals. This stance evolves directly out of his conviction that religion plays a crucial role as an autonomous source of authority and value that, on occasion, may require adherents to act otherwise than the law prescribes. The rationale for the accommodation of religion, rather than simply government neutrality, is not primarily to protect the individual conscience, although it also does that. The primary purpose of accommodation is the "preservation of the religions as independent power bases that exist in large part to resist the state" (Carter 1993a: 134).

Carter and Neuhaus have in common a view of religion as an essential check on the tendency of a secular democratic state to enlarge itself continually at the expense of its own best principles. There are also, however, important differences between them. Neuhaus emphasizes the importance of the Judeo-Christian religious tradition specifically for democratic norms and values. Carter, by contrast, focuses on the importance of religion and religious groups more generally as counterweights to state power. He frequently uses small and unconventional religions as positive examples of religious resistance, and is often critical of how the courts have dealt with these groups.

Religion in Public Life: A Composite Proposal

The chapter thus far has reviewed a number of theories about the proper role of religion in politics. Most Americans believe that religion has a role to play in the public arena and in the political life of the nation, but do not see that role in narrowly sectarian terms. As Chapter 7 discussed in detail, their views combine elements of accommodationism and separationism.

There are also a variety of proposals from religious writers that take something of a middle ground between separationism and accommodation (e.g., Castelli 1988; Wogaman 1988; Perry 2003). While most of these writers are themselves Christians, they typically frame their ideas in terms of religion more generally. Of course, each writer's view has its own nuances and distinctive elements; nonetheless, a general composite picture emerges that contains the core elements of this "centrist" view. They are as follows:

- Communities of faith are responsible for educating their own members, so that they in turn will act politically in ways that are consistent with their faith commitments. Beyond this, however, communities of faith are called to more direct involvement in public life. Being a part of civil society entails an obligation to participate in its processes. Faith communities are called upon to oppose social evils and to nurture positive moral values, both among their own members and in the society at large. Religious groups in the United States understand the claims of God to reach every area of human life, public and private—although not all that is good and holy ought to be codified in civil law.
- When organized religion chooses to involve itself in this way, it "must play by the same rules" (Castelli 1988: 21) as everyone else. This means not relying on appeals to divine revelation or to religious authority to make their case, and not claiming to speak authoritatively for God.
- Communities of faith must also realize that the moral relevance of government decisions and social issues varies widely. Thus, they must pick their battles with care. Faith communities should, in other words, take stands on matters in which the outcomes truly do matter in moral terms and on which they are most competent to speak. Thus, fundamental issues of "human worth" ought to take priority over efforts to regulate "human conduct" (Perry 1997).
- Some types of direct political involvement by religious groups are acceptable. Testimony before legislative committees, friend-of-the-court

briefs, lobbying, and mail campaigns are all examples of permissible behaviors. Direct endorsements and campaigns on behalf of specific candidates ought to be avoided, however, both for tax reasons and otherwise.

- Civil disobedience is an option that should not be undertaken lightly, but one that may at times be necessary. If so, it must be done with willingness to accept the penalties for illegal actions (as was the case with the civil rights movement, discussed in Chapters 4 and 9).
- Partisan or issue advocacy, "taking sides," is not the only option. Working for reconciliation between contending parties is also important (see the discussion of common ground politics below).
- Although organized religion must be involved in public life, it must do so with keen awareness of the dangers involved. Becoming too heavily involved in the compromises of politics can impair the ability to maintain a credible moral stance. The greater the involvement, the greater the risk of corruption and worldliness. The danger of idolatry, of conflating secular politics with the will of God, must be guarded against.
- Churches and other faith communities must practice a style of involvement that always reflects respect for both their political opponents and people of other faiths. The objective of political involvement ought never to be sectarian dominance.
- A demand that candidates for public office be "godly" or "born-again" or come from a specific religious tradition violates (in spirit at least) the constitutional prohibition on religious tests for public office. Any stand or action that sends a message of special privilege to adherents of a particular faith, or that sends messages of "outsider" status to non-adherents, is impermissible.

The ethicists from whom this composite portrait is drawn are moderate in their approach. Their view would certainly not win universal agreement among religious believers, let alone non-believers (many of whom would regard it as too accommodationist). Theologians such as Ellul and Yoder would clearly reject it as far too political. Many religious conservatives (and some liberals as well) would see it as insufficiently committed to the profound transformation of society along religious lines. Nonetheless, it represents an increasingly common effort to reconcile the seemingly incommensurable demands of religious faith and secular politics.

"Culture Wars": Two Worldviews at Odds

Chapter 4 discussed the growing gap between liberal and conservative religion, and the increasingly political manifestations of these different worldviews. This phenomenon has come to be referred to by many observers of American politics and society as the "culture wars." The culture wars thesis is not a normative statement about the proper role of religion in public life. It is, rather, an empirical description of a conflict that is perhaps inevitable at this particular cultural moment in America, when two dramatically different worldviews are both strongly held and relatively evenly balanced.

The basic thesis is fairly simple. James Davison Hunter (whose book title brought the term "culture wars" into the public discourse in the early 1990s) uses the terms "orthodox" and "progressive" to define the two poles. The defining feature of orthodoxy is its reliance on and commitment to a transcendent authority that is unchanging, consistent, and stands outside both the individual and the culture. Progressivism, on the other hand, understands moral authority as more subjective and individual, guided by reason rather than authority. Truth is more a process than a body of clearly defined content. Whereas the orthodox base their thinking on time-tested assumptions rooted in tradition, progressives focus more on the "prevailing assumptions of contemporary life" (Hunter 1991: 44–45).

The division that Hunter observes is rooted in differing moral under-standings, each of which desires to dominate all others. It touches the most basic assumptions about how American society should be ordered, and how American individuals should order their lives as well. It is thus inextricably intertwined with discussions of the proper role of religion in American public life.

The Two Opposing Camps

The combatants in the culture war have been identified and labeled differently by different scholars, but usually include a similar constellation of "usual suspects." Arrayed on one side are liberals, leftists, modernists, secularists, secular humanists, feminists, gays and lesbians, those in favor of the welfare state, big-government advocates, peace activists, religious liberals, academics, and the media. They are accused of bulldozing a secular humanist agenda into place (often using the courts) against the wishes of the majority of citizens who have not had the political power to prevent it. Organizations that are often named in this category include the American Civil Liberties Union, National Organization for Women, National Abortion Rights Action League, and People for the American Way.

On the other side are those who favor traditional values, who believe in discipline, public decency, and order, partisans of United States military superiority, supporters of the traditional two-parent monogamous heterosexual family as a normative social ideal, traditional gender roles for men and women, an attitude of respect from children to their elders, and public reinforcement of religious beliefs and moral values. The best-known organizational names in this category, as discussed in Chapter 10, were the Moral Majority in the 1980s, the Christian Coalition in the 1990s, and Focus on the Family today. There are also many single-issue organizations dedicated to goals such as limitations on abortion, cleaning up television, reintroducing organized prayer into public school classrooms, opposition to same-sex marriage, and the passage of other legislation designed to enact traditional values into law. Having had only limited success on the national level, these groups have turned their attention to state legislatures and local school boards, and have been very successful in some instances at getting their supporters on county boards of education.

While some issues have obvious cultural and moral dimensions (abortion, marriage, school prayer, etc.), others would not necessarily appear to break down along these lines. One of the hallmarks of the culture wars, though, is that all sorts of issues get pulled into the maelstrom. Thus, even debates on economics and foreign policy take on cultural dimensions (Leege et al. 2002), and simple life decisions such as what car to drive, what to name a child, and where to eat fast food or buy coffee become badges of identity in the epic cultural struggle.

The culture wars have been raging for decades now, with inconclusive outcomes. On some issues (gay rights and drug legalization, for example), public opinion has clearly been moving in the direction of the "progressives." On others, such as abortion and school prayer, opinion has either moved in the "orthodox" direction or stayed there (Wilcox and Robinson 2011). Short-term demographic trends appear to favor the progressives (because younger people are more liberal on most—but not all—culture wars questions than older people), while longer-term trends may favor the orthodox (because they reproduce at significantly higher rates). What is clear, however, is the existence of stereotyping and hostility on both sides of the "theological fence" that separates the two parties to the debate. But how much of it is just rhetoric?

> [Liberals] look across the theological fence at their conservative cousins and see rigid, narrow-minded, moralistic fanatics; conservatives holler back with taunts that liberals are immoral, loose, biblically illiterate, and unsaved ... Do tensions between religious liberals and conservatives actually run deep? Or are they merely the work of a few highly articulate pressure groups such as Moral Majority and People for the American Way?
>
> (Wuthnow 1988: 215)

As Wuthnow notes, stereotyping and hostility have often lessened as opposing groups interact with each other; this has been the case, for example, with Jewish–Christian tensions, and often with racial animosities as well. In the case of the parties to the current culture war, however, this has not proven to be the case. Those tensions seem to be "rooted more in the presence of contact than in its absence" (Wuthnow 1988: 217) perhaps because inter-actions between cultural liberals and cultural conservatives do more to highlight differences than commonalities. Education, traditionally another major factor in lessening prejudice, does not seem to ameliorate liberal–conservative tensions, either. Like contact, it may in fact exacerbate them.

The belief that such tensions exist seems to have become something of a self-fulfilling prophecy. The tensions do indeed run deep, creating real divisions in American cultural life.

It should be noted, however, that not many people identify completely with either side of the "culture wars" conflict; there is, in fact, a continuum that stretches between the two poles. As Fiorina (2010) has argued, ordinary Americans are not nearly as polarized on cultural and political questions as are the elites. However, as Hunter (1991) points out, elites matter, and the argument over American culture and who will define "America's soul" (Wuthnow 1989) has ramifications that will touch everyone. They reflect honest, deeply felt concerns about issues that are central to determining the direction that American civic life will take.

The Culture Wars and the Civil Religion

Chapter 1 described civil religion as a hybrid of secular and religious ideas and symbols that provides a national narrative and, at least to some extent, unifies the nation. Wuthnow (1988) argues that the noise of the culture war battle reaches the civil religion as well as the churches. Rather than uniting people around a common set of values, it echoes the deep differences reflected by the culture wars thesis.

The Christian conservative version of the civil religion maintains that America stands in an unique relationship to God, with its form of government and economy divinely legitimated. America is responsible for bringing the whole world to Christ, and has been given extraordinary resources and divine favor for that purpose. The secular liberal version, by contrast, rejects the "one nation under God" concept as an affront to pluralism. America as God's greatest tool for evangelizing the world is not mentioned, and the United States is at least as likely to be named as a cause of the problems facing the world as their solution. Basic human rights are cited as the grounds of this civil religion more often than Judeo-Christian particularity (Wuthnow 1988).

The two civil religions differ in their presuppositions, their methods, and their end goals. The conservative vision resembles what Max Weber called the "priestly" function of religion, creating a sense of sacredness and purpose and legitimizing the existing order. The liberal vision is more like Weber's "prophetic" function of religion, being critical and challenging the status quo in light of larger concerns (Wuthnow 1988).

As with anything that touches on the culture war in the United States, there is rhetorical venom on both sides. A letter from the liberal organization Clergy and Laity Concerned, for example, contrasts the two views of America as "one based on arrogance and a false sense of superiority, the other based on ethical, biblical principles" (cited in Wuthnow 1988: 397).

Proponents of civil religion in the United States think of it as a unifying ethos that underlies and unites the various denominational religions that flourish in such great plurality here. Clearly, a civil religion fragmented along the same lines as the broader culture war cannot perform this unifying function. If people cannot agree on a basic narrative about the nation's history, purpose, and core values, the cultural chasm is wide indeed.

Common Ground Politics: Beyond Left and Right?

Despite the apparently irreconcilable divisions between religious, political, and cultural elites, many ordinary Americans have some sympathy for (and some exasperation with) both sides, and would like to find a way beyond the gridlock and culture wars. As Jim Wallis (1996b: 20), founder of the liberal evangelical organization Sojourners, writes:

> The old solutions of the Left and the Right and the bitter conflict between liberals and conservatives seem increasingly irrelevant and distasteful to people in their own communities. Many people care both about the moral values that have concerned the conservatives and the issues of justice and equity that have preoccupied the liberal agenda.

Wallis' conviction expressed here, which shares much with Fiorina's (2010) more secular insight, forms the basis for a movement that seeks to move beyond the politics of Left versus Right. Sojourners is one of the organizations seeking to bring about an end to the "culture war." The constituency of this movement is diverse, and includes both conservative and more liberal Protestants as well as Catholics and non-Christians. Wallis refers to this as a movement for "common ground politics" (Wallis 1997, 2005).

Three Premises

Advocates of this approach base their thinking on three premises: (1) Both liberals and conservatives have something important to offer, something that the majority of Americans support. (2) Equally, however, both approaches have serious flaws. (3) Although the federal government does have a responsibility for the building of a good society and the moral nurture of its people, especially its young, much more needs to be done at the local level, closer to where people live and work.

What do liberals and conservatives offer that is helpful and desirable? Liberals have worked hard for "racial, economic, and gender justice." They have stood for peace and against undue corporate power. Liberalism has consistently advocated government provision of a social safety net and upheld the importance of civil liberties. Conservatives, for their part, have demanded a "values-based politics." They have emphasized the need for strong families and for personal responsibility more than reliance on government (Wallis 1997).

On the other hand, both groups have serious flaws and have made serious mistakes. Liberal interests have not upheld crucial social and personal moral values, and have not taken seriously the fraying of traditional family ties. Too often, their message has been one of moral relativism in the name of individual liberty. They have relied too heavily on government solutions to social ills. The conservatives have been in error on important matters as well. They have not always been concerned with racial justice, nor have they defended the poor and the vulnerable. Although they attack big government, they favor big business and military growth (Wallis 2005). They have verbally promoted family values while working to enact economic policies that undercut families. Too often, their near-absolute faith in free markets has blinded them to the needs of those that the market economy has left behind.

Finally, most Americans (and certainly the proponents of common ground politics) do not believe that the government can solve all of the country's problems (either economic or moral), especially not without imposing even more burdensome regulations. This approach sees government at all levels—federal, state, and local—and the private sector working together to bring about solutions that transcend the politics of right and left.

Practical Implications

Of course, as the dates of some of these writings suggest, the effort to transcend left and right with "common ground politics" has been going on for nearly twenty years to little avail. The culture wars rage on unabated, and liberals and conservatives seem more polarized and embittered toward one another than ever. As Fiorina (2010) points out, Wallis's basic intuition remains true —there are plenty of Americans who would like a more centrist, cooperative politics, and whose positions on values issues fall in between the secular left and the religious right. Unfortunately, however, from this perspective, there are relatively few politicians in either party who embrace this sort of political and cultural centrism. As a result, the practical implications and results of the quest for "common ground politics" have so far been quite limited. Nevertheless, the effort by Wallis and others to promote this sort of political transformation continues, because they see the reshaping of American politics to promote civil discourse, and to pursue both social justice *and* moral values, as a genuine calling.

Summary and Conclusions

The question of how religion should be involved in politics is, as this book has stressed repeatedly, a complex one. This chapter has reviewed the following range of viewpoints on the issue:

- Organized religion does not belong in public life. Mixing the two is either bad for government, bad for religion, or bad for both.
- Government and organized religion both benefit from a working partnership between them. Some theorists hold that religion provides necessary

support for democracy. Others believe that religion has within itself the call for cooperation.

- Rejecting the extremes of both separation and accommodation, religious centrists have offered proposals for a limited, constrained involvement of faith in politics. In general, although political involvement will always be problematic for religious institutions, there are ways that churches can be involved without compromising either their own beliefs and practices or the constitutionally mandated separation of church and state.
- For at least twenty-five years, many observers have maintained that a "culture war," with significant religious dimensions, characterizes American politics.
- This situation has led to a call by some for a new politics that transcends both left and right. The practical results of this call, however, have so far been limited.

What conclusions can be drawn from these reflections? It seems fairly apparent that many theorists want neither a "high wall of separation" between church and state, nor do they want to see the wall torn down completely. This is similar to the situation in the general public, as discussed in Chapter 7. The most concern arises in applying ideas that would require fairly extensive cooperation between government and organized religion. It seems certain that questions and litigation about the proper role of religion in public life will continue for the foreseeable future, perhaps intensifying.

This chapter began by noting that attitudes toward the role of religion in public life can be described as running along two vectors, one for each of the two religion clauses. It appears that the establishment clause vector has taken a more accommodationist direction in recent years, encouraging and allowing for the sorts of cooperation between government and religion that have been discussed above (as exemplified by government funding of faith-based charitable initiatives).

It is somewhat more difficult to sort out the fate of the free exercise clause vector, because there seem to be forces pulling in both directions. On one hand, the prevalence of social movements in which previously marginalized groups (such as homosexuals) are demanding rights may lead to a continued libertarian movement. On the other hand, there seems to be an increasing call for community standards that would lead in a communitarian direction (seen, for example, in the resistance to granting these rights). On balance, however, the libertarian impulse would seem to be ascendant, at least for now.

The combination of the religion clauses in the First Amendment with the often-noted religiosity of the American people virtually guarantees that the role of religion in public life will be continually subject to renegotiation. It will never be a fixed and settled entity.

12 Conclusion

Is America a Secular or a Religious Nation?

In the American experience, the separation of church and state . . . does not necessarily mean the separation of religion from public life. Another way of saying this is that America has a strong commitment to secularism, but it is secularism of a particular kind, understood in a particular way.

(Wilfred McClay, Pew Forum Faith Angle Conference, December 3, 2007)

A common thread has run through all the examinations in this book, both historical and contemporary: the tension between America's long-standing religious pluralism and commitment to institutional secularism, and the profound role that religious faith has played in American history and continues to play in the lives of many Americans. Strong voices for both secularism and religion can be found in the nation's heritage and in contemporary public opinion.

The analyses presented here have provided ample evidence for each position. The strong religious mission of the Pilgrims, the Puritans, and Patrick Henry are balanced by the separationism of Roger Williams and Thomas Jefferson. Contemporary Americans' desire to accommodate religious expression in the public square is accompanied by a wariness of sectarian impositions. The political power of a resurgent evangelical Protestantism, so prominent over the last thirty years, is beginning to be offset by an increasingly large and self-consciously secularist constituency.

As this book has shown, the religious and political realms have been thoroughly intermingled throughout the history of the United States. Prior to American nationhood, religion and politics were woven together in the colonies (though in different ways and to different degrees in different places). Even before that, they were inextricably linked in those countries from which settlers came to what would become the United States. Over time, however, Americans have managed and negotiated those links in complex and at times contentious ways, seeking to respect both the nation's religious devotion and its religious diversity.

Politics and Religion: A Common Concern with Values

A significant reason for the close relationship between religion and politics is that they deal with overlapping human concerns. Religion, for example, strongly influences what people take to be right or wrong, moral or immoral, just or unjust. Politics exists because people—whether religious or not—have conflicts concerning these values. Not everyone agrees about a vision for the good society; hence, value disputes must be bindingly adjudicated by recognized authority. One of government's most important roles is conflict resolution. A value dispute arises, there is public conflict on the question, and at some point an authoritative decision is reached on the issue (which, however, may not be permanent). An example is the conflict over the legality of abortion, an issue about which religious groups and individuals have been deeply concerned. Although the question was "resolved," at least provisionally, by the Supreme Court's decision in *Roe* v. *Wade*, the conflict continues today.

The points at which politics and religion overlap often concern those things upon which people place the greatest value; religion provides ways that people can live their lives in conscious relationship with principles of ultimate importance. For many people, it seems only natural, right, and reasonable that their highest values should be enshrined and advanced by the culture in which they live, and that is where politics comes in. As noted in Chapter 1, politics provides one vehicle—perhaps the primary vehicle— by which people can work to give force to their conceptions of what is right and just. This enduring concern with socially relevant values has emerged throughout the book. For example:

- Chapter 2 discussed how many people came to this country because of their desire to live in keeping with their religious values, and how in some cases they attempted to impose those values on others. It also showed that the founders had complex and at times inconsistent visions of the role of religion in the new nation.
- Throughout history, as reviewed in Chapters 3 and 4, religious values have been interwoven with the issues of the day, at times being used to support opposing viewpoints and strategies. For example, some people supported the war in southeast Asia as a battle against "godless communism," while others demonstrated for peace based on their religious convictions.
- In examining the ways in which the Supreme Court has interpreted the two religion clauses of the First Amendment (Chapters 5 and 6), it is clear that the justices have been guided by diverse values, resulting in distinctive interpretations at different times in the history of religious liberty litigation.
- Chapter 7 demonstrated that public opinion about the proper relationship between religion and politics reflects a wide range of values on the part of the American public. Chapters 8 and 9 further showed that religious

commitments can sometimes lead to dramatically differing political values among black and white Americans.

- Chapter 10 dealt with how religious communities function as political interest groups, seeking to translate their values and their conceptions of the right and the just into public policy.

Culture Wars . . . and Beyond?

The last half century has seen increasing polarization between the values upheld by the "conservative right" and those of the "liberal left." Some commentators have even described this conflict as a "culture war," as discussed in Chapter 11. The debate concerns the core values of the two sides, the sources of those core values, and views about how values should affect the public realm. The conflict, in other words, is wide-ranging, involving substantive, epistemological, and procedural disagreements.

One of the ways that religion and politics have been intertwined throughout much of the history of the United States is expressed in the concept of "civil religion," a nationally shared creed and story that combines religious and patriotic elements. Civil religion was originally thought of as an underlying, commonly accepted fund of moral and political values that unified the nation despite its many partisan and sectarian differences. Recent investigators, however, have highlighted the extent to which the civil religion—or, in this case, religions—have themselves become involved in the fragmentation that has characterized values in the United States since the 1960s. There are now at least two civil religions, a conservative and a liberal version, with quite different views of America's origins, its national meta-narrative, its foundational values, and the goals for its future. Generally speaking, religion—and certainly Christianity—is much more central to the conservative account than to the liberal one.

As discussed in Chapter 11, common ground politics is one attempt to resolve this conflict and bring about a new politics that transcends the "culture war" divisions of left and right. It seems inevitable that both the liberal and conservative dimensions of political and religious discourse in the United States will continue for the foreseeable future. The dialectic between the two poles has been a feature of our national life for decades now, and has taken on a self-perpetuating character. At the same time, there does seem to be genuine interest in moving beyond it, in trying to find some commonality of values and priorities between liberal and conservative, secular and religious narratives of America. The success or failure of those efforts will dictate the tone of American politics in decades to come.

The Proper Role of Religion: Private, Public, or Both?

It seems safe to predict that America will see continuing debate about the role of religion in national life. Is its only proper location the private sphere—

family and home and community of faith—or does it have a place in the "public square" as well? For those who hold, as most Americans currently do, that religion does indeed belong, at least to some degree, in the public square, what ought its presence there look like? How should it relate to the other institutions—most notably government—that occupy that space? This discussion will surely continue, and likely intensify, as government takes on more and more responsibilities in areas such as health care that touch on people's most deeply held moral values.

The majority of citizens believe that religion does have a valuable role to play in the public realm. Although some people maintain that religion and politics simply cannot or should not mix, this sort of absolute separationism has always been the minority view in America. The challenge for the majority, then, is to define what the boundaries are for religious influence in public life. In what instances ought they to seek to give their moral convictions the force of law, and when should they draw a line between personal belief and state imperative? When does a morally derived belief that, for example, health care is a universal right, or life begins at conception, or warfare is categorically wrong, or pornography degrades human dignity, transcend the bounds of private conscience and become the basis for government action? How broad a moral consensus is necessary before the majority can legitimately give its view of right and wrong the force of law? These are all critical questions touching on the limits of religion's influence in a pluralistic society.

A second set of important questions, from the standpoint of the state, concerns how to draw on all of the benefits that religion can offer to national life (greater altruism, more civic participation, more charitable giving, a sense of virtue, etc.), while avoiding its potentially negative features (narrow dogmatism and sectarian strife). Both are very real; serious studies have demonstrated both the virtues of religion (Brooks 2006; Smidt et al. 2008; Putnam and Campbell 2010) and its vices (Harris 2004; Hitchens 2007), while others have given compelling examples of both (Stark 2003). From the standpoint of religious groups, there is concern over how to participate in the secular politics of the nation, forming coalitions with people of all faiths and of none, without compromising doctrinal integrity and the unvarnished proclamation of religious truth. Both sacred and secular institutions in America will continue to grapple with the question of how best to approach each other.

Interpreting the Religion Clauses

Given the strong constitutional basis of American law and society, much of the definition of religion's public role in years to come will take place not in the legislative arena, but in the judicial one. A perennial concern in the United States is how the two religion clauses of the First Amendment are to be interpreted and related to one another. In the final analysis, do they work together, or are they inevitably in tension? What kinds of interpretations are best for politics, and which are best for religion? Might the answer be the same for both, or is a tradeoff inevitable? Again, these questions will continue to be raised as the Supreme Court struggles to define the boundaries of the relationship between religion and politics, and the role of religion in the life of the nation. Given the increasing number of arenas in which religious institutions and government agencies come in contact with one another (education, health care, social welfare, etc.), legal conflicts in this area can only be expected to proliferate.

In terms of public opinion about these constitutional questions, Americans show very mixed attitudes. People strongly favor the idea of separation of church and state in the abstract, while being more likely to favor accommodation in concrete instances such as support for school prayer and public religious displays. Public support for free exercise depends largely on the nature of the specific practice and the perception of the group involved; people are more likely to support free exercise for groups and practices with which they are relatively comfortable, and to favor restrictions when they distrust the group involved or when the religious practice conflicts with community norms. Cultural elites—both secular and religious—are generally more likely to favor separation and (especially) free exercise than is the public at large. All three of these patterns—the mixed attitudes of the general public, the stronger support for both separationism and free exercise among elites, and hence the discrepancy between the two groups—can be expected to remain features of the national landscape.

Religion Variables as Predictors of Political Attitudes and Behavior

Chapters 8 and 9 demonstrated that three religious variables—religious identification, attitudes toward the Bible, and religious commitment—are important predictors of various political attitudes and behaviors. The religious variables are certainly not the only predictors, and sometimes they are not even the strongest ones. However, to varying degrees, religious factors have come to influence profoundly what Americans think and how they act politically. Numerous factors influence the exact nature of that relationship; two of the most important are race and the political or social issue itself. It is safe to say, however, that the values Americans hold will continue to be shaped in large part by their religious beliefs and commitments, and that these values will in turn help to motivate their political choices. Religion is among the most intensely personal of all human characteristics, but it can also become intensely political, a dynamic that has been demonstrated repeatedly throughout American history and will be for the foreseeable future.

Religious Groups and the Political Process

One of the major ways that religion has been and continues to be involved in politics is that religious groups function as interest groups and attempt to influence the political process and shape legislation and regulation. This occurs on both a grand, social movement scale (in the crusades against slavery and segregation, for example), but also at the more modest level of "routine" policy lobbying. For example, in relatively recent history, religious groups have functioned as interest groups in trying to affect public policy concerning prayer in public schools, apartheid in South Africa, aid to Israel, and embryonic stem cell research, to name but a few policy areas.

Evolving policies at both the federal and state levels will inevitably bring religious institutions and government into more frequent contact and, in all likelihood, tension. Already, the contraception coverage mandate imposed by the Department of Health and Human Services under "Obamacare" has led to intensive lobbying and, ultimately, legal action by the Catholic Church and other religious groups. Lobbying efforts are ongoing in various states regarding proposed school voucher programs, and the eligibility of religious schools to participate in those programs (and the restrictions on them if they choose to do so). Conscience protections for pharmacists who object to contraception, doctors and nurses who oppose abortion, and various business owners who believe that homosexuality is immoral are the subject of intense lobbying at both the state and federal level, just as provisions for conscientious objection to military service have been in times past. As religious groups feel more and more that their ability to live in fidelity to their teachings is impacted by national, state, and local legislation, they will have no choice but to play, at least to some extent, the lobbying and political influence game.

A Secular State or a Godly Nation?

In the end, one is left with the question of whether the United States is a religious nation, a secular one, or, somehow, both. Although the latter answer is by far the most complex, it is the only one that accurately describes the United States in the twenty-first century, as well as throughout most of its history.

In many ways, the United States is obviously a secular country. There is clearly no established church. Tax monies generally do not go to support religious organizations, and people of any religious persuasion or of none can hold public office. The founding documents of the nation were conceived and written by people who held many different religious views, including deism and even agnosticism. Religion may be taught about, but not preached, in the public schools, which are barred from advocating for or against any religion. American public education—arguably the greatest tool a culture has for inculcating its values—is decidedly secular. The elites and gatekeepers of American culture—the media, academics, and business elites—are consistently less religious than the public as a whole. Survey research indicates that a substantial segment of the population has low religious commitment, and those with low commitment are very much like their avowedly non-religious counterparts. Thus, the social and political views of even some nominally religious people may be effectively secular. Adherents of all religions live in this country on an equal legal footing with each other, and with those of no religion. By and large, Americans support civil liberties such as free speech for those who are against churches and religion, and a majority now report that they would be willing to consider voting for an atheist for president.

All of that said, however, the United States is in very profound ways a religious nation. Churches, temples, and synagogues thrive. Adherents of all the world's religions live here, and many attract American converts. Books on religious topics frequently appear on the best-seller list, and *The Bible* miniseries in 2013 was one of the most successful offerings in the history of cable television (O'Connell 2013). The overwhelming majority of Americans profess belief in God, and people continue to turn to their communities of faith for support, especially in times of crisis and important life passages such as birth, marriage, and death. Despite some decline in denominational religious identification among the young, American college students are interested in religion, and interdenominational parachurch organizations flourish on campuses around the country (Jacobsen and Jacobsen 2008). Conservative religious organizations, especially, have become much more active in politics in the past several decades, and enjoy much greater prominence than they do in most advanced industrial democracies. Across the political spectrum, religion motivates individuals to work and to protest for causes that concern their core moral values—in the spirit of a long tradition of religiously inspired American social and political movements. American theologians and ethicists discuss frequently discuss the "how to" of religion's involvement in the public life of the nation. Many Americans continue to think of their country as "one nation under God," and our coins and currency proclaim trust in a divine being. Political leaders routinely include religious themes in their remarks, and the last several presidents (from both parties) have spoken quite openly about their Christian faith.

What, then, is one to make of these conflicting signals? Do we live in a religious or a secular nation? The answer, as this book has shown, is complex, nuanced, and debatable. America is neither the Holy Commonwealth envisioned by the Puritans nor the secular polity imagined by some Enlightenment rationalists. In sum, however, one might say that the United States is an institutionally secular nation populated mostly by religious people. Some Americans are profoundly and devoutly religious, others are irreligious, and most fall somewhere in between. Collectively, however, they continue the political quest for an America that simultaneously respects religious conviction and religious difference, whose politics can be informed by faith without being dominated by it. That struggle has defined the history of religion and politics in America, and will continue to shape their future.

Appendix A

Major American Religions

As is discussed repeatedly throughout this book, the United States is one of the most religiously diverse countries in the world. Virtually every faith known to humankind has adherents in America. Still, some traditions are obviously much larger than others. In fact, seven major categories—Catholics, mainline Protestants, evangelical Protestants, black Protestants, Mormons, Jews, and the unaffiliated or "nones"—make up 95 percent of the U.S. population, according to data from the Pew Forum on Religion and Public Life's U.S. Religious Landscape Survey (http://religions.pewforum.org/pdf/report-religious-landscape-study-full.pdf). All statistics referred to in this appendix are drawn from that detailed and comprehensive study.

Because these groups collectively generally shape the interaction of religion and politics in America, each merits a brief description here. Limiting the discussion to these groups reflects, of course, an interest in brevity, not a theological statement. Other significant and ancient world religions, such as Eastern Orthodoxy, Islam, Buddhism, Hinduism, etc., are also present in the United States, but none has even half the American adherents of the smallest groups mentioned above (Jews and Mormons). Even for the seven groups discussed, the descriptions are necessarily general and schematic; for a much fuller and more nuanced discussion, one should consult Julia Corbett-Hemeyer's (2010) *Religion in America* as well as the various chapters of this book, where the history and politics of these groups in America is discussed in some detail. Nonetheless, the profiles below should provide a sense of the origins and basic theological orientation of each of these major groups, as well as an estimate (based on the Pew data) of their share of the U.S. population.

Catholics

According to the Pew data, 24 percent of the U.S. population identifies as Catholic. The Roman Catholic Church is the world's oldest Christian religious body, tracing its origins to the apostolic community surrounding

Jesus himself, and more than half of the world's Christians are Catholic. Within Catholicism, the principle of "apostolic succession" is quite important, as every bishop in the Church was consecrated by another bishop, in an unbroken line stretching back to the apostles. This is especially important with regard to the Pope, whom Catholics regard as the "Vicar of Christ" and the heir to Saint Peter. In Matthew's Gospel (16:18-19), Jesus said to Peter:

> You are Peter, and upon this rock I will build my church, and the gates of the netherworld shall not prevail against it. I will give you the keys to the kingdom of heaven. Whatever you bind on earth shall be bound in heaven; and whatever you loose on earth shall be loosed in heaven.

This grant of authority forms the basis of the Catholic belief that the Pope is the temporal head of the universal church.

An affirmation of the Church's teaching authority goes along with the institution of the papacy and the principle of apostolic succession. Catholicism regards both the Bible *and* the tradition of the Church as binding sources of moral authority. This body of authoritative teaching, promulgated by the Church over the centuries, is known as the *magisterium*. On a very few core matters of faith and doctrine, when the Pope speaks *ex cathedra* in his capacity as heir to Saint Peter, he is believed to be protected by the Holy Spirit from error. This is the much-discussed (and widely misunderstood) doctrine of "papal infallibility."

Along with its views on Church structure and authority, Catholicism is also distinctive in the nature of its worship. The Catholic Church is highly liturgical, meaning that it has a set order of worship (which is the same worldwide) and follows a religious calendar, with liturgical seasons (lent, advent, etc.) and designated saints' days and holy days (Christmas, the Ascension, the Assumption, etc.). Also, the core of Catholic worship is sacramental, centering principally on the Eucharist, which Catholics believe to be the actual body and blood of Christ in the form of bread and wine. In addition to the Eucharist, Catholics also recognize the sacraments of Baptism, Reconciliation (penance), Confirmation, Matrimony (marriage), Holy Orders (ordination), and Anointing of the Sick. Finally, Catholicism is distinctive in its veneration of Mary, the mother of Jesus, who is honored in Catholic prayer, art, and feast days.

Mainline Protestants

According to the Pew data, mainline Protestants comprise 18 percent of the U.S. population. While this is clearly an appreciable presence, it represents a significant contraction for what was historically America's predominant religious tradition. Mainline Protestants are now the nation's third-largest religious grouping, behind evangelical Protestants and Catholics and just ahead of the unaffiliated.

The mainline Protestant churches have their origins in the Reformation's break with Catholicism in the sixteenth century, which produced the Lutheran, Presbyterian, and Anglican traditions (Methodism, a major part of mainline Protestantism, was an eighteenth-century offshoot of Anglicanism). Like all Protestants, they reject the authority of the Pope and the very idea that a single leader can speak authoritatively for the Church. They have also, at least for the last century, generally rejected biblical literalism. While the Bible and church tradition are both important sources of moral insight, they are to be applied in conjunction with reason by the individual believer to discern right and wrong in a given situation. As a result, there is considerable variation in doctrinal interpretation both within and among the mainline Protestant churches.

In terms of worship style, mainline Protestants share much with Catholics. These are, for the most part, liturgical churches that have a set order of worship (generally similar to the Catholic Mass) and regular communion, as well as other sacramental rites that vary from denomination to denomination. They do, however, generally reject the Marian devotions of the Catholic Church (with Anglicans as a partial exception to this rule).

Over the course of American history, the mainline Protestant churches have been characterized by social activism. Involvement in the world on behalf of the poor and marginalized has been an increasingly central emphasis, particularly on the part of clergy. In America today, perhaps no other religious tradition is as fully heir to the reformist, "social Gospel" legacy as is mainline Protestantism. This has given these churches an increasingly liberal cast, particularly at the elite level. Generally speaking, social justice takes precedence over doctrine in these churches, and service is stressed more than proselytism.

It should finally be noted that mainline Protestantism is perhaps the most difficult religious tradition about which to generalize. There is wide social, theological, and political variation within the group, such that non-trivial elements of these churches approach very close to Catholicism, evangelicalism, and Unitarianism in their theology and worship style. Generally speaking, however, mainline Protestantism can be thought of as non-Catholic Christianity with a moderate to liberal theological and political approach.

Evangelical Protestants

Evangelical Protestants comprise the largest share of the American religious pie, with 26 percent of the respondents in the Pew survey (this includes only those in predominantly *white* evangelical churches; while many black Protestants share much with white evangelicals, they are generally regarded as a separate religious tradition, discussed below). Like mainline Protestants, their origins are in the Reformation of the sixteenth century, but they really began to emerge as a religious tradition distinct from their mainline cousins in the early twentieth century. Today, groups such as the Southern Baptist

Convention, the Assemblies of God, the Church of Christ, and the Church of the Nazarene would fall under the evangelical umbrella, as would most of the independent, non-denominational "Bible churches."

Evangelicals are distinct from mainline Protestants in several important respects. Theologically, they place much more emphasis on the Bible as the centerpiece of religious life. Evangelicals are much more likely than either mainline Protestants or Catholics to take a literalist reading of the Bible, and scripture clearly takes precedence over reason, revelation, or tradition (all of which they regard as fallible) as a source of binding doctrinal authority. Evangelical theology, while clearly praising charity and other good works, focuses more on individual conversion, repentance, righteousness, and redemption than on the "social Gospel" so prominent in mainline Protestantism. Evangelicals are also much more likely than those in other Christian traditions to regard explicit confession of faith in Jesus Christ to be a necessary condition for salvation; as a result, they place a strong emphasis on missionary and proselytizing activities (second only to Mormons in this regard).

In their worship, evangelicals generally eschew the liturgical and sacramental trappings of Catholicism and mainline Protestantism in favor of services centered on preaching and scripture reading. Tellingly, the pulpit, not the altar, is usually the architectural center of an evangelical church. While they typically do have communion services at least periodically, evangelicals generally do not see them as the centerpiece of religious life. Traditionally, evangelicals have favored a simple religious aesthetic; it would thus be highly unusual to find stained glass windows, religious statuary, votive candles, incense, and the like in evangelical churches (whereas these elements would be commonplace in Catholic and, to a lesser extent, mainline Protestant worship).

Evangelicalism, over the course of the last fifty years, has become the predominant manifestation of Protestantism in America. While they are under-represented among the cultural elites (particularly in entertainment, academia, and the media), they are over-represented in church—which, they would argue, is where it really matters. A clear majority of the Protestants in church on any given Sunday in the United States will be evangelicals, making this group the dominant force in shaping the overall direction and tenor of American Protestant Christianity.

African American Protestants

According to the Pew survey, about 7 percent of the U.S. population identifies with historically black Protestant churches—principally black Baptist (the National Baptist Convention U.S.A., the National Baptist Convention of America, and the Progressive National Baptist Convention), black Methodist (the African Methodist Episcopal Church, the African Methodist Episcopal Zion Church, and the Christian Methodist Episcopal Church), and black

Pentecostal (the Church of God in Christ). These churches generally were formed in the nineteenth century, as a result both of African Americans' desire to develop their own distinctive theology and worship and of white Protestant churches' tendency to encourage or impose racial segregation. The historical development of African American Christianity is discussed extensively in Chapter 9.

Theologically, black churches (like white evangelical ones) tend to be very Bible-centered, and African American Protestants are even more likely than white evangelicals to be biblical literalists. They also tend to reflect the characteristically evangelical emphasis on personal conversion and righteous living. They differ, however, in often bringing strong themes of social reform, racial solidarity, and group struggle into the religious mix as well. As a result, while black Protestants and white evangelicals are *religiously* very similar in many respects, they are *politically* quite different (as discussed in Chapters 8 and 9).

As with all of these traditions, it is important not to over-generalize about black Protestantism. As discussed in Chapter 9, congregations and clergy influenced heavily by black liberation theology differ significantly both from the traditional Black Church and from the new "Prosperity Gospel" congregations. Despite these differences, however, scholars generally view the predominantly African American churches as having enough distinctive elements in common, in terms of shared history, worship style, and race-conscious theology, to constitute their own religious tradition.

Mormons

As discussed in Chapter 3, The Church of Jesus Christ of Latter-day Saints (also known as the Mormons) is the largest religious tradition with specifically American origins. The faith was founded in the 1820s by Joseph Smith, who claimed to have received a divine revelation and a mandate to restore the Christian religion to its true apostolic character, from which he believed it had fallen away. According to the Pew survey, Mormons are about 2 percent of the U.S. population, and that figure will likely grow over time as a result of both conversions (Mormons have famously extensive missionary efforts) and natural increase.

Mormons consider themselves to be Christians; they regard the Bible as authoritative scripture, and they acknowledge both the divinity and the sacrificial atonement of Jesus Christ. They do, however, differ theologically in several significant ways from Catholic, Protestant, and Orthodox Christians, and are thus generally regarded as outside the bounds of Christianity by members of these traditions. Mormon theology is not Trinitarian; it regards the Father, the Son, and the Holy Spirit as three distinct (and not fully co-equal) entities. Mormons also accept as authoritative extra-biblical scripture, including most notably the Book of Mormon, and believe that Jesus appeared to people in the Americas after his death and resurrection in Israel. Finally, Mormons differ substantially from both Catholics and Protestants in their understanding of the cosmos, the afterlife, and the nature of Jesus.

The LDS Church is governed by a President (generally referred to by Mormons as "The Prophet"), who church members regard as a "prophet, seer, and revelator." He is assisted by other counselors (usually two) who form the First Presidency, and beneath them by the Quorum of the Twelve. Collectively, these Church officials exercise a binding authority over both doctrine and administration that resembles Catholicism much more closely than Protestantism. The Mormon faith is marked by the observance of "ordinances," such as baptism, confirmation, and marriage and sealing (roughly equivalent to what other churches would call sacraments), some of which can only be performed in LDS temples (to which those outside the faith are not admitted).

In everyday life, Mormons are distinguished by their exceptionally strong emphasis on family ties; they are significantly less likely to be divorced and significantly more likely to have large families than are other Americans. Mormons also follow a distinctive dietary and lifestyle code called the Word of Wisdom, which forbids (among other things) the consumption of alcoholic beverages, tobacco, coffee, and tea.

Because of their heterodox theology and distinctive practices (including, until the 1890s, polygamy), Mormons have been persecuted and regarded with suspicion to varying degrees throughout American history, as discussed in Chapter 3. Nonetheless, they have endured and thrived, and are now the nation's fastest-growing major religious group.

Jew

Throughout American history, Judaism has been the nation's largest non-Christian religious faith. This remains true today, as Jews are about 2 percent of respondents to the Pew survey (more than twice as many as there are Muslims, Buddhists, or Hindus). Moreover, Jews are represented at a much higher rate among America's economic, political, and cultural elites, so their influence in the nation's life is greater than their modest numbers would suggest.

Judaism is an ancient faith, with roots stretching back thousands of years. It places great emphasis on the Patriarchs Abraham, Isaac, and Jacob as the spiritual and literal fathers of the Jewish people. Probably the most obvious difference between Jews and Christians is that Jews do not regard Jesus as divine or as the savior of humanity. Most Jews do not doubt the existence of Jesus as a historical person (there is considerable non-biblical corroboration for this), but they do not believe him to be the Messiah.

The core spiritual texts of Judaism are the Tanakh (what Christians would call the Old Testament) and, secondarily, the Talmud (a collection of laws and commentaries on the Tanakh). Different traditions and movements within Judaism, however, take varying approaches to the laws contained within these sacred texts.

There are a number of subdivisions within American Judaism, though the three major ones are Orthodox Judaism, Conservative Judaism, and Reform Judaism. Orthodox Jews follow all of the moral precepts and ceremonial laws of the faith strictly, and believe that the entire Tanakh is God's literal word to the Jewish people, with absolute authority. Orthodox Jews believe that their way of practicing the religion best embodies historical Jewish belief and identity, and they are generally suspicious of the authenticity and legitimacy of other forms of Jewish worship.

At the other end of the spectrum are Reform Jews, who represent the most liberal major sector of American Judaism. Reform Jews make a clear distinction between the moral law (as embodied, for example, in the Ten Commandments) and the ceremonial or ritual law (such as strict Sabbath observance and the kosher dietary rules), and believe that only the moral law is binding. The observance of ritual and ceremony is, in their view, a matter of cultural identity and personal choice, not divine command.

Conservative Jews take a middle position between Orthodoxy and Reform. Conservative Jews seek to preserve and respect the traditions of the faith and to remain in continuity with historic Judaism, but allow for more adaptation to modernity than do the Orthodox. They will typically keep kosher and observe the Sabbath, for example, but not with the scrupulousness of the Orthodox. Currently, Conservative and Reform Jews in the United States significantly outnumber Orthodox Jews, but the Orthodox are the fastest-growing segment.

The Unaffiliated

A rapidly growing segment of the American population does not identify with any particular religious tradition. According to the Pew survey, 16 percent of Americans are religiously unaffiliated, including 25 percent of those under thirty years old. This is up from around 10 percent as of 1990, and around 5 percent in 1970, establishing a clear growth trajectory for religious non-affiliation.

This is a very difficult group about which to generalize. While a component of the religiously unaffiliated population is made up of self-described atheists and agnostics, they are only about a fourth of the group (or about 4 percent of the total U.S. population). The remaining three fourths (about 12 percent of the U.S. population) are split about evenly between what Pew calls the "secular unaffiliated" and the "religious unaffiliated." The former are people who seldom (if ever) pray, attend religious services, or read the Bible, and for whom religion is not a significant part of daily life. The latter are people who do exhibit signs of conventional religious devotion and for whom religion may be important, but who for whatever reason do not express an affiliation with any particular religious denomination or tradition.

Who are these religious "nones?" In most ways, they are not as different from their more religious counterparts as popular wisdom often assumes. They have about the same average educational attainment, though the distribution is slightly different—the religiously unaffiliated are somewhat over-represented at both the lowest and the highest educational levels. They are found in all occupational categories, as well as in all income categories. They are somewhat less likely than others to be married and, if married, they have slightly fewer children. They are more urban than rural or small-town, and are more heavily white than the population at large.

Usually, members of this group were not non-religious in childhood (though this is more common than it once was), but became so at some later point, whether by a simple drift away from religion or a sort of "reverse conversion" experience, in which they made a conscious turn away from faith. Socialization may be the key factor in this process, as secular orientations are often acquired from people in one's social environment. Spouses and "significant others" can be especially important in this regard.

Appendix B

Information on NORC GSS Questions

Chapters 8 and 9 of this book rely heavily on questions drawn from the 2006 through 2012 iterations of the National Opinion Research Center's General Social Survey. The GSS has been conducted at least every other year since 1972. Full details about the survey, its history, and its administration can be found at www3.norc.org/gss+website/.

Some of the questions referred to in the chapters are straightforward and self-explanatory (vote choice, party identification, etc.), or else have been fully reproduced in the text, and thus do not require elaboration here. Others, however—particularly those reported in Tables 8.2, 8.4, and 8.6—require more information to establish the full scope and context of the queries. These items are detailed below.

Social Welfare Index

The social welfare index is a composite of two equally weighted items. The first asks:

> "We are faced with many problems in this country, none of which can be solved easily or inexpensively. I'm going to name some of these problems, and for each one I'd like you to tell me whether you think we're spending too much money on it, too little money, or about the right amount. [First] welfare . . . are we spending too much, too little, or about the right amount on welfare?"

The second item asks:

> "Some people think that the government in Washington ought to reduce the income differences between the rich and the poor, perhaps by raising the taxes of wealthy families or by giving income assistance to the poor. Others think that the government should not concern itself with reducing this income difference between the rich and the poor.
>
> Here is a card with a scale from 1 to 7. Think of a score of 1 as meaning that government ought to reduce the income differences between rich and poor,

and a score of 7 meaning that the government should not concern itself with reducing income differences. What score between 1 and 7 comes closest to the way you feel?"

These items are then combined and scaled such that someone who gives the most conservative possible answers (i.e., we are spending too much on welfare and government should not concern itself with income differences) is scored 0, and someone who gives the most liberal possible answers (i.e., we are spending too little on welfare and government ought to reduce income differences) is scored 100, with others arrayed in between.

Gender Equality Index

The gender equality index is a composite of two equally weighted items (which, as discussed in Chapter 8, are less than ideal). The first asks:

"If your party nominated a woman for President, would you vote for her if she were qualified for the job?"

The second asks:

"Tell me if you agree or disagree with this statement: Most men are better suited emotionally for politics than are most women."

These items are then combined and scaled such that someone who would not vote for a woman for president and thinks that men are better suited for politics is scored 0, and someone who would vote for a female presidential candidate and disagrees that men are better suited for politics is scored 100, with others arrayed in between.

Racial Liberalism Index

The racial liberalism index is formed from three equally weighted items. The first asks:

"We are faced with many problems in this country, none of which can be solved easily or inexpensively. I'm going to name some of these problems, and for each one I'd like you to tell me whether you think we're spending too much money on it, too little money, or about the right amount. [First] improving the condition of blacks. . .are we spending too much, too little, or about the right amount on improving the condition of blacks?"

The second asks:

"Suppose there is a community-wide vote on the general housing issue. There are two possible laws to vote on. One law says that a homeowner can decide

for himself whom to sell his house to, even if he prefers not to sell to African-Americans. The second law says that a homeowner cannot refuse to sell to someone because of their race or color. Which law would you vote for?"

The third asks:

"Some people say that because of past discrimination, blacks should be given preference in hiring and promotion. Others say that such preference in hiring and promotion of blacks is wrong because it discriminates against whites. What about your opinion—are you for or against preferential hiring and promotion of blacks? Do you favor/oppose preference in hiring and promotion strongly or not strongly?"

These items are then combined and scaled such that the most racially conservative responses (we are spending too much on blacks, homeowners should be able to sell to whomever they want, and strong opposition to preferential hiring and promotion) are scored zero, and the most racially liberal responses (spending too little, equal housing rights, and strong support for preferential hiring and promotion) are scored 100, with others arrayed in between.

Political Tolerance Index

The political tolerance index is built from respondents' expressed willingness to tolerate various activities by various groups. For each group, respondents are asked whether a member should be allowed to give a public speech, teach in a college, and have a book that he or she had written in a public library. The groups asked about are:

1. *"Somebody who is against all churches and religion"*
2. *"A person who believes that Blacks are genetically inferior"*
3. *"A man who admits he is a Communist"*
4. *"A person who advocates doing away with elections and letting the military run the country"*
5. *"A man who admits that he is a homosexual"*
6. *"A Muslim clergyman who preaches hatred of the United States"*

Responses are combined and scaled such that the minimum tolerance score (opposition to all activities by all groups) is 0, and the maximum score (tolerance for all activities by all groups) is 100, with others arrayed in between.

Issue Items

In addition to the indices described above, Chapters 8 and 9 also make reference to positions on a variety of individual issues. They are described below.

Defense Spending: *"We are faced with many problems in this country, none of which can be solved easily or inexpensively. I'm going to name some of these problems, and for each one I'd like you to tell me whether you think we're spending too much money on it, too little money, or about the right amount. [First] the military, armaments, and defense . . . are we spending too much, too little, or about the right amount on the military, armaments, and defense?"*

Homosexuality: *"What about sexual relations between two adults of the same sex—do you think it is always wrong, almost always wrong, wrong only sometimes, or not wrong at all?"*

Birth Control: *"Do you strongly agree, agree, disagree, or strongly disagree that methods of birth control should be available to teenagers between the ages of 14 and 16 if their parents do not approve?"*

Abortion: *"Please tell me whether or not you think it should be possible for a pregnant woman to obtain a legal abortion if the woman wants it for any reason."*

Death Penalty: *"Do you favor or oppose the death penalty for persons convicted of murder?"*

Gun Control: *"Would you favor or oppose a law which would require a person to obtain a police permit before he or she could buy a gun?"*

Marijuana: *"Do you think the use of marijuana should be made legal or not?"*

Pornography: *"Which of these statements comes closest to your feelings about pornography laws: There should be laws against the distribution of pornography whatever the age; There should be laws against the distribution of pornography to persons under 18; or there should no laws forbidding the distribution of pornography?"*

Euthanasia: *"Do you think a person has the right to end his or her own life if this person has an incurable disease?"*

References

Abraham, Harry J. 1989. "The Status of the First Amendment's Religion Clauses: Some Reflections on Lines and Limits." In James E. Wood, Jr., Ed., *Readings on Church and State* (pp. 109–126). Waco, TX: J. M. Dawson Institute of Church–State Studies.

Adams, James L. 1970. *The Growing Church Lobby in Washington*. Grand Rapids, MI: Eerdmans.

Ahlstrom, Sydney E. 1972. *A Religious History of the American People*. New Haven, CT: Yale University Press.

Albanese, Catherine L. 1976. *Sons of the Fathers: The Civil Religion of the American Revolution*. Philadelphia, PA: Temple University Press.

Allitt, Patrick. 1993. *Catholic Intellectuals and Conservative Politics in America, 1950–1985*. Ithaca, NY: Cornell University Press.

Allitt, Patrick. 2009. *The Conservatives*. New Haven, CT: Yale University Press.

Asher, Herbert A. 2010. *Polling and the Public: What Every Citizen Should Know*, 8th ed. Washington, DC: CQ Press.

Atkeson, Lonna Rae. 1999. "'Sure, I Voted for the Winner!' Overreport of the Primary Vote for the Party Nominee in the National Election Studies." *Political Behavior* 21: 197–215.

Audi, Robert, and Nicholas Wolterstorff. 1997. *Religion in the Public Square: The Place of Religious Convictions in Political Debate*. Lanham, MD: Rowman & Littlefield.

Baer, Hans A., and Merrill Singer. 2002. *African American Religion in the Twentieth Century: Varieties of Protest and Accommodation*, 2nd ed. Knoxville, TN: University of Tennessee Press.

Balmer, Randall. 2000. *Mine Eyes Have Seen the Glory: A Journey into the Evangelical Subculture in America*, 3rd ed. New York, NY: Oxford University Press.

Barry, John M. 2013. *Roger Williams and the Creation of the American Soul: Church, State, and the Birth of Liberty*. New York, NY: Penguin.

Bates, Vernon L. 1991. "Lobbying for the Lord: The New Christian Right Home-schooling Movement and Grassroots Lobbying." *Review of Religious Research* 33: 3–17.

Bellah, Robert. 1967. "Civil Religion in America." *Daedalus* 97: 1–21.

Ben Zion, Ilan. 2012. "Jewish Donors Prominent in Presidential Campaign Contributions." *The Times of Israel*, October 20. www.timesofisrael.com/jewish-donors-prominent-in-presidential-campaign-contributions/.

Bergan, Daniel E. 2009. "Does Grassroots Lobbying Work? A Field Experiment Measuring the Effects of an e-Mail Lobbying Campaign on Legislative Behavior." *American Politics Research* 37: 327–352.

Berger, Peter L. 1967. *The Sacred Canopy: Elements of a Sociological Theory of Religion.* Garden City, NY: Doubleday.

Bernstein, Phillip S. 1950. *What Jews Believe.* New York, NY: Farrar, Strauss, & Young.

Berry, Jeffrey M. 1977. *Lobbying for the People: The Political Behavior of Public Interest Groups.* Princeton, NJ: Princeton University Press.

Berry, Jeffrey M., and Clyde Wilcox. 2008. *The Interest Group Society,* 5th ed. New York, NY: Pearson/Longman.

Berry, Mary, and John Blassingame. 1982. *Long Memory: The Black Experience in America.* New York, NY: Oxford University Press.

Bolce, Louis, and Gerald De Maio. 1999. "Religious Outlook, Culture War Politics, and Antipathy toward Christian Fundamentalists." *Public Opinion Quarterly* 63: 29–61.

Bolce, Louis, and Gerald De Maio. 2007. "Secularists, Antifundamentalists, and the New Religious Divide in the American Electorate." In J. Matthew Wilson, Ed., *From Pews to Polling Places: Faith and Politics in the American Religious Mosaic* (pp. 251–276). Washington, DC: Georgetown University Press.

Boller, Paul F. 1963. *George Washington and Religion.* Dallas, TX: Southern Methodist University Press.

Boorstein, Michelle. 2012. "One in Five Americans Reports No Religious Affiliation, Study Says." *The Washington Post,* October 8. www.washingtonpost.com/local/one-in-five-americans-reports-no-religious-affiliation-study-says/2012/10/08/a7599664–11c8-11e2–855a c9ee6c045478_story.html?hpid=z3.

Boston, Rob. 1994. "Happy Birthday, RFRA (Religious Freedom Restoration Act)." *Church and State* 47: 8–11.

Brooks, Arthur C. 2006. *Who Really Cares: The Surprising Truth About Compassionate Conservatism.* New York, NY: Basic Books.

Bruni, Frank. 2011. "Race, Religion and Same-Sex Marriage." *New York Times,* October 31. www.nytimes.com/2011/11/01/opinion/bruni-same-sex-marriage-and-blacks.html?_r=0.

Bucher, Glenn R., and L. Gordon Tait. 1988. "Social Reform Since the Great Depression." In Charles H. Lippy and Peter W. Williams, Eds., *Encyclopedia of the American Religious Experience: Studies of Traditions and Movements* (pp. 1463–1475). New York, NY: Charles Scribner's Sons.

Bunderson, Carl. 2013. "Second Fortnight for Freedom to Highlight Marriage, Mandate." *National Catholic Register,* May 14. www.ncregister.com/daily-news/second-fortnight-for-freedom-to-highlight-marriage-mandate.

Burden, Barry C. 2007. *Personal Roots of Representation.* Princeton, NJ: Princeton University Press.

Bushman, Richard Lyman. 2008. *Mormonism: A Very Short Introduction.* New York, NY: Oxford University Press.

Byrnes, Timothy A. 1993. *Catholic Bishops in American Politics.* Princeton, NJ: Princeton University Press.

Calhoun-Brown, Allison. 1996. "African American Churches and Political Mobilization: The Psychological Impact of Organizational Resources." *Journal of Politics* 58: 935–953.

Calvin, John. 1559. *Institutes of the Christian Religion.* In John T. MacNeill, Ed., *Library of Christian Classics.* 1960. Trans. Ford Lewis Battles et al. (pp. 1–1800). Philadelphia, PA: Westminster Press.

Camp, Bayliss J. 2008. "Mobilizing the Base and Embarrassing the Opposition: Defense of Marriage Referenda and Cross-Cutting Electoral Cleavages." *Sociological Perspectives* 51: 713–733.

Campbell, David E., and J. Quin Monson. 2008. "The Religion Card: Gay Marriage and the 2004 Presidential Election." *Public Opinion Quarterly* 72: 399–419.

Carter, J. Scott, Shannon Carter, and Jamie Dodge. 2009. "Trends in Abortion Attitudes by Race and Gender: A Reassessment Over a Four-Decade Period." *Journal of Sociological Research* 1: E3.

Carter, Stephen L. 1993a. *The Culture of Disbelief: How American Law and Politics Trivialize Religious Devotion.* New York, NY: Basic Books.

Carter, Stephen L. 1993b. "The Resurrection of Religious Freedom?" *Harvard Law Review* 107: 118–142.

Castelli, Jim. 1988. *A Plea for Common Sense: Resolving the Clash between Religion and Politics.* San Francisco, CA: Harper & Row.

Cayton, Mary A. 1988. "Social Reform from the Colonial Period through the Civil War." In Charles H. Lippy and Peter W. Williams, Eds., *Encyclopedia of the American Religious Experience: Studies of Traditions and Movements* (pp. 1429–1440). New York, NY: Charles Scribner's Sons.

Chidester, David. 1988. *Patterns of Power: Religion and Politics in American Culture.* Englewood Cliffs, NJ: Prentice Hall.

Cillizza, Chris. 2013. "The Republican Problem with Hispanic Voters—in 7 Charts." *The Washington Post*, March 18. www.washingtonpost.com/blogs/the-fix/wp/2013/03/18/the-republican-problem-with-hispanic-voters-in-7-charts/.

Cleage, Albert B., Jr. 1968. *The Black Messiah: The Religious Roots of Black Power.* New York, NY: Sheed & Ward.

Cleage, Albert B., Jr. 1972. *Black Christian Nationalism: New Directions for the Black Church.* New York, NY: William Morrow.

Cleary, Edward L., and Allen D. Hertzke, Eds. 2006. *Representing God at the Statehouse: Religion and Politics in the American States.* Lanham, MD: Rowman & Littlefield.

Cohen, Steven M. 1989. *The Dimensions of American Jewish Liberalism.* New York, NY: American Jewish Committee.

Cohen, Steven M., and Charles S. Liebman. 1997. "American Jewish Liberalism: Unraveling the Strands." *Public Opinion Quarterly* 61: 405–430.

Combs, Michael W., and Susan Welch. 1982. "Blacks, Whites, and Attitudes Toward Abortion: A Research Note." *Public Opinion Quarterly* 46: 510–520.

Cone, James H. 1969. *Black Theology and Black Power.* New York, NY: Seabury.

Cooney, John. 1984. *The American Pope.* New York, NY: Times Books.

Corbett, Michael. 1991. *American Public Opinion: Trends, Processes, and Patterns.* New York, NY: Longman.

Corbett-Hemeyer, Julia. 2010. *Religion in America*, 6th ed. Upper Saddle River, NJ: Prentice Hall.

Corey, David D., and J. Daryl Charles. 2012. *The Just War Tradition: An Introduction.* Wilmington, DE: Intercollegiate Studies Institute.

Covert, Tawnya J. Adkins, and Philo C. Wasburn. 2009. *Media Bias? A Comparative Study of Time, Newsweek, The National Review, and The Progressive Coverage of Domestic Social Issues, 1975–2000.* Lanham, MD: Lexington Books.

Cowing, Cedric B. 1971. *The Great Awakening and the American Revolution: Colonial Thought in the 18th Century.* Chicago, IL: Rand McNally.

Curry, Thomas J. 1986. *The First Freedoms: Church and State in America to the Passage of the First Amendment.* New York, NY: Oxford University Press.

Dabney, Virginius. 1949. *Dry Messiah: The Life of Bishop Cannon.* New York, NY: Alfred A. Knopf.

Dahl, Robert A., and Bruce Stinebrickner. 2003. *Modern Political Analysis,* 6th ed. Upper Saddle River, NJ: Prentice Hall.

Davis, Derek. 1991. "The Supreme Court, Public Policy, and the Advocacy Rights of Churches." In James E. Wood, Jr. and Derek Davis, Eds., *The Role of Religion in the Making of Public Policy* (pp. 101–125). Waco, TX: J. M. Dawson Institute of Church–state Studies.

Davis, Molly. 2011. "Louis Farrakhan: U.S. Lacks Moral Authority to Attack Gadhafi." *Chicago Sun-Times,* March 26. www.suntimes.com/news/nation/4517685-418/louis-farrakhan-u.s.-lacks-moral-authority-to-attack-gadhafi.

Davis, Reginald F. 2010. *The Black Church: Relevant or Irrelevant in the 21st Century?* Macon, GA: Smyth & Helwys.

Dawkins, Richard. 2006. *The God Delusion.* Boston, MA: Houghton Mifflin.

Dawson, Michael C. 1994. *Behind the Mule: Race and Class in African-American Politics.* Princeton, NJ: Princeton University Press.

Deckman, Melissa M. 2004. *School Board Battles: The Christian Right in Local Politics.* Washington, DC: Georgetown University Press.

DeSipio, Louis. 2007. "Power in the Pews? Religious Diversity and Latino Political Attitudes and Behaviors." In J. Matthew Wilson, Ed., *From Pews to Polling Places: Faith and Politics in the American Religious Mosaic* (pp. 161–184). Washington, DC: Georgetown University Press.

DeVoto, Bernard. 2000. *The Year of Decision: 1846.* New York, NY: Saint Martin's.

Dillenberger, John, and Claude Welch. 1988. *Protestant Christianity: Interpreted Through its Development,* 2nd ed. New York, NY: Macmillan.

Djupe, Paul A. 2007. "The Evolution of Jewish Pluralism: The Public Opinion and Political Preferences of American Jews." In J. Matthew Wilson, Ed., *From Pews to Polling Places: Faith and Politics in the American Religious Mosaic* (pp. 185–212). Washington, DC: Georgetown University Press.

Djupe, Paul A., and John C. Green. 2007. "The Politics of American Muslims." In J. Matthew Wilson, Ed., *From Pews to Polling Places: Faith and Politics in the American Religious Mosaic* (pp. 213–250). Washington, DC: Georgetown University Press.

Drakeman, Donald L. 1991. *Church–State Constitutional Issues: Making Sense of the Establishment Cause.* New York, NY: Greenwood Press.

Dunn, Charles W., Ed. 1984. *American Political Theology: Historical Perspective and Theoretical Analysis.* New York, NY: Praeger.

Eastland, Terry, Ed. 1993. *Religious Liberty in the Supreme Court: The Cases That Define the Debate Over Church and State.* Washington, DC: Ethics and Public Policy Center.

Easton, David. 1965. *A Systems Analysis of Political Life.* New York, NY: Wiley.

Ebersole, Luke Eugene. 1951. *Church Lobbying in the Nation's Capital.* New York, NY: Macmillan.

Edel, Wilbur. 1987. *Defenders of the Faith: Religion and Politics from the Pilgrim Fathers to Ronald Reagan.* New York, NY: Praeger.

Eisgruber, Christopher L. 1994. "Why the Religious Freedom Restoration Act is Unconstitutional." *New York University Law Review* 69: 437–476.

Ellul, Jacques. 1967. *The Political Illusion.* New York, NY: Alfred A. Knopf.

Ellul, Jacques. 1972a. *The Politics of God and the Politics of Man.* Grand Rapids, MI: Eerdmans.

Ellul, Jacques. 1972b. *Violence: Reflections From a Christian Perspective.* New York, NY: Seabury Press.

Ellul, Jacques. 1976. *The Ethics of Freedom.* Grand Rapids, MI: Eerdmans.

Endy, Melvin B., Jr. 1988. "War and Peace." In Charles H. Lippy and Peter W. Williams, Eds., *Encyclopedia of the American Religious Experience: Studies of Traditions and Movements* (pp. 1409–1429). New York, NY: Charles Scribner's Sons.

Erikson, Robert S., and Kent L. Tedin. 2010. *American Public Opinion: Its Origins, Content, and Impact,* 8th ed. Upper Saddle River, NJ: Pearson.

Esposito, John L., and Sheila B. Lalwani. 2010. "The Reality of Islamophobia in America." *Los Angeles Times,* September 9. http://articles.latimes.com/2010/sep/09/opinion/la-oew-esposito-islamophobia-20100909.

Fairbanks, David. 1977. "Religious Forces and 'Morality' Policies in the American States." *Western Political Quarterly* 30: 411–417.

Falwell, Jerry. 1980. *Listen America!* Garden City, NY: Doubleday.

Faust, Drew Gilpin. 2008. *This Republic of Suffering: Death and the American Civil War.* New York, NY: Alfred A. Knopf.

Finke, Roger, and Rodney Stark. 1992. *The Churching of America, 1776–1990: Winners and Losers in Our Religious Economy.* New Brunswick, NJ: Rutgers University Press.

Finucane, Martin. 1995. "Christian Coalition Asks Catholic Support." *Seattle Times,* December 10. http://community.seattletimes.nwsource.com/archive/?date=1995121 0&slug=2157016.

Fiorina, Morris P. 2010. *Culture War? The Myth of a Polarized America,* 3rd ed. New York, NY: Longman.

Fletcher, Joseph F. 1966. *Situation Ethics: The New Morality.* Philadelphia, PA: Westminster Press.

Flowers, Ronald B. 1994. *That Godless Court? Supreme Court Decisions on Church–State Relationships.* Louisville, KY: Westminster John Knox Press.

Floyd-Thomas, Stacey, Juan Floyd-Thomas, Carol B. Duncan, Stephen G. Ray, and Nancy Lynne Westfield. 2007. *Black Church Studies: An Introduction.* Nashville, TN: Abingdon Press.

Ford, Peter. 2001. "Europe Cringes at Bush 'Crusade' Against Terrorists." *Christian Science Monitor,* September 19. www.csmonitor.com/2001/0919/p12s2-woeu.html.

Fowler, Robert Booth. 1985. *Religion and Politics in America.* Metuchen, NJ: Scarecrow Press.

Fowler, Robert Booth. 1988. *Unconventional Partners: Religion and Liberal Culture in the United States.* Grand Rapids, MI: Eerdmans.

Fowler, Robert Booth, Allen D. Hertzke, Laura R. Olson, and Kevin R. den Dulk. 2010. *Religion and Politics in America: Faith, Culture, and Strategic Choices.* Boulder, CO: Westview.

Frankel, Marvin E. 1994. *Faith and Freedom: Religious Liberty in America.* New York, NY: Hill & Wang.

Frazier, E. Franklin. 1963. *The Negro Church in America.* New York, NY: Alfred A. Knopf.

Frazier, E. Franklin, and C. Eric Lincoln. 1974. *The Negro Church in America.* New York, NY: Schocken Books.

Fuchs, Lawrence. 1956. *The Political Behavior of American Jews.* Glencoe, IL: Free Press.

Gaffney, Edward M., Jr. 1991. "The Abortion Rights Mobilization Case: Political Advocacy and Tax Exemption of Churches." In James E. Wood, Jr. and Derek Davis, Eds., *The Role of Religion in the Making of Public Policy* (pp. 127–158). Waco, TX: J. M. Dawson Institute of Church–State Studies.

Gallup Center for Muslim Studies. 2010. "In U.S., Religious Prejudice Stronger Against Muslims." www.gallup.com/poll/125312/religious-prejudice-stronger-against-muslims.aspx.

Gallup, George, Jr., and Jim Castelli. 1989. *The People's Religion: American Faith in the 90s*. New York, NY: Macmillan.

Gaustad, Edwin S., and Leigh E. Schmidt. 2002. *The Religious History of America*. San Francisco, CA: Harper & Row.

Gelm, Richard J. 1994. *Politics and Religious Authority: American Catholics Since the Second Vatican Council*. Westport, CT: Greenwood Press.

Gibson, Troy, and Christopher Hare. 2012. "Do Latino Christians and Seculars Fit the Culture War Profile? Latino Religiosity and Political Behavior." *Politics and Religion* 5: 53–82.

Gilgoff, Dan. 2009. "James Dobson's Political Surrender." *U.S. News & World Report*, May 14. www.usnews.com/news/blogs/god-and-country/2009/05/14/james-dobsons-political-surrender.

Gill, Sam. 1988. "Native American Religions." In Charles H. Lippy and Peter W. Williams, Eds., *The Encyclopedia of the American Religious Experience: Studies of Traditions and Movements* (pp. 137–151). New York, NY: Charles Scribner's Sons.

Ginsberg, Benjamin. 1982. *The Consequences of Consent: Elections, Citizen Control, and Popular Acquiescence*. Reading, MA: Addison-Wesley.

Glendon, Mary Ann. 1993. "Religion and the Court: A New Beginning?" In Terry Eastland, Ed., *Religious Liberty in the Supreme Court: The Cases That Define the Debate Over Church and State* (pp. 471–481). Washington, DC: Ethics and Public Policy Center.

Glock, Charles Y., and Rodney Stark. 1965. *Religion and Society in Tension*. Chicago, IL: Rand McNally.

Goldman, Susan Sachs. 2012. *Friends in Deed: The Story of Quaker Social Reform in America*. Washington, DC: Highmark.

Goodstein, Laurie. 2002. "War on Iraq Not Yet Justified, Bishops Say." *New York Times*, November 14. www.nytimes.com/2002/11/14/national/14WAR.html.

Graber, Mark A. 2005. "Counter-Stories: Maintaining and Expanding Civil Liberties in Wartime." In Mark Tushnet, Ed., *The Constitution in Wartime: Beyond Alarmism and Complacency* (pp. 95–123). Durham, NC: Duke University Press.

Grebler, Leo, Joan Moore, and Ralph Guzman. 1970. *The Mexican American People: The Nation's Second Largest Minority*. New York, NY: Free Press.

Green, John C. 1995. "The Christian Right and the 1994 Elections: A View From the States." *PS: Political Science and Politics* 28: 5–8.

Green, John C. 2007. *The Faith Factor: How Religion Influences American Elections*. New York, NY: Praeger.

Green, John C., and James L. Guth. 1989. "The Missing Link: Political Activists and Support for School Prayer." *Public Opinion Quarterly* 52: 41–57.

Green, John C., James L. Guth, Lyman A. Kellstedt, and Corwin E. Smidt. 1996. *Religion and the Culture Wars: Dispatches from the Front*. Lanham, MD: Rowman & Littlefield.

Greenberg, Anna, and Kenneth D. Wald. 2001. "Still Liberal after All These Years? The Contemporary Political Behavior of American Jews." In L. Sandy Maisel and Ira Forman, Eds., *Jews in American Politics* (pp. 162–193). Lanham, MD: Rowman & Littlefield.

Griffith, Ernest S., John Plamenatz, and J. Roland Pennock. 1956. "Cultural Prerequisites to a Successfully Functioning Democracy." *American Political Science Review* 50: 107–137.

Gross, Neil, and Solon Simmons. 2009. "The Religiosity of American College and University Professors." *Sociology of Religion* 70: 101–129.

Grossman, Cathy Lynn. 2011. "Number of U.S. Muslims to Double." *USA Today*, January 27. http://usatoday30.usatoday.com/news/religion/2011-01-27-1Amuslim 27_ST_N.htm.

Guth, James L. 2009. "Religion and American Public Opinion: Foreign Policy Issues." In Corwin E. Smidt, Lyman A. Kellstedt, and James L. Guth, Eds., *The Oxford Handbook of Religion and American Politics* (pp. 243–265). New York, NY: Oxford University Press.

Guth, James L., and John C. Green. 1993. "Salience: The Core Concept?" In David C. Leege and Lyman A. Kellstedt, Eds., *Rediscovering the Religious Factor in American Politics* (pp. 155–174). Armonk, NY: M.E. Sharpe.

Guth, James L., John C. Green, Lyman A. Kellstedt, and Corwin E. Smidt. 1995a. "Faith and the Environment: Religious Beliefs and Attitudes on Environmental Policy." *American Journal of Political Science* 39: 364–382.

Guth, James L., John C. Green, Lyman A. Kellstedt, and Corwin E. Smidt. 1995b. "Onward Christian Soldiers: Religious Activist Groups in American Politics." In Allan J. Cigler and Burdett A. Loomis, Eds., *Interest Group Politics*, 4th ed. (pp. 55–76). Washington, DC: Congressional Quarterly Press.

Guth, James L., John C. Green, Corwin E. Smidt, Lyman A. Kellstedt, and Margaret M. Poloma. 1997. *The Bully Pulpit: The Politics of Protestant Clergy*. Lawrence, KS: University Press of Kansas.

Hadden, Jeffrey K. 1969. *The Gathering Storm in the Churches*. Garden City, NY: Doubleday.

Haider-Markel, Donald. 2001. "Morality in Congress? Legislative Voting on Gay Issues." In Christopher Z. Mooney, Ed., *The Public Clash of Private Values: The Politics of Morality Policy* (pp. 115–126). Chatham, NJ: Chatham House Press.

Hallowell, Billy. 2013. "What Is Farrakhan's Nation of Islam and What Do Its Members Really Believe?" *The Blaze*, March 7. www.theblaze.com/stories/2013/03/07/what-is-the-nation-of-islam-and-what-do-its-members-really-believe/.

Hanna, Mary T. 1979. *Catholics and American Politics*. Cambridge, MA: Harvard University Press.

Hanna, Mary T. 1989. "Bishops as Political Leaders." In Charles W. Dunn, Ed., *Religion in American Politics* (pp. 75–86). Washington, DC: Congressional Quarterly Press.

Harris, Frederick C. 1999. *Something Within: Religion in African-American Political Activism*. New York, NY: Oxford University Press.

Harris, Sam. 2004. *The End of Faith: Religion, Terror, and the Future of Reason*. New York, NY: W. W. Norton.

Harris-Lacewell, Melissa. 2004. *Barbershops, Bibles, and BET: Everyday Talk and Black Political Thought*. Princeton, NJ: Princeton University Press.

Harris-Lacewell, Melissa. 2007. "From Liberation to Mutual Fund: Political Consequences of Differing Conceptions of Christ in the African American Church."

In J. Matthew Wilson, Ed., *From Pews to Polling Places: Faith and Politics in the American Religious Mosaic* (pp. 131–160). Washington, DC: Georgetown University Press.

Heim, David. 2012. "The Persistent God Gap." *The Christian Century*, November 9. www.christiancentury.org/blogs/archive/2012-11/persisent-god-gap.

Hennesey, James J. 1981. *American Catholics: A History of the Roman Catholic Community in the United States*. New York, NY: Oxford University Press.

Henriques, Diana B., and Andrew W. Lehren. 2007. "Religious Groups Reap Federal Aid for Pet Projects." *New York Times*, May 13. www.nytimes.com/2007/05/13/business/13lobby.html?pagewanted=all&_r=0.

Hertzke, Allen D. 1988. *Representing God in Washington: The Role of Religious Lobbies in the American Polity*. Knoxville, TN: University of Tennessee Press.

Hertzke, Allen D. 1989. "Faith and Access: Religious Constituencies and the Washington Elites." In Ted G. Jelen, Ed., *Religion and Political Behavior in the United States* (pp. 259–274). New York, NY: Praeger.

Hertzke, Allen D. 1991. "An Assessment of the Mainline Churches Since 1945." In James E. Wood, Jr. and Derek Davis, Eds., *The Role of Religion in the Making of Public Policy* (pp. 43–80). Waco, TX: J. M. Dawson Institute of Church–State Studies.

Hertzke, Allen D. 2004. *Freeing God's Children: The Unlikely Alliance for Global Human Rights*. Lanham, MD: Rowman & Littlefield.

Hertzke, Allen D. 2009. "Religious Interest Groups in American Politics." In Corwin E. Smidt, Lyman A. Kellstedt, and James L. Guth, Eds., *The Oxford Handbook of Religion and American Politics* (pp. 299–329). New York, NY: Oxford University Press.

Himmelfarb, Milton. 1985. "Another Look at the Jewish Vote." *Commentary* 80: 39–44.

Hirschman, Albert. 1970. *Exit, Voice, and Loyalty*. Cambridge, MA: Harvard University Press.

Hitchens, Christopher. 2007. *God Is Not Great: How Religion Poisons Everything*. New York, NY: Twelve.

Hofrenning, Daniel J. 1995. *In Washington But Not of It: The Prophetic Politics of Religious Lobbyists*. Philadelphia, PA: Temple University Press.

Holden, Andrew. 2002. *Jehovah's Witnesses: Portrait of a Contemporary Religious Movement*. New York, NY: Routledge.

Hoover, Dennis R., and Kevin R. den Dulk. 2004. "Christian Conservatives Go to Court: Religion and Legal Mobilization in the United States and Canada." *International Political Science Review* 25: 9–34.

Hudson, Winthrop S., and John Corrigan. 1992. *Religion in America: An Historical Account of the Development of American Religious Life*. New York, NY: Macmillan.

Huey-Burns, Caitlin, and Carl M. Cannon. 2013. "Evangelicals May Be Key to Immigration Reform." *Real Clear Politics*, March 26. www.realclearpolitics.com/articles/2013/03/26/evangelicals_may_be_key_to_immigration_reform_117646.html.

Hunter, James Davison. 1991. *Culture Wars: The Struggle to Define America*. New York, NY: Basic Books.

Hunter, Jeannine. 2012. "Who Are the 'Nones'?" *The Washington Post*, October 9. www.washingtonpost.com/blogs/under-god/post/who-are-the-nones/2012/10/09/e3669952-1238-11e2-ba83-a7a396e6b2a7_blog.html.

Hutcheson, John D., and George A. Taylor. 1973. "Religious Variables, Political System Characteristics, and Policy Outputs in the American States." *American Journal of Political Science* 17: 414–421.

Inglehart, Ronald F. 2008. "Changing Values among Western Publics from 1970 to 2006." *West European Politics* 31: 130–146.

Jacobsen, Rhonda Hustedt, and Douglas Jacobsen. 2008. *No Longer Invisible: Religion in University Education.* New York, NY: Oxford University Press.

Jacobson, Gary C. 2012. *The Politics of Congressional Elections,* 8th ed. New York, NY: Pearson/Longman.

James, Vaughn E. 2007. "The African-American Church, Political Activity, and Tax Exemption." *Seton Hall Law Review* 37: 371–411.

Jelen, Ted G. 1987. "The Effects of Religious Separatism on White Protestants in the 1984 Presidential Election." *Sociological Analysis* 48: 30–45.

Jelen, Ted G. 1991. *The Political Mobilization of Religious Beliefs.* New York, NY: Praeger.

Jelen, Ted G. 1992. "Political Christianity: A Contextual Analysis." *American Journal of Political Science* 36: 692–714.

Jelen, Ted G. 1993. *The Political World of the Clergy.* Westport, CT: Praeger.

Jelen, Ted G. 1995. "Religion and the American Political Culture: Alternative Models of Citizenship and Discipleship." *Sociology of Religion* 56: 271–284.

Jelen, Ted G. 2005. "Ambivalence and Attitudes toward Church–state Relations." In Stephen C. Craig and Michael D. Martinez, Eds., *Ambivalence, Politics, and Public Policy* (pp. 127–144). New York, NY: Macmillan.

Jelen, Ted G. 2009. "Religion and American Public Opinion: Social Issues." In Corwin E. Smidt, Lyman A. Kellstedt, and James L. Guth, Eds., *The Oxford Handbook of Religion and American Politics* (pp. 217–242). New York, NY: Oxford University Press.

Jelen, Ted G., and Clyde Wilcox. 1995. *Public Attitudes Toward Church and State.* Armonk, NY: M. E. Sharpe.

Johnson, Joseph A. 1993. "Jesus, the Liberator." In James H. Cone and Gayraud S. Wilmore, Eds., *Black Theology: A Documentary History* (pp. 203–216). Maryknoll, NY: Orbis.

Johnston, Henry P., Ed. 1891. *Correspondence and Public Papers of John Jay, Volume III.* New York, NY: G. P. Putnam's Sons.

Johnston, Michael. 1989. "The Christian Right and the Powers of Television." In Michael Margolis and Gary A. Mauser, Eds., *Manipulating Public Opinion* (pp. 203–221). Pacific Grove, CA: Brooks/Cole.

Johnstone, Ronald L. 1969. "Negro Preachers Take Sides." *Review of Religious Research* 11: 81–89.

Jones, Jeffrey M. 2007. "Some Americans Reluctant to Vote for Mormon, 72 Year Old Presidential Candidates; Support Strong for Black, Women, Catholic Candidates." *Gallup News,* February 20. www.gallup.com/poll/26611/some-americans-reluctant-vote-mormon-72yearold-presidential-candidates.aspx.

Jones, Jeffrey M. 2012. "Atheists, Muslims See Most Bias as Presidential Candidates." *Gallup News,* June 21. www.gallup.com/poll/155285/Atheists-Muslims-Bias-Presidential-Candidates.aspx?utm_source=alert&utm_medium=email&utm_campaign=syndication &utm_content=morelink&utm_term=All%20Gallup%20Headlines%20-%20Politics.

Jones, Woodrow, Jr., and K. Robert Keiser. 1987. "Issue Visibility and the Effects of PAC Money." *Social Science Quarterly* 68: 170–176.

Jones-Correa, Michael, and David Leal. 2001. "Political Participation: Does Religion Matter?" *Political Research Quarterly* 54: 751–770.

Jorstad, Erling. 1993. "New Generation of Preachers Guiding Televangelism in the 1990s." *Religion Watch* 9: 3–4.

Kaplan, Jeffrey. 2006. "Islamophobia in America? September 11 and Islamophobic Hate Crime." *Terrorism and Political Violence* 18: 1–33.

Kaufman, David. 2012. "Tensions between Black and Gay Groups Rise Anew in Advance of Anti-Gay Marriage Vote in N.C." *The Atlantic*, May 4. www. theatlantic.com/politics/archive/2012/05/tensions-between-black-and-gay-groups-rise-anew-in-advance-of-anti-gay-marriage-vote-in-nc/256695/.

Kaufmann, Eric P. 2010. *Shall the Religious Inherit the Earth? Demography and Politics in the Twenty-first Century.* London, UK: Profile Books.

Kearns, Laurel. 1996. "Saving the Creation: Christian Environmentalism in the United States." *Sociology of Religion* 57: 55–70.

Kelley, Dean M. 1991. "The Rationale for the Involvement of Religion in the Body Politic." In James E. Wood, Jr. and Derek Davis, Eds., *The Role of Religion in the Making of Public Policy* (pp. 159–190). Waco, TX: J. M. Dawson Institute of Church–State Studies.

Kellstedt, Lyman A., and Mark A. Noll. 1990. "Religion, Voting for President, and Party Identification: 1948–1984." In Mark A. Knoll, Ed., *Religion and American Politics: From the Colonial Period to the 1980s* (pp. 355–379). New York, NY: Oxford University Press.

Kellstedt, Lyman A., and Corwin E. Smidt. 1993. "Doctrinal Beliefs and Political Behavior: Views of the Bible." In David C. Leege and Lyman A. Kellstedt, Eds., *Rediscovering the Religious Factor in American Politics* (pp. 177–189). Armonk, NY: M. E. Sharpe.

Kellstedt, Lyman A., John C. Green, James L. Guth, and Corwin E. Smidt. 1994. "Religious Voting Blocs in the 1992 Election: The Year of the Evangelical?" *Sociology of Religion* 55: 307–326.

Kerrine, Theodore M., and Richard John Neuhaus. 1979. "Mediating Structures: A Paradigm for Democratic Pluralism." In Dean M. Kelley, Ed., *The Uneasy Boundary: Church and State* (pp. 10–18). Philadelphia, PA: The American Academy of Political and Social Science.

Key, V. O. 1958. *Politics, Parties, and Pressure Groups*, 4th ed. New York, NY: Thomas Y. Crowell.

Key, V. O. 1961. *Public Opinion and American Democracy.* New York, NY: Alfred A. Knopf.

Kidd, Thomas S. 2010. *God of Liberty: A Religious History of the American Revolution.* New York, NY: Basic Books.

Kinder, Donald R., and Lynn M. Sanders. 1996. *Divided by Color: Racial Politics and Democratic Ideals.* Chicago, IL: University of Chicago Press.

King, Martin Luther, Jr. 1963. *Why We Can't Wait.* New York, NY: Harper & Row.

Knutson, Katherine E. 2013. *Interfaith Advocacy: The Role of Religious Coalitions in the Political Process.* New York, NY: Routledge.

Kohut, Andrew, John C. Green, Scott Keeter, and Robert C. Toth. 2000. *The Diminishing Divide: Religion's Changing Role in American Politics.* Washington, DC: Brookings Institution Press.

Kosmin, Barry A., and Seymour P. Lachman. 1993. *One Nation Under God: Religion in Contemporary America.* New York, NY: Harmony Books.

Kurtz, Paul, Ed. 1973. *Humanist Manifestos I and II.* Buffalo, NY: Prometheus Books.

Kurtz, Paul, Ed. 1981. *A Secular Humanist Declaration*. Amherst, NY: Prometheus Books.

Landsberg, Mitchell. 2010. "Nuns in U.S. Back Healthcare Bill Despite Catholic Bishops' Opposition." *Los Angeles Times*, March 18. http://articles.latimes.com/2010/mar/18/nation/la-na-healthcare-nuns18–2010mar18.

Langbein, Laura I. 1986. "Money and Access: Some Empirical Evidence." *Journal of Politics* 48: 1052–1064.

Lasswell, Harold. 1936. *Politics: Who Gets What, When, and How?* New York, NY: McGraw-Hill.

Layman, Geoffrey. 2001. *The Great Divide: Religious and Cultural Conflict in American Party Politics*. New York, NY: Columbia University Press.

Lazerwitz, Bernard, J. Allen Winter, and Arnold Dashefsky. 1988. "Localism, Religiosity, Orthodoxy, and Liberalism: The Case of Jews in the United States." *Social Forces* 67: 229–242.

Leal, David, Matt Baretto, Jongho Lee, and Rodolfo O. de la Garza. 2005. "The Latino Vote in the 2004 Election." *PS: Political Science and Politics* 38: 41–49.

Lee, Jongho, and Harry P. Pachon. 2007. "Leading the Way: An Analysis of the Effect of Religion on the Latino Vote." *American Politics Research* 35: 252–272.

Leege, David C., and Paul D. Mueller. 2004. "How Catholic Is the Catholic Vote?" In Margaret O'Brien Steinfels, Ed., *American Catholics and Civic Engagement: A Distinctive Voice* (pp. 213–250). Lanham, MD: Rowman & Littlefield.

Leege, David C., Kenneth D. Wald, and Lyman A. Kellstedt. 1993. "The Public Dimensions of Private Devotionalism." In David C. Leege and Lyman A. Kellstedt, Eds., *Rediscovering the Religious Factor in American Politics* (pp. 139–156). Armonk, NY: M. E. Sharpe.

Leege, David C., Kenneth D. Wald, Brian S. Krueger, and Paul D. Mueller. 2002. *The Politics of Cultural Differences: Social Change and Voter Mobilization Strategies in the Post-New Deal Period*. Princeton, NJ: Princeton University Press.

Lerner, Robert, Althea K. Nagai, and Stanley Rothman. 1989. "Marginality and Liberalism among Jewish Elites." *Public Opinion Quarterly* 53: 330–352.

Levy, Leonard W. 1994. *The Establishment Clause: Religion and the First Amendment*, 2nd ed. Chapel Hill, NC: University of North Carolina Press.

Libby, Ronald T. 1986. "Listen to the Bishops." In Stephen D. Johnson and Joseph B. Tamney, Eds., *The Political Role of Religion in the United States* (pp. 263–278). Boulder, CO: Westview Press.

Lillback, Peter. 2006. *George Washington's Sacred Fire*. King of Prussia, PA: Providence Forum.

Lincoln, C. Eric, and Lawrence H. Mamiya. 1990. *The Black Church in the African American Experience*. Durham, NC: Duke University Press.

Lindsay, Michael D. 2007. *Faith in the Halls of Power: How Evangelicals Joined the American Elite*. New York, NY: Oxford University Press.

Lipset, Seymour Martin. 1964. "Three Decades of the Radical Right: Coughlinites, McCarthyites, and Birchers." In Daniel Bell, Ed., *The Radical Right* (pp. 373–446). Garden City, NY: Doubleday Anchor.

Lischer, Richard. 1997. *The Preacher King: Martin Luther King, Jr. and the Word that Moved America*. New York, NY: Oxford University Press.

Lockwood, Robert P., Ed. 2000. *Anti-Catholicism in American Culture*. Huntington, IN: Our Sunday Visitor.

Lohmann, Susanne. 1995. "Information, Access, and Contributions: A Signaling Model of Lobbying." *Public Choice* 85: 267–284.

Lund, Christopher C. 2010. "Religious Liberty After *Gonzales*: A Look at State RFRAs." *South Dakota Law Review* 55: 466–478.

Luttbeg, Norman R., and Michael M. Gant. 1985. "The Failure of Liberal/Conservative Ideology as a Cognitive Structure." *Public Opinion Quarterly* 49: 80–93.

Lytle, Mark Hamilton. 2006. *America's Uncivil Wars: The Sixties Era from Elvis to the Fall of Richard Nixon.* New York, NY: Oxford University Press.

McClosky, Herbert. 1964. "Consensus and Ideology in American Politics." *American Political Science Review* 58: 361–382.

McClosky, Herbert, and Alida Brill. 1983. *Dimensions of Tolerance.* New York, NY: Russell Sage Foundation.

McConnell, Michael W. 1990. "Free Exercise Revisionism and the *Smith* Decision." *University of Chicago Law Review* 57: 1109–1153.

McConnell, Michael W. 1993. "Taking Religious Freedom Seriously." In Terry Eastland, Ed., *Religious Liberty in the Supreme Court: The Cases That Define the Debate Over Church and State* (pp. 498–508). Washington, DC: Ethics and Public Policy Center.

McDaniel, Eric. 2008. *Politics in the Pews: The Political Mobilization of Black Churches.* Ann Arbor, MI: University of Michigan Press.

McGuire, Ashley E. 2012. "HHS Mandate: President Obama's Broken Promise." *The Washington Post,* August 2. www.washingtonpost.com/blogs/guest-voices/post/hhs-mandate-president-obamas-brokenpromise/2012/08/02/gJQAyoNrSX_blog.html

Magleby, David B. 1989. "Opinion Formation and Opinion Change in Ballot Proposition Campaigns." In Michael Margolis and Gary A. Mauser, Eds., *Manipulating Public Opinion* (pp. 95–115). Pacific Grove, CA: Brooks/Cole.

Marsden, George M. 1991. *Understanding Fundamentalism and Evangelicalism.* New York, NY: Oxford University Press.

Marsden, George M. 2006. *Fundamentalism and American Culture,* 2nd ed. New York, NY: Oxford University Press.

Marshall, William P. 1991. "In Defense of *Smith* and Free Exercise Revisionism." *University of Chicago Law Review* 58: 308–328.

Marx, Gary. 1967. *Protest and Prejudice.* New York, NY: Harper & Row.

Marx, Gary. 1969. "Religion: Opiate or Inspiration of Civil Rights Militancy among Negroes?" *American Sociological Review* 32: 64–72.

Masci, David, Ira Lupu, and Robert Tuttle. 2006. *The "Christmas Wars": Holiday Displays and the Federal Courts.* Washington, DC: Pew Forum on Religion and Public Life.

Massa, Mark S., S.J. 2003. *Anti-Catholicism in America: The Last Acceptable Prejudice.* New York, NY: Crossroad Publishing.

Mayer, Henry. 1998. *All On Fire: William Lloyd Garrison and the Abolition of Slavery.* New York, NY: Saint Martin's.

Mayer, John A. 1988. "Social Reform After the Civil War to the Great Depression." In Charles H. Lippy and Peter W. Williams, Eds., *Encyclopedia of the American Religious Experience: Studies of Traditions and Movements* (pp. 1441–1461). New York, NY: Charles Scribner's Sons.

Meacham, Jon. 2006. *American Gospel: God, the Founding Fathers, and the Making of a Nation.* New York, NY: Random House.

Mead, Sidney E. 1977. "Neither Church nor State: Reflections on James Madison's 'Line of Separation'." In James E. Wood, Jr., Ed., *Readings on Church and State* (pp. 41–54). Waco, TX: J. M. Dawson Institute of Church–State Studies.

Mead, Sidney E. 1978. "American Protestantism During the Revolutionary Epoch." In John M. Mulder and John F. Wilson, Eds., *Religion in American History: Interpretive Essays* (pp. 162–180). Englewood Cliffs, NJ: Prentice Hall.

Mearsheimer, John, and Stephen Walt. 2007. *The Israel Lobby and U.S. Foreign Policy.* New York, NY: Farrar, Straus & Giroux.

Mellman, Mark S., Aaron Strauss, and Kenneth D. Wald. 2012. *Jewish American Voting Behavior 1972–2008: Just the Facts.* Storrs, CT: Mandell L. Berman Institute.

Menendez, Albert J. 1977. *Religion at the Polls.* Philadelphia, PA: Westminster Press.

Michels, Robert. 1962. *Political Parties.* Tr. Eden Paul and Cedar Paul. New York, NY: Free Press.

Middleton, Richard. 2002. *Colonial America: A History, 1565–1776*, 3rd ed. Oxford, UK: Blackwell.

Miller, Glenn T. 1976. *Religious Liberty in America: History and Prospects.* Philadelphia, PA: Westminster Press.

Miller, Perry, and Thomas H. Johnson, Eds. 1938. *The Puritans.* New York, NY: American Book Company.

Miller, Robert. 1989. "Religious Conscience in Colonial New England." In James E. Wood, Jr., Ed., *Readings on Church and State* (pp. 9–24). Waco, TX: J. M. Dawson Institute of Church–State Studies.

Milyo, Jeffrey, David Primo, and Timothy Groseclose. 2000. "Corporate PAC Campaign Contributions in Perspective." *Business and Politics* 2: 75–88.

Mockabee, Stephen T. 2007. "The Political Behavior of American Catholics: Change and Continuity." In J. Matthew Wilson, Ed., *From Pews to Polling Places: Faith and Politics in the American Religious Mosaic* (pp. 81–104). Washington, DC: Georgetown University Press.

Mockabee, Stephen T., Joseph Quin Monson, and J. Tobin Grant. 2001. "Measuring Religious Commitment among Catholics and Protestants: A New Approach." *Journal for the Scientific Study of Religion* 40: 675–690.

Moen, Matthew C. 1994. "From Revolution to Evolution: The Changing Nature of the Christian Right." *Sociology of Religion* 55: 345–357.

Moen, Matthew C. 1995. "The Fourth Wave of the Evangelical Tide: Religious Conservatives in the Aftermath of the 1994 Elections." *Contention* 5: 19–38.

Moen, Matthew C. 1996. "Evolving Politics of the Christian Right." *PS: Political Science and Politics* 29: 461–464.

Moormann, Jonathan. 2012. "Evangelicals Voting in Record Numbers During GOP Primaries." *Christian Post*, March 19. www.christianpost.com/news/evangelicals-voting-in-record-numbers-during-gop-primaries-71693/.

Morgan, Richard E. 1972. *The Supreme Court and Religion.* New York, NY: Free Press.

Morris, Aldon D. 1984. *The Origins of the Civil Rights Movement.* New York, NY: Free Press.

Murray, John. 1957. *Principles of Conduct: Aspects of Biblical Ethics.* Grand Rapids, MI: William B. Eerdmans.

Murrin, John M. 1990. "Religion and Politics in America from the First Settlements to the Civil War." In Mark A. Noll, Ed., *Religion and American Politics: From the Colonial Period to the 1980s* (pp. 19–43). New York, NY: Oxford University Press.

Myrdal, Gunnar. 1944. *An American Dilemma: The Negro Problem and American Democracy.* New York, NY: Harper & Row.

Neal, Meghan. 2012. "Number of Muslims in the U.S. Doubles Since 9/11." *New York Daily News,* May 3. www.nydailynews.com/news/national/number-muslims-u-s-doubles-9-11-article-1.1071895.

Neuborne, Burt. 1996. "An Overview of the Bill of Rights." In William J. Brennan and Alan Morrison, Eds., *Fundamentals of American Law* (pp. 83–128). New York, NY: Oxford University Press.

Neuhaus, Richard John. 1984. *The Naked Public Square: Religion and Democracy in America.* Grand Rapids, MI: Eerdmans.

Neuhaus, Richard John. 1985. "A Crisis of Faith." In Raymond English, Ed., *Ethics and Nuclear Arms: European and American Perspectives* (pp. 61–67). Washington, DC: Ethics and Public Policy Center.

Nichols, Arland K. 2012. "Voting According to Catholic Principles, not Partisan Politics." *Crisis,* October 16. www.crisismagazine.com/2012/voting-according-to-catholic-principles-not-partisan-politics.

Noah, Timothy. 2012. "'Acid, Amnesty, and Abortion': The Unlikely Source of a Legendary Smear." *New Republic,* October 22. www.newrepublic.com/blog/plank/108977/acid-amnesty-and-abortion-revisited#.

Noll, Mark A., Nathan O. Hatch, and George M. Marsden. 1989. *The Search for Christian America.* Colorado Springs, CO: Helmers and Howard.

Noonan, John Thomas. 1998. *The Lustre of Our Country: The American Experience of Religious Freedom.* Berkeley, CA: University of California Press.

Norrander, Barbara, and Clyde Wilcox. 2001. "Public Opinion and Policymaking in the States: The Case of Post-*Roe* Abortion Policy." In Christopher Z. Mooney, Ed., *The Public Clash of Private Values: The Politics of Morality Policy* (pp. 143–155). Chatham, NJ: Chatham House Publishers.

Norris, Pippa, and Ronald Inglehart. 2004. *Sacred and Secular: Religion and Politics Worldwide.* Cambridge, UK: Cambridge University Press.

Novak, Michael. 2000. "The Influence of Judaism and Christianity on the American Founding." In James H. Hutson, Ed., *Religion and the New Republic* (pp. 159–185). Lanham, MD: Rowman & Littlefield.

Novak, Michael, and Jana Novak. 2006. *Washington's God: Religion, Liberty, and the Father of Our Country.* New York, NY: Basic Books.

Obama, Barack. 2006. *The Audacity of Hope: Thoughts on Reclaiming the American Dream.* New York, NY: Crown.

O'Brien, David J. 1968. *American Catholics and Social Reform: The New Deal Years.* New York, NY: Oxford University Press.

O'Brien, David M. 2011. *Constitutional Law and Politics: Civil Rights and Civil Liberties,* 8th ed. New York, NY: W. W. Norton.

O'Connell, Michael. 2013. "TV Ratings: History's 'The Bible' Pulls 11.7 Million Viewers with Easter Ender." *The Hollywood Reporter,* April 1. www.hollywoodreporter.com/live-feed/tv-ratings-historys-bible-pulls-432045.

O'Connor, Thomas H. 1998. *Boston Catholics: A History of the Church and Its People.* Boston, MA: Northeastern University Press.

O'Daniel, Patrick L. 2001. "More Honored in the Breach: A Historical Perspective of the Permeable IRS Prohibition on Campaigning by Churches." *Boston College Law Review* 42: 733–773.

O'Hara, Thomas J. 1990. "The Catholic Lobby in Washington: Pluralism and Diversity among U.S. Catholics." In Mary C. Segers, Ed., *Church Polity and American Politics: Issues in Contemporary Catholicism* (pp. 143–156). New York, NY: Garland.

Oldfield, Duane M. 1996. "The Christian Right in the Presidential Nominating Process." In William G. Mayer, Ed., *In Pursuit of the White House: How We Choose Our Presidential Nominees* (pp. 254–282). Chatham, NJ: Chatham House Publishers.

Oldmixon, Elizabeth Anne. 2005. *Uncompromising Positions: God, Sex, and the U.S. House of Representatives*. Washington, DC: Georgetown University Press.

Oldmixon, Elizabeth Anne. 2009. "Religion and Legislative Politics." In Corwin E. Smidt, Lyman A. Kellstedt, and James L. Guth, Eds., *The Oxford Handbook of Religion and American Politics* (pp. 497–517). New York, NY: Oxford University Press.

Oldmixon, Elizabeth Anne, and Brian Calfano. 2007. "The Religious Dynamics of Decision Making on Gay Rights Issues in the U.S. House of Representatives, 1993–2002." *Journal for the Scientific Study of Religion* 46: 55–70.

Olson, Laura R. 2002. "Mainline Protestant Washington Offices and the Political Lives of Clergy." In Robert Wuthnow and John H. Evans, Eds., *The Quiet Hand of God: Faith-Based Activism and the Public Role of Mainline Protestantism* (pp. 54–79). Berkeley, CA: University of California Press.

Olson, Laura R. 2007. "Whither the Religious Left? Religiopolitical Progressivism in Twenty-first Century America." In J. Matthew Wilson, Ed., *From Pews to Polling Places: Faith and Politics in the American Religious Mosaic* (pp. 53–80). Washington, DC: Georgetown University Press.

Olson, Laura R., and John C. Green. 2006. "The Religion Gap." *PS: Political Science & Politics* 39: 455–459.

Olson, Laura R., and Adam Warber. 2008. "Belonging, Behaving, and Believing: Assessing the Role of Religion in Presidential Approval." *Political Research Quarterly* 61: 192–204.

Page, Benjamin I., Robert Y. Shapiro, and Glenn R. Dempsey. 1987. "What Moves Public Opinion?" *American Political Science Review* 81: 23–43.

Paris, Peter J. 1985. *The Social Teachings of the Black Churches*. Philadelphia, PA: Fortress Press.

Paulson, Michael. 2008. "U.S. Religious Identity is Rapidly Changing." *Boston Globe*, February 26. www.boston.com/news/nation/articles/2008/02/26/us_religious_identity _is_rapidly_changing/.

Peck, Janice. 1993. *The Gods of Televangelism: The Crisis of Meaning and the Appeal of Religious Television*. Cresskill, NJ: Hampton Press.

Perry, Michael J. 1997. *Religion in Politics: Constitutional and Moral Perspectives*. New York, NY: Oxford University Press.

Perry, Michael J. 2003. *Under God? Religious Faith and Liberal Democracy*. Cambridge, UK: Cambridge University Press.

Peterson, Steven A. 1992. "Church Participation and Political Participation: The Spillover Effect." *American Politics Quarterly* 20: 123–139.

Pew Forum. 2012. *Preaching Politics From the Pulpit: 2012 Guide to IRS Rules on Political Activity by Religious Organizations*. Washington, DC: Pew Forum on Religion and Public Life.

Piehl, Mel. 1982. *Breaking Bread: The Catholic Worker and the Origins of Catholic Radicalism in America*. Philadelphia, PA: Temple University Press.

Pinn, Anthony B. 2002. *The Black Church in the Post-Civil Rights Era*. Maryknoll, NY: Orbis.

Pipes, Daniel. 2012. "Obama: 'My Muslim Faith'." *Washington Times*, September 11. www.washingtontimes.com/news/2012/sep/11/obama-my-muslim-faith/?page=all.

Pitkin, Hanna Fenichel. 1967. *The Concept of Representation*. Berkeley, CA: University of California Press.

Prendergast, William B. 1999. *The Catholic Voter in Amerian Politics: The Passing of the Democratic Monolith*. Washington, DC: Georgetown University Press.

Preston, Julia. 2013. "For Evangelicals, a Shift in Views on Immigration." *New York Times*, April 13. www.nytimes.com/2013/04/14/us/evangelical-christians-increasingly-favor-pathway-to-legal-status-for-immigrants.html?pagewanted=all&_r=0.

Prothro, James W., and and Charles M. Grigg. 1960. "Fundamental Principles of Democracy: Bases of Agreement and Disagreement." *Journal of Politics* 22: 276–294.

Putnam, Robert D., and David E. Campbell. 2010. *American Grace: How Religion Divides and Unites Us*. New York, NY: Simon & Schuster.

Quinley, Harold E. 1974. *The Prophetic Clergy: Social Activism Among Protestant Ministers*. New York, NY: Wiley.

Raboteau, Albert J. 2004. *Slave Religion: The "Invisible Institution" in the Antebellum South*, 2nd ed. New York, NY: Oxford University Press.

Rawls, John. 1993. *Political Liberalism*. New York, NY: Columbia University Press.

Reed, Adolph, Jr. 1986. *The Jesse Jackson Phenomenon: The Crisis of Purpose in Afro-American Politics*. New Haven, CT: Yale University Press.

Reed, Ralph. 1994. *Politically Incorrect: The Emerging Faith Factor in American Politics*. Dallas, TX: Word Publishing.

Regnerus, Mark D., David Sikkink, and Christian Smith. 1999. "Voting with the Christian Right: Contextual and Individual Patterns of Electoral Influence." *Social Forces* 77: 1375–1401.

Reichley, A. James. 1985. *Religion in American Public Life*. Washington, DC: Brookings Institution Press.

Reichley, A. James. 2002. *Faith in Politics*. Washington, DC: Brookings Institution Press.

Reimer, Neal. 1989. "Religious Liberty and Creative Breakthroughs: The Contributions of Roger Williams and James Madison." In Charles W. Dunn, Ed., *Religion in American Politics* (pp. 15–24). Washington, DC: CQ Press.

Reimer, Sam. 2000. "A Generic Evangelicalism? Comparing Evangelical Subcultures in Canada and the United States." In David Lyon and Marguerite Van Die, Eds., *Rethinking Church, State, and Modernity: Canada between Europe and America* (pp. 228–248). Toronto, Canada: University of Toronto Press.

Roberts, J. Deotis. 1974. *A Black Political Theology*. Louisville, KY: Westminster John Knox Press.

Rozell, Mark J., and Clyde Wilcox. 1995. "The Past as Prologue: The Christian Right in the 1996 Elections." In Mark J. Rozell and Clyde Wilcox, Eds., *God at the Grass Roots: The Christian Right in the 1994 Elections* (pp. 253–263). Lanham, MD: Rowman & Littlefield.

Rubenstein, Richard L. 1964. "Church and State: The Jewish Posture." In Donald A. Gianella, Ed., *Religion and the Public Order* (pp. 150–169). Chicago, IL: University of Chicago Press.

Sachs, Susan. 2002. "Baptist Pastor Attacks Islam, Inciting Cries of Intolerance." *New York Times*, June 15. www.nytimes.com/2002/06/15/national/15BAPT.html.

Saison, Tania. 1995. "Restoring Obscurity: The Shortcomings of the Religious Freedom Restoration Act." *Columbia Journal of Law and Social Problems* 28: 653–690.

Sanchez, George. 1993. *Becoming Mexican American: Ethnicity, Culture, and Identity in Chicano Los Angeles, 1900–1945.* New York, NY: Oxford University Press.

Savage, Barbara Dianne. 2008. *Your Spirits Walk Beside Us: The Politics of Black Religion.* Cambridge, MA: Belknap.

Schattschneider, E. E. 1960. *The Semisovereign People: A Realist's View of Democracy in America.* New York, NY: Holt, Rinehart, & Winston.

Scherer, Lester B. 1975. *Slavery and the Churches in Early America, 1619–1819.* Grand Rapids, MI: Eerdmans.

Schlozman, Kay Lehman, and John T. Tierney. 1986. *Organized Interests and American Democracy.* New York, NY: Harper & Row.

Schlumpf, Heidi. 1996. "How Catholic Is the Catholic Alliance?" *Christianity Today,* May 20. www.christianitytoday.com/ct/1996/may20/6t6076.html.

Schneider, Herbert W. 1958. *The Puritan Mind.* Ann Arbor, MI: University of Michigan Press.

Schwartz, Barry. 1987. *George Washington: The Making of an American Symbol.* New York, NY: Free Press.

Second Vatican Council. 1966. "Declaration on Religious Freedom." In Walter M. Abbott and Joseph Gallagher, Eds., *Documents of Vatican II.* New York, NY: Guild Press.

Secret, Philip E. 1987. "The Impact of Region on Racial Differences in Attitudes Toward Legal Abortion." *Journal of Black Studies* 17: 347–369.

Segers, Mary C., Ed. 1990. *Church Polity and American Politics: Issues in Contemporary Catholicism.* New York, NY: Garland.

Segers, Mary C., and Timothy A. Byrnes, Eds. 1995. *Abortion Politics in the American States.* Armonk, NY: M. E. Sharpe.

Servin-Gonzalez, Mariana, and Oscar Torres-Reyna. 1999. "Trends: Religion and Politics." *Public Opinion Quarterly* 63: 592–621.

Sherry, Suzanna. 1992. "*Lee v. Weisman:* Paradox Redux." In Dennis J. Hutchinson, David A. Strauss, and Geoffrey R. Stone, Eds., *1992: The Supreme Court Review* (pp. 123–153). Chicago, IL: University of Chicago Press.

Sigelman, Lee. 1991. "Jews and the 1988 Election: More of the Same?" In James L. Guth and John C. Green, Eds., *The Bible and the Ballot Box: Religion and Politics in the 1988 Election* (pp. 188–203). Boulder, CO: Westview Press.

Sklare, Marshall, and Joseph Greenblum. 1967. *Jewish Identity on the Suburban Frontier.* New York, NY: Basic Books.

Slayton, Robert A. 2001. *Empire Statesman: The Rise and Redemption of Al Smith.* New York, NY: Simon & Schuster.

Smidt, Corwin E., Ed. 2004. *Pulpit and Politics: Clergy in American Politics at the Advent of the Millennium.* Waco, TX: Baylor University Press.

Smidt, Corwin E. 2007. "Evangelical and Mainline Protestants at the Turn of the Millennium: Taking Stock and Looking Forward." In J. Matthew Wilson, Ed., *From Pews to Polling Places: Faith and Politics in the American Religious Mosaic* (pp. 29–52). Washington, DC: Georgetown University Press.

Smidt, Corwin E., Lyman A. Kellstedt, John C. Green, and James L. Guth. 1994. "The Characteristics of Christian Political Activists: An Interest Group Analysis." In William R. Stevenson, Jr., Ed., *Christian Political Activism at the Crossroads* (pp. 133–171). Lanham, MD: University Press of America.

Smidt, Corwin E., Kevin R. den Dulk, James M. Penning, Stephen V. Monsma, and Douglas L. Koopman. 2008. *Pews, Prayers, and Participation: Religion and Civic Responsibility in America.* Washington, DC: Georgetown University Press.

Sniderman, Paul M., and Edward G. Carmines. 1999. *Reaching Beyond Race.* Cambridge, MA: Harvard University Press.

Spector, Stephen. 2008. *Evangelicals and Israel: The Story of American Christian Zionism.* New York, NY: Oxford University Press.

Stanley, Paul. 2011. "'Moment of Silence' Allowed After Court Rejects Atheist Lawsuit." *Christian Post*, October 21. www.christianpost.com/news/moment-of-silence-allowed-after-court-rejects-atheist-lawsuit-58884/.

Stark, Rodney. 2003. *For the Glory of God: How Monotheism Led to Reformations, Science, Witch-Hunts, and the End of Slavery.* Princeton, NJ: Princeton University Press.

Stark, Rodney, and Charles Y. Glock. 1968. *American Piety: The Nature of Religious Commitment.* Berkeley, CA: University of California Press.

Steinfels, Margaret O'Brien, Ed. 2004. *American Catholics and Civic Engagement: A Distinctive Voice.* Lanham, MD: Rowman & Littlefield.

Stouffer, Samuel. 1955. *Communism, Conformity, and Civil Liberties.* New York, NY: Doubleday.

Suro, Roberto, Richard Fry, and Jeffrey Passel. 2005. *Hispanics and the 2004 Election:Population, Electorate, and Voters.* Washington, DC: Pew Hispanic Center.

Swatos, William H., Jr., and Daniel V. A. Olson, Eds. 2000. *The Secularization Debate.* Lanham, MD: Rowman & Littlefield.

Sweet, Leonard I. 1988. "Nineteenth-Century Evangelicalism." In Charles H. Lippy and Peter W. Williams, Eds., *Encyclopedia of the American Religious Experience: Studies of Traditions and Movements* (pp. 875–899). New York, NY: Charles Scribner's Sons.

Swieringa, Robert P. 1990. "Ethnoreligious Political Behavior in the Mid-Nineteenth Century: Voting, Values, Cultures." In Mark A. Noll, Ed., *Religion and American Politics: From Colonial Period to the 1980s* (pp. 146–171). New York, NY: Oxford University Press.

Tamney, Joseph B., Ronald Burton, and Stephen D. Johnson. 1989. "Fundamentalism and Economic Restructuring." In Ted G. Jelen, Ed., *Religion and Political Behavior in the United States* (pp. 67–82). New York, NY: Praeger.

Taylor, Paul, Ana Gonzalez-Barrera, Jeffrey S. Passel, and Mark Hugo Lopez. 2012. *An Awakened Giant: The Hispanic Electorate Is Likely to Double by 2030.* Washington, DC: Pew Hispanic Center.

Taylor, Robert Joseph, Michael C. Thornton, and Linda M. Chatters. 1987. "Black Americans' Perceptions of the Sociohistorial Role of the Church." *Journal of Black Studies* 18: 123–138.

Thomas, Cal, and Ed Dobson. 2000. *Blinded by Might: Why the Religious Right Can't Save America.* Grand Rapids, MI: Zondervan.

Tyack, David, and Elisabeth Hansot. 1986. *Managers of Virtue: Public School Leadership in America, 1820–1980.* New York, NY: Basic Books.

USCCB (Conference of Catholic Bishops). 1968. *Human Life in Our Day.* www.priestsforlife.org/magisterium/bishops/68–11–15humanlifeinourdaynccb.htm.

USCCB. 1983a. *The Challenge of Peace: God's Promise and Our Response.* http://old.usccb.org/sdwp/international/TheChallengeofPeace.pdf.

USCCB. 1983b. *The Hispanic Presence: Challenge and Commitment.* Washington, DC: United States Catholic Conference.

USCCB. 1986. *Economic Justice for All: Pastoral Letter on Catholic Social Teaching and the U.S. Economy.* www.usccb.org/upload/economic_justice_for_all.pdf.

USCCB. 2003. *Strangers No Longer: Together on the Journey of Hope.* www.usccb.org/issues-and-action/human-life-and-dignity/immigration/strangers-no-longer-together-on-the-journey-of-hope.cfm.

U.S. Commission on Civil Rights. 1983. *Religion in the Constitution: A Delicate Balance.* www.eric.ed.gov/PDFS/ED243236.pdf.

Vartanian, Aram. 1991. "Democracy, Religion, and the Enlightenment." *The Humanist* 51: 9–45.

Verbeeten, David. 2006. "How Important Is the Israel Lobby?" *Middle East Quarterly* 13: 37–44.

Vick, Karl, and Ashley Surdin. 2008. "Most of California's Black Voters Backed Gay Marriage Ban." *Washington Post*, November 6. http://articles.washingtonpost.com/2008-11-07/politics/36807003_1_marriage-issue-gay-rights-advocates-civil-rights.

Vitello, Paul. 2010. "On Israel, Jews and Leaders Often Disagree." *New York Times*, May 5. www.nytimes.com/2010/05/06/us/politics/06jews.html?pagewanted=all&_r=0.

Wald, Kenneth D., Lyman A. Kellstedt, and David C. Leege. 1993. "Church Involvement and Political Behavior." In David C. Leege and Lyman A. Kellstedt, Eds., *Rediscovering the Religious Factor in American Politics* (pp. 121–138). Armonk, NY: M. E. Sharpe.

Walker, J. Brent. 1997. "Church–State Intersection." *The Report From the Capital*, February 1: 3.

Walker, J. Brent. 2008. *Church–State Matters: Fighting for Religious Liberty in Our Nation's Capital.* Macon, GA: Mercer University Press.

Wallis, Jim. 1996a. "The Courage of Conviction." *Sojourners*, September–October. http://sojo.net/magazine/1996/09/courage-conviction.

Wallis, Jim. 1996b. "A Crisis of Civility." *Sojourners*, September–October. http://sojo.net/magazine/1996/09/crisis-civility.

Wallis, Jim. 1997. "Common Ground Politics." *Sojourners*, January–February. http://sojo.net/magazine/1997/01/common-ground-politics.

Wallis, Jim. 2005. *God's Politics: Why the Right Gets It Wrong and the Left Doesn't Get It.* San Francisco, CA: HarperCollins.

Wallis, Jim. 2008. "The Bible Is Neither Conservative or Liberal." *Sojourners*, June 12. http://sojo.net/blogs/2008/06/12/bible-neither-conservative-or-liberal.

Walton, Hanes, Jr. 1985. *Invisible Politics: Black Political Behavior.* Albany, NY: SUNY Press.

Ward, Nathaniel. 1647. "The Simple Cobbler of Aggawam." Reprinted in Perry Miller, Ed., *The American Puritans: Their Prose and Poetry* (pp. 95–108). 1956. Garden City, NY: Doubleday.

Warren, Mark R. 2001. *Dry Bones Rattling: Community Building to Revitalize American Democracy.* Princeton, NJ: Princeton University Press.

Weber, Paul J., and T. L. Stanley. 1984. "The Power and Performance of Religious Interest Groups." *Quarterly Review* 4: 28–50.

Weber, Paul J., and W. Landis Jones. 1994. *U.S. Religious Interest Groups: Institutional Profiles.* Westport, CT: Greenwood Press.

Weber, Paul J., Ed. 1990. *Equal Separation: Understanding the Religion Clauses of the First Amendment.* New York, NY: Greenwood Press.

Welch, Michael R., David C. Leege, Kenneth D. Wald, and Lyman A. Kellstedt. 1993. "Are the Sheep Hearing the Shepherds? Cue Perceptions, Congregational

Responses, and Political Communication Processes." In David C. Leege and Lyman A. Kellstedt, Eds., *Rediscovering the Religious Factor in American Politics* (pp. 235–254). Armonk, NY: M. E. Sharpe.

Wilcox, Clyde. 1987. "Religious Orientations and Political Attitudes: Variations Within the New Christian Right." *American Politics Quarterly* 15: 274–296.

Wilcox, Clyde. 1991. "Religion and Electoral Politics among Black Americans in 1988." In James L. Guth and John C. Green, Eds., *The Bible and the Ballot Box: Religion and Politics in the 1988 Election* (pp. 159–172). Boulder, CO: Westview Press.

Wilcox, Clyde. 1993. "The Dimensionality of Public Attitudes Toward Church–State Establishment Issues." *Journal for the Scientific Study of Religion* 32: 169–176.

Wilcox, Clyde, and Leopoldo Gomez. 1990. "Religion, Group Identification, and Politics among Black Americans." *Sociological Analysis* 51: 271–285.

Wilcox, Clyde, and Carin Robinson. 2011. *Onward Christian Soldiers? The Religious Right in American Politics*, 4th ed. Boulder, CO: Westview Press.

Wilcox, Clyde, Joseph Ferrara, John O'Donnell, Mary Bendyna, Shaun Geehan, and Rod Taylor. 1992. "Public Attitudes Toward Church–State Issues: Elite–Mass Differences." *Journal of Church and State* 34: 259–277.

Wilcox, Clyde, Rachel Goldberg, and Ted G. Jelen. 2002. "Public Attitudes on Church and State: Coexistence or Conflict?" In Mary C. Segers, Ed., *Piety, Politics, and Pluralism: Religion, the Courts, and the 2000 Election* (pp. 221–233). Lanham, MD: Rowman & Littlefield.

Williamsburg Charter. 1988. "The Williamsburg Charter, 1988: A Reaffirmation of the First Amendment." http://religiousfreedom.lib.virginia.edu/const/Willburg.html.

Wills, Garry. 1990. *Under God: Religion and American Politics*. New York, NY: Simon & Schuster.

Wilmore, Gayraud. 1998. *Black Religion and Black Radicalism: An Interpretation of the Religious History of African Americans*, 3rd ed. Maryknoll, NY: Orbis.

Wilson, Catherine E. 2008. *The Politics of Latino Faith: Religion, Identity, and Urban Community*. New York, NY: New York University Press.

Wilson, J. Matthew. 1999. "'Blessed Are the Poor:' American Protestantism and Attitudes Toward Poverty and Welfare." *Southeastern Political Review* 27: 421–437.

Wilson, J. Matthew. 2007. "The Changing Catholic Voter: Comparing Responses to John Kennedy in 1960 and John Kerry in 2004." In David E. Campbell, Ed., *A Matter of Faith? Religion in the 2004 Election* (pp. 163–179). Washington, DC: Brookings Institution Press.

Wilson, J. Matthew. 2009. "Religion and American Public Opinion: Economic Issues." In Corwin E. Smidt, James A. Guth, and Lyman A. Kellstedt, Eds. *Oxford Handbook of Religion and American Politics* (pp. 191–216). New York, NY: Oxford University Press.

Wilson, J. Matthew. 2012. "How Are We Doing? Group-based Economic Assessments and African American Political Behavior." *Electoral Studies* 31: 550–561.

Wilson, John F. 1990. "Religion, Government, and Power in the New American Nation." In Mark A. Noll, Ed. *Religion and American Politics: From the Colonial Period to the 1980s* (pp. 77–91). New York, NY: Oxford University Press.

Winters, Michael Sean. 2010. "Anti-Religious Bigotry: Sharia." *National Catholic Reporter*, August 27. http://ncronline.org/blogs/distinctly-catholic/anti-religious-bigotry-sharia.

Wisse, Ruth R. 2012. "Obama, Romney, and the Jews." *The Wall Street Journal*, October 16. http://online.wsj.com/article/SB10000872396390444799904578051070780537396.html.

Wogaman, J. Philip. 1988. *Christian Perspectives on Politics*. Philadelphia, PA: Fortress Press.

Woocher, Jonathan S. 1986. *Sacred Survival: The Civil Religion of American Jews*. Bloomington, IN: Indiana University Press.

Wood, James E., Jr. 1987. "Religious Fundamentalism and the New Right." In John F. Wilson and Donald L. Drakeman, Eds., *Church and State in American History*, 2nd ed. (pp. 246–250). Boston, MA: Beacon Press.

Wood, James E., Jr. 1993. "The Restoration of the Free Exercise Clause (Religious Freedom Restoration Act)." *Journal of Church and State* 35: 715–722.

Wright, Gerald C. 1990. "Misreports of Vote Choice in the 1988 NES Senate Election Study." *Legislative Studies Quarterly* 15: 543–563.

Wuthnow, Robert. 1988. *The Restructuring of American Religion: Society and Faith Since World War II*. Princeton, NJ: Princeton University Press.

Wuthnow, Robert. 1989. *The Struggle for America's Soul: Evangelicals, Liberals, and Secularism*. Grand Rapids, MI: Eerdmans.

Wuthnow, Robert, and John H. Evans, Eds. 2002. *The Quiet Hand of God: Faith-Based Activism and the Public Role of Mainline Protestantism*. Berkeley, CA: University of California Press.

Yamane, David. 2005. *The Catholic Church in State Politics: Negotiating Prophetic Demands and Political Realities*. Lanham, MD: Rowman & Littlefield.

Yoder, John H. 1972. *The Politics of Jesus*. Grand Rapids, MI: Eerdmans.

Young, Jeffrey Robert, Ed. 2006. *Proslavery and Sectional Thought in the Early South, 1740–1829*. Columbia, SC: University of South Carolina Press.

Zaller, John R. 1992. *The Nature and Origins of Mass Opinion*. New York, NY: Cambridge University Press.

Zwier, Robert. 1989. "Coalition Strategies of Religious Interest Groups." In Ted G. Jelen, Ed., *Religion and Political Behavior in the United States* (pp. 175–186). New York, NY: Praeger.

Zwier, Robert. 1994. "An Organizational Perspective on Religious Interest Groups." In William R. Stevenson, Jr., Ed., *Christian Political Activism at the Crossroads* (pp. 95–119). Lanham, MD: University Press of America.

Index